Foreign Policies of the Great Powers

FOREIGN POLICIES OF THE GREAT POWERS

Foreign Policies of the Great Powers

Volume X

From Nationalism to Internationalism
U. S. Foreign Policy to 1914

Akira Iriye

London and New York

First published 1977 by Routledge

Reprinted 2002 by Routledge
2 Park Square, Milton Park, Abingdon, Oxon, OX14 4RN

Simultaneously published in the USA and Canada
by Routledge
270 Madison Ave, New York NY 10016

First issued in paperback 2010

Routledge is an imprint of the Taylor & Francis Group

British Library Cataloguing in Publication Data
A catalogue record for this book is available from the British Library

Library of Congress Cataloging in Publication Data
A catalog record for this book has been requested.

ISBN 978-0-415-27374-9 (hbk) (Volume 10)
ISBN 978-0-415-60619-6 (pbk) (Volume 10)
ISBN 978-0-415-26597-3 (set)

Publisher's Note
The publisher has gone to great lengths to ensure the quality of this
reprint but points out that some imperfections in the original book
may be apparent.

From Nationalism to Internationalism

US Foreign Policy to 1914

Akira Iriye

Professor of History
University of Chicago

Routledge & Kegan Paul

London, Henley and Boston

Contents

Preface

In writing this interpretative survey of American foreign policy before the First World War, I have been influenced by several considerations. First, in view of the ready availability of excellent textbooks, I have not felt it necessary or even desirable to recount familiar facts and episodes in a straightforward chronological fashion. Second, I have viewed 'foreign policy' rather broadly and tried to discuss not merely governmental decisions but also people-to-people relations. Third, ideas, assumptions, and images have been stressed so as to give the reader a conceptual tool to analyse specific foreign policy issues. Fourth, in choosing episodes for purposes of illustration, I have sought to avoid repeating well-known events, not because they are unimportant but because many incidents that are hardly mentioned in conventional textbooks often reveal with striking vividness important characteristics of American foreign affairs.

The title of the book is a shorthand to summarize the changes that took place in United States diplomacy between 1776 and 1914. To be more precise, it would have to be entitled 'From Internationalistic Nationalism to Nationalistic Internationalism.' These terms are defined and described in the book. Basically, my view is that it is possible to trace the course of American foreign relations as a story of a nation which initially combined a traditional formulation of national interests with internationalist aspirations, but which, on the eve of First World War, had come to exemplify a major force for the reshaping of the world while at the same time retaining more conventional concerns as a nation-state. Such a transformation must, of course, be related to the country's economic development and domestic politics, as well as to the external environment of the world community. My purpose in writing the book will have been served if it conveys some idea of the complexity of these various factors as determinants of foreign policy.

As always in the past, I am indebted to my former teachers, friends, colleagues and students for their advice and encouragement over the years. I have benefited particularly from the warm friendship and professional co-operation of diplomatic historians in the United States and abroad. I shall be satisfied if the book contributes in however small degree to their collective efforts to enlighten the past. I must also express my thanks to Harriet Pearl, Kathy Murphy, Marne Deering and Beverly Smith for having typed the manuscript in its various stages.

Chicago   A.I.

Chapter 1

Introduction

What were the characteristics of United States foreign
relations before World War I? Too often American foreign
policy in the nineteenth century has been described in
simplistic terms, such as geographical isolation,
withdrawal from European politics, continental expansion,
and the like. According to such interpretations,
American foreign relations were unique because the United
States was different from other countries in size,
population and history. By the same token, every
country's foreign policy would be distinct. But to stress
these intrinsic differences does not help much when one
explores the interaction between nations and tries to
examine their responses in some comparative perspective.
The study of international relations, after all, is a
study in comparative history; one analyzes why a nation
acts in a particular manner by contrasting it with the
ways other countries behave. It is not enough, or even
meaningful, to say that American foreign affairs were
determined by the country's existential conditions and
domestic forces, for the same would be true of all
countries.

One must, then, begin by establishing an analytical
scheme in terms of which United States foreign policy may
be studied in a comparative framework. Several
conceptualizations have been proposed for studying the
period under consideration, of which two stand out. One
stresses a 'realistic' nature of American foreign policy
in much of the nineteenth century. The history of United
States foreign relations was on the whole a success story;
the nation acquired territories and amassed wealth at
little cost, and managed to avoid foreign complications
of serious magnitude. Such achievements, according to
this interpretation, were due to a great extent to the
adroit handling of foreign policy by the country's leaders

who had a clear idea of what they wanted and a pragmatic
sense of the available means to obtain it. As George F.
Kennan has written in his 'Memoirs: 1950-1963' (1972):

> In such casual reading on American diplomatic history
> as I had had occasion to do while in government, I had
> been struck by the contrast between the lucid and
> realistic thinking of early American statesmen of the
> Federalist period and the cloudy bombast of their
> successors of later decades ... I was surprised to
> discover how much of our stock equipment, in the way of
> the rationale and rhetoric of foreign policy, was what
> we had inherited from the statesmen of the period from
> the Civil War to World War II, and how much of this
> equipment was utopian in its expectations, legalistic
> in its concept of methodology, moralistic in the
> demands it seemed to place on others, and self-
> righteous in the degree of high-mindedness and
> rectitude it imputed to ourselves. (1)

American foreign policy, in this instance, can be examined
in terms of the interaction between realism and idealism,
or pragmatism and moralism. Such a dichotomizing scheme
has had an enormous impact on the study of the subject.

The second popular interpretation sees continuity and
unity, rather than discontinuity and diversity, in the way
the United States has related itself to the world. The
nineteenth century saw the country expand territorially
and commercially, according to this view, and expansion
was to be a key theme of twentieth-century American
foreign relations. Expansion was not only territorial
or economic but also political and ideological; Americans
wanted to Americanize the world by disseminating knowledge
and reshaping other societies in accordance with
democratic principles. Such an interpretation stresses
a monolithic thematic unity in the history of the United
States foreign policy and is critical of the dichotomizing
scheme of Kennan and others. As Bruce Kuklick has noted,
in his 'American Policy and the Division of Germany'
(1972),

> there is a serious conceptual confusion in the
> analysis. One must believe that diplomats are a breed
> of schizophrenic robots who have two alternative
> centers of motivation, one quasi-Machiavellian ... the
> other starry-eyed and impractical ... These forms of
> analysis neglect an elementary psychological and
> philosophical insight - that human beings normally
> see the world as a coherent whole and that ideology
> and interest are inseparable. (2)

Instead of the interplay between two opposite behavior
and thought patterns, then, the second interpretation

would emphasize an underlying world-view which was
remarkably unchanging throughout the nineteenth century
and well into the twentieth. Disparate episodes and
events of American diplomacy would become intelligible as
aspects of the ethos of economic, political and cultural
expansionism. Thus, according to Walter LaFeber's
'America, Russia, and the Cold War' (1972).
     In the middle of the nineteenth century, two events
began to reshape American views toward revolutions:
the continental conquest was completed, and Americans
began emphasizing the commercial aspects of their
foreign policy instead of landed expansion. These
overseas commercial interests became especially
important, for stability, peace, and confidence in
the sanctity of contract were essential to any great
trading venture. By 1900, the United States had
burgeoned into a power which combined the interesting
characteristics of being conservative ideologically
and expansive economically. (3)
     Regardless of the merit or demerit of the dualistic
or the monolithic interpretation of American diplomacy,
these conceptual schemes do not seem totally adequate as
analytical tools when one studies United States foreign
relations in a comparative framework and in an international context, which is the aim of this book. Both
of the above approaches emphasize the uniqueness of
American responses to foreign affairs, and they come
close to viewing United States foreign relations as a
function of the national character - whether one stresses
its proclivity to moralism or systematic urge to expand.
But we will never know in what ways the United States may
differ in this respect from other countries. After all,
neither moralism nor expansionism is a monopoly of the
American people, and the question is whether the latter
can be said to be more, or in a distinctive way,
moralistic and expansionist than others. But then, it
may be asked if these categories are really useful in
comparing the foreign policies of the United States,
Britain, Germany and others. Moreover, the emphasis on
certain thematic unity does not help much when one tries
to account for shifts and turns in American foreign
relations. These do not exist in a vacuum but must be
viewed in the context of the overall international system
at a given moment. The international system itself keeps
changing at all times, and one must relate American
attitudes, ideas and policies to the changing framework
and environment. The relationship here is neither
undirectional nor automatic. The American ethos, even if
such a thing existed, would take different shapes and

expressions as it interacted with the environment.
Conversely, the latter would also be affected by the way
the United States perceived the external world.
These interactions and interrelationships are so
complex that a monolithic or a dualistic interpretation
of United States foreign policy is likely to be of limited
usefulness. Still, some conceptual scheme is essential if
one is not merely to intone a myriad of diplomatic
negotiations, decisions and opinions without much
structure but to develop a coherent synthesis. In order
to facilitate our understanding and analysis of United
States foreign relations before 1914, then, it will be
helpful first to consider the period before 1865 and note
the sources of American thinking and behavior in the
international arena.
Americans related themselves to the outside world in a
number of ways. But by the mid-nineteenth century, at
least five levels or modes of this interaction had become
visible: geopolitical factors, internationalist ideas,
national interest considerations, special interests and
mass culture. These are not mutually exclusive
categories, and the same individual may respond to foreign
issues at any one or more of these levels, depending on
circumstances. By the same token, a single foreign
policy decision may be characterized as a manifestation
of several of these factors. But by identifying at least
these five components or levels of American attitudes,
assumptions, ideas and policies - in short, five
dimensions of the American perceptions of the world - we
may be able to appreciate the complexity and diversity of
American foreign affairs and to trace their changing
characteristics over time.

1 GEOPOLITICAL FACTORS

'Our situation invites and our interests prompt us to aim
at an ascendant in the system of American affairs.' So
wrote Alexander Hamilton for the 'Federalist' in 1788. By
'the system of American affairs' he meant international
affairs in the Western Hemisphere. For the United States
to aim at an ascendant position in the hemisphere implied
a geopolitical view of foreign relations. According to
Hamilton, 'The world may politically, as well as geo-
graphically, be divided into four parts, each having a
distinct set of interests.' These four were: Europe,
Africa, Asia and America. As he saw the world situation,
he was persuaded that 'Europe, by her arms and by her
negotiations, by force and by fraud, has, in different

degrees, extended her dominion over them all. Africa,
Asia, and America, have successively felt her domination.'
Such a situation was not conducive to the peace, welfare,
or security of the United States. In order to ensure
these goals, then, it was incumbent upon the latter to
strengthen itself through unity and to extend its
influence to other parts of the American continent so as
to balance the growing power of the European nations.
Let Americans disdain to be the instruments of
European greatness! [he exclaimed,] Let the thirteen
States, bound together in a strict and indissoluble
Union, concur in erecting one great American system,
superior to the control of all transatlantic force
or influences, and able to dictate the terms of the
connection between the old and the new world! (4)
Here was the essence of 'realpolitik' or globalistic
thinking which provided one component of American foreign
policy. As Hamilton saw it, the crucial thing was to view
the United States in the context of world politics as a
whole and to ask in what kind of international system
the nation's security and interests could best be safeguarded. And he had no doubt that given the superiority
of the European powers, the best strategy for the United
States was to promote a regional system in the Americas.
This could conceivably take the form of American hegemony
over the Western Hemisphere. But the key factor was the
willingness of the American people to play a role in
international politics so as to 'dictate the terms of the
connection' between Europe and America - in other words,
to establish a balance between the Old world and the New.
Hamilton had nothing to say about the role of the United
States in Asia and Africa, presumably because these were
already under European domination and the United States
was too weak to do much about it. But at least in the
Western Hemisphere the country had, or should have, the
power and will to limit the extension of European power.
This continent should be marked as America's sphere of
influence.
    Geopolitical globalism had, of course, characterized
one facet of European diplomacy since the seventeenth
century. As they pondered the question of the 'reason of
state,' European statesmen invariably thought of the
balance of power not only in their part of the world but
also elsewhere. Colonial wars of the seventeenth and the
eighteenth centuries were in part caused by power-
political thinking; capturing another country's colony
would automatically lessen its power, and since this was
considered a relative thing, it followed that a state must
do what it could to reduce the relative power of the

others.   (5) Such considerations had been particularly
pertinent to European diplomacy vis-à-vis the American
continent in the eighteenth century, as exemplified by
William Pitt's foreign policy which regarded imperial
interests as even more important than purely European
interests. From his point of view French power could be
reduced by attacking Canada and reducing French influence
in North America. Thus the policy of seeking to sustain
a balance of power necessitated a geopolitical
perspective. American leaders were heirs to this
tradition, and it was not surprising that Hamilton, whose
views of politics and foreign affairs approximated those
of the British, should have been the first to enunciate a
doctrine of American power politics.

As will be seen, power politics was by no means the
only framework in which Hamilton perceived international
affairs; nor was it the sole basis on which the Americans
viewed the New World as distinct from the Old. But it
should be noted that from its earliest inception the
United States exhibited a power-oriented, geopolitical
tendency in its foreign policy. This theme was not the
major thread in American foreign relations before the
Civil War, but it was present in several key episodes and
decisions of the first decades of the nineteenth century.

Geopolitical thinking was a factor behind the
assertive and highly successful American policy toward the
Spanish empire in the Western Hemisphere, as the latter
began to break up during the Napoleonic Wars. The
Spanish-French alliance of 1795, reversing Spain's
alliance with Britain, involved the country in Napoleon's
wars and made its overseas colonies vulnerable to British
attack. Spain relaxed its mercantilistic policies and
opened up the colonial ports to neutral shipping in order
to provide the colonies with foodstuffs and other
materials. This gave an impetus to American commercial
expansion in the Caribbean region. Havana and New Orleans
flourished with American merchants. Equally important,
some of the Spanish colonies in America took advantage of
the European wars to set themselves adrift from the
imperial bondage. Moreover, the identification of Spanish
and French colonial interests induced the Spanish government to retrocede Louisiana to France; this territory had
been ceded to Spain by France in 1762, but the former had
never made much use of it and was willing to part with it
for a substantial sum of money. Napoleon, however, was
more interested in challenging the British empire in the
East - the Red Sea, India, and beyond. Although Louisiana
was formally given back to France in 1801, Napoleon's
global strategy had no specific scheme for the New World.

Here was an opportunity to try to implement the Hamiltonian concept of geopolitical regionalism - the United States would be the key power in the Western Hemisphere. President Thomas Jefferson, a bitter enemy of Hamilton in domestic politics, was in full agreement with such a view. He was convinced that the United States must try to reject European interference in American affairs and to prevent the rise of a strong European power in the New World. Louisiana and New Orleans, in particular, worried him, the former because of its huge size astride the North American continent and the latter because it provided an entrepot for American commerce with the Caribbean. In his famous letter to Robert R. Livingston, Jefferson declared, 'The day that France takes New Orleans ... we must marry ourselves to the British fleet and nation.' Contrary to his fears, New Orleans remained in Spanish hands, but he was determined to obtain it along with lands in the lower Mississippi. When Napoleon instead offered to sell the entire territory of Louisiana, Jefferson eagerly grasped the opportunity. While territorial expansionism was certainly a factor, considerations of power politics - as Gouveneur Morris said, 'No nation has a right to give to another a dangerous neighbor without her consent' (6) - played a decisive role in the decision to obtain Louisiana.

The Louisiana purchase (1803) and the simultaneous decline of French and Spanish power in the Western Hemisphere meant a relative increase of American power, and by the second decade of the nineteenth century it was not uncommon to conceive of the United States as the predominant member in the American system of international affairs. The independence of the Spanish American colonies, whose new governments the United States recognized one after another, served to enhance America's relative position vis-à-vis that of the European powers. Certainly after the War of 1812 (to be discussed below), it could be said that no European power would try to alter drastically the developing equilibrium in the international system in the Americas, where the European nations still retained some of their colonies and played the most important economic roles, but where the predominant position of the United States would be acknowledged. Great Britain, the strongest European and world power, admitted as much when, after the War of 1812, its government expressed its readiness to see the United States develop as the strongest power in the New World. Without British support or acquiescence, no European power would be able or willing to challenge America's position.

Thus, for instance, while France was interested in
helping Spain crush the independence movement in Latin
America, they would not move for fear of British
retaliation. By 1823 the French government was formally
denying that it had designs on the former Spanish America.
Well might John Quincy Adams boast of 'our natural
dominion in North America.' (7)

Such dominion fitted well with Britain's global
strategy in the post-Napoleonic world, when the Vienna
Conference system of international affairs had brought
about the new status quo. A balance of power was maintained among the great nations which shared the same
proclivity towards stability, conservatism, and order.
The United States was not a member of the system, but the
new international order necessarily involved a definition
of regional stability in the Western Hemisphere, and
after the independence of the Spanish colonies it was
generally perceived in terms of the central position of
the United States. The British government was
particularly anxious to recognize this fact and
incorporated it into its vision of global power structure;
by acknowledging the emerging status quo in the New World,
Britain could ensure peace and order in that part of the
world, which in turn would serve to perpetuate the Vienna
system. As Lord Castlereagh said in 1820, 'there are no
two States whose friendly relations are of more practical
value to each other, or whose hostility so inevitably and
so immediately entails upon both the most serious
mischiefs.' (8) Such thinking induced London to approach
Washington for formalizing the new status quo in the
Western Hemisphere as part of the global order. That the
United States government rejected the overtures and
instead proclaimed unilaterally the so-called Monroe
Doctrine (1823) does not detract from the fact that a
regional system of international affairs in the New World
was being visualized as a separate entity from the Old
World. Actually, by refusing to join Britain in
enunciating the principles of hemispheric autonomy and
opposition to European interference, the United States
failed to have the Monroe Doctrine recognized as international law. It was merely a unilateral assertion which
bound no other country. Moreover, there was no danger of
European intervention in the New World, and American
predominance there was more an ideal than accomplished
fact. All the same, the Monroe Doctrine was an example
of geopolitical thinking and, whether or not the United
States intended it, became an integral part of the Vienna
system.

For over twenty years after 1823 the Monroe Doctrine

remained dormant, and the successive administrations in
Washington did not base its foreign policy explicitly on
that doctrine. Nevertheless, the idea of the hemispheric
system of international affairs in which the United
States played the leading role was always there, and
whenever this principle appeared threatened, the government in Washington was quick to act. The most serious
challenge seemed to come after Texas declared its
independence of Mexico in 1836 and sought incorporation
into the United States immediately thereafter. Britain
and France recognized the Republic of Texas, and they
preferred that the latter remain independent not only of
Mexico but of the United States. The British government
under Lord Aberdeen expressed the hope that slavery
would be abolished in Texas, while France under Premier
François Guizot made speeches stressing the desirability
of maintaining an equilibrium among independent states in
North America. In the meantime, the Mexican government
was reported to be giving land grants in California to
British subjects and attempting to draw Britain into
intervening in the Mexico-United States dispute over the
region. Historians disagree whether the United States
government took these alleged moves by the European
powers seriously, or whether they merely provided a
pretext for pursuing a belligerent foreign policy which
culminated in the Mexican War (1846-8). (9) Neither
Britain nor France was prepared to go to war to deny
Texas or California to the United States, and they never
offered serious opposition to the principles underlying
the Monroe Doctrine. But the United States government,
especially during the administration of President
James K. Polk (1845-9), found it desirable and expedient
to reassert the Monroe Doctrine as a foundation of
American foreign policy. The next effect was to confirm
the geopolitical tradition of Hamilton and
John Quincy Adams and to establish, once and for all, as
it was hoped, the regional autonomy of the American
continent as a separate system of international relations.
     In the decade preceding the Civil War, geopolitical
regionalism became even clearer and defined, at least in
part, the nation's approach to Central America and the
Pacific Ocean. The administrations of Millard Fillmore,
Franklin Pierce and James Buchanan asserted the unique
position of the United States in the Caribbean and sought
to tie the region more closely together. Although there
were many reasons for such a policy, one crucial factor
was the desire to weaken steadily the position of the
European powers in the Western Hemisphere. In 1849 the
United States negotiated a treaty with Nicaragua which

granted to the former an exclusive right to build an
isthmian canal across the latter's territory. This came
to nothing, as the British government objected to giving
up its interests in Central America, and the Clayton-
Bulwer treaty (1850) stipulated that no nation was to
have exclusive control over such a canal. Not to be
daunted by this failure, the United States under
President Buchanan (1857-61) sought a right to maintain
the security of Central America by placing American
troops in the region and explicitly committing the
nation to assist the local regimes to maintain law and
order. There was also a strong interest in the fate of
Cuba, concerning whose future the United States wished
to have a freedom of action without European interference. The principle of 'no transfer' was frequently
reiterated, opposing the transfer of a European colony
in the Western Hemisphere to another European power.
Ultimately, it was hoped by the Buchanan administration
that the island might be offered by the Spanish government
for purchase by the United States. None of these
attempts at extending American dominion came to fruition
at this time, but they nevertheless indicated the
continued functioning of one strain - geopolitical
considerations - in American foreign policy. It was
becoming axiomatic that the United States would seek to
establish its identity in international relations through
assertion of its predominant position in the Western
Hemisphere, in particular in the Caribbean and Central
America.

The 1850s also saw the extension of American power and
interest in the Pacific Ocean. Here again various
factors were involved, and many types of ideas and
interests were behind American approaches to Hawaii,
Japan, and other lands in the Pacific. Power politics
was clearly one of them. As the United States government
and people looked beyond California to Hawaii, or beyond
the Indian Ocean to Taiwan, the Liuchiu islands (Okinawa)
and Japan, there was a sense that the nation was destined
to play a key role in the international politics of the
Pacific Ocean. Commodore Matthew C. Perry, for instance,
was convinced that this was the region where rivalries
among the great powers would take place in the future,
and that the United States must prevent the European
nations from establishing their hegemony there by
adopting an assertive policy of its own. His expedition
to Japan (1852-4) was to him just the beginning; he
insisted that the United States acquire or at least
establish control over Taiwan and the Liuchiu islands to
deny them to Great Britain or other European powers.

Very few of his contemporaries held such a grandiose
vision of the United States as an Asian power, but the
government in Washington was at least willing to
enunciate a clear-cut policy toward Hawaii; the islands
were not to fall under the control of one or other
European nations. President Pierce wanted an eventual
annexation of Hawaii by the United States, and the
reciprocity treaty of 1855 was designed to tie the
island kingdom economically to America. The treaty was
rejected by the Senate, and Congress on the whole
remained indifferent to the Perry expedition and other
acts of American assertiveness in East Asia. The country
was not prepared to play a role in the politics of the
Asia-Pacific region. Nevertheless, the emergence of a
power-oriented view in American diplomacy in the area was
significant. Next to the Western Hemisphere, the Pacific
Ocean and East Asia were already being considered by some
as a theater of active American participation in international affairs, whereas the same could not be said of
Europe, the Middle East, and other parts of the world.
Just once, during the Crimean War, the State Department
decided to act like a world power by offering mediation.
The timid overtures met with no positive response, the
French foreign minister reminding the Americans that
'the United States can hardly hope to solve the Eastern
Question for which the European powers have been unable
to find a solution during the last twenty-five years.' (10)
Europe and the Middle East were beyond reach of American
policy in geopolitical terms, but this, after all, had
been foreseen by Hamilton and reflected the thought that
these areas were within the European spheres of predominance. In the Caribbean and the Pacific, on the other
hand, the United States would assert its power and be
counted as one of the main actors in world politics.

2   INTERNATIONALIST IDEAS

The view of the world in terms of power politics and
global balances characterized only a segment of American
perceptions and policies before the Civil War. Another
key theme in American foreign affairs was a tendency to
universalize foreign relations and conceptualize them in
some internationalist language. Whereas power, the basic
theme in geopolitics, was amoral, non-ideological and
particularistic, this second approach was more ideological, aspirational and universalistic. It sought to
define America's relations - political, economic, and
cultural - with other countries through some concepts of

allegedly universal application. Such an attitude may be
termed internationalism, although, as it will become
clear, presumably universalistic values applied primarily
to culturally Western and economically advanced countries.
Still, it is important to distinguish this from other
strains in the making of United States foreign relations.
For instance, the ideas of reciprocity and equality
among Western nations were central to American foreign
policy after 1776. It was considered important, now that
the colonies had declared their independence of the
fetters of British mercantilism, that they should
enunciate the principle of unrestricted commercial
relations among all countries, especially between the
United States which produced an agricultural surplus
and the European countries at their initial stages of
industrialization. But commercial opportunities would
also be sought in less developed areas of the world, and
the new nation would insist that most-favored-nation
treatment be accorded it in treaties of commerce and
navigation it negotiated with other countries. American
foreign affairs thus began by stressing the internationalist nature of commercial pursuits. This was a
revolt against the particularism of the British empire
and reflected the ideal that there should be unrestricted
and unlimited commercial intercourse among all nations.
The 1778 treaty with France, whereby the signatories
accorded most-favored-nation treatment to their mutual
citizens and several ports were opened up in France and
the French West Indies to American produce, was a signal
achievement to be followed by similar treaties with
Holland, Sweden, and Prussia. The American negotiators
in Paris, discussing peace terms with the British in
1782, were anxious to include commercial reciprocity as
part of the settlement, but in this instance they were
unsuccessful, as the British government was unwilling to
give up the mercantilist policies and practices.
    Internationalism had also a political aspect. After
Concord and Lexington, Americans proclaimed themselves
to be in 'the state of nature.' They were now outside
the protection of British law, and their rights would
cease to be those of Englishmen. Instead, they began
universalizing their experience; they spoke of 'rights
of men' - not simply for American or British but for
human rights. Such revolutionary idealism was of course
never the whole picture, and was not allowed to eclipse
totally more mundane considerations or power-oriented
notions. Political internationalism in fact might soon
have been relegated to a minor place in American foreign
policy if not for the almost concurrent development of

another revolution, that in France. The spread of
universalistic vocabulary in the 'age of the democratic
revolution,' combined with the circumstances of the birth
of the American republic ensured that idealism and internationalism would continue to play an inordinately
important role in the formulation and perception of
United States foreign policy.

'The American Revolution was the mother of the French
revolution,' said Jacques Pierre Brissot. 'Shall all the
nations of the earth,' wrote Marquis de Condorcet on the
eve of his death, 'some day achieve that stage of civilization to which have arrived the freest and most
enlightened peoples, the French and the Americans?' (11)
Such expressions reflected the image that the revolutions
in America and France were intimately linked because they
were but two manifestations of mankind's struggle for
freedom and human rights. As Joseph Garat wrote in 1783,
'Every eye today is fixed upon North America; it is there
that the greatest interests of the Universe are at stake
... The philosophers of all Europe see in the new
constitutions [in the various states] the noblest, and
perhaps the last, hope of the human race.' (12) The
implications were unmistakable. The independence and
consolidation of the United States would have significance
for the entire world, and the example of America would be
followed first by France and ultimately by all other
countries.

The American people generally reciprocated such a
sentiment and welcomed the coming of the revolution in
France - which became a 'sister republic.' There was
real enthusiasm after 1792, which saw the abolition of
monarchy in France and the defeat of the invading armies
of the European powers. There were public celebrations
throughout the United States, and Americans took to
wearing 'caps of liberty.' Even those who did not
succumb to revolutionary fervor or accept the identification of the two revolutions readily subscribed to an
image of America as a champion and disseminator of the
blessings of civilization and progress. They were convinced that the United States was a different kind of
nation, destined to influence world history by its
example and through the spread of these blessings to other
lands. America was a nation not only dedicated to the
principle of free intercourse among peoples but also to
certain universalistic notions such as liberty and
rights. The American people, it followed from such a
self-image, were an instrument for promoting these
principles and disseminating knowledge to the rest of the
world. American citizens abroad were not just subjects

of a government; far more important, they were agents of
ideas and principles which were considered of universal
applicability. They stood not only for a state in the
technical sense but were also representatives of common
human concerns and champions of their aspirations.

Because these developments took place when the central
government was still weak and before there was an opportunity to clarify what constituted the national interest,
internationalist concepts were bound to have strong
repercussions on American foreign policy during the era
of the Napoleonic Wars. At least initially American
sentiment was predominantly pro-French, and many spoke
out in favor of forming an alliance with France. It is no
accident that the sentiment began to wane when Americans
came to see French policy as less universalistic than
particularistic, designed to promote France's own self-
interest rather than broader concerns of mankind. But
pro-French feelings persisted and grew into an active
political movement within the United States when the
administration of President George Washington proclaimed
official neutrality in 1793. Washington was accused by
James Madison of his 'seeming indifference to the cause
of liberty' - to which Alexander Hamilton replied in a
characteristic fashion, saying that 'generosity' was a
good thing in individuals but not for international
relations. In 1794, when Jay's treaty was concluded with
Britain, providing for the dismantling of the remaining
British garrisons in the Northwest and the referral to
joint commissions of most other disputes between the two
countries, it was fiercely opposed by those Americans
who considered the terms of the treaty a national disgrace
and designed to befriend the British at the expense of
the French. American opinion became split between the
Federalists, favoring the treaty, and the Democratic-
Republicans who opposed it, and the latter represented
the current of pro-French sentiment. The nation-wide
debate on Jay's treaty was the first instance where a
foreign policy question divided American opinion between
internationalist views and their opponents. In the end
the latter prevailed, with President Washington lending
his prestige to the Federalists and cautioning his
countrymen, in his 'farewell address' of 1796, against a
sentimental attachment to any particular country.

Internationalism was not strong enough to be translated into official policy, but it continued to constitute one facet of American attitude toward foreign
countries. In the first decades of the nineteenth
century, one can best see this in the sentiment supporting the revolt of the Spanish colonies in Latin America.

In 1811 the House committee on Spanish American colonies
adopted a resolution declaring, 'as neighbors and inhabitants of the same hemisphere, the United States feels
great solicitude for their welfare.' After the Congress
of Vienna, Henry Clay expressed the fear that the
European principle of legitimacy might work to the
destruction of 'every principle of liberty' in the
Western Hemisphere. (13) He was instrumental in persuading the House of Representatives to adopt a resolution in
1821 expressing sympathy with the newly independent Latin
American republics. Such ideas, seeing in the independence movements of the Spanish colonies the continuation
of the struggle for freedom that had begun in North
America but which had been frustrated in France, created
a strong pressure on the government to recognize the
Latin American republics. Although ideology was by no
means the only factor, the United States under President
James Monroe was ready to do so, and by 1826 seven of
them had been recognized. Nearly thirty years later
William H. Seward boasted, in a speech entitled 'The
Physical, Moral, and Intellectual Development of the
American People,' that the 'influences of the United
States on the American continent have resulted already in
the establishment of the republican system everywhere,
except in Brazil, and even there in limiting imperial
power.' He added in a significant passage: 'heretofore
nations have either repelled, or exhausted, or disgusted
the colonies they planted and the countries they conquered. The United States, on the contrary, expand, not
by force of arms, but by attraction.' (14)
    This was the essence of American internationalism. The
United States was an example to the entire world, and its
experiences, institutions and activities were relevant to
other countries and peoples because they were part of the
evolving drama of human history. What happened in America
had universal significance. Conversely, events elsewhere
became meaningful in terms of their relevance to the
universalistic values which the United States embodied.
It is no accident that in the above speech Seward did not
confine himself to mentioning Latin America as an example
of American expansion 'by attraction.' The same values
and principles that spread from North to Central and South
America could not fail to have their impact on other parts
of the world. As he said, the 'influences of the United
States' had in Europe 'awakened a war of opinion, that,
after spreading desolation into the steppes of Russia,
and to the base of the Carpathian mountains, has only
been suppressed for a time by combination of the capital
and of the political forces of that continent.' In Africa

'those influences, aided by the benevolent efforts of our citizens, have produced the establishment of a republic [Liberia] which ... is going steadily on toward the moral regeneration of its savage races.' In Asia, Seward asserted,

Those influences have opened the ports of Japan, and secured an intercourse of commerce and friendship with its extraordinary people ... The same influences have not only produced for us access to the five ports of China, but also have generated a revolution there, which promises to bring the three hundred millions living within that vast empire into the society of western nations.

What Seward characterized as expansion by attraction has sometimes been referred to as liberal expansionism, or informal expansionism. In the history of United States foreign relations, it represented a world-view which envisioned an unlimited and universalistic expansion of American ideas and goods, not only through individual Americans acting as their transmitters but also through other peoples following the American model of progress. In contrast to the geopolitical vision which stressed power, the internationalist concept impelled Americans to think of their country's mission, duties, and responsibilities because of its unique existence as an embodiment of universalistic values and progressive ideas. The two strains developed side by side, and it would be wrong to single out either one of them as the dominant theme in American foreign relations. The image of the United States as a power existed together with the idea of America as a civilization, and along with other themes to be discussed later, characterized the way the American people and government viewed international affairs.

The internationalist strain was especially visible in American writings of the 1830s through the 1850s, when men often discussed their national experience in terms of the themes of progress and civilization. 'The history of humanity is the record of a grand march, more or less rapid, as it was now impeded by obstacles, and again facilitated by force, at all times tending to one point - the ultimate perfection of man,' wrote the 'Democratic Review' in 1839. (15) The 'American Whig Review,' not to be left behind, defined progress in terms of civilization, which it defined as 'the complete harmonious development of man in all his appropriate relations to this world.' The mission of civilization was 'to bring into one, the past, the present and the future - all nations and all generations.' (16) Writing for the 'North American Review,' Jonathan Chapman declared in 1834 that all

events of the past, the present and the future were
interrelated as they revealed the steady march of man
from barbarism to civilization. In this grand panorama
of human progress, all artificial boundaries between
nations and continents were insignificant, and ultimately
there was to dawn upon earth the reign of a utopia, toward
which man had ceaselessly been pressing forward. Such a
utopia had not yet arrived, but at least in the United
States civilization had reached a stage where one could
see a concrete manifestation of human progress. As he
said, 'the undefined something to which man has tended
is none other than that whose reality is now ours; - ours
because the human race has been struggling for it.' (17)
    These ideas of progress and civilization, and the
confident self-image of American history and society were
frequently a basic determinant of the way Americans, in
and out of government, viewed their country's external
affairs. In Europe, Seward's above speech referred to
the revolutionary waves of 1848 which he attributed to the
influence of American ideas and example. Toward France,
the United States Senate unanimously adopted a resolution
'tendering the congratulations of the American to the
French people' on the successful launching of their second
republic. George Bancroft, American minister in Prussia,
went to Paris to offer advice as the French worked on
their new constitution. When popular movements spread to
Germany and culminated in an attempt at Frankfurt to
create a united German nation, Secretary of State Buchanan
sent a minister to that city to recognize the emerging
new state. The mission had to be withdrawn in 1849 as
the unification movement failed, but this act was severely
criticized by Lewis Cass and other Democratic leaders.
Farther east, when revolt against Austria took place in
Hungary, its leader, Louis Kossuth, was likened by
Americans to George Washington, and there was widespread
public clamor for recognition of Hungary. The administration of President Zachary Taylor sent an emissary
to observe the situation in that country, and when the
Austrian government protested, Secretary of State
Daniel Webster replied that the revolutionary events in
Europe 'appeared to have their origin in those great
ideas of responsible and popular governments on which the
American constitutions themselves are founded.' The
United States, therefore, had the right to be interested
in the development of democratic institutions in Europe.
Even after the failure of the revolution of 1848 in many
countries in Europe, American interest did not decline.
George Sanders, United States consul in London, maintained
a rendezvous for political exiles from the continent and

used a diplomatic pouch for sending inflammatory letters,
and Pierre Soule, minister to Spain, loudly proclaimed
his sympathies with the anti-monarchists. (18) Underlying
these acts and statements was the belief that ideas and
institutions that had developed and matured in the United
States were relevant to other countries, and that America,
standing at the apex of human progress, had the duty to
share them with the rest of the world. Although this type
of internationalism was by no means the sole determinant
of official policy, it provided one basic framework for
viewing events overseas.

Similarly in Asia, Americans often viewed the 'opening'
of China and Japan to foreign trade and intercourse
through the lens of internationalism. The whole East
admirably fitted into the American conception of history
and civilization because of its ancient glory and modern
stagnation. Asia was the land where civilization was
born and which had since decayed or remained stagnant,
while the West progressed and in time surpassed it. As a
writer for the 'Southern Literary Messenger' put it in
1854: 'It is eminently the *past*, looking down from her
few broken and time-stained columns, that alone tells us
of what it once was, but is no more.' (19)
Bayard Taylor, talking of the Ottoman empire, wrote in
1855 that 'the life of the Orient is nerveless and effete;
the native strength of the race has died out.' (20) The
Chinese were described by Francis Warrier as a people
who 'have handed down their customs, from time as far back
as the lights of tradition reach,' and who 'even now ...
seem to be in a primitive state, both as to manners and
customs.' (21) According to the 'Democratic Review''s
characterization of Asia,

A dull, dead, stationary, uniformity encrusts society.
The history of today was the history of yesterday, and
will be the history of tomorrow, occasionally relieved
by the march of devastating armies, and more frequently
by the tyrannous freaks of local pride and power ...
Languor, sluggishness, and apathy take possession of
the general mind. (22)

In contrast to the stagnant East was the image of a
progressive, vigorous West. As S.A. Mitchell said in
1843, 'Asia, at a very early period ... appears to have
made a vast stride in civilization; but then she stopped,
and has suffered herself to be far outstripped by the
originally less advanced nations of Europe.' (23) Since,
in the generally accepted view of human progress, the
United States was placed ahead of Europe, it followed
that the people of Asia were far behind the Americans in
the scale of civilization. But nineteenth-century

American internationalism did not stop here. A
corollary of the image of a stagnant Asia was the
rationalist faith that the latter could once again resume
the march toward higher civilization if given impetus
from the outside. 'Let it be understood,' said the
'Democratic Review' in 1839, 'that the same nature is
common to all men, that they have equal and sacred
claims, that they have high and holy faculties.' (24)
It followed that if only those elements in the East which
impeded its progress were removed and replaced by those
which had contributed to Western advance, the former
would be able to regain its ancient vigor and join the
march of history. As 'DeBow's Monthly' put it in 1859,
'Left to themselves, the Asiatic, African, and Polynesian
races seem to be as unchangeable in their habits as the
bee; but they are readily modified and revolutionized
by contact with superior civilization.'(25)
     It was this task of 'regenerating' or 'awakening'
Asia that the United States, as the vanguard of modern
civilization, could and should perform through its
example and through the activities of enterprising
Americans overseas. 'It was up to the Americans,'
declared 'Knickerbocker' in 1840, 'whether our fellow
men shall reach the elevation whereof they are capable,
and ... whether or not [we shall] confer on them the most
inestimable of all earthly boons, the boon of
Civilization.' (26) Was Asia, asked a writer in the
'Christian Examiner,' to remain unchanged? 'Certainly
not,' was the answer; Western commerce and technology
were bound to change Asia. 'To nourish and water,
without inundating, all this growth and progress, there
will be colonies of Europeans and Americans, wherever
commerce attracts and climate favors.' (27)
     Such perceptions enabled Americans to comprehend the
'opening' of China and Japan in a familiar framework of
internationalism. While there was some initial
criticism of the British use of force during the Opium
War, the overwhelming sentiment in the decades before
the Civil War was to favor the establishment of
commercial relations with and the sending of American
merchants, missionaries, and educators to China and to
other countries of Asia. The same impetus had sent
Americans to the Near East, where by the middle of the
century they were conspicuous as missionaries and
governmental advisors to the Ottoman empire and its
dependencies. But it was the Perry expedition and the
opening of Japan that particularly aroused interest in
the United States. It seemed to be a perfect example of
what America could do in and for the world. The United

States would induce a people, hitherto stubbornly refusing to associate themselves with the outsiders, to open their land for foreign contact, and the Americans would take a lead in bringing them the benefits of civilization. While, as seen above, Commodore Perry had also geopolitical intentions, one basic framework in which his expedition was viewed by Americans was internationalist; it was seen as an attempt to relate the two peoples through the universalistic medium of commercial and cultural intercourse. Americans would not only bring civilization to Japan, but also disseminate knowledge about Japan to the rest of the world. The assumption, of course, was that both the Japanese and the other peoples would appreciate such an endeavor by the Americans. They would all come together more closely knit as members of the world community.

The success of the Perry mission and the subsequent opening of commercial and diplomatic relations with Japan ensured that the Japanese would remain the favorites of Americans, as exemplars of what American internationalism could produce. Those who went to Japan discovered that its people had 'an aptitude for acquiring the civilization of the West to which no other Oriental race can lay claim.' The Japanese seemed to possess 'real vigor, thrift, and intelligence.' (28) When the Japanese government, only six years after the signing of an official agreement with Perry, sent its first mission to Washington, there was tremendous curiosity and favorable comment in the United States. The embassy, said the 'New York Times,' was the first Asian mission to a Christian state since the empire of Siam sent its envoys to the court of Louis XIV. (29) The Japanese mission involved consequences 'the most momentous to the civilization and the commerce of the world for ages to come.' (30) Henry Wood, who accompanied the Japanese as chaplain, noted that 'American customs, ideas and spirit have found their way' even to Japan. 'It cannot be told how much American intercourse in Japan ... will modify the spirit and institutions of that country, while the present Japanese Mission to the United States is certain to carry back a still stronger and more beneficent influence. The lowest official, and every cook and servant, will go back a missionary.' (31) A more characteristic expression of mid-nineteenth century American internationalism would be hard to find. Americans conceived themselves as missionaries to promote commerce, spread knowledge and increase goodwill among men; foreigners who came under their influence would in turn become agents of change in their societies, so that

there would be greater interdependence and understanding among nations.

3 NATIONAL INTERESTS

Not all Americans, however, responded to the Japanese
embassy of 1860 solely in an idealistic, internationalist
manner. Many of them would have agreed with the 'New
York Times' editorial of 21 April that

The Japanese Ministers are to be welcome as the
forerunners of a wonderful expansion in the intercourse of maritime Asia with the United States; and
we are already confidently counting upon our growing
influence with the Chinese and Japanese nations, to
give us certain immense future advantages over our
European rivals in the opulent commerce of the Orient.

Such an opinion reflected the view that America's
commercial interests were involved in the embassy, and
that the nation could conceivably gain at the expense
of its rivals. Implicit was a perception of commercial
competition in the world, in which a country had to
struggle hard to promote its interests. It would
seize any and all opportunities for promoting specific
material objectives, and its response to a foreign-policy
issue would be dependent on its relevance to these
interests.

This type of attitude is different both from power
politics and from internationalist assumptions. Rather,
it is a nationalistic response to a specific situation.
One reacts to it not in terms of some grandiose concept
of world politics or of universalistic principles, but in
a narrow, pragmatic framework of how best to achieve
particular objectives. What matters is how the
interests of the nation in the immediate circumstances
will fare. This is essentially a pragmatic and limited
definition of the nation's relations with other
countries, best summed up by the phrase 'national
interest.'

'National interests,' of course, may include concern
with a global balance of power or with the spread of
knowledge and civilization throughout the world. But it
will not help to discuss all manifestations of foreign
policy as aspects of the national interest, since one
will then have to examine these various aspects and
propose a conceptual scheme for analyzing them. It
seems more useful to consider a pragmatic response to
foreign affairs in terms of specific national interests
as one ingredient of United States relations with the

rest of the world. This ingredient may be termed
'national interest.' It connotes a narrow range of
concerns with the nation's security, economic interests
andprestige, in contrast to the larger preoccupations
with global strategy or internationalism.

Many instances of early American diplomacy can be
explained as products of such nationalism. The idea of
national interest was first forcefully expressed in the
'Federalist' papers, where Alexander Hamilton, John Jay,
George Washington and others stressed the need to take
a 'national' as against a sectional view of the country's
interests. As Hamilton said, the individual states
comprising the new nation were 'incapable of enhancing
the general interests of the Union,' and only a central
government could speak and work for the promotion of the
'national interest.' The establishment of a federal
authority was particularly important in the conduct of
foreign affairs, and the Federalists urged that the new
government be vested with powers over 'security against
foreign danger' and 'regulation of intercourse with
foreign nations.'

These two objectives would be common to all
governments, and in asking that the American people
support the creation of a federal agency to exercise
these powers, the Federalists were able to draw upon the
practices and precedents of European diplomacy since the
seventeenth century. The basic assumption had been the
existence of sovereign nations in a perpetual state of
potential rivalry. Each country had to look after its
own security and interests, and employed all available
means, including warfare, to attain the ends. All
aspects of a nation's interests were interrelated as it
struggled for greater power. As William Mildmay said
in 1765, 'A Nation cannot be safe without Power; Power
cannot be obtained without Riches; nor Riches without
trade.' (32) Or, according to Jean-Baptiste Colbert,
'Trade is the source of finance and finance is the vital
nerve of war.' (33) Power, security and trade were
thus closely linked together, and statesmanship consisted
in making certain that the nation's needs were served in
all three areas.

American leaders in the late eighteenth century were
heirs to this tradition, and when they talked of national
interest their model was undoubtedly the European powers.
There was essentially no difference between them and the
United States in their conception and pursuit of national
interests. It is true, as has been often argued, that the
United States enjoyed 'free security' in the first century
of its history in the absence of powerful and ambitious

neighbors. In contrast to Europe, where nations shared
frontiers and the distance of only a few miles separated
one country's army from another's, the American continent
was thinly populated, and one could travel hundreds of
miles without crossing into another country. Aliens were
usually immigrants who arrived to become American
citizens, not foreign officials, soldiers or mercenaries.
There were battles with Indian tribes, but they were not
considered conventional wars as defined in European
usage. In time there grew the conviction, as Alexis de
Tocqueville put it, 'that [America's] only safeguard
against itself lies in itself.' (34) In other words,
national security came to mean not so much the safeguarding of the country from external threat, as the
prevention of domestic disintegration. It depended on
the American people's ability to compromise various
interest groups and preserve national unity, rather than
on diplomacy and warfare to prevent foreign invasions.

It would be wrong, however, to ignore security
considerations as one ingredient of American foreign
policy. From the very beginning, the federal government
was concerned with ensuring the safety of Americans both
at home and abroad. What little naval strength the new
republic had was put to use in the Caribbean, the Pacific
Ocean, the Mediterranean, and even in the Asian waters
to extend protection to Americans overseas. It was
considered a sign of national respectability to protect
citizens away from home, and one of the first acts of the
United States government was to seek to safeguard
commercial activities along the North American coast.
The Tripoli War (1801-5) demonstrated willingness to use
force to protect Americans as far from home as Tripoli.

What is less obvious but of even greater significance
was the protection of citizens in the American wilderness.
Because the United States chose to be a vast continental
nation-state, instead of a more compact country or a
vastly extended empire made up of disparate parts,
citizenship entailed federal protection. An American was
entitled to the protection of the state anywhere within
the national boundary, even though much of the country
was still wilderness. Protection by state authority
ultimately meant the extension of the power of the
federal government, and the history of the westward
movement amply demonstrates the close connection between
'exploration and empire.' (35) An American penetrating
the western lands carried with him his citizenship,
entitling him to constitutional guarantees of life and
property. He was within the jurisdiction of the
government in Washington, and he operated within the

legal system of the American nation. The national
interest in this sense amounted to the protection of
Americans as they sought to found new homes in the
wilderness. It is important to remember that in disputed
territories such as the Pacific Northwest and the
Southwest, American settlers, traders, and explorers
looked to distant Washington, rather than to closer
authorities of the Hudson Bay Company or the Mexican
government, for protection. They did not establish
their communities within foreign jurisdiction. Instead,
they remained Americans legally as well as morally.
There was a kind of particularism about their behavior
and convictions. By acting within the American political
and legal process, they were extending the limits of the
nation, and the latter in turn justified its claim over
the wilderness by extending its authority and protection
to them.· The lands they occupied became part of the
American nation, not simply distant trading posts to
bring riches to the country's coffers, or frontier
forts to safeguard an empire. The fact that there was
relatively little threat to national security from
without should not obscure this internal nature of
American nationalism. National-interest considerations
were first and foremost concerned with the safety of the
life, property and enterprises of Americans at home.
National strengthening hinged on the government's
ability to provide it.

It is for this reason that there grew a tendency in
the United States to view foreign affairs in terms
primarily of their impact upon the welfare of Americans at
home. Since the main objective of the federal
government was considered to lie in safeguarding the
security and well-being of the citizens, foreign policy
issues were apt to be seen in the domestic context.
Events occurring thousands of miles away overseas did not
seem relevant so long as they left the Americans
undisturbed in their pursuit of economic development.
They expected their government to exercise its power and
authority more at home than abroad. So long as there was
peace, liberty and welfare within the national
boundaries, America should not bestir itself to seek
involvement in foreign affairs. It is obvious that this
type of response - often described, too loosely, as
isolationism - was a reflection of a peculiar brand of
American nationalism, derived from a peculiar conception
of national interest. It was not that the Americans
lacked a foreign-policy outlook, but rather that their
vision of an ideal world stressed an environment in which
they would be free to engage in their private endeavors.

A foreign policy which created and strengthened such possibilities was to be welcomed and supported, but a policy which was not immediately related to them was viewed with skepticism.

This does not mean that there were no foreign-policy questions that affected the welfare of the country as a whole. From the very beginning there arose practical issues involving the new nation's relations with other countries which had to be dealt with by the government in Washington and their representatives overseas. In doing so they had to formulate some basis for policy, and explicitly or implicitly they developed conceptions of American national interests as guidelines to action. For instance, during the 1780s and 1790s, the key question in the country's external relations was the issue of navigation on the Mississippi river. The use of the river was an extremely important matter for American trade, especially the export of agricultural produce from the western states, and the federal government after 1789 consistently sought to have Spain recognize the Americans' right to navigate the river and to store goods at its mouth on the Gulf, New Orleans. Pinckney's treaty (1795), stipulating these points, was a product of ten years' negotiations with Spain.

American response to the European crisis of the 1790s was another instance where considerations of pragmatic national interests provided a determinant of policy. Although, as seen above, there was an ideological sympathy with the French Revolution, it alone did not determine United States foreign policy. Policy makers were keenly aware that the United States was intimately linked to Britain economically and commercially; the country exported vast quantities of raw materials, especially cotton, to England and its colonies, it supplied the bulk of foodstuffs to the British West Indies, and three-fourths of foreign imports into America originated in Britain and its empire. England was also a source of capital for the United States, as Englishmen purchased land, bank stock, governmental bonds and securities in the United States. British exports to the United States were a main source of tarriff revenue, the principal income for the federal government. Some efforts were made to diversify America's economic relations to lessen dependence on the British economy, but the existing obligations, the availability of ready credit and sheer habit tended to tie Americans closely to Britain.

Under the circumstances, George Washington's policy of neutrality was best calculated to protect America's commercial interests. It would protect the nation's economic ties with Britain by refusing to side with France, although it meant sacrificing idealistic and sentimental attachment to the cause of the French Revolution. The victory of John Adams over Thomas Jefferson to succeed Washington as president confirmed general acceptance of this line of reasoning; Adams was an advocate of the policy of neutrality, and he also supported Jay's Treaty (1795) which was greeted favorably by those who stressed the importance of maintaining conciliatory and mutually profitable relations with Britain, even if that implied coolness toward France.

Until about 1805 such a pragmatic policy seemed to suffice. American trade and shipping flourished, as the nation took advantage of the European war as a middleman in economic relations. There were tremendous increases in the volume of re-exports, indicating that foreign products, once brought to American shores, were taken by American ships once again to other ports. The United States followed the principle of 'free ships free goods' - the idea that neutral ships could carry non-contraband goods free of molestation by belligerents at sea - and France, Britain and other powers on the whole tolerated America's neutral shipping. It seemed to benefit a belligerent without seriously helping its opponent. The situation changed after 1805, when Napoleon imposed the continental system in order to close the European continent to British trade and choke off England economically. Britain retaliated by denying American trade with France. The position of the United States, which hitherto had profited from the war between the European powers, became untenable, as American ships going to England would be seized by the French navy, and those trying to enter France would be captured by the British. Between 1807 and 1812, 389 American ships were seized by Britain, and 352 by France.

The situation compelled the Jefferson administration to confront the question of priorities, which presented itself in such stark seriousness for the first time in the nation's history. The United States had to clarify what its essential interests and policies were, and how to implement them. While there were many factors that eventually resulted in the war with Britain in 1812, the events after 1805 demonstrated the importance of a psychological dimension of the national interest. Quite apart from the fact that American ships were being captured, causing hardships to their owners and exporters, here was a challenge to the national will.

America was being humiliated by the great powers, who
so cavalierly seemed to disregard the sensitivities of
the republic across the ocean.   This type of nationalism
was different from the more optimistic, internationalist
strain of the earlier years.   Now it was a question of
being taken seriously by other countries.   To succumb to
indignities, and to be treated as if American sentiments
did not matter, was a direct challenge to the very idea
of the United States as a respectable nation among
nations.   The country could not forfeit its right to be
treated with dignity and consideration on high seas.   It
was this kind of nationalistic feeling, which transcended
sections and interest groups, that provided the
psychological background of the coming of the War of 1812.
  The war settled little, but it served as a catalyst for
overcoming national frustration over being regarded as a
second-class nation by the great powers.   In that sense
it demonstrated the importance of national honor, prestige
and pride as ingredients of the national interest.   The
country - at least individuals and groups that supported
the war policy - would rather fight than accept cavalier
treatment by others.   As Henry Clay said in 1816, '[We
have gained] Respectability and character abroad -
security and confidence at home.' (36) Although the
peace of Ghent (1814) was basically a truce arrangement,
leaving aside Anglo-American disputes on shipping,
blockade and other matters, the coming of peace coincided
with the end of the Napoleonic Wars, and the United
States emerged from the experience with self-confidence
and respectability.   In a world of sovereign states vying
with one another for promoting their respective 'reasons
of state,' the United States had proved itself up to the
European powers in defining and fighting for what it
considered its vital national interests and honor.
  The United States, however, did not participate in the
European international system that was structured out of
the ruins of revolution and warfare.   With a few exceptions, some of whom have been noted, Americans continued
to consider their national interests narrowly, and
their government dealt with foreign-policy questions on
the whole in a pragmatic fashion, without concerning
itself with geopolitical issues.   For over a quarter
century after 1815, the national interest tended to be
viewed predominantly in economic terms.   It was
considered to be a basic objective of policy to foster
economic development at home and expanding trade
overseas.   With this in mind, successive administrations
devised various ways to assist individuals and groups to
compete with foreigners.   The tariff of 1816, for

instance, was the first instance of peacetime
protectionism, designed to stimulate domestic production,
especially of textiles and iron and thus to lessen
dependence on imports. The United States government
also sought to enter the West Indies market by
negotiating with Britain for the right of American ships
to enter ports in the British West Indies. In 1816 and
1817 Congress passed laws forbidding the coming of
British ships to the United States on their way to or
from the West Indies. These measures were attempts at
breaking British monopoly in Caribbean shipping and
trade, and through such initiatives American shipping
gradually gained entry into hitherto closed markets.
Since the United States remained a net importer of goods
despite protectionist measures, it was all the more
important to encourage a merchant marine. Receipts from
Americans carrying trade could make up the trade deficits,
and the government sought energetically to protect the
right of the American merchant marine to engage in
shipping in all parts of the world. One interesting
aspect of such a drive concerned shipping on the African
coast. Britain sought co-operation with the United States
to suppress the slave trade, but the latter was suspicious
of British interference with legitimate shipping,
especially as Britain wanted the 'right of search' to
suppress the ocean traffic in slaves. The government in
Washington was reluctant to have American ships submit
to a search by the British.

    In the decade of the 1840s, the American national
interests became bound up with expansion and with the
dispute with Mexico, culminating in the war of 1848.
There was a geopolitical strain in the expansionism of
President James K. Polk, as noted earlier; on the other
hand, the ideology of manifest destiny was as much
derived from sectional interests as from a nationalistic
vision, as will be seen. But there were also some
specific issues that were dealt with in the framework of
national-interest considerations. In Oregon and
California, for instance, American settlers had to be
protected from other nationals and sometimes from each
other. Moreover, it was considered most desirable to
have an outlet on the West coast, a harbor or a base, in
order to enter the trade of the Pacific Ocean. Both in
Oregon and California, Polk desired suitable harbors such
as San Diego, San Francisco, or in the Strait of Juan de
Fuca, which could be turned into entrepots of American
commerce in the west. His definition of the national
interest, in other words, included these specific
objectives, all related to his conception of the United

States as a maritime and trading nation. Once he set his
eyes on the commercial possibilities of the West coast, he
conducted his diplomacy with Britain and Mexico to win
from them at least the minimun concessions - the right of
Americans to establish themselves as traders on the
Pacific coast. He was all too successful; not only did
he win Oregon territory, to the 49th parallel, from
Britain, and California from Mexico, but he also acquired
lands connecting the West coast with Texas, the vast
territory of New Mexico. These, and the annexation of
Texas, completed the continental expansion of the United
States and created a host of internal problems,
accentuating differences between regions. The addition
of such vast areas was bound to complicate the governing
of the whole country, and at first it was not clear in
what ways the acquisition of the arid wilderness west of
the Great Plains contributed to the national interest.
But as far as Polk was concerned the primary objective
was the securing of harbors on the West coast and of the
land routes across the wilderness to reach it.

By the middle of the nineteenth century, then, certain
characteristics of American national interests were
becoming visible. Like the European states, the United
States government was concerned with the safety of its
citizens, especially in areas where they mingled with
nationals of other countries. The issue was bound up with
the search for clearer demarcation of national boundaries,
and by 1850 the problem had been settled to America's
great satisfaction. No longer would there be serious
boundary disputes, and Americans within the newly defined
territorial limits would be accorded the rights and
privileges of citizenship, including federal protection
and the jurisdiction of Anglo-Saxon law. Apart from
these issues, the United States would seek to develop
economically through encouraging domestic industrialization and agriculture, and by promoting overseas trade
and shipping.

These factors provided a more 'rational' basis for
American foreign relations, compared with the European
powers. Having solved the frontier question both with
Mexico and Britain (Canada), foreign policy no longer
needed to be preoccupied with boundary disputes.
Extending the rights of citizenship to all, except of
course slaves, within its territorial limits, the
government was relatively free of nationality and ethnic
problems that plagued some of the larger European
countries. Moreover, there was no cause for concern
over an increasing population as was the case elsewhere,
and no necessity to look for an overseas colony to

resettle a surplus population. As an English visitor
noted, 'with Malthus in one hand and a map of the back
country in the other [the American] defies us to a
comparison with America as she is to be, and chuckles his
delight over the splendors the geometrical ratio is to
shed over her story.' (37) Under the circumstances,
the task of America's foreign-policy officials was
considerably less complex than those for their European
counterpart. Consular representatives of the State
Department would look after the interests of Americans
abroad, but otherwise there seemed little need for
constant vigilance or professional interest in the art of
diplomacy. The United States sent to foreign countries
not ambassadors but only ministers, who technically
represented the government, not the sovereign, of the
nation. The implication was that America's foreign
relations would be primarily a matter of technical
details, not of high policy involving personal relations
with sovereigns in Europe and elsewhere.

This did not mean that there were no longer serious
national-interest issues to be negotiated with foreign
governments. In the 1850s the attention shifted to the
Caribbean, where the United States was interested in
protecting the lives, property and activities of
Americans. They were beginning to view Central America,
especially the isthmian region, as a key to commercial
expansion. American ships frequented there, and men like
Cornelius Vanderbilt were interested in building a
railroad across the isthmus. There was even an instance
of gunboat diplomacy in 1854, when President Pierce sent
a gunboat to Greytown, a British base in Nicaragua, after
the American minister was involved in a fight with a
local mob. Greytown was shelled and completely demolished
when the local authorities refused to accept America's
demand for apologies and reparations. Britain protested
and tension mounted, but fortunately the crisis was
aborted because of the coming of the Crimean War. These
incidents did not amount to a serious new departure in
United States foreign policy, but they revealed that even
after the completion of continental expansion the country
would not be free of foreign complications. It would be
called upon from day to day to make decisions involving
Americans abroad, and the basic attitude was to consider
their protection a cardinal ingredient of the national
interest. Even when no geopolitical or ideological
factors were involved, the government had to cope with
the problem in the framework of the traditional
definition of national interest.

The same observations may be made about America's

initiative in the opening of Japan in the 1850s.   At the
level of national interest, the Perry expedition was a
response to the plight of shipwrecked sailors and whalers
in the far reaches of the Pacific Ocean, who had been at
the mercy of Japan's exclusionist policy.   It was,
initially at least, no different from similar missions
undertaken to ensure the protection and well-being of
Americans abroad.   In China, too, the United States
entered into treaty relations to formalize trade
transactions between the two countries.   Beyond that the
government in Washington was unwilling to go.   It
adhered to the policy of non-interference during the
Taiping Rebellion (1850-64) that shook the Ch'ing
dynasty and killed millions of Chinese.   The policy
makers in Washington rejected the idea of taking
advantage of China's turmoil to seize territory, or to
join forces with the European powers to extract further
concessions from the Manchu government.   This did not
mean that the United States would not avail itself of
the most-favored-nation clause and seek to obtain the new
rights and privileges gained by other countries.   In
China as in Japan, American policy insisted on equal
opportunity so that Americans would be protected against
discriminatory treatment as they engaged in commercial
and other activities.   Such a definition of national
interest was in perfect harmony with the requirements of
an economically developing and expanding country, at a
time when no fierce contradiction was perceived between
developed and underdeveloped countries, or among
advanced capitalist economies.

4   SPECIAL INTERESTS

Three strands of United States foreign policy - factors
underlying American perceptions of the world - have thus
far been noted.   They comprise three key determinants of
any government's foreign policy, but in American foreign
relations before the Civil War, it may be observed that
the narrowly constructed definition of the national
interest usually sufficed as a guide to foreign policy.
Some policy decisions were derived from geopolitical
considerations, while others by implication envisioned
an internationalist world-view.   But these factors did
not usually produce a cohesive doctrine of United States
foreign policy which remained by and large pragmatic and
narrowly focused.
    These three ingredients produced - or, as was often
the case, were products of - certain conceptions of United

States foreign relations. They implied some assumptions
as to the role and position of the United States in the
world. They pictured the nation as an actor in international relations. Thus their visions of America were
macroscopic, viewing the country as a total entity, in
the aggregate, in a world community made up of other
entities.

Foreign relations, however, comprise more than state-
to-state or government-to-government affairs. Private
citizens, groups and socio-economic interests also
interact with their counterpart overseas. The sum total
of all such individual and group interactions constitute
an essential part, and quite often even the bulk, of
foreign affairs. In a country such as the United States,
with a relatively small foreign-policy establishment but
a democratic polity where personal and group views and
wishes (often through the mediation of Congress) can be
articulated and identified, these aspects of foreign
intercourse are particularly important. Any discussions
of United States foreign policy, therefore, must take
them into consideration.

To take group interests first, allusion was made
earlier to the Federalists' concern in the 1780s to
define a national as against a particularistic interest
as the basis for foreign policy. In Hamilton's words,
the country must think of the 'general interest' and the
'aggregate interests' rather than of 'local interest.'
That was why he supported the formation of a stronger
central government. The separate states, he said, were
'incapable of embracing the general interests of the
Union.' Even after the organization of the federal
government in 1787, however, the particularism of
individual states and sections exerted a powerful
influence on the evolution of American foreign policy.
While they were never completely dominant, some foreign-
policy decisions by the United States government before
the Civil War could only be understood as products of
this geographical particularism. For instance, during
the 1790s, as the United States negotiated a settlement
of outstanding disputes with Britain, culminating in Jay's
Treaty, one issue which pitted the Southern against the
Northern states was the question of compensation for
slaves carried away by the British armies during the
Revolutionary War. The South was unhappy over Jay's
failure to press the issue, and this accounted in part for
its objection to the treaty that bore his name. The
North, on its part, was unhappy over Jefferson's policy
of the embargo which stifled Northern commerce and
shipping. The War of 1812 brought about a near-revolt by

some Northern states, who viewed their interests to be
closely linked to trade with Britain.

By far the most significant instance of North-South
differences was the question of territorial expansion.
The Northern states were interested in acquiring
commercial bases on the Pacific coast, and they strongly
supported establishing the boundary of Oregon territory
at the 'fifty-four forty' parallel - all the way to
Alaska. On the other hand, they objected to the
extension of slave territory in the South, and resented
the annexation of Texas, causes that were energetically
pushed by the Southern states. If new territories
were to be incorporated into the Union, the North wanted
to make sure that they would be free of slavery - as was
demonstrated in 1846, when David Wilmot, a Congressman
from Pennsylvania, introduced an amendment to an
appropriation bill, stipulating that slavery be barred
from territories seized from Mexico as a result of the
war. The 'Wilmot proviso' passed the House by a vote
of 87-64, but it failed passage in the Senate. The
controversy did not die down, however, and in 1850 a
typical North-South compromise was devised, whereby
California was to be admitted as a free state, while the
rest of the lands acquired from Mexico were not to be
restricted with regard to the introduction of slavery.

While slavery was principally a domestic question,
sectional differences over the matter affected the
development of American relations with Britain and
Mexico. Britain, which abolished slavery in its colonies
during the 1830s, came to be seen as the world leader in
the anti-slavery movement. The Southern states,
therefore, tended to view it with growing alarm and
disdain. During the 1840s some Southern expansionists
conjured up an image of British interference with slavery
in Texas in order to justify their call for Texas
annexation. President Polk also utilized that argument
as a partial justification for the war with Mexico. He
presented his incorporation of Texas as a defensive
measure to prevent a violation of the Monroe Doctrine,
indicating that he viewed British policy as anti-slavery
and thus anti-South and ultimately as a threat to
American rights. This kind of reasoning showed the impact
of sectional thinking upon foreign policy. Another
example was the failure of the Senate, because of
Southern opposition, to endorse the policy of joint action
by Britain and the United States to suppress slave trade.

In the decades before the Civil War, Northern
spokesmen against the extension of slavery were apt to
characterize the South as an impediment to America's

national unity and greatness. In their view, following
the Hamiltonian dictum, pro-slavery interests were doing
great damage to the cause of the aggregate national
interest. Some used the term 'slave power' to describe
the particularism of Southern slave-owners, who were
pictured as the enemy of America's common interests and
aspirations. Others bemoaned the fact that the slavery
question was dividing the nation and hoped to preserve
the union through whatever means was available - whether
through some compromise between sections or through the
extension of federal authority over the South. In the end
this latter view - that the Union must be preserved at all
cost - emerged strongly, and the North became identified
with the cause of national union. The Whig-Republican
concept of the United States as a 'consolidated empire'
rather than a federation of semi-autonomous communities,
as Southern expansionists believed, triumphed when it came
to be viewed as a fundamental precondition for national
greatness. (38)

This was a remarkable feat for the North. It
succeeded in identifying itself with the national
interest. Such an outcome was in part due to the growing
awareness that 'union' and 'liberty' were inseparable. As
Seward said, unless new states were admitted as free
states, 'they will become independent and foreign states,
constituting a new empire to contend with us for the
continent.' Should the United States admit any more slave
states,

> there will be a division of the great American family
> into two nations, equally ambitious for complete
> control over the continent, and a conflict between
> them, over which the world will mourn, as the greatest
> and last to be retrieved of all the calamities that
> have ever befallen the human race. (39)

If the nation were to stand as an integrated whole and
to exert its influence in world affairs, then it must not
perpetuate the institution of slavery, which,
Charles Sumner said, 'degrades our country, and prevents
its example from being all-conquering.' (40) Here was a
merging of anti-slavery sentiment and nationalism,
enabling the North to speak for the national interest
by invoking moral principles.

The North succeeded in picturing the South as
particularistic, as an enemy of American national
interests. It would be more correct to say, however,
that the North was no less particularistic than the
South, but that its conception of the United States was
more in line with the general trends inside and outside
the country that were tending to create larger economic

units. The Northern conception - at least as expounded
by Federalists, Whigs, and Republicans - was the idea of
the United States as an economically integrated unit, in
which the national government as well as separate regions
worked together for the enrichment and development of the
whole country. Such a vision befitted the interests of
Northern merchants, manufacturers and speculators. In a
sense the history of American politics before the Civil
War was a story of the gradual evolution of this type
of Northern particularism so that in the end it would
give the impression of standing for the national interest.
Such a development had obvious implications for foreign
affairs.

The tariff question provides a good example. With a
few exceptions, Northern industrialists and wheat growers
tended to favor protective tariffs, and their influence
was felt upon the high-tariff policies of the Whigs and
the Republicans. The tariffs of 1828, 1832 and 1842 were
frankly protectionist, much to the chagrin of Southern
cotton growers who were dependent on export to Britain
and advocated a freer trade policy. The Democrats, both
in the North and South, on the whole opposed protectionism, not the least because they saw it as a means of
strengthening federal government at the expense of
states' rights. But here again, American domestic
politics steadily crystallized itself during the 1850s
so that high-tariff interests came to dominate the
Northern scene. As Northern Democrats parted company
with their Southern colleagues on the slavery issue and
joined forces with Whigs to form the Republican Party,
protectionism became a main policy for the North and the
West. The Republican plank of 1860 on tariff, written by
John A. Kasson of Iowa, an ex-Democrat, called for 'an
adjustment of imports ... to encourage the development of
the industrial interests of the whole country.' (41)

Apart from geographical sections and their special
interests, other groups within the United States related
themselves to external affairs from their particularistic
points of view. New England merchants, for instance,
were overwhelmingly opposed to alienating Britain during
the Napoleonic wars and were resentful of Jefferson's
embargo. At the same time, they were strong advocates
of an aggressive commercial policy in the Middle East and
Asia. They time and again called for the protection of
American merchants in distant lands, and they were
insistent that the government take the initiative to
open the door of Japan to American trade. For the same
reason, they were enthusiastic exponents of the 'no
transfer' doctrine as it applied to the West Coast; they

sought to obtain American sovereignty for Oregon and
California in order to expand commercial opportunities in
the Pacific Ocean. Likewise, agrarian interests in the
Old Northwest and beyond the Mississippi often acted as
a group, through their spokesmen in Congress, for a
strong commercial policy. They supported a Canadian
reciprocity treaty (1854), providing for free exchanges
of agricultural and other commodities. The treaty was
also favored by another interest group, the fishing
industry, as it granted Americans off-shore fishing
privileges on the coast and inlets of Canada. Another
reciprocity treaty - with Hawaii (1855) - was, however,
defeated in the Senate; it provided for duty-free entry
of Hawaiian sugar into the United States and would have
injured domestic sugar growers.

Economic interests by no means exhausted the list of
special interest groups. Missionary bodies, for instance,
were among the most vocal from the beginning of the nineteenth century. Protestant missionaries went to Siam,
Hawaii, China and other countries with or without
the protection of United States gunboats, but they were
virtually unanimous in insisting on obtaining a treaty
right to proselytize among pagan populations. Those in
Hawaii were particularly influential. After the 1820s,
some of them were calling for Hawaiian annexation to the
United States, and they had the support of some leaders
back home, such as President Pierce and Secretary of
State W. L. Marcy. Another interest group of a special
category was Americans who interested themselves in the
colonization of ex-slaves in Africa. The American
Colonization Society was organized in 1817, including
as vice-presidents prominent figures like Henry Clay
and Andrew Jackson, and it was instrumental in founding
the republic of Liberia in 1822. The idea was to send
free Negroes to America so that they would not be an
inassimilable element in American society, while at the
same time establishing themselves as the hope of the
African continent. Such a venture had obvious
implications for American foreign affairs; its advocates
wanted governmental support for the project, and because
Liberia would be an outpost of the United States in
Africa. Fortunately, there were few foreign
complications at this time as a result of the Liberian
experiment, both because only a handful of blacks ever
partook of it, and because the European powers were
unconcerned. It would have constituted more of a
domestic issue if black Americans had been better
informed and organized about the matter, but at this time
(and until well into the twentieth century) they did not

function as a self-conscious interest group with regard
to foreign affairs.

These, then, were some of the particularistic interests
which had a bearing on the course of American foreign
relations. Before the Civil War, however, their impact
upon policy seems to have been much more limited than was
the case in the European countries. There were few vested
interest groups with strong biases in foreign policy, and
apart from the tariff matter, which is as much a domestic
as a foreign-policy question, private interests neutral-
ized one another and left few traces of their direct
influence upon the government's dealings with foreign
countries. Certainly, after the Congress of Vienna at
any event, there was no phenomenon comparable to the
pressure exerted by Lancashire cotton mills upon British
policy in Asia, by 'Anglo-Indians' upon the Foreign
Office, or by silk merchants in Lyon upon the Quai
d'Orsay.

5 MASS CULTURE: INFORMAL CONCERNS AND PREJUDICES

Apart from the pockets of special-interest groups which
related themselves to external affairs in terms of their
perceived interests, there were individual Americans
whose attitudes toward foreign affairs were at bottom
a function of their personal traits, prejudices and
preoccupations. Of course, it would probably be true
that the bulk of the population remained indifferent to,
and ignorant of, world affairs. To the extent that they
showed an interest in politics, they were likely to be
preoccupied with domestic issues. Provincialism or
parochialism is an elusive phenomenon, and to make a
meaningful observation, one would have to indulge in the
comparison of parochial outlooks among different
countries, a task which is even more difficult in the
absence of reliable documentation. At least a beginning
may be made, however, if one examines the question: how
did the mass of Americans relate to foreigners? The
people-to-people aspect of foreign relations comprises
a vital part of a country's international affairs, and
it may be conveniently distinguished from more formal
relations and from particularistic influences upon
policy. For nineteenth-century America, informal,
private concerns were particularly important in shaping
the nation's outlook on foreign affairs at the mass-
culture level.

Individual Americans came into contact with individual
foreigners in a number of ways. Probably the most common

manner of encounter was through Europeans in the United
States - merchants, tourists, or, most important,
immigrants. American views of European countries could
be shaped by the way their behavior and customs were
perceived by those Americans who came into contact with
them, either directly or indirectly through hearsay or
mass media. To the extent that there was a parochial,
anti-foreign strain in American attitude, it manifested
itself in mid-century nativism, which was against
Catholics and immigrants - the two coincided, of course,
in the case of Ireland and parts of Germany and
Scandinavia. They were seen as an alien force, a threat
to American ideas and institutions. On the whole,
however, there was general acceptance of the idea of
unrestricted immigration, regardless of one's religion
or nationality. Despite their strong sense of national
pride and belief in a progressive image of world
civilization, their perception of American society was
not that of a closely-knit, homogeneous community in
which alien elements made themselves conspicuous.
Rather, there was open-mindedness about the coming of
foreigners and their participation in the task of nation-
building in the United States. So long as they worked
hard, contributed to economic development, and were
willing to assume the duties as well as privileges of
American citizenship, they were to be welcomed. As the
Republican platform of 1860 summed it up, the party was
opposed

> to any change in our naturalization laws, or any state
> legislation by which the rights of citizenship
> hitherto accorded to emigrants from foreign lands
> shall be abridged or impaired; and [it was] in favor
> of giving a full and efficient protection to the
> rights of all classes of citizens, whether native or
> naturalized, both at home and abroad.

European immigrants, however, were after all racially
akin to the native Americans, and the latter could com-
fortably talk of unrestricted immigration so long as the
immigrants were from Europe. Before the Civil War they
did not have to face the problem of non-European
immigration, and it was all but taken for granted that the
United States would continue to be a white man's country.
Certainly the debate on slavery indicated that for most
Northern abolitionists the vision of a free America was
one in which the nation would develop as 'an empire of
free white men,' as Seward said. 'The white man needs
this continent to labor upon,' he spoke in the Senate,
'[he] must and will have it ... The white man, whether
you consent or not, will make the states to be admitted,

and he will make them all free states.' (42)
David Wilmot, the author of the famous proviso, told the
House that his proposal to bar slavery from lands to be
ceded by Mexico was intended to preserve them 'for the
sons of toil, of my own race and own color.' (43)
Within the Caucasian race, some Americans disliked
Catholics and organized the Know-Nothing Party, but the
movement had no direct bearing upon foreign relations.
So long as Americans were accustomed to think of
foreigners as Europeans who might settle and become
Americans like themselves, their personal proclivities
and prejudices did not compromise the generally
favorable attitude toward free intercourse with other
peoples.

Whether the American people were similarly disposed
toward non-Europeans is difficult to determine. On the
one hand, their white-supremacist assumptions meant that
they had a racial view of the world which was
hierarchical. In the mid-nineteenth century, there
steadily grew in influence a view that held that
the various races of mankind were distinct entities,
even traceable, according to some writers, to the very
beginnings of man. Josiah Nott, for instance, argued
that different races were created separately, instead
of being all descendants of Adam and Eve. Thus human
racial diversity could be traced to the origins of
mankind. The white race alone descended from Adam and
Eve, and it was eternally unchanging in its position
of superiority. Other races were developed separately
and were by definition inferior to the whites. Unlike
the latter they were not as capable of progress or
civilization. The white race could only degenerate
through mixed marriages with them. Samuel Morton's
famous 'Crania Americana' (1839) spelled out what
he took to be the characteristics of the various races.
Physical peculiarities of the races, he wrote, were
'independent of external causes' but were immutable
traits they inherited from generation to generation.
Moreover, they produced distinct differences in the
cultural and intellectual capabilities. The Caucasian
race, for instance, was characterized by 'the highest
intellectual endowments,' and the Mongolian race was
'ingenious, imitative, and highly susceptible of
cultivation,' whereas the Negro race (what Morton
referred to as the 'Ethiopian') was 'joyous, flexible,
and indolent - the lowest grade of humanity.' (44)

Such an inflexible race theory conflicted with the
internationalist assumption, noted earlier, that man was
perfectible, that all men were capable of growth and

change. It seems likely that the internationalist
doctrine was embraced as a hopeful view of world history
and of foreign affairs in which the United States would
play a leading and inspirational role, whereas individual
Americans may have retained race prejudice as they came
into contact with foreigners or as they pondered the
future of their country. Because such contacts were
overwhelmingly with Europeans, collective internationalism
and individual parochialism did not necessarily have to
collide. One could believe both in human progress and in
the idea of a free, white America, since Western
civilization was considered to be the most advanced, and
America the most civilized of Western countries. As for
non-white, non-Western peoples, their backwardness would
not prevent them from rejoining the march of progress once
they came under the influence of the West, but whether
individual Americans appreciated their company depended
on specific circumstances. On the whole it would seem
that foreigners were tolerated to the extent that they
exhibited their ability to assimilate Western civilization
or demonstrated certain traits which Americans admired.

The American people, however, were not xenophobic.
They learned about distant lands in school geography and
world history (usually referred to as 'history of all
nations') and they cherished arts and crafts imported
from abroad. A good example of American response to non-
Westerners may be seen in the opening of direct contact
with the Japanese. Before the Perry expedition,
knowledge about Japan was extremely limited and perfunct-
ory, usually a minor part of information about Asia on
the whole. For instance, the 1830 edition of
'Encyclopedia Americana' had a four page article on 'Asia'
and mentioned Japan in passing. 'All the forms of
society,' it said, 'are displayed in the existing Asiatic
nations, from the savage state of the wandering hordes
to the most effeminate luxury; but liberty, founded on
law and the moral and intellectual education of man, is
wanting.' None of the Asian countries was presented in
complimentary terms, least of all Japan and China:
'Ancient forms are preserved most rigidly, and the
intellect is least progressive in China and Japan.' (45)
Samuel Goodrich's 'The Tales of Peter Parley About Asia,'
a popular textbook, described the variety of Asians this
way: 'Many of them are as dark as our Indians, and some
of them are much darker. The women of Japan, and the
Caucasian women, are nearly as white as the women of
America.' But the author reminded the reader that 'The
sun rises on them as well as on us. The skies are over
their heads, the moon and the stars shed their light on

them; they, as well as we, have hopes and fears, joys and sorrows.' The implication was that they were fellow human beings worthy of study. (46) Goodrich conveyed the same message in another book, 'A History of All Nations', published in 1851. He explained that Asia included 'the roving Arab, the horse-mounted Tartar, the superstitious Hindoo, the fierce Malay, the ingenious Chinese, the polite Japanese, the bear-hunting Kamtschadale, the fish-eating Samoiede, and many others.' While the author characterized Asians on the whole as 'slavish,' 'super-stitious,' and 'treacherous,' and described their moral qualities as 'generally ... below those of Europeans,' he praised their highly developed arts. 'All the efforts of European art and capital,' he wrote, 'have been unequal fully to imitate the carpets of Persia, the muslins of India, the porcelain of China, and the lacquered ware of Japan.' (47)

It may be assumed that these bits of information were about all that Americans had at their disposal when, if at all, they thought about Japan. It was superficial knowledge, but they were by no means devoid of curiosity or open-mindedness. Their sense of superiority was clearly present, but this did not mean they would be averse to all dealings with strange people or prevent them from being genuinely interested in learning about other societies. Because direct Japanese-American contact began virtually 'de novo,' it is illuminating to turn to some accounts of the Japanese embassy of 1860, the first time that a group of Japanese officials ever visited the United States. When the ship 'Kanrinmaru' arrived at San Francisco, carrying an advance party of Japanese samurai, the 'New York Times' correspondent on the West coast described the strange encounter in minute detail. People of San Francisco, he wrote,

> have been a good deal puzzled as to the degree of enthusiasm they should exhibit over their distinguished strangers. In our ignorance we have treated them with abundant courtesy, but very little speech-making ... The Japanese have availed themselves of these court-esies only to see some of our foundries and large manufacturing establishments, and to meet on shore our dignitaries.

As for their appearance, the correspondent noted that they 'were all men of small stature, but tough and hearty, and well-knit ... There is an impression that they are more cleanly than the Chinese.' This last was an allusion to the Californians' initial comparison between Chinese and Japanese. After enumerating various physical differences between the two, the writer concluded that the

'differences I have named must suffice for our making
"distinguished strangers" of the one, and a degraded,
inferior class of the other.' (48)   On 28 April, the
'New York Times' issued a special supplement on 'Japan
and the Japanese Embassy' and offered to its readers a
description of that country, its people and Americans in
Japan.   It included the latest dispatch from San
Francisco, where the ambassadors from Edo had just
arrived.   'It made a white man blush,' he wrote, 'to see
how much more simple, tasteful and sensible they were in
their uniform than our grandees were in theirs.'   East-
coast Americans had their first glimpse of the visitors
in May, and the 'New York Times' made a top article of
'The Japanese in America.'   The ambassadors, it noted,
'are dignified, polite and amiable gentlemen ... all the
officers and employes [sic] are intelligent, and
disposed, every one of them, to cultivate our close
friendship and good understanding.' (49)   In Washington,
where the emissaries were to present themselves to
President Buchanan, people waited anxiously for their
arrival, 'on tiptoe of expectation,' as a correspondent
reported,

> in view of the coming delegation from the Empire of
> the Rising Sun ... the ladies are all on the look-out
> for good places to see the sights; correspondents are
> flocking thither, with 'Perry's Expedition' and sketch-
> books under their arms; bootblacks making investments
> in 'Japanese polish'; landlords gloating over the
> prospect of full houses ... while the population
> generally holds its breath in the interval of
> suspense. (50)

The 15 May issue of the newspaper was covered by
descriptions of the embassy's arrival in the capital, the
top article presented under five bold headlines, such as
'The Military and Popular Display' and 'Intense
Excitement and Enthusiasm.'   The previous day, it
reported, there was a slim attendance at the Senate
'owing to a general interest felt in the arrival of the
Japanese.'   Senator John J. Crittenden moved the Senate
to adjourn in view of the occasion.   When Senator
William P. Fessenden objected, saying he 'was opposed to
adjourning for every show that came along,' Crittenden
'explained that this rose far above an ordinary show.'
Whereupon the Senate adjourned by a vote of 19 to 11.
   The versatile correspondent for the 'New York Times'
has recorded for posterity some of the comments the men in
the streets of Washington made on the Japanese visitors:
'Ain't they like women?' 'What do they wear two swords
for?'   'They look like Chinese.'   'Look at his head

shaved.'   'He's got trousers like a Turk.'   'And a coat
like a butcher's shirt.'   'See his white sandals.'
'Guess he's one of the cooks.'   'Wonder if he's a Prince.'
'Can he eat rats?'   Some of the crowd, 'rugged, dirty,
black and white, poked their filthy digits into the
carriage for the Ambassadors - Princes, be it remembered -
to shake hands with them.' (51) Such behavior caused the
'Boston Daily Advertiser' to caution Americans not to
forget that 'these are not barbarians or half-civilized
men, but representatives of a nation whose civilization
in many respects - putting it so as to save our national
pride - is equal to our own.' After the Japanese
ambassadors went through tumultuous receptions in
Washington, Philadelphia and Baltimore, the newspaper
expressed its concern that 'they should be treated in
our principal cities as though they were savages instead
of enlightened men, or Fejee Islanders instead of
representatives of a nation which possessed a high and
elegant civilization before this continent was settled.'
(52) On the eve of the departure of the embassy for
their homeland, the Boston paper summed up the meaning
of the historic visit:

> Not from any particular display of good judgment
> on the part of those who managed the visit, but from
> the inquisitive and imitative disposition of the
> Japanese themselves, we look for some valuable results
> from them, for us and for civilization in general ...
> They have shown themselves to be very inquisitive in
> all matters of mechanics, curious as to machinery,
> quick to perceive the utility of inventions, and ready
> to admit the superiority of new processes ... We have
> no doubt that the path has now been opened, through
> which commerce shall carry to that secluded people the
> arts of civilization which they still lack and the
> religion which they now reject. (53)

One may detect in the episode an example of popular
American response to strangers. A typical reaction was a
mixture of curiosity and ignorance, a sense of superiority
and open-mindedness. Their general lack of knowledge or
their racial particularism did not prevent them from
flocking to the streets to have a glimpse of the visitors,
writing and reading about them, and otherwise extending
their hospitality to them. Their visit to Washington
coincided with the convening of the Republican national
convention and with the heightening drama of an
extraordinary election year, but the embassy was such a
popular phenomenon that, according to the 'New York
Times,' it 'drew better than [Senator Stephen] Douglas.'
(54) This was certainly not a response of an

ethnocentric, indifferent people. Whatever may be said
of United States foreign relations on the eve of the
Civil War, it would be misleading to ignore the episode.
By the same token, the embassy points up the need to
take popular attitudes and perceptions into account as
an important ingredient of American foreign affairs.
There was readiness to engage in people-to-people
relations, and the press performed its educational
function extremely well. That these are an extremely
crucial factor in foreign relations can be readily
demonstrated when one reads what the Japanese visitors
were recording in their diaries. One of them noted,
'In Japan papers are printed once or twice a month but
in western countries they are printed daily although
the news is only slightly different. The fact that the
Japanese have come to America is printed in several
papers.' Of the American hosts, he wrote, 'The people
of America are big hearted, honest and faithful. The
Americans do not scorn foreigners and are kind to
strangers. The American people are simple and honest like
Japanese born in the mountains or on the farm who have
never been spoiled by the big city.' On the day before
they departed from Washington, he recorded, 'many people
came at night to say good-bye. When we met them we all
wept. Seeing them also weeping we realized that they
are tender-hearted people.' Upon arriving at
Philadelphia, people 'came up, shook hands to welcome us,
and went home very happy. We see by this conduct that
the Americans respect the people of other countries.' (55)
The sum of such personal contacts, while by no means the
totality of a country's foreign affairs, constitutes a
vital element and often has a lasting impact upon
subsequent events. In this sense, it is imperative for
the historian of American foreign policy not to lose
sight of this fifth ingredient of national attitudes. It
can connote cosmopolitanism or xenophobia, a high level of
knowledge about foreign countries or superficiality,
friendliness or indifference. But it is their emotions,
ideas and attitudes as they interact with foreigners
that create an environment in which more formal
activities of diplomacy and commerce operate.

6   THE CIVIL WAR

The decade 1850-60 saw a simultaneous development of all
the ingredients of American foreign relations. The
United States asserted itself more strongly than ever
before as a Caribbean power, while beginning to make

itself felt in the Pacific Ocean. Its trade and
shipping expanded rapidly, while the nation delighted
in a self-image as a disseminator of the blessings of
civilization to less fortunate countries. Individual
Americans, although increasingly preoccupied with
domestic politics, found time and resources to meet and
entertain foreign visitors. In the meantime special-
interest groups busied themselves to seek further
opportunities for profit, through a protective tariff at
home, or through the opening-up of more treaty ports for
trade abroad.

The deepening crisis between North and South had vital
implications for America's standing and role in the world,
as perceptive observers readily noted. William H. Seward,
for instance, was an opponent of slavery because he was
convinced that the institution hindered the growth of the
country as a great power. An eloquent speech he made in
Columbus, Ohio, in 1853 gives testimony to this
connection:

> If the Future which you seek consists in this: that
> these thirty-one states shall continue to exist for a
> period as long as human foresight is allowed to
> anticipate after-coming events; that they shall be all
> the while free; that they shall remain distinct and
> independent in domestic economy, and nevertheless be
> only one in commerce and foreign affairs; that there
> shall arise from among them within their common domain
> even more than thirty-one other equal states alike
> free, independent , and united; that the borders of
> the federal republic, so peculiarly constituted, shall
> be extended so that it shall greet the sun when he
> touches the tropic, and when he sends his glancing
> rays toward the polar circle, and shall include even
> distant islands in either ocean; that ... mankind
> shall come to recognize in us a successor of the few
> great states which have alternately borne commanding
> sway in the world -- if this, and only this, is
> desired, then I am free to say that if ... our public
> and private virtues shall be preserved, nothing seems
> to me more certain than the attainment of this
> future, so surpassingly comprehensive and
> magnificent. (56)

Given such a vision of national grandeur, it readily
followed that a sectional conflict, dividing the country
just at the moment when great-power status seemed within
reach, would be nothing less than a catastrophe.
Because of this very reason, such leaders as
Daniel Webster, Henry Clay and Stephen Douglas sought to
minimize the crisis through some sort of compromise

between North and South. In the short run, at any event,
their efforts failed, as did those by Seward and the
Republicans, to maintain national unity. In the context
of American foreign affairs, this failure was
fundamentally attributable to the importance of ideology;
the vision of the United States as a great and united
country came to mean, to Northern leaders at least, a
country standing for principle. The Union must be
preserved, but it was not a sufficient condition of
greatness. The country could not bear 'commanding sway in
the world' unless it purged itself of the taint of
tyranny and degradation. As Abraham Lincoln said in
1854, slavery 'deprives our republican example of its just
influence in the world - enables the enemies of free
institutions to taunt us as hypocrites.' (57) The
assumption here was that the country could be both united
and free. This optimism proved to be premature, but it
is to be noted that for Lincoln and his supporters the
idea of America in the world, standing for certain ideals,
was a very vital part of their thinking. Thus the slavery
question inevitably had implications in their minds for
American foreign relations. It seemed self-evident to
Seward, Lincoln and others that if the United States was
to play a major role as a great power, it could not long
tolerate slavery.

Paradoxically, the North-South rift widened during the
1850s precisely because there was no external threat to
national union. None of the European powers was
interested in actively intervening in American domestic
politics, nor was there any overt threat to national
security. A clearly recognizable danger from the
outside, or openly interventionist attempts by a foreign
power, would have had the effect of turning national
attention to external affairs and might have prevented,
however temporarily, a show-down between North and South.
Just as plausibly, foreign affairs might have divided the
country, as they had during the 1790s, and the
contending factions might have accused each other of
succumbing to, or courting with, an alien power. These
possibilities were remote in the decade before the Civil
War, and the sectional conflict tended to take a purely
domestic form. This had the effect of aggravating
tension in American politics, since the domestic crisis
could not be related to foreign issues. Instead,
sections, groups and individuals within the United States
had to cope with one another on their own terms. This
simplified the matter for them, but at the same time it
provided the nation with few alternatives.

Against such a background, the meaning of the Civil

War in the evolution of American foreign policy becomes
quite apparent. In terms of global politics, any
pretensions the United States might have entertained as a
world power were checked because of the primacy of
domestic politics over external affairs. During the
1850s the country had pursued a rather active policy in
the Caribbean, the Pacific and Asia, and it was on the
threshhold of emerging as a power with global interests
and commitments. All this had now to wait the outcome
of the Civil War, as can be seen in the following excerpt
from an instruction Secretary of State Seward sent in
November 1861 to Minister Robert H. Pruyn in Japan:

> When we gently coerced Japan into friendship with us
> we were a united nation. We did not admit that there
> then was, or, indeed, that there ever had been, a
> stronger one in the world. Our mercantile and our
> naval marine vindicated this high pretension on every
> sea, however distant from our own continent. Nine
> months have wrought a great and melancholy change in
> this proud position. We are divided by faction, and
> engaged in civil war. (58)

One consequence of such changed circumstances was an
abrupt halt in the expansionist thrust of the preceding
decades. The Civil War sorely tested the vision, as
articulated by Seward, of an unlimited expansion of the
United States in all parts of the world. If expansion
within the continental limits alone had brought about
division and conflict, thereby shattering the faith that
expansion and unity were compatible, it could easily be
questioned whether the extension of American power abroad
might not likewise produce friction and crisis at home.
The Lincoln administration, moreover, associated prewar
territorial expansion with Southern slavery, and both
President Lincoln and Secretary of State Seward intensely
disliked the idea of expansion in the Caribbean region
because of these connotations.

Even with respect to more immediate national
interests, the United States government became aware of
the disastrous consequences of the domestic upheaval
almost as soon as it broke out. American shipping, which
had registered remarkable growth and even overtaken
British merchant marine just on the eve of the Civil War,
plummeted, as Northern ships had to be engaged in block-
ading the Southern coast, and were captured by Southern
forces, or were transferred to foreign registry to avoid
capture. Insurance rates on American ships became
prohibitive, while foreign ships entered the lucrative
business of neutral shipping. The result was a
precipitous decline of American merchant marine, from

which it was never really to recover. Whereas in 1860
nearly two-thirds of total United States trade was carried
on American ships, by 1864 the ratio had declined to 27.5
per cent. The government was powerless to check the
decline. For one thing, export trade from North and West
needed to be promoted, and foreign bottoms had to be
utilized to carry American goods, mostly grains, to
Europe. There was an increase in Northern trade because
of a shortage of grains in Europe during the 1860s, and
the export trade was an important source of revenue for
the North. In addition, the Republican administration
imposed high tariffs on imports to raise revenue for the
prosecution of the war, and it also increased tonnage
dues on foreign ships. In a sense, then, there was a
congruence of interests between foreign shippers and
American officials.

More ·serious was the impact of the Civil War upon the
protection of American interests overseas. The above-
cited instruction by Seward to the minister in Japan
continued:

what will be the influence of the news of our
divisions among the semi-barbarians of Japan,
magnified and painted, as they will doubtless be,
by strangers, enemies of the republic, its prosperity,
and its power? Will the government of Japan retain the
fear which, perhaps, was the best guarantee of its good
will towards us? Will the misguided faction in Japan,
so hostile to all foreigners, suffer the government
to remain in friendship with a nation that will seem
to them to have lost the virtue of patriotism so
essential to command the respect of other nations?
Already we have heard that the Chinese authorities,
informed of our divisions, have come to underrate our
power, and to disregard our rights. Is this evil to be
experienced also in Japan? To prevent it is the
responsibility of your mission -to watch and guard the
national interests there, while the storms of faction
are spending their force against the government at
home, will be your chief duty.

As if to justify Seward's fear that American interests
abroad might be jeopardized by the Civil War at home,
Henry Heusken, a Japanese-speaking aide to Consul
Townsend Harris, was murdered by a group of Japanese
fanatics in 1861. Two years later an American gunboat,
'Pembroke,' was attacked off the coast of Choshu in
western Japan. In the first incident, Harris opposed the
use of force, preferring to let the Japanese government
handle the case. The rationale was that American
interests could best be protected through a policy of

co-operation with officials in power in Japan, whose
position was increasingly coming under attack from more
openly anti-foreign factions. The 'Pembroke' affair
was considered a manifestation of the latter group's
assault on all foreign rights, and the United States
joined the other powers in a bombardment of the coastal
regions of Chōshū in 1864. An American ship joined nine
British, three French and four Dutch gunboats and
demolished the area. In addition, they forced the
central government to pay reparations amounting to three
million dollars.

Such a show of force, in co-operation with the
European powers whose ambitions the United States had
often suspected, may have reflected the judgment that
the nation could not afford to have its rights and
interests cavalierly disregarded by a country it
considered 'semi-barbaric.' It was ironic that this,
about the only instance of forceful policy by the United
States during the Civil War, should have been possible
only because it acted together with the European nations.
It was as if national interests depended on collaboration
and understanding with them. If so, it constrained the
freedom of American diplomacy. Seward was fully aware of
the constraints and did not indulge in an adventuristic
foreign policy lest it should unnecessarily irritate
America's potential antagonists. But there was a real
crisis closer home which revealed the vulnerability of the
United States during the Civil War. This was the French
adventures in Mexico.

Before 1861 the United States had tended to view its
southern neighbor as less than a first-rate power, one
where American interests were taken for granted, and
President Buchanan had even been willing to consider the
use of land and naval forces to protect Americans in
transit across Mexico. With the coming of the Civil War,
the table had turned, and the North had to worry about
foreign intervention in that country. That the United
States was now less feared was demonstrated when France
under Napoleon III occupied Mexico City in June 1863 and
placed Archduke Maximilian of Austria on the throne as
emperor of Mexico in April 1864. It was hopeless for
the North to oust the French or Maximilian from Mexico
by force, and Seward had to resort to diplomatic means
to try to prevent an alliance between Mexico and the
South. The latter, for obvious reasons, wanted such an
alliance, but Maximilian hesitated, thinking that his
political survival depended on the future attitude of
Washington. Because of Seward's shrewd diplomacy, never
threatening Maximilian with speedy retaliation and not

once mentioning the Monroe Doctrine, neither Maximilian nor Napoleon felt pushed into a belligerent stand against the North. A South-Mexican alliance would have brought about French recognition of the South and possible intervention in the Civil War. But Napoleon III was reluctant to act without Britain. On several occasions he proposed joint action between France and Britain, and in 1865 he proposed an alliance between the two so that they would come to each other's aid in case of aggression by the United States against either of them. Nothing of the sort materialized, but even the fact that such an alliance and other measures were contemplated by a great European power indicated to what extent the power and prestige of the United States had suffered because of the civil strife.

Since foreign influence inevitably increased during the Civil War, it was to be expected that Great Britain would play a pivotal role in affecting the course of American foreign relations. Ultimately British policy defined the extent of foreign intervention, and the unwillingness of the government in London to take measures against the North proved to be a crucial factor in the history of the Civil War.

American-British relations during the Civil War offer a fascinating mixture of power and ideological and national interest considerations. The ideological component, in particular, was extremely important because both North and South sought to appeal to British support in idealistic terms, and because the British had always been interested in the slavery question, having abolished the institution in the 1830s. There had also arisen, as in the United States, a debate on race, concerning the question of whether freed slaves would ever make progress and reach the state of civilization attained by the white race. Moreover, the British had always been interested in the question of national organization, having experienced sessionist movements in America, India, Ireland and elsewhere. They saw in the American Civil War issues that were obviously relevant to their own country.

From the Northern point of view, Britain's anti-slavery policy was a great asset; the North could obtain British support - or at least a non-interventionist policy - by portraying the Civil War as involving the slavery dispute. The South, on its part, presented itself as a nation struggling for independence. It justified its secession in terms of a compact theory of government which Americans had used in the 1770s. When in 1863 Poland staged an uprising against Russia to seek independence, the Confederate regime could view it as another example of the struggle for freedom for which it, too, was fighting. Britain in fact supported Polish aspirations and proposed a joint mediation by Britain, France, Austria and the United States. The latter declined out of deference to Russia, but in so doing it opened itself to charges of indifference to the fate of the heroic Poles, just as it suppressed Southerners' desire to establish a nation of their own.

Fortunately for the North, Britain was divided ideologically between pro-North and pro-South sympathies. Many, like Lord Acton, supported the freedom of the Southern states to secede, while men like Richard Cobden and John Bright saw the Civil War as a struggle between democracy and privilege and actively campaigned on behalf of the Northern cause. But neither viewpoint had overwhelming support among British public opinion, and key officials were drawn by both these arguments. They accepted the idea of Polish independence, implying agreement with the Southern stand, while at the same time they welcomed Lincoln's emancipation proclamation as a worthy step in the eradication of slavery. Under the circumstances, strict neutrality was the least objectionable alternative, a policy that was also dictated by considerations of British national interests. These interests were essentially commercial, and British trade seemed best protected through a policy of neutral- ity. Many, to be sure, expected unhappiness over the Northern blockade of the Southern coast, bringing to a halt the traffic in cotton that had comprised as much as a half of annual American exports to Britain before 1861 and provided jobs for mill-hands in Lancashire. They were bitter over the economic distress which they experienced with varying degrees of intensity; and those who suffered most were the strongest exponents of a more positive policy on the part of Britain, at least looking toward recognition of the South. (59) But there were other interests which would have been adversely affected by such a policy. England depended on American wheat, supplied and shipped from the West and the North. There was a brisk export of British arms and munitions to the Union. While the Republican tariffs discouraged the growth of overall British exports to the United States, the potential loss was offset by an increasing flow of goods to France, a flow which resulted from the British-French treaty of 1860, stipulating very low duties on mutual imports.

London did not initially intend to favor the North explicitly, but by refraining from recognizing

Confederate independence and from challenging the
blockade of the Southern coast by the Union, British
policy in effect helped the Northern cause.   After 1863,
with the issuing of the emancipation proclamation, both
self-interest and ideology seemed to dictate that
Britain should at least implicitly favor the North.   The
French offer of joint intervention was rejected,
indirectly frustrating the Confederate government's
scheme to obtain European and Mexican support.

The Civil War thus forced Americans to take foreign
affairs much more seriously than had been the case for
several decades.   They discovered that their nation's
fate was bound up with the policies of other governments.
They could no longer take for granted national survival,
security or protection of interests.   The Civil War
provided a unique opportunity to consider the
implications of different angles of American policy -
power, ideals, interest - and to take foreign countries
with utmost seriousness.   Perhaps this was the ultimate
if unforeseen paradox: the United States, which had
largely ignored foreign affairs and concentrated on
domestic development and expansion, found itself rent
by civil strife and forced to recognize the importance
of foreign relations.

Chapter 2

European Imperialism and U S Expansionism

The decades after the Civil War coincided with the Age of
Imperialism in European diplomacy. Practically within
a generation world politics was transformed as the
European powers one by one extended the limits of their
political and economic empire, so that by the turn of the
century much of the globe had been divided up among them
as colonies and spheres of influence. And yet for the
United States this was a period of relative inactivity
in the world arena, and before the mid-1890s it did not
join the European nations in imperialistic politics.
This gap constitutes an essential characteristic and a
conceptual framework for comprehending United States
foreign relations during the years 1865-90.

1 POST-CIVIL WAR AMERICAN DIPLOMACY

The United States was conspicuously absent from much of
the drama of imperialist politics before the 1890s. It
alone of the major Western countries did not participate
in the scramble for colonies, concessions and spheres of
influence in Asia, Africa and the Middle East. Only
infrequently did it attend international conferences or
become party to big-power understandings and agreements
over colonial issues. It fought no wars and made no
conquests, the purchase of Alaska from Russia in 1867
being the last instance before 1898 of territorial
aggrandizement. In contrast to the European powers,
American diplomacy was generally quiescent.

The twenty-five-year period between the end of the
Civil War and 1890 thus offers a fascinating contrast
between European and American foreign affairs. Some
historians refuse to be impressed with the apparent
inactivity and passivity of United States foreign policy

after the Civil War, and argue that this was a period of preparation for what was to come, that underneath the superficial lack of interest in imperialistic adventures, there continued the urge to expand, commercially if not territorially, that had characterized the earlier decades and that was to blossom into active and aggressive expansionist policies in the last years of the century. It is undoubtedly possible to discuss the post-Civil War period from the vantage point of the 1890s, but one must not forget that the United States during the 1870s and the 1880s was acting within a specific international environment and that it had to relate itself, not to its future existence, but to other contemporary powers. In other words, one must compare American policy of these decades with the foreign policies of the European nations, not simply with the United States as it came to play a more assertive role in the 1890s. It then becomes evident that, at the level of formal diplomacy at least, American policy hardly made much difference in the developing drama of imperialistic politics in most regions of the world. The United States, to be sure, maintained its strong interest in the Caribbean and the Pacific, but in Asia, the Middle East or Africa, the main theaters of European diplomacy, America's role was either non-existent or extremely limited.

To account for this gap, it is necessary to examine the perceptions of world affairs by American officials and opinion-makers. How did they perceive the country's position in the world after the devastating Civil War? Did they still maintain the traits from the earlier days - nationalistic views with a strong component of internationalism? What did they think of European imperialism? Were there parallels between European and American expansionist thought? What did Europeans in turn think of the United States after the Civil War?

For twelve years after the Civil War - 1865-77 - two Secretaries of State were in charge of America's foreign affairs: William Henry Seward under President Andrew Johnson and Hamilton Fish under President U. S. Grant. They had both been active in American politics and government before the Civil War and had long formed their ideas about the country's external relations. They saw no particular need to change them in the post-bellum period. Essentially, they perceived foreign policy in terms of traditional national interests that were defined rather specifically and, in the case particularly of Fish, narrowly. They would want the United States to enjoy security from aggression, to maintain its special position in the Caribbean, to expand

commercial opportunities overseas and to avoid
unnecessary foreign complications. To this list Seward
would add territorial expansionism through purchase if it
could be achieved without causing much domestic or foreign
opposition. Seward's expansionism had its roots in the
pre-Civil War days, when he envisioned a gigantic American
'empire' consisting of all freedom-loving countries in the
world. After 1865 his immediate goals were more modest,
but he was still interested in acquiring lands close to
the United States so that the nation could build a huge
open market. He was dreaming of an America that would
promote economic development through domestic
industrialization and foreign immigration. In 1867
he was instrumental in negotiating for the purchase of
Alaska from Russia and the Danish West Indies (now the
Virgin Islands) from Denmark. He was successful in both
instances, but the Senate refused to ratify the Danish
treaty providing for the acquisition of the West Indies
for $7,500,000, considering the price too high. However,
Seward was able to persuade enough Senators to agree to
the Alaskan purchase for $7,200,000. He continued to
evince an interest in annexing Canada through peaceful
means, for he thought it would be more economical to
join the two countries together than to have them maintain a separate existence, in view of their economic
compatability. But the British government was determined
to maintain the empire, and in 1867 created a unified
regime of the Canadian Confederation.

Hamilton Fish was not as keen about territorial
expansion as Seward, although he too held aspirations
for Canadian annexation. But both of them were alike in
conducting foreign affairs more or less in a pragmatic
framework of national interests. First of all, they
wanted to safeguard the country's security from external
aggression. This was an easy task, since at that time
no hostile forces were in the environs of the United
States. The only exception was Mexico, where Maximilian
had established himself as emperor in 1863. Seward had
no difficulty in pressing France to withdraw its forces
from Mexico and thus to dismantle Maximilian's regime.
This was done in 1867, and thereafter there was no serious
foreign complication to the detriment of national
security. Second, they supported means to expand trade
opportunities abroad. The Hawaiian reciprocity treaty
of 1875 was a good example. It was seen not only as an
opportunity for increasing American-Hawaiian trade but
also as a major inducement for expanding United States
commerce in the wider Pacific region as well as Asia.

Both Seward and Fish continued the tradition of

viewing the Caribbean as a region of special importance
to American interests, and they sought to preserve the
position that the country had attained in the area before
the war. Seward wanted the Danish West Indies in part
because he was interested in a naval base in the West
Indies. Secretary Fish on his part enunciated a 'no
transfer' principle as part of the Monroe Doctrine,
asserting that no territory in the Western Hemisphere
should be transferred to a European power. The principle
itself went back to the eighteenth century, but in 1870
Fish applied it to Santo Domingo after the Senate
defeated an annexation treaty. The annexation of Santo
Domingo was sought by Presidents Andrew Johnson and
U. S. Grant, but neither Fish nor other Republican
leaders were enthusiastic. For Secretary Fish the 'no
transfer' doctrine was useful as a way of preventing
premature territorial aggrandizement by the United
States, for he could argue that there would be no danger
of the island's being transferred to a European power,
which might jeopardize national security and thus
necessitate measures by the United States.

Fish's handling of the Cuban crisis was another
instance of a cautious Caribbean policy. In 1868 Cuban
insurgents, led by De Cespedes, staged an uprising
aimed at independence and the abolition of slavery on the
island. There was atrocious fighting between the rebels
who destroyed sugar crops in order to eradicate what they
believed to be the foundation of Spanish colonialism, and
the plantation owners who wanted to perpetuate the
existing regime. In the United States there was
considerable sympathy with the rebel cause, and voices
in and out of the Grant administration began calling
for some assistance, at least recognition of the
insurgents as belligerents. Such a step would enable them
to obtain arms in America. Segments of public opinion
were influenced by the anti-slavery sentiment and by
expansionism, envisaging an economic union of the two
countries.

Fish refused to be stampeded into taking precipitous
action. Cuba for him was part of the Caribbean policy of
the United States, which stressed tranquility and
stability in the region as prerequisite to American
security and economic interests. He did not desire to
adopt a policy that might bring about European
intervention. Between uncertainties produced by American
policy, no matter how well-intentioned, and the status
quo, he would choose the latter. Moreover, he did not
believe that the United States was prepared for war with
Spain, which could result from a premature crisis if the

former intervened in Cuba. He was not at all convinced, unlike some of his countrymen, that the insurgents were united and possessed a veritable government which could function in place of the colonial regime. At the same time, he was opposed to slavery, and believed that peaceful and mutually beneficial relations between Cuba and the United States were possible only through emancipation, which might ultimately lead to the island's independence. But he did not force these measures upon Spain by threatening war. The only step he was willing to take at this time, partially in response to mounting Congressional and public clamor, was to call on Spain to abolish slavery. But the latter was slow to respond, and the rebellion was ultimately crushed in 1878.

Once, in 1873, a serious crisis threatened American-Spanish relations when Spanish authorities in Cuba captured the ship 'Virginius' and executed the crew, including some Americans. The ship was engaged in transporting arms from the United States to the Cuban rebels, and was illegally flying the American flag. There was an instantaneous outburst of public indignation in the United States, newspapers and some Congressmen calling for retaliation. Here again, Fish showed moderation, believing that war was undesirable and unnecessary for both countries. He pressed Spain to agree to a speedy solution of the incident, and he was ready to soften American demands on reparations. The Madrid government responded favorably and at the end of November, within a month after the incident occurred, accepted a settlement involving the payment of an indemnity to the families of the American crew who had been shot.

In adopting a cautious policy, Secretary Fish was well aware of the nation's unpreparedness for war even against a relatively weak European country like Spain. After the Civil War American armed forces had visibly and spectacularly dwindled, and arms and weapons were becoming obsolete. Army appropriations, which used to amount to billions of dollars during the Civil War, were a mere $35 million in 1871. What was left of the Union army was primarily employed to defend Western lands against Indians. The navy, too, had let its fleet decay, and it did not seem to be in a position even to consider war over Cuba. Under the circumstances, the only means Fish had at his disposal was patient and moderate diplomacy. It succeeded against Spain, but it was by no means clear that it would work toward the great European powers that were steadily building up their armies and navies.

The 'Virginius' incident serves as a good index of
American thinking about external affairs.   Twenty-odd
years later, such a crisis might have brought about a
more bellicose foreign policy and created a popular
movement for American intervention.   In 1873, too, the
press expressed the mood of the public through such
headlines as 'the people aroused,' 'America arming,' and
'a burst of wrath.'   However, there were enough calmer
voices to restrain national sentiment from becoming
boiled to the point of creating a crisis atmosphere, as
was to be the case in the 1890s.   Hamilton Fish succeeded
in his moderate policy because he did not antagonize
too many opinion leaders.

Among the anti-interventionists, the 'Nation' provides
an excellent example.   In the postbellum days it
functioned as the leading journal on public issues,
almost always calling for patience, reason and moderation
in foreign affairs and opposing external adventures and
complications.   It opposed territorial expansionism, and
was particularly vociferous against the annexation of
Santo Domingo and other Caribbean lands, arguing that
the American nation could not 'stand the indefinite
expansion of this awful volume of ignorance and
corruption' represented by these peoples. (1)   During the
'Virginius' episode, the 'Nation' editorially supported
the Spanish contention that it had every legal basis for
seizing a ship belonging to the rebels and engaging in
carrying arms to the insurgents in Cuba.   Moreover, like
Fish, the editors were skeptical of the rebels' claims as
revolutionary leaders.

> What reason have we [asked the magazine] for supposing
> that the descendants of Spaniards, bred to a tropical
> climate, under the teaching of tropical Catholicism,
> in contact with negro slavery, and under a military
> government, have become the sober, chaste, self-
> restrained, brave, and humane patriots who are usually
> held up for popular admiration at indignation meetings?

Moreover, the 'Nation' pointed out, 'there ought to be ...
a certain relation between our diplomatic tone and our
means of offence and defence.'   If the United States were
to adopt a belligerent stance toward Cuba and Spain, it
must be prepared to go to war.   But 'we have, according
to the best authority, no navy.'   A war with Spain might
'leave our ports at the mercy of the enemy, and produce
a most disastrous effect on our commerce and finances.'

This last point was developed in a cogently argued
editorial entitled, 'How Should We Fight Spain?'   It was
a considerate exposition of factors involved in foreign
policy decisions.

A nation may regulate its demeanor toward foreign
powers either by Quaker principles or by feudal - that
is to say, military - principles. It may adopt a
policy of patience and long-suffering, and may rely
wholly or in part for redress of injuries on
argument, or in appeals to the conscience or to the
opinion of the civilized world; or it may adopt a
policy based on the feudal theory of 'honor,' or, in
other words, the theory that in all disputes it is
itself the sole and best judge of the extent of the
injury received and of the nature of the atonement to
be exacted, and that self-respect requires a prompt
resort to force for the redress of wrongs.

During the 'Virginius' affair, the editorial went on, the
United States had tended to act according to the second
principle, but without adequate military preparedness.
This was an extremely dangerous thing to do. If the
nation were to be really concerned with revenging the
wrongs committed against its citizens or were interested
in defying foreign powers, then it must build up its
armaments. If, on the other hand, the United States was
not going to maintain a powerful navy, 'we must also
make up our minds to be very peaceful in our demeanor,
and to bear insults and "outrages" and "dungeon" troubles
patiently, and to give up the luxury of speedy
vengeance.' (2)

American diplomacy in the years immediately following
the Civil War was neither totally pacifist nor totally
bellicose. The 'Nation' was right to point out the
disparity between the sorry state of military strength
and the belligerent rhetoric mouthed by the public and
officials alike. On the whole, however, Seward and Fish
conducted the country's external affairs with due regard
to the lack of adequate armed forces. Fish, in
particular, abhorred impetuous adventurism and kept
foreign-policy concerns to narrowly defined limits.

The same observations may be made about America's
response to European power politics during the 1870s.
After the Franco-Prussian War, German foreign policy under
Chancellor Bismarck sought to isolate France, while
at the same time preventing the extension of British and
Russian power. It served Bismarck's purposes to
encourage Anglo-Russian rivalry in the Middle East and
Central Asia, so that neither of the two would find it
easy to come to the aid of the revengeful French against
Germany. Bismarck was also interested in the United
States in the context of European politics. He was
desirous of keeping up American-British tensions wherever
possible so as to neutralize the latter as a potential

friend of France, and of encouraging Russia's pro-American stance so that the United States might be able to take a strong stand against Great Britain in various issues pending between the two countries.

These developments created an international environment favorable to the United States, enabling the latter to persist in a policy of non-involvement in European affairs. None of the major European powers wanted trouble with America, and almost all the newly arising issues affecting the powers occurred outside the Western Hemisphere: Alsace-Lorraine, the Balkans, the Middle East, Central Asia or Africa. The result was that the United States could afford to stand more or less outside European politics. Only with respect to Great Britain did there arise a fleeting sense of crisis from time to time, abetted no doubt by German and Russian policies. Anglo-American relations were marred by much unfinished business carried over from the Civil War. Influential segments of the American press believed that but for British policy, the Civil War would have ended one year or more earlier. The 'Alabama' case, involving American claims against Britain which had built this and other ships during the Civil War for use as Confederate raiders, aroused often bitter nationalistic feelings, and the 'New York Times,' among others, went as far as to call for the annexation of Canada in lieu of indemnity payments by Great Britain. The Grant administration and especially Secretary Fish did not want to exacerbate Anglo-American relations, and they were willing to moderate America's demands. The Gladstone ministry in London, too, was anxious to avoid friction with the United States, and in 1871 a treaty was concluded, providing for an international arbitration of the dispute.

The only area where Fish showed a geopolitical concern was, as had been the case with virtually all his predecessors, the Caribbean. Although he was lukewarm toward territorial aggrandizement, he wanted to maintain the principle of 'no transfer.' During 1871-7 he addressed as many as seven inquiries to Germany and Denmark to ascertain whether the latter was going to part with its West Indies colonies and cede them to the former. Echoing a sentiment going back to Alexander Hamilton and John Quincy Adams, and anticipating James G. Blaine and Theodore Roosevelt, Fish declared in 1870:

> The United States by the priority of their independence, by the stability of their institutions, by the regard of their people for the forms of law, by their resources as a government, by their naval

power, by their commercial enterprise, by the
attractions which they offer to European immigration,
by the prodigious internal development of their
resources and wealth, and by the intellectual life
of their population, occupy of necessity a prominent
position on this continent which they neither can
nor should abdicate, which entitles them to a leading
voice, and which imposes on them duties of right and
honor regarding American questions, whether those
questions affect emancipated colonies or colonies
still subject to European dominion. (3)

Since the strengthening of American power and influence
in the Caribbean region would be empty rhetoric without
an isthmian canal, it was not surprising that the Grant
administration should have been strongly concerned with
expediting the matter. In 1872 an Interoceanic Canal
Commission was created to survey possible canal routes
through Central America. Four years later it reported
in favor of a route across Nicaragua. But the Clayton-
Bulwer treaty of 1850 stood in the way of the construction
and maintenance of a canal under unilateral American
control. While the United States government was
interested in having the treaty modified or repudiated,
no positive step was taken at this time. Nor, for that
matter, was there a build-up of armed forces in the
United States, despite Fish's mention of 'naval power.'
Military expenditures continued to dwindle as if to
belie his sanguine assertion about America's leading
position in the Western Hemisphere. But such a
discrepancy all the more vividly confirms the
geopolitical vision which he shared with his countrymen
that the United States must claim the American continent
as a sphere of special concern. Despite the relative
inactivity of American foreign policy in the years
immediately following the Civil War, this maxim was
never given up.

Apart from the pursuit of national interests and the
assertion of primacy in the Western Hemisphere, postbellum
foreign relations were also characterized by the
continuation of certain internationalist themes in the
way Americans viewed external problems and envisioned
their country's role in the world. First of all, it may
be noted that the Civil War caused no drastic change in
the ideas of history, progress or civilization that had
provided an intellectual foundation of the American
visions of foreign affairs. There was pride at seeing
the nation survive the bloody Civil War and stand as the
country that had both abolished slavery and maintained
unity. George Bancroft reiterated a familiar theme when

he declared, in an 1866 memorial address on
Abraham Lincoln, 'In the fulness of time, a republic rose
in the wilderness of America ... From whatever there was
of good in the systems of the former centuries she drew
her nourishment; the wrecks of the past were her warnings.'
(4)   Likewise, John Lothrop Motley, the historian who
served as minister to London in the second Grant
administration, wrote in his 'Historic Progress and
American Democracy' (1869), 'In the fulness of time,
after so many errors, crimes, and disappointments,
civilization seemed to find a fresh field for its
endeavors, as the discovery of this continent revealed a
virgin world.' He talked of human progress in exactly
the same way that Americans of the early decades had done:

> I believe it possible to discover a law out of all this
> apparently chaotic whirl and bustle [of the past]; this
> tangled skein of human affairs as it spins itself
> through the centuries. That law is progress - slow,
> confused, contradictory, but ceaseless development,
> intellectual and moral, of the human race. (5)

As before the Civil War, these remarks reflected optimism
that man's history was the story of the progress of
civilization, and that America stood at the forefront of
the march upward of humanity. In international relations,
too, the United States was conceived to be a very special
member of the world community, embodying the principles
and ideals that had contributed to progress. 'The proper
place of the country,' declared the 'Nation' as it
celebrated the coming of the centennial year, 1876, 'is at
the very head of the civilized world; and if we of this
generation cannot claim it, let us hope our sons and
grandsons will be more fortunate.' Comparing the
situation then with that a hundred years earlier, the
editorial noted:

> In the last hundred years the advance of Europe in
> the matter of providing better protection for the
> individual man, and freer play for his faculties,
> has been very great ... In this very important matter,
> therefore, the Old World has really caught up with us.
> America does not now enjoy the pre-eminence in it she
> did then, although it ought to be said that much of the
> improvement in Europe is neutralized by the growth of
> large standing armies and the attendant
> conscription. (6)

Such an assertion revealed the faith that history was
still progressing in one, upward direction, and that the
United States remained at the forefront of the march of
human civilization. It was a cause for satisfaction and
celebration that the European nations had one by one

followed America's lead in emancipating man, but they
seemed to be taking a backward step by increasing
armaments. By the same sorts of criteria, American
officials and media generally rejoiced over German
unification, the formation of the Third Republic in
France, or the creation of a modern government in Meiji
Japan - developments which took place within a short
span of time in the early 1870s. They all appeared as
evidence that nations were becoming more and more
civilized, and that mankind on the whole had made vast
strides during the last one hundred years.

One intriguing question in connection with American
ideals and universalistic visions at this time is their
relationship to the developing rhetoric of imperialism
in Europe. The imperialists, as seen above, had their
own brand of idealism and internationalist ideologies.
They justified expansion at least partially in the name
of civilization and progress. While the Americans did
not undertake overt territorial expansion after 1867,
they saw before their eyes the unfolding drama of
European imperialism in the subsequent decades. How they
viewed the phenomenon, and what vocabulary they used in
describing what they witnessed, are fascinating questions
that have not been adequately explored by historians. A
glance at a range of American writings seems to indicate,
however, that there was some willingness to accept the
rhetoric of civilization in discussing European
imperialism.

The 'Nation' magazine, in speaking of the Russian
push toward Central Asia in the direction of India,
stated in January 1873,

> even after Russia becomes possessor of all Central
> Asia, as it is to be hoped, in the interests of
> civilization, she will be before long, it would take
> a generation to make it a basis for operations against
> so well organized a military empire as British India
> now is, even if it is to be believed that the
> barbarous view of the relations of civilized powers
> to each other is to be indefinitely maintained. (7)

The first part of the sentence referred to 'the
interests of civilization' which would be served by
Russian imperialism, while the second part described the
relations among 'civilized powers' as 'barbarous.'
Underneath the apparent contradictions in the use of the
term 'civilization,' there seems to have been a coherence
in such an image of world politics. The Western powers -
civilized by definition - were engaged in ancient ways of
diplomacy and warfare in which no improvement could be
discerned, but at the same time their superior

civilization was bound to make an impact upon non-Western peoples once the latter became objects of Western expansion. Although the former aspect was deplorable - and Americans congratulated themselves that their country was free from Old World power politics - the latter idea provided a rationale for imperialism which they could understand and even support.

Civilization in such a context still referred to those characteristics which had manifested themselves in the West. According to John S. Hittell's 'A Brief History of Culture' (1875),

> Civilization, the third stage of culture as distinguished from the lower conditions of savagism and barbarism, is the condition of men possessing a literal alphabet, steel edge tools in common use, and a refined taste in literature and the fine arts. Ancient Greece and Rome in their prosperous ages, and the Aryan nations generally of the present time, are civilized. (8)

Henry M. Field, writing his best-selling 'From Egypt to Japan' in 1877, fully agreed with the definition. For instance, talking of the Islamic world, he remarked:

> When the iron crust of Islam is broken up, and the elements begin to melt with fervent heat, the Eastern world may be moulded into new forms. Then will the Oriental mind be brought into an impossible state, in which argument and persuasion can act upon it; and it may yield to the combined influence of civilization and Christianity.

Similarly, Field justified British rule in India in the name of civilization. English magistrates in the colony, he said, 'will educate the Hindoos to the idea of justice, which, outside of English colonies, can hardly be said to exist in Asia.' His views on the matter were very explicit and virtually identical with those of European defenders of imperialism:

> Will anybody tell me that the people of India, if left alone would have built their own railways? Perhaps in the course of ages, but not in our day. The Asiatic nature is torpid and slow to move, and cannot rouse itself to great exertion ... The question of English rule in India is a question of civilization against barbarism. These are the two forces now in conflict for the mastery of Asia ... I believe in modern civilization, and I believe in Christianity. These are the great forces which are to conquer the world. In conquering Asia, they will redeem it and raise it to a new life. The only hope of Asia is from Europe: 'Better fifty years of Europe than a cycle of Cathay';

and the only hope of India is from England. (9)
When in 1873 the Japanese government put pressure upon
China to grant an audience to foreign envoys in Peking,
the 'Nation' congratulated Japan for putting the issue to
China in the form of 'audience or war.' It would appear,
it said, 'that in Japan the civilized world will have the
most efficient helper in breaking down the Chinese
exclusiveness and altering the destiny of the Flowery
Kingdom.' (10)

On the other hand, while Americans might generally
look favorably upon the civilizing aspect of European
imperialism, this did not lead them to advocate forceful
expansion for their own country. Outside the Western
Hemisphere, which was considered more in the context of
geopolitical regionalism, national interests or
traditional expansionism there was no sentiment in the
1870s that the nation must follow the footsteps of the
European powers in establishing colonial control over
other peoples. Such a policy militated against the self-
perception of America as a country standing for peaceful
relations among nations and for civilized manners of
dealing with other peoples. As Richard J. Hinton wrote
in 1869, in connection with European rivalries in Asia:

We cannot follow in the footsteps of our European
cousins, and become aggressors - aggrandizing
ourselves by absorbing what already exists there of
national life. Our triumphs are to be peaceful;
commerce will be the reawakener; the United States
must lead in the regeneration of Asia. (11)

This idea of peaceful expansion, involving the country
primarily in economic and cultural relations with the rest
of the world, and giving its external affairs an idealistic dimension, went back to the 1770s, but it was still
sufficiently potent after the Civil War to provide one
layer of opposition to territorial aggrandizement.

Hinton's stress on 'peaceful triumphs' reflected the
continued faith that America could influence other lands
through education, example and attraction. Even without
resorting to force, the United States could, through its
commerce, missionaries or sheer political influence,
advance the cause of progress and civilization
throughout the world. Such optimism required an
assumption that all men were capable of progress.
Although the post-Civil War years were beginning to see
the rising impact of racial theories which stressed
ineradicable distinctions among races, a strong strain of
universalism remained. For instance, John S. Hittell, who
spoke of the Teutonic race's ability to 'control the
world for a thousand years to come,' could also discuss

progress in a universalistic vein:

> Progress has not yet gained a full consciousness of
> itself ... A large proportion of mankind do not
> understand that society is improving ... [If] they
> were confident that there is a continuous advance even
> at a slow rate toward better conditions, they would
> feel a stimulus to exertion ... Many who now side
> with superstition and oppression, do so in
> ignorance ... A common interest binds all men
> together; as they advance, they learn to work in
> mutual helpfulness and good-will.(12)

As before the Civil War, American perceptions of
Japan provide a good example of this type of thinking.
These coincided with the emergence of Meiji Japan, whose
leaders avidly took to Westernizing their country's
political institutions and education. As seen from the
United States, the Japanese appeared the embodiment of
the spirit of progress, and it was particularly
gratifying that many Americans had had a hand in the
dramatic transformation. Henry M. Field wrote:

> that which is of most interest to a stranger in Japan,
> is not Yedo or Fusiyama, but the sudden revolution
> which has taken place in its relations with other
> countries, and in its internal condition. This is one
> of the most remarkable events in history, which, in a
> few years, has changed a whole nation, so that from
> being the most isolated, the most exclusive, and the
> most rigidly conservative, even in Asia, it has become
> the most active and enterprising; the most open to
> foreign influences; the most hospitable to foreign
> ideas; and the most ready to introduce foreign
> improvements. This change has taken Japan out of the
> ranks of the non-progressive nations, to place it, if
> not in the van of modern improvement, at least not very
> far in the rear. It has taken it out of the stagnant
> life of Asia, to infuse into its veins the life of
> Europe and America. In a word, it has, as it were,
> unmoored Japan from the coast of Asia, and towed it
> across the Pacific, to place it alongside of the New
> World, to have the same course of life and progress.
> (13)

Given the prevailing notions of progress and civilization,
it was not surprising that many writers repeated Field's
refrain that Japan had now rejoined the march of progress.
'Japan is today,' said the 'San Francisco Daily Evening
Bulletin' in 1872, 'all the circumstances of her previous
condition considered, the most progressive nation on the
globe.' (14) According to E. H. House, Japan had leaped
in one stride 'from the twilight of the Middle Ages to a

brightness of purpose not very far behind that of modern
Western civilization.' (15) On the occasion of the visit
of an 1872 Japanese embassy to the United States, the
'Overland Monthly' expressed a popular view that
'contrasting the sunny present of Japan with its dark,
stormy past, we have bright hopes for the future of the
Empire of the Sun.' (16)

Such expressions revealed that after the Civil War
certain ideals and universalistic images continued to
provide a framework for viewing other countries.
Americans rejoiced in Japan's 'progress' and bemoaned
the fate of other peoples who seemed too entrenched in the
past to awaken themselves. Some of these peoples were
coming under European control, and Americans generally
applauded the efforts of Europeans to bring civilization
to them, although America itself would not yet be called
upon to share the task. This was a decision that had to
be made by the next generation of Americans.

One component of America's traditional idealism as it
related to external affairs had been the concept of free
commercial intercourse throughout the world. Peaceful
economic expansionism had constituted a vital aspect of
American foreign relations as perceived by the country's
leaders and people. But the ideal had been compromised
to a great extent by the protectionist sentiment which
had sought to safeguard domestic industry by restricting
imports. The Republican ascendancy after 1861 ensured
the continuation of a high tariff policy, and for years
after the end of the Civil War the United States
maintained a schedule of import duties that were among
the highest in the West. This was due basically to the
fact that the Republican administrations favored
continuation of protectionism which had been necessary
during the Civil War, and that such a policy was supported
by various interest groups who constituted some of the
principal backers of the party. For instance, coal-mine
operators, iron and steel manufacturers, and makers of
carpets, glass or woolen goods sought to protect their
interests through high tariffs. Probably the most
serious consequence of the protectionist sentiment in
American foreign affairs was the refusal of the Senate
to renew the Canadian reciprocity treaty. In 1869 Canada
proposed a new reciprocity agreement to replace the one
which expired in 1866, and the proposal included the
grant to Americans of the free use of the St Lawrence
and duty-free admission of certain manufacturers to one
another. But the Congress was too strongly influenced by
special-interest groups to support the measure. Instead
of clutching at the prospect of a virtual economic union

between the two countries, these groups served their own interests by seeking unilateral governmental protection.

As in Europe, the 1860s and the early 1870s were years of rapid economic development, but unlike the most advanced countries such as Britain and Germany, America was still strongly dependent on foreign sources of supply for capital and labor. Approximately one-third of employees in manufacturing or mechanical industries were immigrants, and the industrialists continued to favor the policy of unrestricted immigration. In 1871 Germany passed a law forbidding emigration of persons under twenty-five years of age and subject to military service. The United States had to seek European labor from all available sources, and generally there was little problem in obtaining immigrants. The only dispute, involving a special-interest group, was the emergence of anti-Chinese movements on the West Coast. The East Coast in general and capitalists in particular had no objection to the coming of Chinese laborers, and they did not question Secretary Seward's view, as he incorporated it into the American-Chinese treaty of 1868, that the United States should welcome immigration of Chinese whose labor could be put to good use in American economic development. By 1873 there were over 80,000 Chinese in the United States, over 62,000 of them in California. This resulted in the appearance of a movement that was to constitute one unique component of American foreign relations in the decades to come. Californians comprised a special-interest group in this case, speaking with a loud voice for a particular policy: Chinese exclusion. The movement was derived from various sources: Californian nativism which opposed the coming of Oriental aliens who seemed to be interested only in making money, the generally low opinion of Chinese, labor hostility to low wage earners, and local politics where Chinese exclusion became a favorite issue for candidates.

This was unquestionably a novel issue confronting the United States. The country had drawn on the continuous inflow of foreign laborers for its economic development but, as the 'Nation' noted in 1876, hitherto the immigrants had been 'from countries which are allied to our own by race, language, religion, or customs.' The editorial conceded every country's 'undoubted right to impose restrictions and regulations, and to exact prerequisites as a means of self-protection,' but insisted on 'the absolute necessity of the whole question being considered and settled from a national point of view.' (17) But it was extremely difficult to adopt 'a

national point of view' when the issue involved questions
of race prejudice, juxtaposition of totally different
life styles, and the nature of American politics where
local issues could exert powerful influence upon
national policy. As a man wrote from San Francisco:

> What [the Chinese] is really guilty of is being a
> Chinaman ... The Chinaman never adopts an iota of our
> civilization, or becomes in any sense an American.
> Universal brotherhood does not and cannot apply to
> him, because he will not be a brother. His
> civilization *displaces* exactly so much of our own;
> it substitutes Mongolianism ... [The Chinese] have no
> ambition for progress, no taste for education or the
> arts and sciences, no possibility of expansion into
> anything but confirmed Mongolianism. (18)

The impact of anti-Chinese sentiment was already felt in
national politics during this period. In the 1876
presidential election, the Republican party demanded
protection for European immigrants and naturalized
citizens, and declared that Congress had a duty to 'fully
investigate the effect of the immigration and importation
of Mongolians upon the moral and material interests of the
country.' The Democratic Party platform likewise
denounced Mongolian immigration. Here was an instance
of a special-interest group exerting pressure upon the
government in an issue of potential importance in American
foreign relations.

Protectionism and Chinese exclusion ran counter to the
credo of free trade and immigration. But the Republican
tariff policy was challenged by low-tariff groups such as
importers in New England and New York, textile
manufacturers, and railroad financiers. They wanted·to
have cheap imported raw materials - Indian linseed,
Russian and Philippine hemps, Scottish and British iron,
and the like. Textile interests in the East also feared
that high import duties on cotton fabrics could
encourage the growth of competitors at home. During the
1870s the movement for lower import duties was generally
unsuccessful, but it began to develop into a national
political issue as the Democratic Party staged a comeback
in the wake of the depression of 1873 and became a vehicle
for promoting views opposed to those of the reigning
Republican Party. Many who had joined the latter before
1861 because of the slavery question now returned to the
Democratic Party to agitate for a low tariff policy.
After the end of the Reconstruction, the tariff emerged
as a key issue dividing the two parties. The Democratic
Party and low-tariff interests looked to one another
for support against Republican power and protectionism.

Among these interests much of the agrarian population
was most conspicuous.

It should be remembered that despite the rapid
industrialization after the Civil War, American trade
still largely consisted of agricultural goods. In 1865,
for instance, 60 per cent of exports and 47 per cent of
imports were in farm products. Ten years later, the
ratios were 77 per cent and 53 per cent, respectively.
In other words, both in American export and import trade,
the importance of agricultural produce increased.
Because general prices began to decline after the panic
of 1873, it is not surprising that farmers should have
been extremely interested in further cultivating
overseas markets. They were among the most vocal
exponents of trade expansion, calling upon the government
to assist them to facilitate the growth of agricultural
exports. Since they were consumers of manufactured
goods, moreover, they tended to favor lower tariffs on
imports. It would be wrong to say that farmers had a
comprehensive strategy for global politics or an overall
conception of the national interest. But as a special-
interest group they had a very articulate notion of what
they wanted. They had always been in favor of market
expansion overseas and for lower tariffs on imported
manufactures, but after the Civil War they became more
insistent because of declining prices and of the
Republican tariff policy. However, on such controversial
issues of the day as the annexation of Santo Domingo or
intervention in Cuba, agricultural interests on the whole
played no decisive role. They were not interested in
these questions so long as they seemed irrelevant to the
growth of their exports.

Finally, there were private individuals and groups
who, while by no means directly involved in the country's
foreign relations, were nevertheless part of them. For
instance, Americans continued to travel abroad and write
accounts of their foreign experiences. Many of them
stayed in a foreign land and worked as missionaries,
advisors and educators in distant lands. A unique
phenomenon of post-Civil War America was the activities
of some fifty veterans in Egypt, in the service of
Ismail Pasha, the reform-minded viceroy. Charles Stone
became chief of the Egyptian general staff, and before the
British occupation of Cairo in 1882, these officers
functioned as one of the most visible groups of Americans
abroad. They did not influence official policy in
Washington in a direct manner, but their presence
undoubtedly contributed to maintaining the tradition of
private individuals assisting various causes throughout

the world.
   At home, at the level of mass culture, Americans came
into contact with foreign objects and persons in a
number of ways. One of the most interesting developments
was the holding of the world's fair in Philadelphia in
1876, commemorating the centennial of the nation's
history. The fair covered 236 acres and contained 249
buildings, and some ten million visitors came to see
the exhibits by foreigners and Americans. More than
thirty countries participated, and the occasion provided
a unique experience to Americans to demonstrate that the
United States could rival European nations in splendor.
One interesting aspect of the organization of the fair
was an underlying racialist ideology in the placing of
various exhibits. Buildings were grouped by race -
Anglo-Saxons, Teutons, Latins and the like.
   Such race consciousness seems to have been a notable
development in American perceptions of the world after
the Civil War. Race prejudice had existed earlier, of
course, but it had not always intruded upon American
consciousness as individuals considered foreign affairs
and looked at the world. After the Civil War, issues of
Santo Domingo, Cuba, Chinese immigration and others seem
to have made Americans more aware of the racial factor
in international relations. At bottom this reflected
the growing influence of biological and anthropological
theories which stressed the fixed characteristics of
races, compelling the thinking that if the United States
were to remain a viable national entity, it could not
ignore its racial composition. By the same token, other
nations seemed to behave in a way determined by their
racial traits. In a typical expression of American
self-perception the 'Quarterly Church Review' in 1865
defined the United States 'as the ultimate habitation
of the Indo-Germanic race, the broad land wherein,
gathered from the many countries of Europe, it will dwell
as one people, and one nation, with all the powers it
has developed, all the good qualities it has evolved
during the two thousand years of its sojourn in Europe.'
'The Americans,' the journal continued, were 'a giant
race,' a people 'of Arian race, one in blood.' (19)
Given such an image of America, it was to be expected
that there would be resistance, on racial grounds, to
the annexation of alien lands such as Cuba and Santo
Domingo. While there were divergent reasons behind the
failure to annex them to the United States, the racial
factor was crucial. As the 'Nation' editorialized in
connection with the Cuban episode,
   when we talk of annexing Cuba, as some of our orators

do most glibly, we mean the admission to a share in
this government of a motley million and a half of
Spaniards, Cubans, and negroes, to whom our religion,
manners, political traditions and habits, and modes of
thought are, to tell the honest truth, about as
familiar as they are to the King of Dahomey. (20)
Opposition to the coming of Chinese laborers has
already been noted. Its racialist rhetoric was quite
similar to that used by opponents of Cuban or Dominican
annexation. As a writer put it,
A quarter of the population of the globe wears the
pig-tail - and it is a terrible and portentous fact
to us. China can as easily send us millions as Ireland
has sent us thousands. And if we make it comfortable
for them here, if we open our doors as wide to them
as to other people, I cannot see why she should not do
so ... We invite [immigrants] to come and join us and
become Americans, not to come in exhaustless swarms
and remain Asiatics. (21)
The dichotomy between Americans and Asiatics was more
generally related to a view of the world divided into
several racial groups. The United States was the home
of the Aryan race, it was pointed out more and more
frequently, and thus its people's characteristics set
them apart from other races. In an interesting article
on the Turkish crisis involving British-Russian rivalries,
George B. McClellan pointed out:
The habits, intellect, religious sentiments, the
civilization of Europe are totally unlike those of
Asia, while the Africans are entirely different from
and vastly inferior to both the others ... Possessing
many of the qualities of Europeans, and an aptitude
for their civilization, the Russians have at the same
time many Asiatic characteristics, and possess a
peculiar facility for conquering and assimilating to
themselves the purely Asiatic countries. (22)
The implication was that Russia was a different country
from other Western countries because of its contact with
Asiatic peoples. While it would be wrong to exaggerate
the significance of such passages, it is none the less
notable that the kinds of racialist thinking that
constituted one ingredient of European imperialist
rhetoric were readily accepted by American writers. At
this time, however, race consciousness tended to turn
Americans inward, to an awareness of their racial
identity and to reject imperialistic adventures that
would result in the amalgamation of divergent races in
America. This was a fundamental part of the atmosphere
of the time which created a milieu for the making and

execution of United States foreign policy. There was no
strong momentum for an aggressive policy, and no
movement for drastically altering the course of the
country's external relations.

2   THE SEARCH FOR IDENTITY

Having celebrated the centennial, the United States after
1877 looked to a new century of its relations with the
rest of the world. During the next twelve years, four
presidents occupied the White House: Rutherford B. Hayes,
James A. Garfield, Chester A. Arthur (who succeeded
Garfield after the latter's assassination) and
Grover Cleveland. All but the last were Republicans,
and the coming to power of Cleveland, a Democrat, in
1885, marked the end of the twenty-year period of
Republican domination of the executive branch.
   These were years of momentous importance in world
politics. It may be said that most, if not all, of the
crucial factors that were to culminate in the First
World War became manifest during this period. First of
all, Germany and Austria-Hungary entered into an
alliance in 1879, and three years later they signed the
triple alliance, including Italy. These alliances
were to remain in force until the beginning of the First
World War and provided a constant factor in international
politics, aligning these powers against potential
enemies to them collectively or individually. Second,
the Russo-Turkish War of 1877-8 conclusively demonstrated
the weakness of the Ottoman Empire and Russia's ambition
to take advantage of any situation to promote pan-Slavic
causes. This alarmed Britain, and the rivalry between
Russia and Britain over Turkey as well as Central Asia
and the Far East constituted another characteristic of
the period. A fourth development was Britain's
momentous decision to occupy Egypt, carried out in 1882.
It reflected a determination to protect the Suez Canal,
a vital link in the British Empire, especially as a route
to India. The occupation of Egypt intensified mutual
suspicion and antagonism between Britain and France, as
the latter was also intent upon protecting its influence
and investment in the area and sought to check the
rising power of Britain in the Middle East. Estranged
from Britain, France undertook expansionist moves in
Indochina, going to war with China during 1884-5 in
order to have the latter recognize French sovereignty
over Annam and Tonkin. Not to be left behind, Britain
annexed Burma to the Indian Empire in 1885. In the

meantime, the powers steadily extended their control over the African continent. They sent expeditions to various parts of Africa, set up protectorates, and entered into various multilateral and bilateral agreements to recognize their respective spheres of influence. A spectacular example of the latter was the Berlin Conference on Congo affairs, held during 1884-5, attended by fourteen nations, which concluded by establishing such principles as the suppression of slavery and freedom of navigation. The Congo Free State, which had been developed under the imperialistic inspiration of King Leopold of Belgium, was recognized by the powers.

While these and other events were taking place with breathtaking rapidity, the United States continued to stand aloof from most theaters of imperialist activities and world politics. In contrast to the definite steps being taken by the European nations to engage themselves in imperialism and 'realpolitik,' American diplomacy, it may even be argued, was never more peacefully oriented and never less imperialistic than during these years. These matters are relative phenomena, and it would be easy to emphasize those aspects of American foreign relations that were expansionist, imperialist or interventionist. On the whole, however, the contrast between European and American diplomacy was extremely significant, and it was never again to be as striking. Because of this, it is not surprising that not a few Americans began writing urgently about bridging the gap so that the United States might act like the great European powers. Whether the nation could afford to remain passive in the face of rapidly changing world realities was a fundamental question that had to be confronted. In struggling with the question, observers inevitably raised the issue of America's identity. Where the United States stood in world politics, what role it desired for itself to play in international relations - these were problems that ultimately led to a search for national identity to suit the Age of Imperialism. The decade of the 1890s was to provide a fascinating debate on the question, and the years before 1889 were basically a period of quiet preparation for the debate.

In terms of the national interest, the United States government did not depart from its traditional conception during these years. It was still considered of fundamental importance to further the nation's trade and other economic interests. A good discussion of the basically commercial definition of the national interest can be found in Eugene Schuyler's 'American Diplomacy and the Furtherance of Commerce', a series of lectures the

author gave at Cornell University and published in
1886. Schuyler was a career foreign service officer and
was consul general at Constantinople during the Russo-
Turkish War. He was instrumental in producing a new
constitution for Bulgaria, which emerged from the war as
an autonomous state. But his main concern was with the
traditional goal of promoting American economic interests.
In the above lectures he gave many instances where
consular officials played key roles in this task, and he
pleaded for greater public recognition of the foreign
service. (23)   American trade, in fact, showed signs of
growth and expansion during the late 1870s and the 1880s.
Except for 1888 and 1889, exports always exceeded imports,
despite the fact that there was a general decline of
prices after the panic of 1873. The bulk of exports still
consisted of agricultural products, but after 1880 iron
and steel manufactures began to be sold in large
quantities abroad. In view of the fierce competion among
the European powers for overseas markets, it was
incumbent upon the United States government and its
representatives abroad to watch jealously for the
protection of foreign commerce. One instance of
diplomatic importance arose as a result of the policies
of France, Germany, Austria-Hungary, Italy and others
to prohibit the importation of pork and pork products
from America, ostensibly for sanitary reasons. Such
restrictions were in part designed to offset the growing
dependence on wheat and other foodstuffs supplied by
the United States. In Germany alone, quantities of wheat
imported from America increased sevenfold between 1879 and
1881, from 422,000 to 3,029,000 bushels. Since the United
States refused to part with its protectionist tariff
policy, the German and other European governments saw
no reason why they should freely admit American products
when other sources of supply were available. Hence the
pork controversy. There was a genuine possibility of a
tariff war when sentiment in Congress was aroused over
the pork issue and a bill was introduced in 1884
providing for prohibition of imports from those countries
that proscribed imports from the United States for
sanitary considerations. (24) Fortunately, sanity
prevailed in Washington, and in 1890 the United States
enacted a law providing for meat inspection, opening the
way for readmission of American pork to Germany.
   An economic issue of some bitterness at this time was
a fishery dispute between America and Canada. This
involved the right of American fishing vessels to catch
and dry fish in Canadian waters in the Newfoundland and
Labrador areas. Tension mounted after 1885, when the

Canadians began capturing American vessels, mostly from
New England, and the United States Congress responded by
urging President Cleveland to take retaliatory measures.
Cleveland called upon Great Britain to settle the dispute
through the establishment of a joint Anglo-American
commission. In 1888 a 'modus vivendi' was arrived at,
and Americans were once again allowed fishing privileges
in Canadian waters. President Cleveland's handling of
the affair revealed his perception of the national
interest: to protect Americans abroad since not to do so
would damage national honor and reputation. It was not
that he was overly concerned with the plight of a
specific group of Americans, but that the matter
involved the whole nation, since its existence and
interests were bound up with the ability of the
government to extend protection to citizens engaged in
legitimate activities overseas. As he wrote to
George Steele, president of the American Fishing Union,
'to maintain the national honor' was to 'protect all our
people.' He went on:

> In this view, the violation of American fishery
> rights and unjust or unfriendly acts towards a
> portion of our citizens engaged in the business is
> but the occasion for action, and constitutes a
> national affront which gives birth to or may
> justify retaliation ... [In] the performance of
> international duties, the enforcement of international
> rights, and the protection of our citizens, this
> Government and the people of the United States must
> act as a unit -- all intent upon attaining the best
> results of retaliation, upon the basis of a
> maintenance of national honor and duty. A nation
> seeking by any means to maintain its honor, dignity,
> and integrity, is engaged in protecting the rights
> of its people. (25)

Apart from protecting economic rights of individual
Americans and of the nation in the aggregate, the United
States government in this period continued the earlier
policy of viewing the Western Hemisphere as a sphere of
special concern to American security and interests. The
succeeding secretaries of state - W. M. Evarts,
James G. Blaine, F. T. Frelinghuysen and Thomas F. Bayard
- followed Hamilton Fish in paying particular attention
to the maintenance of the country's rights in the
Caribbean and South America. Blaine, who resigned after
holding office for less than a year because of
President Garfield's assassination, was nevertheless a
forceful advocate of close ties with Latin American
countries. He believed, as virtually all his

predecessors had done, that the United States should have
control over a future canal through the isthmus. This
involved the abrogation or modification of the Clayton-
Bulwer treaty and the acquisition of a right to build a
canal. The latter objective seemed to have been
achieved in 1879, when a group of Americans obtained a
concession from Nicaragua for canal construction.
Nothing had been done with the concession, however, when
Ferdinand de Lesseps, the builder of the Suez Canal,
began excavations for a canal across the isthmus of
Panama. Blaine sought to forestall any such project, and
declared that a third-power building of an isthmian canal
violated the Monroe doctrine. Three years later,
Secretary Frelinghuysen negotiated with Nicaragua a new
treaty which stipulated the two countries' joint control
over a future canal. The treaty, however, was rejected
by the Senate as it feared embroilment with Great Britain
in view of the existence of the Clayton-Bulwer treaty.

   Outside the Caribbean, the United States was concerned
with the War of the Pacific (1879-83), which involved a
dispute between Chile on the one hand, and Peru and
Bolivia on the other. Blaine and Frelinghuysen were
interested in mediation, and sought to moderate Chilean
peace terms as the victorious nation had territorial
ambitions at the expense of Peru. But there was no
thought of direct United States intervention, although
American creditors to Peru wanted the establishment of
some sort of protectorate over that country. In the
end the combatants settled the war with little regard to
America's good offices. The United States was interested
in this and other disputes in Latin America primarily in
order to prevent European intervention. The rationale
was a traditional one; it was considered imperative to
make sure that a conflict among American states did not
lead to an international crisis inviting interference
by European powers - as could happen, for instance, should
Peru appeal to a European power for help against Chile.
This did not come about, but in the Age of Imperialism
anything seemed possible, and such considerations
strengthened the determination of American policy-makers
to cling to the Hamiltonian concept of supremacy in the
Western Hemisphere. Evarts, Blaine and others were not
opposed to European trade or investment in Latin America,
which were always considerable. Only about 20 per cent
of total Latin American trade was carried out with the
United States, the rest being mostly with European
countries. As for investments, America's share, though
growing, was still minimal. In Mexico, for instance,
total American investment in 1880 amounted to only seven

million dollars. Continued European economic presence,
then, was to be expected in the Western Hemisphere. But
the United States was sensitive to any possibility of
European political or military control, especially in the
vital Caribbean region. Thus, American policy
consistently opposed a neutrality scheme for a projected
canal as an unwarranted extension of European influence
which would have many military implications.

Because of such reasoning, the military component in
America's Caribbean policy became more and more visible
during this period. There was an identity of views
between State Department and naval thinking, as the
United States Navy, too, heightened its awareness of the
strategic significance of the area. There was nothing
new in such a development, but the 1880s saw a definite
movement on the part of naval strategists to reformulate
national military policy to cope with the trends in
Europe and the world. As they looked at the world
situation, they readily recognized the imperialistic
assumptions and 'realpolitik' ideas that were sweeping
over Europe and incorporating the rest of the world
into a European state system. The time seemed opportune,
then, to put an end to the deterioration of American
naval forces after the Civil War and to initiate a
program for a new, revitalized navy. As of 1880 the
United States stood twelfth as a naval power, a fact
which the administration and the Congress regarded with
growing embarrassment and uneasiness in view of
developments elsewhere. In 1883 Congress took the
initiative to modernize the Navy, which had largely
consisted of obsolescent wooden ships, by authorizing the
construction of three steel cruisers. In 1884 a Naval
War College was established at Newport, Rhode Island,
with Commodore Stephen B. Luce as its first president.
It was at the college that Captain Alfred Thayer Mahan
laid the foundation for immortality by giving a series
of lectures on naval history and strategy. His ideas
were not unique, but he functioned as an intellectual
focus for naval aspirations. He emphasized the need for
a mobile modern Navy to protect the sea lanes, which
were needed for trade and shipping, which in turn provided
the material foundation for national security. He
recognized the cardinal importance of the Caribbean
region and of control over an isthmian canal. These were
ideas the State Department and the White House would find
congenial, but Mahan went a step further in advocating
the creation of a global naval force for the United
States, with bases in all parts of the world, a strong
merchant marine which could be transformed into a

fighting fleet, and even colonial possessions to serve as coaling stations and suppliers of raw materials.

Some of Mahan's extreme ideas, echoing European imperialistic thinking, anticipated American imperialism and world politics of the turn of the century, but they were not acceptable to the political leaders of the 1880s. Nevertheless, it is important to note that some of the most important steps in improving the naval forces were taken during the Cleveland administration (1885-9). President Cleveland was a traditional nationalist, intent upon protecting the country's security, interests and honor defined rather narrowly. But he supported a naval reconstruction program, and more ships were built or authorized during his term of office than at any time since the Civil War. Cleveland's secretary of the navy, William C. Whitney, concerned himself with the reorganization of the Navy Department and with rapid construction of more modern ships. By 1889, twenty-two steel ships had been built or placed in planning stages. This program was in entire accord with the administration's foreign policy, which carried on the tradition of safeguarding national interests while recognizing the need to modernize all military power in view of the situation in Europe.

At this time, however, the United States government did not pursue a world policy that went much beyond the traditional concern with the Western Hemisphere and the Pacific. The preoccupation of Blaine and others with asserting American supremacy in the Caribbean has already been noted. There was really no departure from the past. In the Pacific Ocean, however, there was a new beginning in Samoa and a new assertion of American rights in Hawaii. Regarding the Hawaiian kingdom, American policy during the 1880s revealed a desire to consider the islands, once and for all, an area of special interest to the United States. Commercially, of course, Hawaii had always been closely tied to America, a fact which was reinforced by the reciprocity treaty of 1875. That treaty had provided that the islands would not cede its territory to a third power, but Secretary Blaine feared that the character of the islands might change as a result of the importation of 'coolie' laborers, especially from British possessions in Asia and the Pacific. He said in 1881,

> The United States regards the Hawaiian group as essentially a part of the American system of states ... [While] favorably inclined toward the continuance of native rule on a basis of political independence and commercial assimilation with the United States,

we could not regard the intrusion of any non-American
interest in Hawaii as consistent with our relations
thereto. (26)

This was clearly a declaration of American supremacy over
the Hawaiian kingdom, and Blaine was applying the kind of
vocabulary hitherto reserved for the Caribbean and the
Monroe doctrine to enunciate a Pacific policy for the
United States. In 1887 a new reciprocity treaty,
including a provision for giving the United States the
exclusive right to establish a naval base at Pearl
Harbor, was passed by the Senate, further incorporating
Hawaii into the American sphere of security.

None of the European powers seriously stood in the way
of American intrusion in the mid-Pacific, but this by no
means diminishes the vital fact that the United States
reaffirmed its special-interest in the ocean. At a time
when the powers were claiming control over most parts of
the globe, American policy was tantamount to defining
its geopolitical role in the Age of Imperialism. Blaine
repeatedly warned the European powers to keep their hands
off the Hawaiian islands, much as the imperialist powers
would try to establish their spheres of influence in
Africa or the Middle East. Still, it is significant
that an outright annexation of the islands to the United
States was not contemplated at that time, nor was the
use of force considered to establish American claims.
What resulted was a virtual American protectorate over
Hawaii, based on the fact, as Eugene Schuyler said,
that 'commercially speaking, the Hawaiian Islands have
become almost an American possession.' (27) This was
more a case of peaceful expansionism rather than
imperialist power politics.

American hegemony over Hawaii was unquestionably
aided by the willingness of potential competitors to
refrain from active intervention and assertion of their
rights. The matter was far more complex in Samoa,
another Pacific territory in which the United States
became involved. Samoa was situated in the south-western
Pacific, closer to Australia, New Zealand and other
British territories than to the Hawaiian islands, not to
mention the continental United States. The south-western
Pacific was also a theater of German imperialism, as
Germany under Bismarck marked out the region as a target
of its new colonialism. The United States had no
intention of becoming involved in an imperialistic
rivalry so far from the West coast, but the presence of
American merchants and naval ships inevitably created a
situation resembling European power politics. The Samoan
chieftains, desirous of minimizing the extension of

European, especially German, power, looked favorably
upon the United States as a restraining outside
influence.   In 1878 Samoa and America signed a treaty
of amity and commerce, giving the United States rights to
a naval station at Pago Pago on the island of Tutuila.
But German influence gained ascendancy, with Great Britain
supporting its ambitions in Samoa in return for Germany's
recognition of British interests in Africa and the Middle
East.   The United States, without a comparable bargaining
lever, might have totally withdrawn from that part of the
Pacific.   Instead the Cleveland administration, not
known for fondness for world politics, proposed a
conference of the three powers in Washington.   Such a
proposal itself is interesting in that the American
government, while pursuing a far more passive policy than
the European imperialists, was not willing to accept
German hegemony over some tiny islands in the south-
western Pacific.   The United States would discuss the
matter with Germany and Britain and arrive at mutually
satisfactory arrangements.   But America lacked military
power or a world policy outlook to match German
ambitions, and the conference broke up in failure, having
served only to fortify Germany's determination to control
Samoan affairs.   Bismarck was irritated at the failure
of the Washington conference to recognize German claims
and threatened to cause trouble for American interests in
Hawaii unless the United States accepted the German
proposal, backed by Britain, for a government in Samoa
under Germany's control.

The crisis came to a head in 1888 when Germany deposed
the reigning rulers there and established a new government
under its control.   (American and British ships were in
Samoan waters, and the future of the tripartite
relationship seemed extremely precarious.)   President
Cleveland protested, but the settlement of the crisis
was left in the hands of his successor, Harrison, who
agreed to a tripartite protectorate over Samoa.
Cleveland's basic attitude was to avoid unnecessary
entanglement in such far-off places but to impress upon
the European powers America's concern with the protection
of its interests and with the maintenance of the status
quo in Samoa.   As he telegraphed to Rear-Admiral
Lewis A. Kimberly in Samoa in January 1889,

> Protest against the subjugation of the country and the
> displacement of native government by German rule
> enforced by German arms and coercion, as in violation
> of positive agreement and understanding between foreign
> powers interested, but inform the representatives of
> the German and English Governments of your readiness

to cooperate in causing all treaty rights to be
respected and in restoring peace and order on the
basis of a recognition of Samoan rights to
independence. Endeavor to prevent extreme measures
against Samoans and to procure a peaceful
settlement. (28)

In other words, Cleveland was not interested in having
the United States play an aggressive role as an
imperialist power, but he recognized the importance of
the Samoan dispute to American prestige as a Pacific
power. While commercially American interests were
insignificant, it seemed important to have a say in the
disposition of Samoa among the great powers. In opposing
the establishment of German hegemony, the United States
was applying to the islands the same kind of principle
it had maintained with respect to the Western Hemisphere.
In this sense, the Samoan episode may be considered a
step in the direction of deepening American involvement
in the Pacific.

Beyond the Pacific Ocean lay the Far East, where the
United States had engaged in commercial and missionary
activities for decades. Although the 1880s saw the
further intrusion of Britain and France upon Southeast
Asia, and the intensification of Anglo-Russian rivalry
in Korea, American policy on the whole desisted from
following the example of the European imperialists.
American relations with Japan and China were largely
commercial and cultural, and there was little thought of
the United States becoming an active participant in
Asian politics. Both Japan and China viewed America
as less aggressive than the European powers and sought
its support on various issues. For instance, Peking and
Tokyo were turned to the United States to solve their
perennial dispute over the Ryukyu islands (or the
Liuchiu islands, to use Chinese appellation). When former
President Grant conducted a world tour upon leaving
office, he was asked by the two countries to mediate the
dispute. While little came of it, basically because Grant
did not wish to take sides, the episode was a good example
of the image of America held by officials in China and
Japan. The United States seemed to be a fair and
peacefully inclined country, not like the expanding
European powers. During the Sino-French War over
Indochina (1884-5), to cite another instance, the
combatants both sought America's good offices to
terminate the conflict. Although the peace accord was
brought about primarily through the efforts of
Sir Robert Hart, superintendent of the Maritime Customs
Administration in China, the American government and its

representative in China, John Russell Young, were willing
to help, another indication of interest in Asian affairs.

Perhaps the most notable example of active American
policy in the Far East during this period was its
dealings with Korea. In 1882 Captain Robert W. Shufeldt
of the United States Navy was sent to the Korean
kingdom to establish formal relations with that country.
The mission was successful in part because both China and
Korea sought to utilize American influence against other
outside powers. Like Japan before the Perry expedition,
there was hardly any strong commercial reason for the
opening of Korea to American trade. But the United
States was keenly interested in taking the initiative
and was one of the first Western countries to negotiate
successfully for a treaty of commerce with the Korean
dynasty, thus recognizing that country's sovereign status
in international law, much to the chagrin of the Chinese
who considered Korea a tributary state with no
independent status of its own. But America's role did
not stop there, as the Koreans showed an unusual degree
of interest in obtaining American advisors, much as
Japan had done and was doing at that time. In 1883 a
Korean mission headed by Min Yong Ik was successful in
obtaining as an advisor the services of George C. Foulk
who later became naval attaché in the United States
legation. He and a few other Americans, most notably
Horace Allen, a missionary who served as Korea's
official representative in the United States in 1887,
were inevitably involved in the maelstrom of Korean
politics which was shaking the foundation of the
country's dynastic rule. In the midst of factious strife
and international intrigues, Foulk, Allen and others
worked toward aligning the Korean government more with
reform-minded forces than with the conservatives who had
the support of the Chinese government.

All these instances indicated the willingness of the
United States to have some influence in Asian politics.
Basically, however, American policy did not depart from
the traditional one of protecting the country's economic
interests and its citizens abroad. Where political
questions arose, the American policy tended to support
the efforts of the local regimes to maintain their
autonomy against encroachment by the powers. But the
United States would not intervene by force. Samoa was a
significant exception, and it indicated the difficulty,
if not the futility, of trying to have a say in power
politics without a comprehensive global strategy and
without engaging in the imperialistic diplomacy of give-
and-take. Elsewhere in the Pacific and Asia, there was

no desire to establish a new pattern of American
diplomacy. This was the situation which John A. Kasson,
an Iowa politician who served as minister to Germany,
lamented in his renowned letter to Secretary Bayard,
dated 1885:

> I venture to add an expression of my sorrow, bordering
> upon a sense of shame, that the blindness, weakness
> and timidity of a long continuing so-called American
> policy [i.e., the Monroe doctrine] has made our navy
> on the Pacific Ocean insignificant and has led
> foreign nations to ask for our views, if asked at all,
> after the *fait accompli*, instead of before it. The
> Pacific Ocean should have been an American sea ...
> touching at numerous islands having American plant-
> ations, and covered by the American flag ... The
> system of Protectorate, as now understood, if adopted
> by us for such islands as Samoa or for other weak
> governments where we have special interest ... would
> be of special advantage to the beneficiaries of it,
> as it would give to us the control of their foreign
> relations. (29)

He was arguing for a policy that went beyond the
traditional one of adherence to the Monroe doctrine and
primary concern with the Caribbean region. He would like
to see the United States acting like Germany in the
Pacific, with an imperialistic vision and naval force to
back it up. He was not, however, totally right in
depicting such a negative image of American power and
policy in the Asia-Pacific region. In Hawaii, Samoa,
Korea and elsewhere, the United States was engaged in
varying degrees of assertive activities. But they did
not yet amount to a comprehensive strategy of world
politics.

Elsewhere in the world, the United States continued
to stress commercial interests and such private
activities as missionary and educational enterprises by
Americans. In the Middle East, there persisted a strong
concern with the region's educational reform, and in
1885 as many as eight colleges and seventy-five
secondary schools were flourishing in Turkey, all under
the supervision of American missionaries and educators.
But there was no interest in Washington to adapt itself
to the changing circumstances of the 1880s and pursue
a more power-politics oriented policy in the Middle East.
Likewise in Africa, where the decade saw a virtual
partitioning of the continent among the European powers,
the United States was content with seeking commercial
goals. The country was quite interested in affairs in
the Congo, and the Arthur administration took a

unilateral step to recognize Leopold's International
Association of the Congo. However, the basic impetus
was commercial. The region appeared an exciting new
market for American goods, especially textiles. There
was no thought of establishing an American sphere of
interest in Africa, although for historical and
sentimental reasons Liberia always was viewed as a
special case. Secretary Frelinghuysen's instruction to
W. P. Tisdel, commercial agent appointed to the Congo,
explicitly stated, 'Both the people and the Government
of the United States will be much better satisfied with
the early extension and increase of our commerce there
than by any other result of your mission.' (30) The
Cleveland administration was willing to send a delegation
to the Berlin conference on the Congo (1884-5), but this
was primarily to ensure the freedom of trade and the
abolition of slave traffic in Central Africa. These
were traditional objectives, and they did not form part
of a new African policy.

At the end of the 1880s, then, it may be said that the
United States had not gone much beyond the earlier
emphasis on the Western Hemisphere and the Pacific Ocean
in the geopolitical aspect of its foreign policy. Even
in these areas the period left a mixed record.
Territorial expansionist sentiment vis-à-vis Santo
Domingo or Cuba had subsided, while Hawaii was
definitely becoming integrated into the American state
system, and the United States adamantly refused to give
up its prerogatives in Samoa. Compared with the rapid
twists and turns in European diplomacy, the United States
was still largely untouched by a perceived need to adopt
a global and imperialistic strategy.

Internationalist ideologies, too, continued as they
had and provided a vocabulary for comprehending America's
role in the world. As earlier, men talked of
civilization and progress, and these words could still be
used to rationalize European imperialism. As a New York
newspaper put it, 'civilization gains whenever any
misgoverned country passes under the control of a
European race.' (31) The idea that European expansion
represented a gain for civilization, and that the only
alternative was the reign of darkness in much of the
world, was reiterated by characteristic forcefulness by
one of the leading popular writers of the time,
John Fiske. In an article written in 1885 for 'Harper's,'
entitled Manifest Destiny, he advanced the theme that the
history of Europe since the fall of the Roman Empire had
been that of a struggle between civilization and
barbarism. For centuries after the decline of Rome there

had been a tendency toward 'the "asiaticization" of
European life,' but after the fifteenth century, reaction
set in and the cause of European civilization was
resurrected. Fiske summed up modern history in the same
dichotomous way:

> Having at length won the privilege of living without
> risk of slaughter and pillage at the hands of Saracens
> or Mongols, the question now arose whether the Aryans
> of Europe should go on and apply their intelligence
> freely to the problem of making life as rich and
> fruitful as possible in varied material and spiritual
> achievement, or should fall into the barren and
> monotonous way of living and thinking which has always
> distinguished the half-civilized populations of Asia.

The advancing frontiers of European civilization since
early modern times had ensured that the battle would be
won, and that the West would finally impose its higher
standards of life and values upon the rest of mankind.
This was the new 'manifest destiny,' and it amply
justified the expansionist activities being undertaken
by the West. (32)

While in this article Fiske stopped short of calling
on the United States to join the European countries in
expanding their civilization, another popular author,
Josiah Strong, had no such reservations. He identified
the destiny of America with that of Europe, in particular
of the Anglo-Saxon race, and insisted that the Americans
must work together with the British, Germans, and others
to perpetuate Western supremacy in the world. His book,
'Our Country,' initially published in 1885, was the first
in a series of books Strong was to write to spread his
message. 'Is there room for reasonable doubt,' he asked
rhetorically in this book, 'that this race, unless
devitalized by alcohol and tobacco, is destined to
dispossess many weaker races, assimilate others, and
mold the remainder, until, in a very true and important
sense, it has Anglo-Saxonized mankind?' The Anglo-Saxons
were characterized by Protestant Christianity and civil
liberty, and they were so vigorous that they were
destined to overwhelm other races both in quantity and
quality. Such an outcome was only to be welcomed, as it
would enhance the cause of civilization and true
religion. (33)

Other writers were less sanguine. In fact this period
saw the beginning of some skeptical literature about the
alleged supremacy of Western civilization and the
presumably efficacious effects of European imperialism.
For instance, writing for the 'Andover Review' in 1885,
W. Barrows asked, 'Does civilization allow violence, and

may an inferior people be forced by a superior into a
higher grade? ... Conceding that upward movements should
be made among all the barbarous and semi-civilized
peoples, are these common processes of force and
manoeuvre and seizure necessary and justifiable?'
Writing as a theologian, he strongly questioned the
morality of imperialism, even if the result of Western
expansion were to civilize 'inferior' peoples. The essay
was appropriately titled Commerce, Civilization, and
Christianity in Their Relations to Each Other.   Earlier,
and even during the 1880s, most writers assumed that
these three things were mutually compatible - in fact, that
they were aspects of the same Western socio-culture.
Barrows, in contrast, showed awareness of the disparate-
ness of the various elements constituting a civilization,
and was particularly critical of the practices of
imperialism in the name of the West's higher values. As
he said, 'commercial aggressions on the uncivilized, and
... seizures of territory by nations ambitious to enlarge
their domain, affect most seriously the propogation of
spiritual Christianity.' (34) Another critic of
imperialism was former president Grant who toured the
world in 1779. As reported by his travel companion,
John Russell Young, Grant remarked,
     'since I left India I have seen things that made my
     blood boil, in the way the European powers attempt to
     degrade the Asiatic nations ... It seems incredible
     that rights which at home we regard as essential to our
     independence and to our national existence, which no
     European nation, no matter how small, would surrender,
     are denied to China and Japan.' (35)
Inasmuch as the United States too was a treaty power and
American merchants enjoyed all the rights and privileges
in Asia that their European counterpart did, Grant's
condemnation only of the latter was myopic. Nevertheless,
such views represented one type of American reaction to
European imperialism, indicating that the liberal
exceptionalist self-perception was still strong at this
time, and tended to differentiate between European and
American expansionism. In such a perspective, European
imperialism could not be accepted by Americans simply
because it was carried out in the name of civilization,
commerce, or Anglo-Saxonism.
     There is, furthermore, enough evidence to show that
during the 1880s some American observers were no longer
confident of the traditional idea of progress nor
complacent about the superiority of Western civilization.
This was the time when material welfare, power politics,
and the development of the natural sciences were forcing

critical reformulation of familiar concepts about
history and society. To be sure the bulk of writings
still exuded optimism and dealt in standard clichés. A
good example is E. A. Allen's 'History of Civilization',
a four-volume world history published in Cincinnati in
1888. He reiterated the familiar notion that 'A history
of civilization is a history or description of the various
steps by which man passed from the lower stages of
enlightenment to that advanced stage that we call
civilization.' He was confident that man 'has lived a
life of progress' and that 'advance in all departments
of culture will continue.' Even such a popular account,
however, included references to some new themes. For
instance, the above, unilinear view of history was
curiously combined with a cyclical image of civilizations:
'nations and races, no less than individuals, enter into
the struggle of life with diverse faculties; they fulfill
their allotted task and then decline in importance.' He
applied the image to modern history and concluded, 'side
by side with the decline of the Yellow Races, there is to
be seen the increasing importance of the Whites. Taking
widely extended views of past time, the historic period of
the world's history corresponds to the rise of the Whites
to a commanding position in the world.' He was certain
that 'Aryan civilization will continue to grow' and,
'ipso facto', that 'in the future, as in the past, man
will live a life of progress.' (36) Obviously, the
author was influenced by Social Darwinist thinking and
popular racial theories. What is more important, he
identified the progress of mankind essentially with the
predominance of the Aryan race, revealing that even in a
traditional conceptual framework, it was no longer
possible to ignore the racial question that was
fascinating a growing number of writers because of the
deepending interactions between the West and the non-West
in the Age of Imperialism.

There were more acute observers and less optimistic
accounts of civilization. A Catholic author wrote in
1885,

The present age is an uncivilized age, because it
makes materialism its chief good, while caring little
for those who have 'not' that good ... [Both] in
principle and in practice, civilization has dropped to
paganism, or, to what is much the same thing, living
for self. Intellectually, civilization has lost its
object, and, therefore, morally has lost its grace
and its heart. (37)

Obviously, the writer's conception of civilization was
opposed to the prevailing view, but such questioning about

generally accepted simplistic ideas was not confined to
Catholic journals. The prestigious 'North American
Review', for instance, had a series of articles with such
titles as Is Our Civilization Perishable?, Shall Our
Civilization Be Preserved?, and The Coming Civilization.
The first of these articles, published in 1884, answered
the question it posed in the title in the affirmative.
According to the author, John A. Jameson,

It would be very unwise to flatter ourselves that
[Providence] esteems us or our civilization more
highly than he did that of the Chaldeans, the
Assyrians, or their successors ... [Our] civilization
is perishable ... [It] may perish from moral or moral-
physical causes, which are now actually at work in some
countries; which have brought destruction upon many
civilizations, isolated and circumscribed in extent;
and which threaten, in this age of steam, the
printing-press, and electricity, to become universally
operative, and to work their destructive effect
whenever the social conditions facilitate their
malign influence.

While the writer was not a complete pessimist, he noted
that modern civilization had produced 'the prevalence of
crime, social immorality, and the thickening dangers of
industrial discontent and conflict.' The only remedy, he
insisted in his article Shall Our Civilization Be
Saved? , was religion. (38)

These examples indicate that for some writers
civilization and imperialism were synonymous, for others
they were incompatible, while a few were skeptical of the
value of civilization itself. Since at this time the
United States was not engaged in actively pursuing
imperialistic goals, most observers dealt in generalities
or confined their comments to European expansion. To the
extent that Americans thought about such problems, the
bulk of them would have agreed with J.R. Tucker that
'True patriotism, an elevated humanity, a love for real
progress, a devotion to liberty under law and
Constitution, and an earnest purpose to advance the whole
country in Christian civilization, will be attended with
success; the want of these will be followed by disaster
and convulsion, and will result in disgrace to American
history.' (39) In such a perspective, ethical values
and moral precepts must still underlie American action,
and at this time they seemed to dictate a foreign policy
that was more internationalist than power-politically
oriented.   John A. Kasson, the one official who probably
came closer than any other diplomat at this time to call
for America's participation in imperialism and power

politics, wrote enviously of German policy under
Bismarck: 'Fair phrases about traditional friendships,
the progress of liberty and civilization, the brotherhood
of nations [have no more] practical significance than a
blank sheet of state paper.' (40) The implication was
that the Americans still liked to talk about these things,
whereas the imperialist powers preferred to deal in terms
of power and dominion. Another diplomat, Simon Wolf,
consul general at Cairo, wrote in 1882, 'We must war in
the East not with cannon and shot but with schoolbooks,
bibles, and constitutions.' (41) This was a perfect
expression of traditional American expansionism which
took a more economic and cultural than a political and
military form.

The fact that a Democratic administration of
Grover Cleveland was in control of American diplomacy
during the crucial mid-1880s may have served to
perpetuate the rhetoric of universalism and internationalism in the country's external relations. Cleveland's
vision was essentially narrow, exalting national honor
and patriotism as fundamental principles of policy. For
this very reason, however, he was disinclined to
besmirch the country's reputation in engaging in dubious
adventures overseas. He wanted America to stand as an
example to the world, an embodiment of justice and
fairness at home as well as abroad. Moreover, he was
adamantly opposed to Republican protectionism, especially
as the country was going through a prosperous period
and treasury surpluses through lowering import duties.
He recognized the interdependence of the American and the
world economies, and sought to increase the importation
of cheap raw materials and manufactured goods so as to
benefit the American consumer and to lower the cost of
production at home. To pursue these goals, he saw no
justification for undertaking aggressive foreign policies.
The United States would be economically strong enough to
withstand foreign competition even in a free trade
situation.

In taking an anti-protectionist stand, Cleveland set
himself up as the embodiment of the national interest as
against special interests. As he said in 1887,

A nation seeking by any means to maintain its honor,
dignity, and integrity, is engaged in protecting the
rights of its people; and if in such efforts
particular interests are injured and special
advantages forfeited, these things must be patriotically borne for the public good ... [No] sacrifice
of personal or private interests shall be considered
as against the general welfare. (42)

Special interests, however, were still too strongly
entrenched, especially in Congress, to enable Cleveland
to modify the tariff system at this time. As earlier,
manufacturing interests generally favored high tariffs,
and they stifled efforts at reciprocity and most-favored-
nation agreements that were desired by some countries,
such as Canada and Germany. High-tariff advocates often
argued that free trade was a British institution and
designed to undermine the competitive advantages enjoyed
by American agriculture and industry. As Senator
William McKinley declared at the Republican convention
of 1888, the idea of destroying protectionism was un-
American, made 'at the joint behest of the whiskey trust
and the agents of foreign manufacturers.' (43) As such
a quote revealed, the Republican Party was also trying
to portray itself as the party of national unity. It
stood for a greater America through industrialization
which farmers and laborers as well as manufacturers should
support. The Republicans were challenged by the
Democrats who too appealed to these various groups with
a vision of economic welfare and development by means
of freer trade. Here again was an instance of America's
search for identity; special interests were closely
bound up with national politics, and the two major
parties were compelled to clarify their respective
visions of national unity in the age of rapid change.

    With respect to the Chinese immigration question, the
exclusionist groups successfully imposed their image of
a white America upon both political parties. Although
the succeeding administrations opposed a unilateral
imposition of restrictions on Chinese immigration, the
Congress readily acceded to requests from West-coast
exclusionists and passed various measures in that
direction. The Hayes administration, bowing to pressure,
concluded a treaty with China in 1880, which gave the
United States the right to regulate the entry of Chinese
laborers, thus annulling the provisions in the 1868
treaty that had stipulated the right of Chinese to
emigrate to America. In 1882 the Congress, not satisfied
with the new treaty, passed an exclusion act restricting
Chinese immigration for ten years.

    Finally, at the mass level, the period saw the rising
sense of discontent among farmers and laborers with
working conditions, low income and control by the East-
coast business establishment, a sense of frustration that
was to culminate in a nationwide movement of the
People's Party after 1890. The issues involved, however,
were overwhelmingly domestic questions. Except for the
tariff matter, there was no foreign-policy related

question which agitated the masses in this period. One potential source of conflict that was becoming discernible was the influx of 'new immigrants' toward the end of the 1880s. Immigrants from Southern and Eastern Europe were arriving en masse and providing a new source of foreign labor, replacing the dwindling supply of Germans and Scandinavians. To the extent that Americans showed resentment toward foreign labor, it was still largely focused on the Chinese. There were frequent physical assaults upon Chinese miners and workers in the Western states, and both Republicans and Democrats supported the exclusion act of 1882.

There persisted a vaguely defined hostility toward Great Britain that had lingered on after the Civil War. Several segments of the American population were anti-British for one reason or another. Catholics, who by then were constituting politically significant blocs of voters, remained antagonistic toward Britain and toward a foreign policy that gave the appearance of overly identifying the destinies of the two countries. Irish-American suspicions of British interference in American politics were sufficiently strong to cost Grover Cleveland their votes in 1888 when, during the presidential campaign, the British minister in Washington indiscreetly intimated his preference for Cleveland. Agrarian radicals and populists were also anti-British, viewing British capitalism as standing for the same kinds of principles and objectives as the East-coast business establishment. 'Money power,' to which Western farmers and miners bitterly opposed themselves, was as often an East coast as a British phenomenon in their minds. Ironically, however, they favored lower tariffs, equating protectionism with monopoly, whereas some Eastern businessmen and politicians were antagonistic toward British influence in world affairs because it implied freer trade.

These were significant phenomena, but they did not yet create a mass psychology affecting the course of American foreign relations. Neither did they visibly alter the way individual Americans dealt with foreigners or viewed world affairs. They sensed that many things were wrong with the country's economy and political life, but this was not translated into a movement for a different kind of foreign policy. Most Americans undoubtedly remained ignorant of, or indifferent to, foreign affairs, and persisted in a parochial self-image, looking at other peoples with a combination of disdain and open-mindedness. When Rudyard Kipling visited the United States in 1889, it was such aspects of the American character which

impressed him most. Arriving at San Francisco, he
decided to watch the people 'and try to find out in what
manner they differ from us, their ancestors.' Some of
his discoveries touched on the way Americans viewed
themselves and others. Regarding politics, Kipling
wrote, 'the Democrat at a party drinks more than the
Republican, and when drunk may be heard to talk about a
thing called the Tariff, which he does not understand,
but which he conceives to be the bulwark of the country
or else the surest power for its destruction.' But both
Democrats and Republicans 'are ... agreed in thinking that
the other part is running creation (which is America) into
red flame.' Another discovery was that half the people
he met seemed to be carrying pistols. The press reaction
to shooting incidents interested him.

> The Chinaman waylays his adversary and methodically
> chops him to pieces with his hatchet. Then the Press
> roar about the brutal ferocity of the Pagan. The
> Italian reconstructs his friend with a long knife.
> The Press complains of the waywardness of the alien.
> The Irishman and the native Californian in their hours
> of discontent use the revolver, not once, but six
> times. The Press records the fact, and asks in the
> next column whether the world can parallel the
> progress of San Francisco.

In Yellowstone Park, Kipling encountered a German
American - 'a rabid American citizen - one of a very
difficult class to deal with. As a general rule, praise
unsparingly, and without discrimination. That keeps most
men quiet; but some, if you fail to keep up a continuous
stream of praise, proceed to revile the Old Country -
Germans and Irish who are more American than the Americans
are the chief offenders.' Kipling happened to be among
the tourists at Yellowstone Park on 4 July and he
participated in their 'patriotic exercises.' A clergyman
gave an oration, saying the Americans were 'the greatest,
freest, sublimest, most chivalrous, and richest people on
the face of the earth.' This and other speeches amazed
the author, who called their language 'gas, bunkum, blow,
anything you please beyond the bounds of common sense.'
But his American travel companions seemed pleased whenever
he expressed his marvel at American patriotism. One of
them said he should 'get out your letters - your letters
of naturalization.' Kipling was impressed with the
combination of provincialism and friendliness that he saw
in America. (44) No doubt his 'American Notes' contained
exaggerations, but it captured the state of at least one
level of American culture as it related itself to
external affairs. The bulk of people were busy making

money and genuinely believed in America's superior
material progress.   There was no need for such a people
to be concerned with foreign affairs or to be diverted
from domestic problems by exciting adventures overseas.

Chapter 3

The Growth of Nationalistic Expansionism

In 1889 American diplomacy could still be characterized as traditional; it was primarily concerned with national security and the protection of economic interests. They comprised the national interest within fairly clearly defined limits. For over twenty years the country had not acquired additional territory, although this was the time when the European powers were vying with one another to extend their control over distant lands. On the other hand, there was some sense of uneasiness as Americans viewed themselves and the world and saw things happening that did not entirely accord with their customary perceptions of international affairs. The bulk of the population remained complacent and provincial, but various writers were no longer certain that familiar concepts like civilization and progress sufficed as a vocabulary to describe the rapidly changing events in the world.

Within ten years much changed. The United States joined the ranks of imperialist countries, with new overseas possessions and bases, and it considered itself a major world power. Domestically, there was renewed optimism that the nation was at last asserting its vital energies outward, instead of intensifying social strife at home. At the same time, opponents of the new departure engaged its supporters in a fierce debate. National opinion was never united, but at least there was a nationwide debate on foreign policy questions for the first time since the 1840s.

The story of this transformation is a fascinating one, and historians have dealt with it in various conceptual frameworks. Some of their interpretations will be noted in proper places. But the real measure of the change can be taken only if one viewed the 1890s by applying to it the same analytical framework as to the preceding decades.

Here, therefore, we shall look at United States relations with various parts of the world after 1889 in terms of the ingredients mentioned earlier, always keeping in mind the question of comparison with the diplomacy of the European powers.

1 LATIN AMERICA

Of all the areas of the world, American assertion of power and prerogatives in Latin America was the least unexpected. In this region, and especially in the Caribbean, the United States had pursued a policy which at times was quite imperialistic, similar to the European powers' policies in the Middle East or Africa. By 1889 there had developed a strong tradition of American involvement in the Western Hemisphere which was considered an area of special concern to the United States politically, militarily and economically. In the early 1870s there were chances of war with Spain over Cuba, and throughout that decade and the next, the succeeding administrations strongly supported the construction of an isthmian canal which would be placed under American control. The fact remains, however, that after the Civil War the United States had not intervened directly in other American republics, nor had it taken active steps to build a canal. It had not acquired bases nor annexed territories in the Caribbean, although there were always groups of men calling for such moves. The most notable development had rather been the beginning of the construction of a modern navy which, in the event of its completion, would mean a substantial increase in American power in the areas closest to the United States. This, however, was more in a blueprint stage than a reality.

For a while after 1889 American approaches to Latin America did not depart radically from tradition. In the presidential election of 1888 Grover Cleveland lost to Benjamin Harrison, partially because of British Minister Lionel Sackville-West's indiscretion mentioned earlier. With the new Republican administration James G. Blaine returned to the capital as secretary of state. He died in January 1893, shortly after he was replaced by John W. Foster. In 1892 Cleveland and Harrison fought against one another once again, and this time the former won. As secretary of state he appointed W. Q. Gresham and, after the latter's resignation in 1895, Richard Olney. Thus, as one party succeeded another in succession, there was a rapid turnover of diplomatic

personnel. Still, during the first half of the decade,
familiar themes and approaches repeated themselves as the
Harrison and the second Cleveland administrations coped
with various issues in the Western Hemisphere.

First of all, the United States took steps to stress
inter-American ties more closely than ever before. The
idea had geopolitical as well as national security
connotations, but a factor which became increasingly
prominent was economic. As the economic component in the
national interest gained in importance, especially in
view of the shared perception of the need to expand
exports, Latin America attracted attention as an area of
fundamental importance to the United States, an area
where mutually advantageous commercial relations might be
promoted. If the United States could secure a dependable
market in the Western Hemisphere and offered in return
to purchase goods from Latin American countries, imposing
on them relatively low import duties, the result would be
an expansion of America's economic empire without the
burden of political and territorial control.

Such economic expansionism went back to the early part
of the nineteenth century. But at the end of the
century it represented some new initiatives on the part
of the United States since it implied a reversion to a
free trade policy, as against the prevailing Republican
orthodoxy of protectionism. The Democratic
administration of Grover Cleveland had been unsuccessful
in persuading Congress to modify the high tariff policy
that had lasted for over twenty years. Harrison's
victory in 1888, however, did not spell the death of the
anti-protectionist movement. To be sure, Congress in
1890 passed the McKinley tariff, named after Senator
William McKinley who had made a name for himself through
a consistent advocacy of protectionism, which raised the
average level of import duties to 49.5 per cent, an
all-time high. But reaction was quick and for once
effective. Democrats under the leadership of former
President Cleveland mobilized public sentiment, especially
among Western farmers, against the McKinley tariff and
Republican protectionism. As he wrote to J. A. Hill of
the Farmers' Alliance,

> Struggle as they may, our farmers must continue to be
> purchasers and consumers of numberless things enhanced
> in cost by tariff regulations. Surely they have the
> right to say that this cost shall not be increased
> for the purpose of collecting unnecessary revenue, or
> to give undue advantage to domestic manufacturers. The
> plea that our infant industries need the protection
> which thus impoverishes the farmer and consumer is, in

view of our natural advantages, and the skill and
ingenuity of our people, a hollow pretext. (1)
Enough voters agreed with Cleveland; in the Congressional
elections of 1890 the Republicans suffered a severe defeat
and lost their control of the House, a defeat that was
attributed largely to the popular dissatisfaction with
protectionism. For the first time since the end of the
Civil War, there was sufficient public support for a
change in tarriff policy.

The McKinley tariff itself, moreover, contained some
provisions that indicated a departure from strict
protectionism. One put sugar on the free list, allowing
foreign sugar to come in free of import duties. Domestic
sugar growers, however, who would no longer be protected
from foreign competition, were compensated through a
bounty of two cents per pound of sugar cane they produced.
This amounted to subsidizing American sugar-cane growers
while at the same time enabling the consumer to purchase
sugar at the world prices. The only group that suffered
severely from the arrangements was in Hawaii, where the
sugar planters had enjoyed a reciprocity agreement with
the United States enabling them to export their sugar to
America duty-free. The privilege was now wiped out, and
the consequent hardship was to provide one factor in the
story of Hawaiian annexation to the United States. In the
context of United States relations with Latin America,
much more significant was the part of the McKinley tariff
which authorized the government to enter into reciprocal
tariff arrangements with foreign governments through
executive agreement. In case a foreign country imposed
discriminatory duties upon American goods, the United
States would retaliate by raising its tariffs upon that
country's imports, but the American government could also
arrange for mutual lowering of duties with another
country.

In 1890 American policy-makers primarily had Latin
America in mind when they sought such reciprocity
arrangements. The Cleveland administration had supported
the idea of a pan-American conference, which had
originated with Secretary Blaine of the Garfield era, with
a view to discussing just such arrangements. Invitations
were sent out in July 1888. However, by the time the
conference met in Washington - known as the first
International American Conference (or Pan-American
Conference for short) - the Democrats had been turned out
of office, and Blaine had returned to the State
Department. He sought to interest the delegates from
seventeen other countries (Santo Domingo did not
participate) in the idea of a Pan-American customs union,

much like the German customs union or the proposal for a
British imperial customs union being advocated by tariff
reformers in England. They all had in common economic
regionalist thinking, trying to transcend narrow national
limits in promoting foreign trade but stopping short of
free trade within larger geographical units. The proposal
appealed to Americans who wanted a change in the economic
nationalism of the preceding decades, but they repudiated
the McKinley tariff all the same, revealing their desire
for a much more drastic revision in commercial policy.
Latin American countries too were unwilling to consider
setting up a customs union at that juncture. The
conferees in Washington, however, managed to establish an
international bureau of American republics to function as
a central body for exchanging information among the
member states. This was a small but significant first
step in the direction of greater economic integration in
the Western Hemisphere.

If the first Pan-American conference contained
ingredients both of traditional aspirations and new
initiatives, exactly the same was the case with the major
diplomatic incident of 1891: the Chilean controversy. In
October a Valparaiso mob attacked an American cruiser, the
'Baltimore', killing two and injuring seventeen of its
crew. The attack had not been provoked in any direct
sense, although there had been latent anti-American
sentiment among Chile's Congressionalists who rebelled
against the government and took over earlier that year.
This was a case that called for a response within the
traditional framework of diplomacy. President Harrison
did so, at least initially. In his annual message to
Congress in December, he called on the Chilean government
to make amends, saying that the conduct of the sailors and
their commanders had been exemplary and not such as to
justify wanton attacks by a mob. A prompt apology by
Chile would have settled the incident right there, and
it would have passed from memory simply as another affair
in the chronicle of United States foreign relations which
contained similar episodes. This time, however, there
developed a brief period of crisis as the Chilean foreign
minister denounced the 'Baltimore' and President Harrison
for interfering with that country's rights. Secretary of
State Blaine, shaken in his confidence for promoting
inter-American unity, responded in kind. He threatened
Chile with a break in diplomatic relations unless the
latter agreed to a speedy settlement of the affair by
apologizing. In a special message to Congress on
25 January 1892 Harrison supported Blaine's stand and even
intimated that the United States might have to go to war
to defend its honor.

It seems doubtful that Blaine and Harrison really
visualized war with Chile. Rather, they must have
reasoned that through strong language they could persuade
the Chileans to back down. This was not an unusual
practice when a stronger power dealt with a weaker, and
certainly the annals of American diplomacy abounded in
cases where harsh language and a show of force were
resorted to in order to retaliate against wrongs
perpetrated on citizens abroad. However, to intimate
willingness to go to war because of a relatively minor
incident was something few predecessors of Harrison and
Blaine would have done without a long and mature
deliberation. In this sense they were departing from
tradition. They brought war back as a possibility in
American foreign relations for the first time since the
Cuban crisis of the early 1870s. It does not appear,
however, that in doing so they were driven by any long-
range objectives of American diplomacy or motivated by
systematic geopolitical concerns. The whole episode
was a manifestation of nationalistic foreign policy.
They, and the public that expressed indignation at Chile,
were reacting to the event in the framework of nationalism
and viewing it as a case where American lives and
reputation were involved. They were not interested in
warring upon Chile to seize its territory, or in
establishing America's claim to world-power status. These
would come later. At the beginning of the 1890s, the
primary consideration was the traditional one of maintaining the national interest with all available means.
National-interest considerations, of course, could lead
to foreign adventures and involvement in distant lands,
as had just happened in Samoa. Chile was like Samoa in
that sense. But the Samoan dispute concerned Britain
and Germany, whereas the Chilean episode was a strictly
bilateral affair. Given the by then ancient doctrine of
hemispheric regionalism, American policy toward Chile was
not very surprising.

The Harrison administration's Latin American policy,
with its willingness to engage in rhetorical devices to
stress hemispheric ties and special American interests,
might have caused the United States to enlarge further its
scope of foreign affairs if the Republicans had been
returned to the White House in 1893. But Cleveland's
victory in 1892 brought back a Democratic administration
whose primary concern was with tariff reform. Moreover,
the atmosphere of the country changed drastically after
the depression of 1893. Precipitated by a depletion of
the United States gold reserve and the failure of the
Philadelphia and Reading Railroad, but ultimately related

to the long-term decline of wholesale prices and the rising tide of agrarian and industrial radicalism, the crisis revealed a loss of confidence in the future of the national economy on the part of both foreigners and Americans. Foreign investors found the United States a less attractive capital market than earlier, especially because of the partial remonetization of silver in 1890, which caused fear that the gold standard as it was practiced in England might come to an end. Throughout 1893 nearly five-hundred American banks were in trouble, as well as countless commercial establishments and railroads. The official declaration that as of the census of 1890 the frontier had disappeared in America added fuel to the sense of uncertainty, as did mass unemployment and increasingly radical agitation against East-coast capitalists by Western farmers and miners, most of them demanding 'free silver,' that is, a bimetallic standard of money where silver as well as gold would be legal tender.

It was amid such furor that a new tariff, the Wilson-Gorman tariff, passed Congress in 1894. It lowered the average level of import duties to 39.9 per cent, as compared with 49.5 per cent in the McKinley tariff. Certain commodities, such as wool, copper and lumber were put on the free list. The revised schedule was still too high to meet with Cleveland's approval; he refused to sign it. But the tariff went into effect all the same. Although it lowered the average duties on imports, the Wilson-Gorman tariff did away with the reciprocity provisions in the McKinley tariff. This seeming contradiction - lowering of tariffs combined with removal of reciprocity that had aimed at freer trade with Latin American countries - was essentially a result of partisan politics. The Democrats and President Cleveland did not support the reciprocity principle, considering it Blaine's brain child and tinged with Republican vested interests. In the fall Congressional and local elections of 1894, William McKinley, now running for the second term as governor of Ohio, castigated the new tariff as a Democratic heresy and damaging to the Latin American trade that had been fostered through the operation of Republican reciprocity. When the Democrats talked of free trade and open world markets, McKinley countered with the slogan, 'protection, patriotism, and prosperity.' (2) This was a perfect expression of Republican ideas of American foreign relations. It summed up the prevailing theme of the 1870s and the 1880s that the United States would be entirely capable of managing its own affairs and ensuring prosperity without extensive

foreign trade. Markets were to be found at home rather
than abroad, and they must therefore be protected against
foreign imports. Such an inward-looking outlook
fostered patriotism, a belief in the nation's ability
to avoid foreign entanglement and maintain its autonomy
and integrity. There was perfect thematic unity between
protection, patriotism and prosperity, which constituted
the edifice of Republican orthodoxy and high-tariff
non-imperialism. There was no need to go beyond
elementary tenets of patriotism - that is, national
interests narrowly defined - as a guide to the conduct of
foreign affairs, and there certainly was no imperative
necessity to expand territorially or to extend the
nation's military and political control over distant lands
and peoples. Due in part to such reasoning and the
Republicans' fierce attack on the Wilson-Gorman tariff,
the elections of 1894 resulted in their recapturing of
the House and many state houses and legislatures from
Democrats.
   It may be noted that this Republican consensus,
symbolized by McKinley's ideas, was a uniquely American
phenomenon in the Age of Imperialism. The European
governments and public opinion were also extremely
interested in the tariff question, but they tended to
support both protectionism and imperialism. This was
certainly the case in Germany and France, where imperialistic foreign policies were coupled with trends away from
mid-nineteenth century free-trade expansionism. More
often than not, support for protection implied support for
empire, and vice versa. McKinley and the Republicans,
on the other hand, were by and large for protection and
against empire. The uniqueness of this position becomes
evident when it is compared with various currents of
thought in Great Britain at that time. British opinion,
in and out of government, during the 1890s, was divided
into three positions concerning the questions of the
tariff and imperialism. First, there were the vestiges
of free-trade anti-imperialists, heirs to the Manchester
liberal tradition. Then there were 'Liberal imperialists'
like Lord Rosebery, who insisted on the preservation of
the British empire but also retained a free-trade
attitude concerning the trade of the colonies and
imperial possessions. Third, 'tariff reform imperialists'
like Joseph Chamberlain came close to continental
advocates of protection and imperialism, arguing that the
empire should be an economic unit to enhance its
efficiency and serve the interests of the people at home.
McKinley's views fell into none of the three categories.
He believed that the United States really did not need

overseas markets, describing the Democrats' preoccupation with open world markets as 'a great free-trade shadow-dance' devoid of substance.

The Democratic followers of Grover Cleveland came closer to Britain's liberal anti-imperialists in their opposition both to empire and to protection. But their outlook on international affairs was more nationalistic and parochial than the British liberals', as can be seen by their rejection of the reciprocity arrangements in the McKinley tariff which should have won their support. The Wilson-Gorman tariff was also an anomaly in that it put sugar back on the duty list, whereas in 1890 it had been made duty-free. This was because of the Democratic sentiment against the sugar trust in America, which seemed to have been the primary beneficiary of the bounty provision in the McKinley tariff. For all these reasons, the tariff of 1894 was not a clear-cut victory for the exponents of freer and more extensive foreign trade, although the Republicans were only too glad to make a partisan issue out of it. Cleveland was as much a nationalistic thinker as McKinley in foreign-policy matters; patriotism was a word he was fond of using as frequently as McKinley. For the latter's 'protection, patriotism, prosperity,' he would have only substituted 'lower tariffs, patriotism, prosperity.' In advocating lower tariffs, he was not visualizing, as were the radical liberals in England, an international economic order where men everywhere freely moved and exchanged goods and capital. Rather, his primary concern was with 'patriotism and ... justice and fairness toward all interests' in the United States, as he wrote in 1894.

> When we give to our manufacturers free raw materials
> [he said in defence of freer trade] we unshackle
> American enterprise and ingenuity, and these will open
> the doors of foreign markets to the reception of our
> wares and give opportunity for the continuous and
> remunerative employment of American labor ... Tariff
> reform will not be settled until it is honestly and
> fairly settled in the interest and to the benefit of
> a patient and long-suffering people. (3)

His reference was all to domestic factors.

The second Cleveland administration's Latin American policy reflected such nationalism. In contrast to Blaine who had sought to take the initiative to bring together the countries of the Western Hemisphere into some sort of meaningful cohesion, no matter how superficial, Cleveland and his secretaries of state were satisfied with a more traditional policy of maintaining the nation's essential interests and honor in the region, shunning risky

initiatives and careless adventures. Such a stance was
well reflected in two key episodes of the mid-1890s: the
Venezuelan crisis and the Cuban uprising. Although
outwardly Cleveland reacted in a contradictory manner to
these events - taking a bellicose stand on the former
instance but persisting in patient diplomacy in the latter
- there was underlying unity to his foreign policy,
derived from his perception of the national interest.

The Venezuelan crisis arose as a result of a long-
standing dispute between Venezuela and British Guiana
over a boundary. It became more serious when gold was
discovered in the area in question, and neither Britain
nor Venezuela would back down from its contentions.
Ordinarily such a dispute would have been settled through
war, arbitration or some sort of compromise. War was out
of the question because of the relative proximity of the
region to the United States, which would consider British
military action a grave infringement upon its
prerogatives. Venezuela preferred arbitration through
America's good offices, but London was unwilling to accept
this approach because of the fear that the United States
would favor Venezuela and that its intervention would set
a precedent for similar acts elsewhere in the Western
Hemisphere. Britain would have been happy to see the
dispute drag on and to work out some sort of modus
operandi with Venezuela. This might have happened, but
quite suddenly the United States under President Cleveland
decided to intervene. In his annual message to Congress
in 1894 he initiated action by offering arbitration.

Reasons for Cleveland's initiative and concern are not
hard to find or understand. His action was entirely
within the customary framework of the defense of the
national interest. Although his perception of the
national interest always stressed the protection of the
American people's rights and honor at home and abroad, and
although Venezuela was not immediately relevant to America
in that sense, its location was of crucial importance.
Cleveland shared his predecessors' concern with American
supremacy in the Western Hemisphere and with rejecting
further European encroachment upon the area. Venezuela
was heavily indebted to European creditors, and he feared
European imperialism would try to extend itself by using
military power in support of investments in Latin America.
As he wrote to Thomas F. Bayard, now ambassador in London,
President Cleveland viewed the crisis primarily in terms
of the Monroe doctrine. 'I am entirely clear,' he said,
'that the Doctrine is not obsolete, and it should be
defended and maintained for its value and importance *to
our government and welfare*, and that its defence and

maintenance involve its application when a state of facts
arises requiring it.' The Doctrine was essentially a
matter of national security and interests, for 'the
extension of European systems, territory, and jurisdiction,
on our continent, may ... be effected as surely and as
unwarrantably under the guise of boundary claims as by
invasion or any other means.' Furthermore, he conceived
of his and the country's role as a defender of the
principle of peaceful settlements of international
disputes, against military interventionism and arbitrary
behavior by the great powers. The Venezuelan boundary
dispute was a test-case of whether the United States
could persuade Britain to adjust the problem without
recourse to war. Once conceived this way, his
intervention began to assume a moral tone, reflective
of his ardent nationalism, that the United States stood
for certain principles of behavior and meant to speak out
for them, even against the strongest power in the world.
In his words, 'instead of threatening war for not
arbitrating, we simply say, inasmuch as Great Britain
will not aid us in fixing the facts, we will not go to
war, but do the best we can to discover the true state
of facts for ourselves' to settle the dispute. (4)

This was a thoroughly traditional approach. So,
essentially, was Secretary of State Olney's bellicose
rhetoric during the Venezuelan dispute. In a note to the
British government, which was soon made public in the
United States to the delight of a nationalistic opinion,
Olney asserted:

> Today the United States is practically sovereign on
> this continent, and its fiat is law upon the subjects
> to which it confines its interposition. Why? ... It
> is because ... its infinite resources combined with
> its isolated position render it master of the situation
> and practically invulnerable as against any or all
> other powers.

Despite his effort at the beginning of the statement to
impress upon the reader the novelty of such an assertion,
the content of the note revealed the traditional nature
of its author's ideas. The last sentence quoted above
said nothing that had not been reiterated time and again
by other Americans. This was the language of nationalism
which', combined with a geopolitical preoccupation with
American power in the Western Hemisphere, constituted
the sum of American policy during the crisis.

That the Venezuelan dispute nevertheless became a
landmark was due basically to the fact that the nationalistic tone of American policy found a receptive audience
at home that was particularly pleased that the target of

the nationalistic policy was none other than the greatest
power in the world, Britain. Neither Cleveland nor Olney
had any notion of global strategy, and they did not set
out to devise a world policy on the basis of hostility
towards Great Britain. They were simply being nationalistic. But their acts and statements had anti-British
implications and served to crystallize opinions both in
the United States and in Britain concerning their mutual
relations. In this way, quite unwittingly the Cleveland
administration lent its hand to an ultimate emergence
of an Anglo-American entente. In the immediate
circumstances of 1895, however, President Cleveland's
handling of the dispute had a great deal of appeal to a
populace that was becoming more and more restive because
of the domestic economic and social crisis. There had
been an undercurrent of Anglophobia in American opinion
at the mass cultural level, but in the 1890s this was
reinforced with a sense of socio-economic crisis that
affected certain segments of the population. For those
who were self-consciously poor, alienated or excluded
from opportunities for advancement in American society,
foreign affairs for the first time began to assume some
importance. This was particularly true of farmers,
miners, silver interests, and other followers of
William Jennings Bryan who perceived themselves in
opposition to the Eastern establishment and to the
orthodox theories and practices of the American economic
system. As they pondered the crisis of the nineties,
they became entrapped in an anti-British rhetoric,
attributing to Britain and its supporters in the United
States most of the ills of that day. They identified
Britain with the gold standard, the target of their ire
as they advocated the remonetarization of silver as the
best solution for the economic crisis. The silverites
and Bryanites accused the East-coast business community
of lack of patriotism in meekly submitting to the British-
dominated gold-standard system in international trade and
domestic economic development. In 1893 Bryan made a
speech in Congress declaring that the United States still
seemed to be a British colony, and that the nation must
now be determined to wrest autonomy and freedom from
Great Britain. The 'Rocky Mountain News' hailed the
speech and said Bryan should be nominated for president
on 'a people's platform' that included opposition to the
gold standard, Britain and 'Eastern despotism.' (5)
   With such a climate of opinion, it was not surprising
that Cleveland's bellicose attitude toward Britain during
the Venezuelan dispute should be immensely popular among
segments of the population that found Bryan's rhetoric

pleasing. For those who tended to identify their plight
and the ills of American society with British and
Eastern 'monopolists,' the administration's staunch
support of the Monroe Doctrine and forceful attitude
toward Great Britain were thoroughly praiseworthy. While
it is doubtful that Cleveland deliberately sought to
arouse mass patriotism to enlist its support for his
nationalistic foreign policy, the impact upon the two
countries was little short of being stunning. Some
American leaders were led for the first time to articulate
their pro-British sentiment. Others felt the need to
speak out openly and strongly to reaffirm their adherence
to the idea of American-British friendship. They would
oppose the prevailing mood of Anglophobia with a
reasoning which had geopolitical as well as ideological
components.

As seen earlier, after 1865 there had been some
instances of friction with Britain, but they had largely
been related to the unfinished business left over from
the Civil War. As Europe entered the Age of Imperialism,
segments of American opinion had favored and often identified itself with the rhetoric of European expansion, of
which there was a visible British strain. By the late
1880s they had become convinced of the need to consolidate
the ties between the two countries not only in terms of
American national interests as traditionally defined,
but also of providing the basic framework for American
thought and action in the international arena. The trend
continued in the nineties, as America's leaders saw what
they took to be dangerous revolutionary tides sweeping
through the country. For them Britain symbolized
stability and order, not only at home but abroad. In
international affairs, they were advocates of an entente
between the United States and Great Britain; together,
they believed, the two powers could provide a peaceful
world order and spread the blessings of civilization to
the four corners of the earth. Their rift and division
would be a calamity not only at the national level but
also to world peace and civilization.

Ambassador Thomas F. Bayard, representing the United
States in London, was one of the staunchest advocates of
Anglo-American friendship. Although a Democrat, whereas
most exponents of the idea were found among the
Republicans, he was deeply chagrined at the eruption of
the Venezuelan dispute and did what he could to calm the
atmosphere. In January 1896 he wrote to President
Cleveland about the absolute necessity to maintain
'friendly competition in the onward march of civilization
of the two great branches of English-speaking people.'

His use of the term 'civilization' was in accordance
with the way a growing number of commentators were
describing American relations with other countries,
especially Britain. To them it appeared axiomatic that
the friendship of the two countries in their separate and
joint endeavors was a vital condition for the advancement
of human civilization. It was nothing short of insanity,
therefore, that the American people should be so stirred
by an anti-British mood as to talk of retaliation and
even of war, on an issue of relatively minor importance
like the Venezuelan boundary dispute. 'Every now and
then,' Bayard said, 'the tide of civilization seems to
ebb, and mankind go backward.' His reference was to the
trends of opinion within the United States advocating
policies that 'would wrap the world in flames if carried
out.' (6) Henry White, who preceded Bayard in London as
American representative, was another ardent supporter of
Anglo-American entente. He criticized Cleveland's
handling of the dispute, attributing it to his 'ignorance
of diplomacy.' On the other hand, White was more willing
than Bayard to see American power more strongly asserted
in the Western Hemisphere in the name of the Monroe
Doctrine. Far from embittering Anglo-American relations,
he believed that such a step would only cement ties
between the two nations by removing causes of friction.
As he wrote, 'it is in the interest of both American
continents, otherwise there will always be questions
between the two countries.' (7) Basically, therefore,
White was one with Bayard in supporting a policy of
rapprochement and friendship with Britain. Moreover,
both couched their policy statements in the language of
Anglo-Saxon civilization. White's close friends such as
Theodore Roosevelt and John Hay could not have agreed
more with such a position. Roosevelt wrote White,

> I feel it is to the interest of civilization that the
> English-speaking race should be dominant in South
> Africa, exactly as it is for the interest of
> civilization that the United States themselves, the
> greatest branch of the English-speaking race, should
> be dominant in the Western Hemisphere. (8)

Hay, who was soon to succeed Bayard as ambassador to
Britain, was emotionally and intellectually even more
committed to a pro-British stand. He identified with
British upper-class values, which to him included law
and order as well as cultural sophistication and
industrial progress. Viewing London as his second home,
he looked at American foreign relations from the
perspective of an Anglo-American rather than a purely
nationalistic standpoint. Naturally he was horrified by

Cleveland's and Olney's belligerent rhetoric and by what appeared to be his countrymen's ignorant anti-British hysteria.

Fortunately for these supporters of Anglo-American friendship, the government in London did what it could to accommodate American sensitivities about the Western Hemisphere. It is true that Lord Salisbury, then prime minister and foreign secretary, refused to give international legal recognition to the Monroe Doctrine, considering it merely a unilateral enunciation of policy by the United States without any force of law. But he was as convinced as his American friends of the wisdom of avoiding a crisis across the Atlantic. British foreign policy had not been overly concerned with the United States for over a decade, and for this reason the commotion in America was totally unexpected. Britain's political and social elites had mingled with their counterpart in America, who shared a similar intellectual outlook. Some prominent leaders, such as Joseph Chamberlain, William Harcourt and Randolph Churchill were married to Americans. It had never occurred to them that a serious crisis would arise between the two countries. The sudden eruption of the Venezuelan crisis, then, served as a catalyst to confirm their commitment to Anglo-American friendship. It was not that they understood or even pretended to understand the volatile nature of American public opinion and politics. Rudyard Kipling, who had married an American and tried to start a new life in Vermont in the early nineties, was about to leave the United States, confessing his inability to fit into an American way of life. Moods in America were a mystery. But Britain could turn to John Hay, Henry White, Henry Adams and others and work through them to maintain a relationship of sanity with the United States. They had the same notion of 'civilization,' and agreed that world peace, stability and civilization depended to a large extent upon co-operation between the two branches of the Anglo-Saxon race. It was unthinkable - 'an absurdity as well as a crime,' as Chamberlain had said - that the two should clash anywhere in the world, least of all in such a relatively remote area as Venezuela. Although Salisbury was not as passionately devoted as Chamberlain to the cause of American friendship, he did not hesitate, once the furor broke out in the United States, to accept the Cleveland administration's renewed proposal for an arbitration. In January 1896 a boundary commission was appointed, leading ultimately to the settlement of the dispute through a board of arbitration in 1899.

In contrast to the Venezuelan dispute, the Cuban crisis did not directly affect American-British relations, and in part for this reason there was no outburst of patriotic, anti-British sentiment over the matter. But the Cuban affair just as strongly touched a responsive chord in American public opinion and served to raise fundamental questions about the nature of the country's foreign policy and commitments overseas. The crisis arose as the Cuban insurgents, suppressed in 1878, had continued to agitate underground and in the United States. Open hostilities broke out again in 1895, and readers of American newspapers were treated to almost daily reports on the civil war for the next three years. Press coverage, however, had been extensive during the ten-year civil war in Cuba (1868-78), and at that time there had also been much agitation among segments of congressional and opinion leaders for some positive action by the United States government. Hamilton Fish, as noted earlier, had conducted his diplomacy in the traditional framework of caution and of Caribbean regionalism. During the 1890s, in contrast, the United States government and people found themselves steadily drawn into the Cuban crisis until the country was on the brink of war in the winter of 1897-8. How does one account for the change?

Until the beginning of 1897, President Cleveland was in office and dealt with the Cuban civil war in an essentially routine manner, stressing the protection of American national needs and interests. Cleveland was as cautious and non-interventionist as Fish, and for basically the same reasons. It was obviously important to prevent possible European intervention, and to protect American economic interests, consisting largely of investments in Cuban sugar plantations and real estate, and of trade with the island which exceeded 100 million dollars in 1893. Continuation of the civil war, both sides employing increasingly desperate and devastating methods of destruction, would cause hardship to these interests. The United States, therefore, was inclined to offer mediation between rebels and Spanish rulers. But Cleveland persisted in a policy of neutrality, refusing to take sides in the civil war. He did not believe that the rebels were representative of the Cuban population any more than the existing regime, and concluded that to recognize their belligerent or semi-autonomous status, not to mention independence, was tantamount to intervening in Cuban affairs. In trying to protect American commercial interests and to bring the civil war to an end, the only conceivable weapon, as far as he was concerned, was diplomacy. And that implied continued dealings with the Spanish government in Madrid. It did not make sense to antagonize Spain when the latter's support and concurrence were needed to restore peace to the island and create a stable environment for American business to flourish. As in the case of the Venezuelan dispute, moreover, Cleveland was convinced that his cautious, patient approach was in line with the preservation of the honor of the nation as a country that eschewed bellicosity and imperialism. As he said in the December 1896 message to Congress, 'The United States has ... a character to maintain as a nation, which plainly dictates that right and not might should be the rule of its conduct.' Thus, here again there was a unity in American foreign policy under President Cleveland; the country's security, interests and dignity were all bound up in a policy of prudence, shunning adventurism and excess.

This was an attitude that had prevailed in the 1870s and won approval of substantial portions of the population. Twenty years later, however, support for such a policy could not be taken for granted. This was fundamentally due to a changed political-social milieu which made the execution of a traditional policy more difficult and complicated. There were emerging groups of men who would not be satisfied with Cleveland's cautious stand and sought to force a departure in American foreign policy. For one thing, he was a Democratic president deeply believing in the righteousness of his party. He took delight in partisan politics, castigating the Republicans for their alleged responsibility for the ills of American society. Some Republicans, therefore, seized upon the Cuban crisis as a partisan issue and attacked the president's seeming indifference to humanitarian and nationalistic considerations which, in their view, should dictate a more forceful attitude toward Spain. In the election year 1896 the Republican Party adopted a platform calling for America's good offices to bring about Cuban independence. The Democratic Party, in contrast, was satisfied with reiterating support for the principles of the Monroe Doctrine. The Democrats themselves, however, were divided. Although they generally loyally backed the official stance of their leader, Cleveland, some of them, especially followers of William Jennings Bryan, expressed strong sympathy for the Cuban insurgents. They identified themselves with the Cubans in so far as the latter seemed to be struggling for goals such as self-determination and people's rights against monopoly and privilege, just as they themselves were doing. Their clamor for action grew after the victory of McKinley over Bryan in November.

Democrats in the South and West, regions of strong populist sentiment, were burnt with a crusading spirit to come to the aid of the oppressed and the under-privileged, an image of Cubans that corresponded to their own self-perception.

Thus the traditionalism of Cleveland's Cuban policy was opposed at various levels. At one level, there was geopolitical thinking, perceiving the Cuban crisis as an opportunity not only to reassert American power in the Caribbean - a goal with which Cleveland could not have agreed more - but also to play a more active role in world politics. Young and vigorous Republicans, such as Theodore Roosevelt and Henry Cabot Lodge, were the strongest exponents of this, what Lodge called a 'large policy.' They differed from their leaders such as Harrison and McKinley in wanting to go much beyond the latter's definition of national commitments. Instead of defining the national interests, as McKinley did, in terms of 'protection, patriotism, prosperity,' Roosevelt, Lodge, and their friends would look outward and demand that the nation become an active member of international politics. To do so it was imperative to respond positively to a crisis such as the Cuban civil war and to be willing to take risks, even the risk of war with Spain. Only then would the United States be able to carry weight as a power and be an equal of the great powers of Europe. Not unnaturally, therefore, the exponents of the 'large policy' were also strong advocates of a bigger and better navy. They agreed completely with their friend, Alfred Thayer Mahan, that status and power went hand in hand in world politics, and that the building of a great modern navy was essential if the United States was to exert its influence in the international sphere beyond its immediate environs.

In stressing the need for a larger navy, these men were giving their blessing to military strategists who had never given up their hope that the nation would regain the power it had possessed at the end of the Civil War. Naval officers, as Peter Karsten has shown, never wavered in their devotion to an idealized image of themselves, even during the decades of neglect by the federal government, and they had preserved a tradition of fierce patriotism. Their 'patriotism' was different from McKinley's and Cleveland's, although the latter two used the word just as frequently as the military. Naval patriotism involved readiness to use force in distant quarters of the globe in defense of national honor and rights, and it implied an elitism in viewing national destiny as bound up with the state of the navy. An

international crisis meant an opportunity to demonstrate
patriotism and to enhance national power, and for over
twenty years after 1873 these patriots bemoaned the
absence of serious international complications involving
the United States. They envied their British counterpart,
whom they took as their model. The British navy was
visible everywhere in the world, extending the domain over
which the flag established control. The deepening crisis
in Cuba was thus an occasion for reasserting the
military's role in national policy as well as their raison
d'être in American life. As Captain H. C. Taylor, who
succeeded Mahan as president of the Naval War College,
said in February 1896, 'Not only do nations that practice
too long the arts of peace in forgetfulness of war become
enfeebled ... but they grow corrupt internally as well as
race decadence hastens its steps.' (9)

Such a remark might have been condemned as petulant
and unbecoming a responsible citizen in ordinary
circumstances. But in the context of the Cuban crisis
bellicosity was no longer suspect. It became even
respectable as public sentiment was itself turning more and
and more belligerent. This conjunction of navalism, an
age-old phenomenon, and an aroused mass psychology defined
the environment in which foreign policy operated and
tended to narrow the range of alternatives open to the
government. Mass sentiment was basically ideological;
there were humanitarian concerns with the plight of the
Cubans and anger at the brutal way in which Spanish
authorities were dealing with the uprising. But idealism
and humanitarianism were not new. They had always
characterized one aspect of American foreign relations.
More fundamental was the sentiment that somehow
domestic issues and foreign crisis were linked. Farmers,
workers and others who were self-consciously poor,
deprived, disadvantaged or alienated, had for years
concentrated their attack upon what they took to be the
domestic causes of the country's social and economic ills
- the trusts, the 'monopolists,' the Eastern bankers, and
the like. But the Venezuelan crisis and the tariff
dispute had helped to turn their attention outward and
made them realize that there were connections between
domestic and external issues. The Cuban case fitted their
perception and their imagination perfectly well. The
United States, which was going through a serious economic
crisis after the depression of 1893, appeared to be
headed for a disaster unless drastic steps were taken to
reconstruct the society. Somehow the nation, once the
symbol of hope for humanity, had degenerated into a
society of contentious groups and class struggles. Given

such an image, there was receptivity to ideas calling for
an innovation, for a departure, and for a drastic
solution.   It was in such a context that there grew
psychological readiness to act decisively at home and
abroad.

The joining of domestic and foreign issues was
calculated to mobilize public sentiment, to mould it into
a tangible force that had to be reckoned with by decision-
makers.   There were two areas in which internal and
external affairs perceived in conjunction.   First, as
happened during the Venezuelan crisis, public clamor for
intervention in Cuba was sustained by an image of
privilege in American society against which the people
were pictured as revolting.   Second, by standing for
human rights in Cuba, one could hope to transform the
United States to become once again the symbol of justice
and freedom.   In both instances, the nation as it stood
in the mid-1890s was seen as not what it should be; it
was controlled by corrupt politicians and businessmen and
was unmindful of the ideals for which it had been
renowned.   To intervene on behalf of the Cubans, in such
a context, was to challenge the situation at home and
seek to restore an America that was good, just and
honorable.

Interestingly enough, President Cleveland and his
supporters often defended the official policy of caution
and neutrality in much the same way.   They argued that in
order to preserve national integrity and traditional
virtues, it was imperative to shun extremism and
emotionalism in dealing with foreign disputes.
Conservative leaders, skeptical of mass emotionalism and
patriotic excesses, stood behind Cleveland.   They stressed
the need to maintain the tradition of non-intervention in
external affairs and to uphold the president's
prerogative to conduct foreign policy rather than letting
mass opinion dictate national behavior.   As Edward Chapman
said, the country was animated by 'pseudo patriotism' and
'military imperialism,' but true patriotism lay in
eschewing facile solutions and persisting in a prudent
course of action.   Moreover, Cleveland's supporters
argued, in an intellectual framework not very different
from McKinley's, that the basic national interest to
protect was the country's prosperity and economic
interests.   Premature intervention and a possible war
with Spain would disrupt the national economy and create
unstable business conditions just when the country was
trying to recover from the depression of 1893.

By the end of 1896, then, American opinion was being
sharply split because of different views of what

constituted the national interest and how far the country
should go to transform itself and its foreign policy.
Both supporters and opponents of Cleveland's Cuban policy
argued for patriotism and nationalism, and they all
referred back to tradition.   But there was no agreement as
to the contemporary implications of the historical past,
some saying that tradition dictated a policy of non-
intervention, while others proclaimed that it was in the
character of the American people to intervene for human
rights and national honor.   Divisions at home, then, were
producing divergent approaches to foreign affairs.

     During the presidential campaign of 1896, however, the
overriding issue was that of silver; the Democratic
candidate, William Jennings Bryan, advocating the
remonetarization of silver in order to alleviate the
financial problems of farmers and laborers.   The silver
issue divided the party, as Cleveland and his followers
refused to accept Bryan's monetary doctrines.   Foreign
policy issues were temporarily submerged under the more
immediate question of silver, and it was only after
Bryan's defeat by McKinley that Cuba came to the fore as
an urgent issue in national politics.   Nevertheless, the
Cuban question alone might not have been sufficient to
alter drastically the nature of American foreign relations.
The island was after all an area of special concern to the
United States, and intervention or even war and annexation
might not have necessitated fundamental rethinking about
the nature of American commitments overseas or the extent
of its power on the global scale.   The significance of
the national debate on Cuba consisted in the fact that it
was not an isolated phenomenon, but that it was part of
the drama of a deepening involvement in affairs of distant
lands that was taking place at that time.   While the
Venezuelan and the Cuban disputes could still be handled
within a familiar framework of Caribbean regionalism or
national-interest considerations, matters in other parts
of the world called for more drastic reformulation.   It is
in such a context that one may now turn to the discussion
of Asia and the Pacific.   It was the conjunction of the
Caribbean crisis with the Asian-Pacific drama which
brought about the age of American participation in
imperialist politics.

2   ASIA AND THE PACIFIC

By the end of the 1880s it was becoming obvious that the
European powers were extremely interested in applying to
Asia and the Pacific the kinds of imperialist politics and

global strategies that they were practicing in the Middle East, Central Asia or Africa. In the Pacific Ocean, Germany and Britain vied with each other to extend their control, and their relations were far from peaceful, as the Samoan dispute revealed. The German encroachment upon Samoa, moreover, was symptomatic of a larger interest in the South-west Pacific. That region, encompassing the corner of the Pacific that lay close to the British, Dutch and French colonial empires, attracted German attention as an avenue of approach to the wider ocean and as a base of operation for its imperial interests elsewhere in Asia. This region was also becoming of crucial importance because of the vulnerability of the Spanish regime in the Philippines. The Filipino population, for over three-hundred years under Spanish control, was no longer passive, and there were undercurrents of discontent and opposition that began to manifest themselves openly just as the world entered the Age of Imperialism. Upper-class Filipinos - the so-called 'ilustrados' - who represented wealth and education, were permeated by Western-oriented reformist ideas and sought greater rights and self-respect in a colonial society. They developed a propaganda movement, seeking to promote change within the framework of Spanish rule. Such a gradualist approach was challenged by more radical revolutionaries led by secret societies, representative more of peasants and workers than of professional classes. One such secret society, the Katipunan, was eventually to lead a revolt in 1896, catapulting the movement for overthrowing the existing regime. Internal turmoil, however, was primarily significant in so far as it might create a power vacuum which foreign powers would be only too interested to fill. Germany, in particular, eyed the islands as a possible base for its expanding navy. More important than insular politics was the renowned wealth of the islands. Their rich mineral and agricultural resources made them a tempting prize to the imperialist powers.

Another area of great interest to the powers was the island of Formosa (Taiwan). The island, under the rule of the Ch'ing dynasty of China for two-hundred years, was strategically situated because of its proximity both to the China mainland and the Philippines. The French attacked Taiwan during the war with China (1884-5), and were interested in permanently occupying part of the island as a condition for settling the war. Nothing came of it, but French action attracted the attention of the other imperialist powers and, most important, of Japan. The Japanese government viewed Taiwan as an important stepping stone as the nation contemplated expansion in

Asia and the Pacific. Already in 1874 an expedition was
sent to the island with a view to demonstrating Japan's
concern with the safety of its nationals visiting or
engaged in various activities in Taiwan. But it was
during the 1890s that Japan joined the ranks of the
imperialist powers.

The development of Japan as an imperialist power,
paralleling the emergence of the United States as a world
power, was an event of fateful significance for the
future of American foreign relations. It is well to
stress that Japanese imperialism, like its European
counterpart, exhibited both geopolitical particularism and
universalistic expansionism. That is to say, the
Japanese government and military strategists were
preoccupied both with establishing a zone of special
interest nearer home in order to guarantee national
security, and with extending the country's political
influence and economic interests wherever possible
throughout the world. Taiwan was more important in
connection with the second than the first consideration.
It appeared to be a gateway to the South Seas, a region
that fascinated Japan's expansionists. As a writer put it
in 1890, what the nation required was a policy of southern
expansion: 'policy for commerce, trade, settlement, and
colonization of the southern islands.' They were rich in
natural resources and enjoyed open spaces. The Japanese
should do in these islands what Germans were doing in
Samoa. The writer specifically mentioned the Philippines
as one of the most desirable objects for Japanese
expansion. Not satisfied with such a vision, another
author called on his countrymen to redouble their effort
to migrate to and work in Hawaii. The Hawaiian islands,
lying in the middle of the Pacific Ocean, seemed a
perfect area for directing Japanese energy and skill with
a view ultimately to bringing them under Japanese
influence if not control. (10)

On the continent of Asia, on the other hand, Japanese
preoccupation was more particularistic. There was concern
with the encroachment of the European powers upon China
and Korea, with the possible result that the security of
the home islands of Japan might become compromised. The
problem of China and Korea were closely linked, since
the Ch'ing dynasty was trying desperately to retain
control over the Korean kingdom lest the latter should
go the way of Indochina, while factions within Korea were
appealing to China, Russia and other countries to provide
them with support as they engaged in a struggle for power
in a political context that was becoming more and more
volatile. The situation became acute when the Russian

government announced the intention of building a trans-Siberian railway traversing three-thousand miles of Siberia and terminating at Vladivostok, a port in the Maritime Provinces, just to the northeast of Korea. Russian penetration of China and Korea was expected to continue, as was Britain's determination to resist it. From the Japanese point of view, big-power rivalries in the near-by kingdom of Korea were an extremely serious matter, and it was considered to be particularly essential to prevent that country from falling under the control of a third power. Korean 'independence' became a basic goal of Japanese policy.

The Sino-Japanese War of 1894-5 was occasioned by a rebellion within Korea that brought about the dispatch of Chinese troops to maintain law and order. The Japanese government and military seized the opportunity to remove Chinese, and hopefully European, influence from the peninsular kingdom. Large forces were sent to Korea, and fighting broke out between Japanese and Chinese troops. The resulting victory by Japan introduced a new factor to Asian-Pacific international politics. Taiwan was ceded to Japan, thus providing an opportunity for further penetration of the South Seas by the Japanese. Having crushed the Chinese navy, Japan's naval force emerged as a key to the balance of power in the Southwest Pacific, with clear implications for the future status of the Philippines and near-by territories. In Taiwan itself, the Japanese army of occupation encountered stiff opposition by residents, some of whom proclaimed a short-lived republic. Government of the island was done through a military administration, and Japan now emerged as a full-fledged colonial power. At the same time, Japanese publicists continued to stress the need to expand peacefully through trade and emigration in other parts of the world, especially the Pacific Ocean and South America, areas of special concern to the United States.

In the meantime, the Sino-Japanese War increased China's dependence on, and control by, the European powers. Japan had initially asked for the cession of Liaotung peninsula, at the southern tip of Manchuria, reasoning that such a possession was necessary to ensure Korean 'independence.' That alone would have entrenched Japanese power in southern Manchuria and almost inevitably brought about a clash between Japan and Russia on Chinese soil. China would have been a helpless bystander in the drama of imperialist politics. A Russian-Japanese war did take place in 1904, but other events occurred during the decade after the Sino-Japanese War, causing further damage to Chinese sovereignty.

Russia, Germany and France decided, immediately after the
peace treaty between China and Japan was signed, to
intervene to compel the latter to give up the rights it
had just obtained in Manchuria. The 'tripartite
intervention,' as it came to be known, aimed at
preventing Japanese control over China, and reflected the
fear - a mixture of geopolitical, economic, and
racialist thinking - that the combination of the
resources and manpower of the two Asian countries would
present an enormous obstacle in the way of Western
influence and interests in that part of the world. The
European powers, of course, had diverse interests in Asia
and elsewhere, but they were agreed on the desirability
of further extending their rights in China, and on the
assumption that such an objective would be made much more
difficult to attain if Japan should be allowed to
establish greater control over China. Great Britain alone
of the major powers viewed Japanese acquisition of
southern Manchuria with relative equanimity, considering
it a possible counterweight to Russian power. But Britain
refused to obstruct the tripartite powers or to come to
the aid of Japan. The intervention succeeded.

This proved to be only a respite from the Chinese
point of view. Between 1895 and 1897, the European
powers turned their attention to the Far East with greater
intensity than ever before, now that China's weakness
had been revealed and a new structure of international
politics in Asia had to be defined. Their strategy was
to obtain economic concessions from, and to establish
political control over, the Ch'ing empire, just as they
were doing in the Middle East. In the immediate
aftermath of the Sino-Japanese War, railway concessions
occupied the center stage; the powers vied with one
another to obtain a right to build railways in China, to
be financed through syndicates formed by foreign bankers.
Often a railway concession was coupled with a loan, as
happened when France offered a loan to China to meet the
latter's needs for indemnity payments to Japan, and was
in turn awarded a right to build a railway across
Manchuria. The Chinese Eastern Railway, as it came to be
called, was of enormous economic and strategic value to
Russia, an ally of France, and had important political
implications, tying China, France, Russia and their
friends closely together. Others such as Germany, Britain
and Italy were not to be left behind. They too sought,
and usually got, similar concessions. Within a few years
after the Sino-Japanese War, nineteen railways had been
contracted away, their total mileage amounting to 6,420
miles. As was happening in the Middle East, a railway

defined a special sphere of interest for the power that
had the concession, and China was fast turning into an
arena that would be divided up into spheres of influence
of the powers.

Such was the situation in Asia and the Pacific that
provided a novel context for the operation of American
foreign policy during the 1890s. Occurring more or less
simultaneously with the Venezuelan dispute, the Cuban
uprising, and other incidents closer to home, events in
Asia and the Pacific served to keep American officials
and opinion leaders interested in foreign-policy matters
and impel them to consider alternative choices facing
the nation in the immediate future. Before 1897,
however, American policy in these areas on the whole
adhered to a traditional framework, much as was the case
with the Caribbean region.

First of all, Hawaii remained within an American
sphere of special interest, but pressures for a drastic
departure of policy - looking toward the islands'
annexation by the United States - were not sufficiently
strong to bring about a change until 1898. American-
Hawaiian ties might have remained as close as they had
been in the past, and there might have been no
territorial incorporation of the latter into the United
States but for the changing environment of international
relations during the 1890s. For one thing, the navalists
and their supporters were now able to make a more
plausible case for their annexationism because of the
increasing tempo of events in Asia and the Pacific.
Alfred Thayer Mahan and his fellow expansionists could
argue with greater force and reasoning, and to a
widening circle of sympathetic listeners, that American
security and interests demanded the possession of bases
and defense posts in the Pacific, and that to reach
China and engage in its trade actively, it was important
to demonstrate American determination and power, backed
up by a sizeable naval force in the ocean. Moreover,
in the Age of Imperialism it was always possible that
unless the United States took over the Hawaiian islands,
some other power, such as Britain or Germany, might do
so.

One new factor in the scene was the growth of Japanese
power and influence. At first this took the form of
Japanese immigrants into Hawaii. Starting from 1885, when
the Japanese and Hawaiian governments signed an agreement
for contract labor arrangements, the number of Japanese
laborers working in sugar plantations registered
phenomenal annual increases. Already in 1890 there were
12,000 Japanese in Hawaii, compared with 15,000 Chinese,

2,000 Americans, and 34,000 natives. The white minority was determined to prevent any weakening of its political influence and economic power, and in 1887 the whites in Hawaii were successful in having the royal government adopt a new constitution which restricted the voting rights to themselves and to the native population. Already the census of 1891-2 showed that Japanese and Chinese were paying 29 per cent of the taxes. The white minority could not long expect to monopolize power, unless they were backed up by the military support of a major nation. That would necessitate annexation to the United States. After 1890, moreover, the movement within Hawaii for joining America was given impetus by the McKinley tariff which put all imported sugar on the free list, wiping out the advantages of Hawaiian sugar which had enjoyed reciprocity arrangements with the United States for over ten years.

The United States government was not officially involved in annexationist moves, but the American minister in Hawaii, John L. Stevens, kept in close touch with members of the 'annexation club,' composed of a handful of whites interested in deposing Queen Liliuokalani. When, at the beginning of 1893, the annexationists resorted to violence and occupied the government buildings, Stevens quickly landed American marines and proceeded to recognize the revolutionary regime without waiting for instructions from Washington. The 'revolution' was bloodless, 160 American marines constituting the major force on the islands, and on 1 February Stevens proclaimed Hawaii a protectorate of the United States. A treaty of annexation was speedily drawn up, specifying a territorial form of government for Hawaii. That the American minority in Hawaii preferred the territorial status to statehood was due basically to its fear of colored races on the islands who would gain American citizenship in the event that Hawaii was annexed as a state. As one of the Hawaiian commissioners sent to Washington remarked, 'There is such a large number of Chinese and other cheap laborers on the islands who cannot be trusted to vote intelligently that if universal suffrage was declared the whites, who represent almost the entire business interests of the country, would be outvoted and powerless.' (11)

These events took place in a period of transition in American politics, just as President Harrison was stepping down, to be replaced by Grover Cleveland in the White House. Harrison, McKinley and most Republican leaders were willing to accept the 'fait accompli' in Hawaii. To them it was more or less a logical step from the reciprocity treaties of 1875 and 1887, making the islands part of the American political system in name as well as in reality. Navalists naturally welcomed the turn of events and looked to the day when the American flag would be raised not only in Hawaii and Samoa but elsewhere in the Pacific. Many were persuaded by commercial reasoning to approve of Hawaiian annexation. In view of the spreading notion about the vast markets of Asia, it was relatively easy to picture Hawaii as a necessary half-way station as the United States participated in the commerce of the Orient. The Republican press on the whole supported annexation, some even going so far as to declare, as the 'New York Sun' did, 'What great nation has ever been anything else than an annexationist?' (12)

The country as a whole, however, was not willing to accept that kind of imperialist rhetoric. The 'New York Herald' was more representative of national thinking than the 'Sun' when it stated, 'there is more sugar than statesmanship and more jingoism than patriotism in the hasty movement' for Hawaiian annexation. (13) To a disinterested observer, it must have seemed that the sudden emergence of the annexationist movement was a direct result of the 1890 tariff and therefore that it was being staged to serve the sugar interests. There was a widespread feeling that the nation should not take a drastic step simply to please them. The distinction between special interests and national interests was on the lips of almost all anti-annexationist spokesmen, as was the distinction between jingoism and patriotism which was noted by the 'Herald'. It seemed that true patriotism was incompatible with emotional jingoism. To make a hasty move to launch the country on an imperial-istic career, the opponents of annexation pointed out, was not an act of patriotism. It was 'pseudo patriotism.' As Senator John Sherman noted in his autobiography, published in 1895, 'If my life is prolonged, I will do all I can to add to the strength and prosperity of the United States, but nothing to extend its limits or add new dangers by acquisitions of new territory.'

In this way the Hawaiian dispute, like the Cuban uprising, compelled Americans to define anew what constituted the national interest and what brought greatness and honor to the country. Sherman's definition was one that would have been accepted by all the traditionalists, whether Republican or Democrat. Harrison's and McKinley's support of Hawaiian annexation indicated, however, that some leaders were willing to go beyond the conventional framework of national policy, although their justification for imperialism was by and

large couched in traditionalist rhetoric.   Both
supporters and opponents of annexation, in other words,
turned to the concept of the country's commercial
interests, prestige and honor to justify their respective
stands.   Under the circumstances, the earlier consensus on
the basic framework of American foreign policy was bound
to dissipate.

Grover Cleveland, returning to the White House in
March 1893, remained a self-conscious traditionalist.   He
refused to be rushed into accepting the 'fait accompli'
in Hawaii.   His basic attitude was similar to Sherman's,
and to his own toward such other diplomatic disputes of
the time as the Venezuelan crisis and the Cuban uprising.
He was an intense nationalist, but his sense of national
greatness included traditional values and virtues such as
justice, the principle of fair play, and self-
determination.   He felt that these values had been
violated by Minister Stevens and by the Harrison
administration when they had so hastily moved to
incorporate Hawaii into the United States.   The only
remedy was to refuse to ratify the treaty of annexation
until a thorough investigation of the revolution was
conducted.   Cleveland therefore dispatched Congressman
James H. Blount to conduct an investigation.   The result
confirmed the President's fears; Blount found that
Minister Stevens' behavior had been highly objectionable
and that there was no popular sentiment among the people
of Hawaii to seek an annexation to the United States.
The American protectorate over Hawaii was speedily
terminated, and the Cleveland administration proceeded
to try to restore Queen Liluokalani to the throne.   This,
however, proved difficult, since she was no more
representative of the popular will than the white
minority, and since the latter objected to Cleveland's
interference with Hawaii's internal affairs.   The upshot
was that the United States recognized the provisional
government of Honolulu, and American-Hawaiian relations
were restored to the state prevailing before 1893.

Thus far the Hawaiian debate had been conducted
largely within the framework of traditional foreign-
policy questions.   Both annexationists and anti-
annexationists insisted that national honor and interests
dictated a certain course of action.   It was an inner-
looking debate.   Increasingly, however, external factors
assumed importance because of the quickening tempo of
imperialist politics in Asia, during and after the Sino-
Japanese War.   The victory in the war gave the Japanese
unprecedented self-confidence which was soon coupled
with a sense of chagrin at the tripartite intervention.

Both reinforced the view that Japan must continue to
expand wherever possible. The war, many publicists
pointed out, was only a first step toward enlarging the
limits of the empire. Now that the nation proved capable
of fighting a formidable enemy, it should turn its
energies to peacetime expansion. Moreover, since Japan
was denied an opportunity to expand to Manchuria, it
seemed logical to undertake the task elsewhere.

Hawaii became important in such a context. Not only
did the islands continue to appear an ideal place for
settling Japanese emigrants, but the growing navy and
national power of Japan began to seem relevant to its
destiny in the Pacific. American residents in Hawaii
were well aware of these trends; Japanese laborers on
the islands impressed them as arrogant and cocky because
of the victory over China, and the fear of Japanese
domination of Hawaii grew more and more intense. Some
sort of confrontation with Japan was not unwelcome
from the point of view of the annexationists. They
reasoned that the United States would not want to be
embroiled in a war with Japan, and that the only way
it could be avoided would be through annexation,
foreclosing the territory to further Japanese immigration.
From the Japanese point of view, however, the logic was
unacceptable because they refused to consider American
annexation of Hawaii inevitable. Some went so far as to
argue that the islands belonged as much to Japan as to
the United States, and that the Japanese government should
do all in its power to foster the growth of the
population outflow across the Pacific. Under the
circumstances, then, the Japanese ingredient in the
Hawaiian problem became clearly visible and gained
importance in the second half of the 1890s. In early
1897, just before Cleveland left the White House to
yield the presidency to McKinley, an incident broke out
that symbolized the tension building up in Japanese-
Hawaiian-American relations. This was the 'Shinshū Maru'
incident, involving the refusal of Hawaiian authorities
to permit the landing of a shipload of Japanese
arrivals. The situation was considered so serious by
Japanese officials, both in Hawaii and Tokyo, that they
determined on a policy of strong protest, backed up by
the dispatch of a warship.

Paralleling the growth of Japanese expansionism
eastward across the Pacific, American interest in Hawaii
also intensified after the Sino-Japanese War. Official
policy toward the war, to be sure, was circumspect, and
generally conducted within the traditional framework of
protecting commercial interests and expressing hopes for

peaceful settlement. Fearing the impact of the war and
the disruption of China upon American commerce, the
Cleveland administration offered mediation to the
belligerents, while at the same time augmenting the size
of the Asiatic squadron from one to eight ships. These
steps were designed to prevent the disintegration of the
Chinese empire which would be detrimental to the furtherance of American commercial interests, but they were not
a new policy. The United States did not involve itself
actively in the war, and it did not combine with other
European powers to try to influence the course of events
during or after the war.

Public interest in Asia, however, had been aroused
because of the war, and it remained strong throughout
the remainder of the decade. Coinciding with the Cuban
uprising and the national debate on intervention, the
Sino-Japanese War served to keep the size of the foreign-
policy public enlarged. There was a great deal of
excitement over the prospects for commercial expansion
once the war was over. Japanese victory over China was
widely interpreted in the United States as a victory of
civilization and enlightenment over backwardness and a
seclusionist foreign policy, and it was expected that
postwar China would prove to be more receptive to foreign
influences and intercourse. Although the myth of the
China market had always existed, in the circumstances
of the mid-nineties when the American economy was going
through a serious crisis, Asia and the Pacific began to
be looked upon as one of the keys to the future of the
United States. Not merely being a valuable but distant
market, the region came to seem quite relevant to the
survival of the national economy itself. Since the
national interest was still largely defined in economic
terms, it is not surprising that many came to link the
destiny of the country to developments in East Asia.
They called upon the government to promote more actively
than in the past the fostering of commercial interests
in China, and the State Department responded by
authorizing the legation in Peking to intercede on behalf
of Americans to obtain contracts from Chinese
authorities. Within the navy, attention turned
increasingly to the question of how best to protect
American interests in Asia and the Pacific at a time when
the European powers as well as Japan were augmenting
their forces in Eastern waters.

The Hawaiian question after 1894 thus became bound up
with the Chinese question, and those Americans who were
concerned with the extension of commercial interests in
China were prone to view Hawaii in this larger context.

They were now more willing than earlier to consider
annexation of Hawaii because the islands appeared an
ideal stepping-stone to the markets of the Orient. To
have a third power establish control over them would be
quite detrimental to the larger objective. At the very
least, it seemed necessary to deny the islands to
another power. At a time when the United States was
trying seriously to extend its interests in East Asia, it
was imperative to make good its long association with
Hawaii and consider it part of America's Asian policy.
In this way, just as the Cuban revolution was forcing
Americans to consider alternative paths for their
foreign policy, the situation in Asia and the Pacific
was compelling them to view foreign affairs from a
fresh perspective. In that process, some were willing to
go beyond the traditional framework of narrowly defined
national interests.

3   THE GREAT DEBATE

The coming of William McKinley to power in 1897
coincided with a mounting crisis in various parts of the
world, confronting the United States with the question
of serious policy choices. It was McKinley's task to
decide whether to continue a more or less traditionalist
approach to the country's foreign affairs or to be ready
to go beyond it and to define a new framework for
relating America to the rest of the world. In performing
this task, he found it more and more difficult to
separate different regions of the globe for consideration;
problems in Asia, the Pacific and the Caribbean were
becoming so interrelated that American action in one
region held immediate implications for other areas.

Relations with Spain over Cuba, for instance, were no
longer an isolated matter but became bound up with events
in Hawaii, China and elsewhere. If Cuba had been the
only major diplomatic issue facing the administration, it
might have continued Cleveland's policy of caution and
prudence. Pressures from interventionist groups, it is
true, were intensifying, and the Bryan Democrats were
particularly vociferous, calling for action to liberate
the Cubans. William Jennings Bryan, after his defeat in
1896, supported belligerent moves as he saw Cuba in terms
of self-determination, identifying the Cubans as the
underdogs like himself and his followers. There was a
crusading spirit in Southern and Western states, the same
spirit of defiance of the East-coast establishment that
had manifested itself in the agrarian reform and the

free-silver movements. McKinley, however, would have
been able to withstand this challenge, as he had in 1896,
if it had not coincided with other developments. In his
inaugural address of March 1897 he declared that 'peace
is preferable to war in almost every contingency.' He
was concerned with the plight of the insurgents in the
island and sympathized with their mistreatment by Spanish
authorities. But he felt these problems could be dealt
with through diplomacy; they were more matters of
humanitarianism than of high policy. He repeatedly
expressed his hope that reform measures would be
undertaken in Cuba, and tried successfully to obtain
permission from Spain to send food and medical supplies
from America to the island. The State Department
solicited contributions to a relief fund, to be
distributed through the consul at Havana, and President
McKinley himself donated $5,000. anonymously. (14)
Fortunately for such a policy of patience and moderation,
liberals were restored in power in Madrid in October,
and they were willing to offer concessions to the
insurgents, including some form of autonomy for the
island. Extreme measures taken against Cubans would be
terminated, and a moderate regime of mutual interdependence between Cuba and Spain would be instituted.
This might have been an expedient and workable solution
of the crisis without a direct involvement of the United
States.

McKinley's moderation toward the Cuban affair,
however, lost part of its plausibility because of his
readiness to act more boldly in Hawaii, looking toward
its annexation to the United States. The 'Shinshū Maru'
incident, noted above, gave impetus to a renewed
annexationist movement both in Hawaii and the United
States, and the argument gained force now that the
Japanese threat was clearly seen. Secretary of the Navy
John D. Long gave instructions to the naval commander at
Honolulu to proclaim a provisional protectorate if Japan
showed signs of resorting to force over the incident,
and the American minister in Hawaii was likewise
authorized to establish a protectorate in case of an
emergency. (15) President McKinley was very much behind
these moves, and he was a positive force for annexation,
prodding reluctant Senators to approve of the treaty of
annexation which was negotiated anew in June. Naval
authorities were naturally delighted with such a turn of
events. To them McKinley seemed to be far more receptive
than Cleveland to the idea of establishing overseas bases
to strengthen naval power and enhance American influence
in the world arena. Certainly, as far as Hawaii was

concerned, McKinley did little to discourage such hopes. For this reason, his cautious policy towards Cuba began to seem less and less plausible. If he was willing to use force to assert America's primacy in Hawaii thousands of miles away, there seemed to be no reason why he should still be reluctant to involve America in affairs of an island just off the coast of the United States.

Furthermore, the Hawaiian issue was intimately linked to events in East Asia, where momentous changes were taking place in China's relations with the powers. Part of McKinley's reasoning for Hawaiian annexation was the trade of the Orient; he believed that the islands would constitute a valuable link in America's expanding commercial empire in Asia. The Senate foreign relations committee, reporting favorably on the treaty of annexation, declared that Hawaii was 'the commercial "Crossroads of the Pacific."' Just at this juncture, however, prospects for expanding commercial interests in Asia were confronted with the drama of what appeared to be an impending partitioning of China. Beginning with the seizure of Kiaochow Bay in Shantung province by Germany in November in 1897, the European powers one after another encroached upon Chinese administrative integrity, seeking bases, leaseholds and concessions in various parts of the Ch'ing empire, and establishing their spheres of influence. By the spring of 1898, Germany, Russia, France and Britain had claimed such spheres in specific regions of China, within each of which a power would have a primary right to obtain a naval base, lease land, build a railway and otherwise engage in commercial and political activities.

The importance of this turn of events for American policy and opinion can be seen in the fact that between November 1897 and April 1898 news from Asia shared a prominent place with Cuban affairs in the press. Sometimes China even overshadowed Cuba in coverage. Readers keenly interested in the Cuban uprising, therefore, were very likely to read accounts of the European powers' imperialistic activities in China. A foreign-policy public which had for several years remained large because of events in Cuba was almost certain to be interested in the news from Asia. Moreover, Hawaii's importance was bound to grow now that attention was turning to East Asia.

Press comments clearly indicated that connections were being established in American minds between disparate episodes of international affairs and efforts were being made to develop a new synthetic framework for comprehending the problems confronting American diplomacy.

The 'American Review of Reviews,' for instance, noted in
February 1898, 'Our acquisition of Hawaii would be
directly useful in helping to keep open Chinese Ports.'
(16) Somewhat more sensationally, the 'Chicago Tribune'
made essentially the same point in the editorial of
19 December 1897:

> Has Congress become so degenerate, cowardly,
> unpatriotic, and pusillanimous as to close its eyes
> to what is going on in China? Is it afraid to
> recognize or to meet the danger which menaces this
> country and the inevitable result - namely: the grab
> of Hawaii, which will follow these Chinese grabs if we
> don't place the islands under our own protection at
> once? Now is the time for this country to put its
> answer to the European powers and show that it is
> aware of the full meaning of their conspiracy. The
> solemn duty of Congress is to annex Hawaii, then
> double, and if need be, treble our naval strength.

The racial theme, which was an important aspect of the
debate over Hawaii, also appeared in connection with the
crisis in China. According to the 'Atlanta Constitution,'
the European powers' thrust into China was but a prelude
to the division and occupation of the entire Asian
continent by the white races who had already established
their hegemony over Africa. '[White] supremacy will be
universal around the world. This is the trend of
history ... The white races have reached the culmination
of their triumph and the colored races, without exception,
have been reduced to a position of subserviency.' (17)

These expressions indicate an attempt to comprehend
disparate events in world affairs in a cohesive
intellectual framework so that they would make some sense
in terms of American relations with them. Concepts such
as race, civilization and commerce were joined to
considerations of national interests and power as various
writers tried to clarify the meaning of the rapidly
changing international affairs for the United States.
Because Cuba, Hawaii, China and other territories in Asia
and the Pacific were racially and culturally different
from America, it is not surprising that a good deal of the
discussion concerning the country's foreign relations
dealt with their interracial and intercultural aspects.
To that extent American writers were coming to
approximate the views of their European counterpart and
echo the same kinds of concern about the implications of
the pervading Westernization of the non-Western world.

In an article for the January 1898 issue of the
'North American Review,' Charles Denby, a long-time
minister in China, declared, 'Asia is the greatest hive of

human beings in the world, the greatest storehouse of
treasures, the greatest unexploited field, and last prize
to conquer for the commerce of the West.' While this was
a standard stereotype, Denby was convinced that after the
Sino-Japanese War things had really begun to move in Asia
and presented a challenging opportunity to the West to
enter the arena. 'Until the war,' he wrote, 'the East
itself continued on its monotonous way, disappointing all
hope of progress, the same from year to year.' The war,
however, 'has done more to open this vast field to
Western commerce and civilization than five hundred years
of foreign trade and one hundred years of missionary
teaching.' (18) The implications for the United States
were obvious. It was to join forces with European
countries at that most favorable moment for the
transformation of the East. In such a context, even the
traditional concern with the extension of commerce came
to assume fresh significance. As the 'New York Times'
commented, 'The extension of our commerce must now become
and continue to be the chief aim of our policy at home
and abroad. This necessity makes our foreign relations
a matter of broader concern than they were in the
decades when we were felling forests and making homes.'
(19) The whole coloration of American foreign policy
must be changed to cope with the situation.

Just as in Europe, moreover, the anticipated contact
of East and West through the latter's determined effort
to spread its commerce and civilization gave rise to
speculation about the nature of Western expansion,
especially now that America seemed at the threshold of
that movement. To be sure, earlier writers had dwelt on
the theme, as seen in the last chapter. Toward the
end of the century, however, Americans discussed the
matter not only in terms of European imperialism, as had
primarily been the case during the 1870s and the 1880s,
but as something that concerned their own country. Even
before they actually undertook colonialist adventures,
they were developing an attitutde that encouraged a sense
of identification with Europe vis-à-vis the non-West.
Increasingly, they were viewing themselves as members
of Western civilization which was spreading its ideas and
institutions to the rest of the world. Questions
Americans raised about their foreign relations would,
therefore, become bound up with perceptions of the interactions between East and West. The vocabulary of
European expansion thus found its way to American
consciousness and prepared Americans emotionally and
intellectually to comprehend the meaning of what their
government would soon undertake.

In June 1897 Benjamin Ide Wheeler, president of the
University of California at Berkeley, wrote an article
for the 'Atlantic Monthly' on 'Greece and the Eastern
Question.' The article was really a discourse on
differences between East and West. The basic question
in the Middle East, he said,
> is a question which in its reality concerns the
> perennial antithesis between Occidentalism and
> Orientalism, and which in its practical statement
> for us and ours means this: Who is to lead, who is
> to represent Occidentalism in its inevitable conflicts
> with the Orient?

To Wheeler it was axiomatic that there was an inevitable
conflict between East and West, as they represented
diametrically opposed principles of life and society. As
he said,
> personality in the Western sense is endowed with the
> right of origination. In the East, action looks to
> continuance, not to creation ... In the West, life is
> a boat, with a rudder and a keel, that can cross the
> stream. In the East, life, personality, is a chip
> swept on the great current ... The West is full of
> creation, progress, restlessness, achievement, failure,
> disappointment, exultation; the East abounds in
> quietism, resignation, and blissful stagnation.

The meaning of Western expansion, in such a context, was
to preserve the precious traditon of individual rights
and self-government against the autocratic institutions
of the Orient. The Anglo-Saxons, Wheeler declared, must
jointly champion the cause of the West. (20)

Wheeler did not elaborate on how the Anglo-Saxon
conceptions of government and personality would affect
life-styles and behavior patterns of non-Western
governments and peoples, should they spread throughout
the world. But at least one writer was keenly interested
in the question of the deepening interaction between the
two civilizations. Writing for the September 1897 issue
of 'Harper's,' Alfred Thayer Mahan took note of the fact
that East and West 'are approaching not only in
geographical propinquity ... but ... in common ideas of
material advantage, without a corresponding sympathy in
spiritual ideas.' Charles Pearson, an Englishman of long
residence in Australia, had analyzed the implications of
this phenomenon in his influential book, 'National Life
and Character, A Forecast' (1893). Mahan echoed Pearson
in presenting a dramatic imagery:
> There will be a stirring of the East, its entrance
> into the field of Western interests, not merely as a
> passive something to be impinged upon, but with a

vitality of its own, formless yet, but significant,
inasmuch as where before there was torpor, if not
death, now there is indisputable movement and life ...
[In] the ebb and flow of human affairs, under those
mysterious impulses, the origin of which is sought by
some in a personal Providence, by some in laws not yet
fully understood, we stand at the opening of a period
when the question is to be settled decisively, though
the issue may be long delayed, whether Eastern or
Western civilization is to dominate throughout the
earth and to control its future.

Since the West was 'surrounded and outnumbered' by the
non-West, the former's survival, not to mention
continued pre-eminence, depended on its ability 'to
receive into its own bosom and raise to its own ideals'
the peoples of China, Japan and elsewhere. Or else,
these latter would remain barbarians even after they had
assimilated the material aspects of Western civilization.
Should they fail to imbibe 'the indwelling spirit' of the
West and merely copy its power and prosperity, then it
might have to use its naked force in the struggle for
survival; '[the] great armies and the blind outward
impulses of the European peoples are the assurance that
generations must elapse ere the barriers can be overcome
behind which rests the citadel of Christian
civilization.' (21)

There was thus crystallizing a sense of urgency as
Americans developed a new awareness of the key importance
of external events. The traditional approach - whether
of the McKinley or the Cleveland variety, both of which
stressed the preservation of national security and
economic interests without extensive involvement
overseas, differing only on the tariff question - seemed
no longer adequate to cope with the new situation.
Economically, politically and intellectually, there
seemed to be ample justification for going beyond
traditionalism and pursuing a more active foreign policy.
Even those who had hitherto supported the Cleveland-
McKinley policy were apt to be captivated by a vision of
the struggle between civilizations, and influenced by a
rhetoric of power. Most important, views of the business
community began to break away from indifference and
caution to active concern with foreign affairs. In order
to protect commercial interests, they perceived a need
to involve the United States in world affairs far more
deeply than in the past.

Had advocates of intervention in Cuba been confined to
navalists, Bryan Democrats and other political dissidents,
and a few jingoistic newspapers, President McKinley might

still have been able to pursue a cautious policy in search
of a peaceful settlement of the dispute in Cuba and the
protection of commercial interests in Asia. Even at the
beginning of 1898 he continued to rely on traditional
means of diplomacy. Hawaii was the only major exception.
He had decided that the United States must annex the
islands. With Spain he would still maintain a friendly
relationship, trying to persuade it to accept American
mediation and undertake necessary reforms in Cuba. This
seemed the only way to stop the bloodshed in Cuba, protect
American interests, and avoid war with Spain. In the
meantime, McKinley dispatched the 'Maine' to Havana to
guard against possible attacks on Americans in the island.
A real test of such a policy came when not only the
Madrid government refused to accept American mediation,
convinced that the rebels must first put down their arms,
but the 'Maine' was blown up in a Havana harbor, causing
the death of 260 American officers and men. The outraged
sense of nationalism and mass commotion might have
impelled McKinley to take speedy retaliatory action, but
he responded cautiously. The United States, he said,
'can afford to withhold its judgment and not strike an
avenging blow until the truth is known. The
Administration ... will not be plunged into war until it
is ready for it.' (22)

That was in February. What happened during the next
two months to cause McKinley to change his mind and
prepared him to decide on war is not altogether clear.
At bottom was his perception of the pressures being
exerted on the White House by various groups in the
country. It is reasonably certain that by the early
spring of 1898 he saw these pressures not only coming
from dissidents and extremists but being generated by
wider circles of men who had in the past supported the
traditionalist approach. The drama involving China was
of particular importance in this connection. February
and March saw Russia and Britain imposing harsh demands
on China for concessions and leases, and by the end of
March the former had obtained leases for Port Arthur and
Talienwan, at the southern tip of Manchuria, and the
latter at Weihaiwei, almost directly south of Talienwan
across Bohai bay. Before the British government took
steps to join Germany and Russia in establishing
strongholds and spheres of influence in that part of
China, causing further intensification of their struggle
for greater power and influence in the rest of Asia,
London sounded out Washington on the possibility of joint
action in China. The McKinley administration was
reluctant to be drawn into such collaboration, especially

when it might give the impression of following the
British lead and thus provide added ammunition to
political opponents whose dislike of Britain had not
abated. Nevertheless, the feeling that the United
States could no longer indulge in the luxury of a
passive foreign policy continued to grow.

> To say [wrote P. J. Morgan, the 'Atlanta
> Constitution's' correspondent in China] that
> 70,000,000 of the bravest, most enterprising and most
> progressive people of the earth will sit quietly by
> and take no advantage of their strength and power is
> to reverse the lesson of history. Whether America
> shall enter into the general partition [of China] which
> is going on at present or whether it is her fate to
> wait until a future time is something which the
> future must disclose. (23)

Should the United States decide to do something in China,
it was almost certain to act in Cuba as well. The
obverse was also true. Events in Asia and the Caribbean
were becoming intertwined in American perception, and
ultimately the question had to be faced whether the
United States was to define for itself a new role in
international affairs.

It was not simply a handful of jingoes or a
groundswell of political malcontents, then, that pushed
McKinley to take a more belligerent attitude toward the
Cuban crisis in April 1898. He had decided that the
nation was now psychologically and intellectually, even
more than militarily, prepared to go to war against Spain.
Writers had harped on such themes as American power,
Western civilization, or white supremacy, so that
McKinley himself did not have to provide leadership in
justifying the new undertakings to the American people.
Most important, the business community, usually his basic
point of reference, now stood behind him, feeling that the
perpetuation of the stalemate in the Caribbean and
inaction in Asia was becoming intolerable. While business
interests did not push for war over Cuba for purely
economic reasons, they welcomed the opportunity to rally
around the flag so as to put an end to the period of
disunity and dissention at home, and to press for an
assertive policy in Asia.

Such was the background of the Spanish-American War.
Purely in terms of diplomacy involving the United States
and Spain over the Cuban rebellion, it was an unnecessary
and perhaps even avoidable war. There was no reason why
the two countries, which had maintained peaceful relations
over all the turmoil in the Caribbean during the previous
decades, could not have solved the issue through rounds of

negotiations. It is primarily in the context of
pressures within America, which in turn were related to
events overseas as perceived by Americans, that one may
account for the ultimate decision by the administration
to go to war. It was a decision calculated to unify
opinion at home and to enable the country to pursue a
more vigorous and comprehensive policy abroad than had
been the case in the past.

In both these objectives, the McKinley administration
was successful, at least in the short run. The war was
enormously popular in the United States, as it appealed
to diverse segments of the population. Political
opponents of Cleveland and McKinley, those who had
followed William Jennings Bryan in demanding a policy of
humanitarian interventionism in Cuba, hailed the coming
of the war as their moral victory, and were eager to join
the war effort. Bryan himself obtained a commission in
the Nebraska regiment and trained in Florida for service
in Cuba - although the war came to an end before he saw
action in the Caribbean. The sight of so many Bryan
Democrats joining forces with Republicans and Cleveland
Democrats at a moment of decision for the country added
symbolic significance to the war. It was as if the
Spanish-American War were helping unite the country in a
common cause. Since nationalism had always lurked just
below the humanitarianism of the interventionist groups,
it was natural that they should have welcomed the new
turn of events as an opportunity to reassert American
nationalism. The American people, declared Bryan just
before the declaration of war, 'Without regard to
political differences, are ready to support the
Administration in any action necessary for the protection
of the honor and welfare of the nation.' (24) From the
Republican camp, an Indiana editor and aspiring
politician, Albert J. Beveridge, used more colorful
language in expressing the same sense of national unity:
'No sections any more but a Nation. At last, my friend,
a Nation. No, not a *Nation* but *the Nation*. *The Nation*,
God's chosen people.' (25) His reference to sections
expressed a common view that the war provided one final
opportunity for the reconciliation of North and South, as
veterans from the two sections vied with one another in
offering their services to fight in the first foreign
war since the Civil War.

If the Spanish war appealed to the humanitarianism and
nationalism of Americans, it also had specific meaning
for those who had longingly looked overseas to extend
the nation's power and prestige. Naval strategists, in
particular, had for over a decade been developing ideas

for augmenting national power by means of warship
construction and more extensive involvement in the
affairs of distant lands.   Their horizon had not been
confined to the Caribbean during the debate on the
Cuban uprising.   Rather, they had been quick to see
implications for American strategy in the rest of the
world once the United States should become embroiled
in hostilities with Spain.   Already in 1896 they had
devised a contingency plan which envisaged an attack on
the Spanish fleet in the Philippines in the event of war,
and the plan was quickly put into effect as crisis
mounted in the early spring of 1898.   Admiral
George Dewey, commanding officer of the Asiatic squadron,
confidently reported on 31 March, nearly a month before
the formal start of armed hostilities, that 'with the
squadron now under my command the [Spanish] vessels
could be taken and the defenses of Manila reduced in one
day.' (26)   It was not, however, merely a matter of
destroying the Spanish fleet in Manila harbor.   The
whole operation would enlarge spheres of action for the
United States navy, which would now have added
responsibilities in the Southwest Pacific.

The annexation of Hawaii, which was finally effected
through a joint resolution of both houses of Congress in
July, had equally enormous strategic significance.   The
value of the islands in the Central Pacific was evident
during the war, as battleships and troops, en route to
the Southwest Pacific, could assemble in Hawaii and be
readied for action in the Philippines.   Likewise, the
Spanish islands of Guam and Wake were attacked and taken
without much resistance from Spanish commanders.   All of
a sudden the armed forces of the United States found
themselves in control of a chain of islands stretching
across the Pacific, bringing to reality one of the fondest
dreams of the military services after the Civil War.
American military power was no longer confined to the
continental United States and the Caribbean.   Vast
opportunities and responsibilities were being added.

The war also had meaning to advocates of a more
ambitious foreign policy.   John Hay, ambassador in London,
serves as a good example.   Like some of his
contemporaries, he was dissatisfied with the
traditionalist definition of American foreign policy and
convinced that the United States should chart a new
course, going beyond the time-honored concern with the
Caribbean and with the extention of commercial interests,
but frankly involving itself in world politics so as
to shape it in a way best calculated to serve its goals.
Hay was particularly eager to have the United States act

closely with Great Britain in various parts of the world.
This was because he felt an Anglo-American definition of
world order would best promote American interests,
whereas friction between the two would be disastrous. At
a time when the European powers were engaging in colonial
ventures and 'realpolitik,' Hay saw no reason why the
United States should not at least show some willingness
to base its policy on geopolitical considerations and
opt for an entente with Britain. From such a perspective,
the Spanish-American War was first and foremost an
opportunity to demonstrate the identity of policies and
interests between the two countries, not only over Cuba
but in Asia, the Pacific and ultimately the whole world.
It was very important that there be co-operation between
London and Washington during the war, and he did his
best, as ambassador in Britain, to obtain such
co-operation.

Fortunately for Hay and others like him, British
foreign policy was almost entirely in accord with their
expectations. Both Britain's official thinking and
public mood sympathized with the American stand for a
number of reasons. After the Venezuelan crisis of 1895,
there had developed a self-conscious movement in England
for fostering Anglo-American amity, and events in the
United States had been closely watched for clues to the
attainment of such a goal. The election of McKinley
over Bryan's opposition had been a gratifying sign from
the point of view of reducing emotional Anglophobia in
America, as was the appointment of John Hay as ambassador
to the Court of St James. In 1897 Lord Salisbury hinted
that this government would not interfere with action
taken by the United States in Cuba. When the European
powers jointly appealed to America and Spain for peace
in April 1898, the note had been drafted by the British
Ambassador in Washington, Julian Pauncefote, and
approved in advance by McKinley. During the war opinion
in Britain was overwhelmingly pro-American, and there
was an approximation of the language used to
characterize it. Both Americans and Englishmen referred
to the conflict as 'a war for civilization,' reflecting
the sentiment that the two peoples shared a common
concern in the interest of preserving and promoting what
they most cherished in the world, and of developing an
international community in which their principles,
interests and life-styles could best be protected against
threats from differently oriented peoples and
governments. Under the circumstances, it could be
expected that the Spanish-American War might prove to be
a crucial occasion for the implementation of an

Anglo-American co-operative policy which had been advocated by a number of officials and publicists on both sides of the Atlantic. This was one of the most important byproducts of the coming of the war. By the mere act of going to war on Spain, the United States was not only forcing the European powers to clarify their relations with America and to work out a global strategy to fit the new situation, but also it was resorting to policies and principles that had characterized European diplomacy in the latter half of the century. In this mingling of American and European diplomacy, the most obvious beneficiary was Great Britain, as well as those in the two countries that were advocates of close co-operation across the Atlantic.

The prosecution of the war, however, could not be long continued without involving the question of empire. Here American public opinion, which was virtually unanimous regarding the war itself, did not achieve the same degree of consensus but remained divided as before the war. The question of empire was bound to arise since the American people and their government had to decide how far they should carry the war, and how they should define the desirable peace aims. Spain was an empire, and war against Spain involved lands in the Pacific as well as the Caribbean. Should the United States continue military action, it would soon find itself attacking and repulsing Spanish forces from these possessions. Should the American government decide to put a halt to hostilities, it would still have to consider what terms it should be willing to accept for a peace settlement. These were problems that were claiming the attention of a growing number of Americans who, even while responding to the call to arms in a nationalistic spirit, were concerned lest such issues should open up a Pandora's box. Unlike the European powers, the United States since the 1840s had never been engaged in a foreign war with specific war aims in view, and thus the very emergence of these questions gave the impression of novelty. It was as if the country was at a threshold of a new chapter in its history, the character of which was in the hands of the American people and their leaders. The 'great debate' which ensued indicates the seriousness with which they grappled with the phenomenon. It also reflects the persistence of various strands that had gone into American perceptions of external events. It will thus be useful to consider the debate of 1898 in the framework we have employed.

Roughly speaking, American opinion was divided into two camps, those for and against territorial expansion in the process or as a consequence of the war with Spain. But the division was never clear-cut, and each argument had components that could easily be transferred to the other side as a justification. The situation was volatile, and one must guard against the temptation, to which many writers have fallen, to speak of 'imperialists' and 'anti-imperialists' as though these were consistently definable, mutually exclusive categories.

Those who saw the war as an opportunity for charting a new course for American foreign relations presented various arguments in support of their view. Some, like John Hay, were mostly concerned with geopolitical factors and insisted that the United States must now behave as a responsible power with interests and commitments throughout the world. The country could no longer afford to be indifferent towards events in distant lands. American military action was a harbinger of positive diplomatic efforts in peacetime, and it would be incumbent on the United States to indicate clearly where it stood with respect to various international problems. In this connection, Hay repeated the thesis that America and Britain must co-operate as world powers; because of their similarity of outlook and interests, they should co-ordinate their policies and contribute to the making of a stable world order. For this reason, the United States should not hesitate to take up the burden of empire. Americans who were advocates of an increased world role for their country were generally admirers of British colonialism and imperialism. Their vision of Anglo-American co-operation was worldwide and included an image of the two countries as imperial powers. While ambassador in London, Hay forwarded to the State Department various articles and pamphlets commenting on the virtues of British colonialism. The implication was that colonialism was part of British power, and that if the United States were now to pursue a more active foreign policy in co-operation with Britain, it must be willing to consider territorial acquisitions. They would enhance American power and status in world affairs, a prerequisite for assuming geopolitical roles and a psychological imperative for bringing about such co-operation.

The idea of Anglo-American co-operation also had an idealistic aspect. The view, as outlined earlier, that certain countries and races stood as guardians of civilization had been articulated in the United States as well as Europe in the last decades of the century, and it had provided Americans with one way of viewing European colonialism. In 1898 it became a matter not

only relevant in Europe but also in America. As they
engaged in the war with Spain, Americans found themselves
speaking of it in much the same way as Europeans had
described their wars, in terms of civilization. The
basic assumption was that through war and victory they
would be able to spread the blessings of civilization -
material as well as spiritual - to other lands with the
result, as so many of them said, that 'all civilization
will profit.' It was but a step from such a supposition
to the thought that civilized nations must carry on the
task of establishing control over the rest of the world.
Americans, too, would be contributing to civilization if
they did not stop at merely defeating Spain but took
over some of the latter's possessions to impart to them
the essence of good government and physical well-being.
While the idea of mission had always been present in
American thinking concerning foreign affairs, the new
idealism of 1898 was notable because there was almost
complete identification between 'civilization' and
territorial expansion. Reflecting an image of mankind's
division between civilized and uncivilized, the concept
implied the West's responsibility for the world as a
whole, which in turn assumed some degree of physical
control over distant lands. The United States, in such a
perspective, was to spread the reign of civilization not
only to the indigenous Indian population or to contiguous
territories as earlier, but also to other parts of the
globe as its share of the responsibilities of the
civilized nations.

Other advocates of expansion were more concerned with
parochial issues closer to home. Nationalism, as was the
case in Europe, was an important ingredient of the
expansionism of 1898. To some supporters of colonialism,
perhaps best exemplified by Senator Henry Cabot Lodge of
Massachusetts, the most crucial question was the
character of the nation. They argued that the martial
spirit that manifested itself during the war showed the
vigor and strength of the nation which had for so long
seemed divided and passive. To bring out the best in
America, it seemed desirable to continue the national
effort in pursuit of large goals. It would be good for
the country to respond positively to the challenges of the
new age and undertake tasks it had not borne before.
With new responsibilities in the world arena would come
nationalistic awareness, and the United States would
regain the sense of fresh excitement and dedication that
had characterized the formative years of its history.
In short, overseas commitments and activities would be a
means of reforming and revitalizing America.

As Lodge said,

> The athlete does not win his race by sitting
> habitually in an armchair. The pioneer does not open
> up new regions to his fellow men by staying in warm
> shelter behind the city walls ... If a man has the
> right qualities in him, responsibility sobers,
> strengthens, and develops him. The same is true of
> nations. The nation which fearlessly meets its
> responsibilities rises to the task when the pressure
> is upon it. I believe that these new possessions
> and these new questions, this necessity for watching
> over the welfare of another people, will improve our
> civil service, raise the tone of public life, and
> make broader and better all our politics. (27)

From such a point of view, imperialism was to be welcome
as it would improve the national character.

Others had more specific interests in mind as they
advocated expansion. Naval and army strategists and
officers were delighted with the coming of the first
foreign war in every military officer's experience. Now
that battles were fought in Cuba, Puerto Rico, the
Philippines, and even Guam, the war gave them a long-
awaited opportunity to demonstrate their service to
the country and to convince the American people of the
need for peacetime preparedness. The possession of
overseas territories and bases would necessitate an
enlarged armed service, a larger fleet and a modernized
staff system. All these would open up numerous career
opportunities for the professional soldier. For all
these reasons, the military spoke with one voice for the
need to retain at least some of lands from which Spanish
forces had been expelled.

Another interest group, the business community,
provided added pressure for expansion, although there
was much less unaminity here than among the military.
It was primarily the commercial and industrial groups
interested in the trade of the East that expressed the
greatest degree of enthusiasm for controlling part or
the whole of the Philippines. Coming on the heels of
what appeared to be an impending partition of China, the
war with Spain and the naval action in Manila bay
impressed businessmen as a providential occasion for
reinvigorating American policy in Asia in order to expand
the China trade. They had been impressed with the
audacity of the European powers to claim parts of China
as their spheres of influence and attributed such acts to
the presence of military power in close proximity to
that country. The possession of a harbor or an island
in the Philippine archipelago would enable the United

States to enter upon the scene and protect American interests with greater vigor and effectiveness than before.

As for public opinion at the mass level, the mood of the American people was not very difficult to guage, as President McKinley found out, or thought he did, when he made an extensive trip of the country to be in touch with the thinking of the nation. At least in the summer and fall of 1898, before the problems and complications of postwar arrangements became more evident, there was general rejoicement at military victories and excitement at undertaking fresh overseas adventures. The mood was a combination of national pride, a sense of duty and responsibility toward inferior races, and a vision of world history and international affairs which placed the United States at a threshold of greatness. The biography of Albert J. Beveridge, an Indianapolis publicist turned politician, gives as good an example as any of the expansive, aggressive mood of the people in 1898. Only two days after the Congress declared war on Spain, Beveridge was in Boston, asserting, 'the first gun of our war for civilization is also the morning gun of a new day in the republic's imperial career.' (28) He was an enormously popular orator, and his support of an 'imperial career' for the nation found such general sympathy that he decided to run for a Senate seat from Indiana almost solely on the basis of his imperialist rhetoric. His victory over a candidate more entrenched in state and national politics was an indication that at least in the summer and fall of 1898 such a man could command widespread support. Beveridge was also instrumental in preparing Indiana opinion for President McKinley's tour, mobilizing pro-expansionist views effectively so that the latter would be convinced of the mood of the public. Beveridge's ideas and his career at this point reflected the existence of a politically articulated body of opinions in the United States which favored some kind of overseas expansion. And his justification of imperialism in the name of nationalism and civilization was probably an accurate echo of mass psychology. The public sentiment welcomed the opportunity to see the country embarking upon an expansive career overseas because it seemed to be the right thing to do to achieve fame and status in international politics, while at the same time dedicating itself to the service of mankind. It became fashionable to 'look outward' and to think of the nation's destiny in terms of seeking frontiers to conquer outside the continental boundaries. 'The spirit of the people once

having looked outward,' a writer noted in the 'Atlantic,'
'American enterprise will seek new fields of conquest -
not by arms, but by trade and legitimate adventure. Our
navy has revealed to ourselves not less than to the rest
of the world our rightful place among the nations.' (29)
Such a juxtaposition of different themes - naval power,
world-power status, trade, and adventure - graphically
pointed to 'the spirit of the people,' who were never
clearly motivated by or driven to one thing but combined
different interests and ideas to embrace an amorphous
sentiment for empire.

One important aspect of the general enthusiasm for
overseas expansion was a sustained interest in the Asian
question. Public attention had been aroused by the Sino-
Japanese War and the German seizure of Kiaochow, but in
1898 China and the rest of Asia seemed to become even
closer to Americans now that their own forces were
occupying the Philippine islands. As William Elliot
Griffis, one of the foremost American authorities on
Japan, wrote in November,

For the people of the United States, the oceanic
event of May 1, 1898 changed their view of the world.
It made the Far East a Near West. Heretofore they
had looked at the Chinas, the Indies, and the Pacific
spice-world, eastward, as if through and beyond
Europe. On that day perspective became prospect.
Now they turn to see the whole Pacific through their
western windows and at their own doors. (30)

Similarly, an editorial for 'Outlook' noted in September,
'No event in the recent history of the world is more
striking than the sudden transference of action from
the nearer to the farther East; the shifting of international interest from Constantinople to Pekin and
Manila.' The United States had had a hand in such a
remarkable development. The war with Spain, therefore,
was far more than another event in the chronicle of
military history. It signaled the fact that 'humanity
has entered a new and momentous stage of development,'
to be characterized by the awakening of the East. The
idea was not new. Generations of writers had spoken
of the transformation of the non-West, and writers like
Pearson and Mahan had pondered the implications of such
a change for the future of the world. But all of a
sudden academic discourse gained immediate relevance.
The battle of Manila signified America's decision to
participate in the drama of Asian transformation, thereby
identifying the United States with other expanding
countries of the West. America, as it were, self-
consciously became part of the West when its guns echoed

in the waters of a Philippine bay. There was thus
reality to an assertion such as contained in the
'Outlook' editorial that 'The West will govern the East
with the ultimate result not only of making the East
self-governing, but of learning new lessons of wise,
pure, and efficient administration.' (31) The editors
had in mind not merely British rule in India and other
cases of European colonialism, but also the establishment
of American government in the Philippines. This was
seen and supported not only in the narrow framework of
American interest and power, but more basically as an
inevitable process of history. It may be noted that
Americans were in fact saying that not only Asians but
they themselves would rejoin the march of world history.
It was impossible not to do so.

These were some of the main arguments put forward by
exponents of an active foreign and colonial policy in the
United States in 1898. It would be wrong to say that
there was any degree of coherence in their position. The
imperialistic expansionists came from all sections of
the country and represented divergent interest groups.
They were united in calling for an agressive, acquisitive
foreign policy, but they did not reflect a single
ideology or an interest group. Nevertheless, there was
some psychological unity in that they sensed imperialism
was a way of life in international politics as well as an
aspect of that particular stage of world history. To
deny the nation this road seemed tantamount to choosing
atrophy and decline instead of progress and power.

The soundness of such a perception of the world and
of history was questioned vehemently by opponents of
expansion. The anti-imperialists, too, derived from
various sources, and it would be impossible to say that
they represented totally different interests, groups, or
ideologies from the imperialists. For one thing, there
were very few 'pure' anti-imperialists; William Jennings
Bryan, for instance, who repeatedly attacked the
administration's expansionist policy, did not oppose the
acquisition of Puerto Rico, and Senator George F. Hoar,
the leading Republican spokesman against empire, endorsed
Hawaiian annexation. It should also be pointed out that
most anti-imperialists were supporters of peaceful
commercial expansionism. What set them apart from the
bulk of imperialists was their opposition, in 1898, to
certain territorial acquisitions, especially Cuba and
the Philippines. And they, too, had a vision of history.

Theodore Roosevelt once characterized the anti-
imperialists as 'men of a bygone age having to deal with
the facts of the present.' (32) The characterization was

too simplistic, but it was quite apt in so far as
different images of the past often distinguished
proponents and opponents of territorial expansion.
Whereas the former, like Roosevelt, would argue that
'[the] guns of our warships have awakened us to new
duties ... [Let] us rather run the risk of wearing out
than rusting out,' the latter responded by saying that
purity and integrity of the American past was being
irrevocably lost through the nation's adoption of
imperialism. Just as the imperialists were eager to
identify the destiny of the United States with Western
power, civilization and history at that juncture, the
anti-imperialists sought to preserve the precious
national tradition which seemed to have been characterized
by distinctive qualities that set the country apart
from all others. By persisting in military action
beyond what was needed to free the Cubans, and by
entrenching American armed forces in distant lands, the
government appeared to have broken from that tradition
and accepted a new policy which made the country no less
aggressive and selfish than the European powers. The
United States, from the anti-imperialists' point of
view, was embracing an ideology and a foreign policy
that were alien both to the nation's history and its
values. It was merely becoming one more power in the
world arena with incalculable damage to the health of
domestic institutions and traditions that had made the
country unique. That was why William Graham Sumner, the
leading academic opponent of territorial expansionism,
wrote of 'the conquest of the United States by Spain.'
Although America had defeated Spain militarily, Sumner
argued, the latter had in fact conquered the former in
that politically and ideologically the war was transforming
the United States into a country oriented toward
colonialism and power politics, just as Spain had been.
America had won the war but lost its senses and its
integrity. It could no longer speak as a voice of
conscience or exist as a beacon of light in the world
of greed and darkness. Likewise, William Jennings Bryan
branded imperialism as an alien doctrine and asserted in
December 1898 that just as the American people had
defended Cuban freedom against foreign rule, they must
defend themselves against 'foreign ideas' such as
colonialism and imperialism. (33)
    Here, too, it may be seen that nationalistic thinking
and idealistic considerations merged imperceptibly to
provide a vocabulary of anti-imperialism. As was the
case with the imperialists, the anti-imperialists were
seriously concerned with the physical and spiritual

health of the nation.   But whereas the former stressed
what Roosevelt called 'the life of action, of strenuous
performance of duty' as a key ingredient of national
character and the national interest, opponents of
empire emphasized the maintenance of stability and
social-ideological equilibrium at home as of the
fundamental importance.   Such a goal included the
preservation of the tradition of anti-imperialism and
self-determination, but it also implied constitutional
conservatism and racial purism.   For example, there
was the fear that the acquisition of overseas territory
would necessitate a larger standing army and a larger
fleet, enhancing the power of the military.   Moreover,
the executive branch of the government would become
inordinately strong compared with the legislature, since
the White House and the various departments would be
charged with governing the colonies.   All of this would
subvert the constitution and might bring about a
dictatorship in the United States.   Such a dictatorship
was the more troublesome as it would derive its authority
from a jingoistic populace.   The anti-imperialists often
feared mob psychology as much as a powerful government,
and sought to preserve what they considered to be an
ideal constitution that had served the county well.
Certainly after the Civil War there had been agrarian
uprisings and industrial strife, but imperialism would
not only not solve these domestic problems but would make
matters worse by catering to mass violence and militarism.

Racially, the anti-imperialists feared that the
extension of control over alien races and the need to
govern subject populations would corrupt and weaken the
United States.   This was an argument that went back to
the 1840s, when opponents of Mexican annexation cited the
fear of racial admixture as a key factor.   Fifty years
later, the concern was still there, this time not so
much with the infusion of blacks and mestizos as with the
anticipated contact with tropical races who seemed to
have no sense of modern nationhood or citizenship.   To
make American citizens out of them was ridiculous, but to
govern them as colonial people was worse, since the
colonizers might eventually come under the subtle
influence of those they controlled and lose their original
vigor and intelligence.   The United States had enough
race trouble as it was, and the anti-imperialists could
see no sense in adding to the trouble by closely
associating the country with more non-white races.

It should be noted that their consideration of
national interest made the opponents of empire less than
doctrinaire purists as they discussed the disposition of

various territories in 1898. They shared with the
imperialists concern for national security and for the
protection and expansion of commercial interests. As
Charles Denby wrote, 'Will the possession of these
islands benefit us as a nation? If it will not, set them
free tomorrow.' (34) Most Americans would have answered
the question pragmatically, distinguishing between various
islands. For instance, there was much less opposition
to the annexation of Hawaii in 1898 than earlier, and even
some staunch opponents of Cuban or Philippine annexation
accepted it. Because of Hawaii's commercial importance
to the United States, which was increasing because of its
location as a gateway to the Oriental trade, and because
the threat to the islands from a third power, especially
Japan, was now easily recognizable, only a minority of
doctrinaire anti-imperialists opposed the incorporation
of Hawaii into the United States on constitutional, racial
and other grounds. Likewise, most of those who opposed
the retention of Cuba as an American possession were
indifferent to the fate of Puerto Rico. Few voices were
raised against its annexation. Bryan even remarked
that the United States might take the island as a
justifiable compensation for the war, in lieu of a war
indemnity. He also supported the idea of retaining a
harbor or two in Cuba to insure American security and
interests. He was as convinced as the navalists of the
importance to maintain American rights and influence
in the Caribbean. But he saw no need for the United
States to take the whole island. It would be wrong
morally, since the country had pledged itself, when
going to war with Spain, to Cuba's freedom, and since it
would be an unnecessary burden on America's economy
and conscience to be charged with the governing of
such a large tropical population. Bryan saw no reason
why national security and interests in the Caribbean
region could not be safeguarded without establishing
a colonial regime upon Cuba.

Against such diverse currents of opinion, the McKinley
administration came to a decision to expand the
territorial limits of the United States and to seek the
cession of Puerto Rico, Guam and the Philippines. These,
and the Hawaiian islands, whose treaty of annexation was
finally passed by Congress during the war, made the
United States an empire and a colonial power with
dependent territories outside the American continent
for the first time in the nation's history. President
McKinley's decision was essentially a pragmatic response
to the new situation brought about as a result of the
war with Spain. He reasoned that having fought battles

and expelled Spanish forces from various islands, the
United States could not simply leave them once the
fighting was over. 'While we are conducting war and
until its conclusion we must keep all we get; when the
war is over we must keep what we want,' he said in the
summer. (35) Now that American troops were occupying
Spanish lands, it would be their responsibility to
maintain law and order so as to prevent Spanish
retaliation or a reign of terror in the absence of
authority. But once American power was thus involved
in the governing of distant territory, it was very
difficult to remove it without causing further confusion
and increasing chances of disorder, which could be
seized upon by unfriendly powers in their own self-
interest.

Such reasoning seemed to suffice as the administration
demanded cession of Puerto Rico and Guam from Spain as
part of the postwar settlement, when the peace conference
met in Paris toward the end of the year. The Philippines,
however, were more complicated because of their larger
size and population. American military control did not
extend to more than part of the island of Luzon, and
even there the situation was complex since there had
been an indigenous movement for autonomy and ultimate
independence, a movement that did not exist in Puerto
Rico or Guam. Whether, under the circumstances, the
United States should insist on obtaining the whole
archipelago, or whether it should seek to retain some
strategic areas alone, was a difficult question that was
not settled until the very end. President McKinley and
most of his advisers, even including Captain Mahan,
initially only wanted Manila and one or two additional
harbors. They seemed sufficient for the purpose of
protecting American interests and preventing Spanish
counter-offensive. The commissioners who represented
the United States at the peace conference in Paris,
including John Hay, were at first not given any specific
instruction concerning the disposition of the Philippines,
but in time McKinley, Hay and a majority of the peace
commissioners came to favor retention of the entire
archipelago by the United States.

This momentous decision was in part a practical one.
If the United States were to retain part of the
Philippines, the same reasoning that supported such
action could be applied to the whole of the islands. If
the protection of American commerce in the Orient, for
instance, was good enough reason for demanding the
cession of Manila, it was also plausible to argue that the
whole of the Philippines might be taken for the same

reason. In fact, the islands might offer an attractive
market for American capital and goods in their own right,
instead of being useful simply as a stepping-stone to the
trade of China. Moreover, American control over a few
ports would still leave the bulk of the Philippines in
a chaotic condition, which could be taken advantage of by
a hostile power and there might be direct confrontation
between the two. Finally, since the United States was
going to be a naval power with bases in the western
Pacific, it did not really seem to matter whether the
nation should take one harbor or larger territory. Once
the decision was made to be an expanding power, the size
of the empire was less important.

There was, however, also something ideological and
abstract about the decision to acquire the Philippines.
When geographical proximity, military necessity or
war-indemnity considerations were not sufficiently
convincing, exponents of Philippine annexation could
readily avail themselves of the imperialist argument,
well established in Europe, in terms of civilization,
duty and responsibility. That necessitated an image
of the Philippines as an area ideally suited for
America's civilizing mission. While the peace
commissioners were in Paris, they held a series of
hearings on the islands, and one of those who testified
was a well-known British writer, John Foreman, who had
done much to popularize the notion of the tropics as a
region of the world that was rich in natural resources
waiting to be exploited by civilized nations. In 'The
Philippine Islands,' published in 1892, Foreman wrote,
'The native is indolent in the extreme, and never tired
of sitting still, gazing at nothing in particular ...
[The Natives] have no real sentiment, honor or
magnanimity, and, apart from their hospitality, in which
they far excel the European in all their actions, they
appear to be only guided by fear, or interest, or both.'
The indolence of the tropics, however, could be a virtue.
Happiness, Foreman said, 'is merely comparative: with a
lovely climate - a continual summer - and all the
absolute requirements of life at hand, there is not
one-tenth of the misery in the Philippines that there
is in Europe, and none of that forlorn wretchedness facing
the public gaze.' (36) As might be expected, Foreman
reiterated these themes before the American commissioners
and urged the United States to obtain and exploit the
resources of the islands which the natives were incapable
of doing.

The argument in terms of civilization could appeal to
those who might not otherwise be convinced of practical

values or specific benefits of colonialism. As one
of the civilized nations in the world, the United
States seemed destined to expand in the tropics.
Otherwise, since native characteristics could not be
altered, being ordained by physical conditions of the
region, change would come only if another civilized
nation assumed control. As a self-respecting country,
America could not give up the opportunity that was
within its grasp.

All these considerations, of course, might have
justified acquisition of Cuba as well as the Philippines,
Puerto Rico and Guam. In the case of Cuba, however,
the McKinley administration was constrained by the
circumstances leading up to the coming of the war with
Spain. The United States, after all, had intervened in
Cuban affairs in order to help the natives gain greater
rights from Spain. It would be awkward after the war
to turn around and refuse to deal with Cuba as an
autonomous entity. At the same time, the island was of
strategic importance to the United States, economically
and militarily. Like the Philippines, Cuba was rent by
internal confusion and instability. They were also
alike in that they were richly endowed with natural
resources and presumably uncivilized inhabitants. What
the United States could do, then, was to seek to maintain
law and order in Cuba through the continued presence of
American forces but to desist from annexing it as a
colony. Some, like Albert J. Beveridge, called for such a
step, arguing that circumstances had changed after the
outbreak of the war. But the administration and the
bulk of Congress were inclined to accept a solution short
of outright annexation.

The treaty of Paris, then, reflected these decisions
by the American government and the acceptance of them by
Spain. Within a few years since the days of Grover
Cleveland's traditionalism, the country was emerging
as a colonial power with territorial possessions in the
Pacific as well as the Caribbean. The earlier Cleveland-
McKinley consensus that had visualized American foreign
relations in the traditional framework of national
security, commercial interests, and passive diplomacy
outside the Western Hemisphere, was giving way to a new
definition of national interest and a new vision of
world affairs vis-à-vis the United States. It remained
to be seen if a sufficiently broad consensus would emerge
within America, and to what extent the nation would
apply the recently acquired power and prestige to its
relations with other countries.

Chapter 4

The United States in World Politics

At the beginning of 1899, the United States stood at a
major turning point in its relations with the rest of
the world. Having established its power and exerted
its influence far beyond the Western Hemisphere, the
country had now to define precisely what roles it
proposed to play in various parts of the globe, and what
conceptions it was to develop as guiding principles for
its foreign affairs.

The first item on the agenda, however, was a domestic
question. The McKinley administration had to seek
ratification of the peace treaty by the Senate and its
acceptance by the voters in the forthcoming Presidential
election. The fifty-fifth Congress had its third
session in 1899 to consider, among other things, the
Treaty of Paris. There were ninety Senators at that
time, representing forty-five states. Their average age
was fifty-six, and twenty-eight of them were fifty years
old or younger. Thirty-eight Senators were veterans of
the Civil War. The conservatism and the sense of
continuity such a large proportion of Civil War soldiers
may have represented was offset by the fact that as many
as thirty-nine Senators had been in the Senate for less
than four years, entering national politics only after
1893. Neither of these two groups, however, was
particularly distinguished in terms of the members'
experience or knowledge of foreign affairs. The
decades after the Civil War had not prepared American
legislative leaders politically or intellectually
for roles that were thrust upon the country as a result
of the Spanish war. It was likely, therefore, that
their voting behavior on foreign-policy questions would
more often than not be determined by considerations
other than their understanding of world politics or
international affairs. (1)

The ninety Senators were divided into forty-four
regular Republicans, six 'silver Republicans' (those from
Western states who agreed with William Jennings Bryan on
monetary matters), thirty-four Democrats, five Populists,
and one Independent. A two-thirds majority for the treaty
would require at least sixty-one votes, assuming that all
members voted, and this was far more than the
Republican Party could muster from among its own ranks.
The party was fairly well disciplined because both
President McKinley and John Sherman, his first secretary
of state, had had long careers in Congress, and the
leaders such as Nelson W. Aldrich, William B. Allison,
and Mark Hanna were able to keep tight reins over the
Republican members of the Senate. Party discipline and
regularity seem to have been the major reason for the
overwhelming support the Republican Senators gave the
peace treaty. Even so, the administration needed some
additional votes from the Democrats to obtain a two-
thirds majority. Here there was no discipline comparable
to the Republicans. The Democratic party was in disarray
following the presidential election of 1896, which had
split the followers and opponents of Bryan. They were
still divided in 1899, and they could not adopt a
uniform policy on the Philippine question, although the
division on foreign policy was not necessarily parallel
to that on the silver question. More than half the
Democratic Senators agreed with Grover Cleveland that
imperialism was a dangerous departure from tradition
and could subvert national values and interests. Others,
especially those from the Southern states, accepted the
Republican rhetoric of expansion. Bryan, whose
opposition to Philippine annexation had been expressed
in 1898, counseled a few wavering Democrats to vote for
the treaty, and thus may have been instrumental in
bringing about its ultimate passage.

The breakdown of the Senate vote on the peace treaty
was as follows:

For the treaty: 39 Republicans, 10 Democrats,
                4 Silver Republicans, 3 Populists,
                1 Independent:
                            Total of 57 votes.
Against the treaty: 2 Republicans, 22 Democrats,
                    1 Silver Republican, 2 Populists:
                            Total of 27 votes.

Since only eighty-four Senators came to the voting, a
two-thirds majority required exactly fifty-seven votes.
One more negative vote, in other words, would have
defeated the treaty. In this sense Bryan's stand may
have been a crucial factor. His reasoning was that the

treaty should be ratified in order to terminate the war
formally and end bloodshed, thus detaching the Philippines
from Spain. The United States, he asserted, could then
grant independence to the Filipinos through subsequent
congressional action. Bryan also hoped that by settling
the matter of the treaty in 1899, the presidential
election of 1900 could once again focus on his favorite
subject, the silver question.

Whether Bryan in fact persuaded a Democratic Senator
to change his vote on the peace treaty, thereby assuring
its passage and ratifying the administration's decision
for empire, remains an interesting question. At least
one staunch anti-imperialist, Senator Samuel D. McEnery,
cast a vote in favor of the treaty, and he may in fact
have been influenced by Bryan's thinking. While voting
to ratify the Treaty of Paris, McEnery also introduced
a resolution calling for Philippine independence, which
did not pass, and another leaving the status of the
islands up to future action by the United States
government, which passed by an unimpressive vote of
twenty-six to twenty-two, basically a meaningless gesture
to assuage the conscience of McEnery and others who
still wanted to identify themselves with anti-imperialism.
But the fact remains that with a barely sufficient
majority the Senate gave its consent to the
administration's decision to retain the Philippines. The
closeness of the vote indicated that there was no
overwhelming sentiment for launching the nation on a
systematic colonialist career. When, for instance,
Senator Albert J. Beveridge, recently chosen to represent
his state, introduced a resolution in January 1900
calling for indefinite retention of the Philippines,
the Republican leadership felt this was going too far.
Beveridge's reasoning, that the Filipinos did not deserve
independence since they were 'a barbarous race -
Orientals, Malays, instructed by Spaniards in the latter's
worse estate,' was considered too extreme. (2) Neither
the administration nor the Senate was willing to
undertake a program of unlimited colonial expansionism
which Beveridge espoused. They were prepared to assume
control over the Philippines and other lands taken from
Spain because there seemed to be no other choice.

The presidential campaign of 1900, under the
circumstances, might have provided an opportunity for
the opponents of empire to coalesce their forces so that
a definite stand might emerge as the favored position of
the American people. The Republican Party, by
renominating McKinley and choosing Theodore Roosevelt,
whose support of imperialism was widely recognized, as

his running-mate, clearly stood for 'the glory of our
arms, which has made us a world power,' according to
Chauncey Depew. (3) The party would appeal to the aroused
nationalism of the electorate and stress the prestige and
world-power status that the country had gained as a result
of the war with Spain. While not supporting unlimited
colonial expansion, it would favor the policy of
governing the new acquisitions in their interest as well
as the interests of the United States.

The Democratic Party, which had been divided on the
Philippine question, tried nevertheless to present a
united view on the matter. Its platform advocated
'expansion by every peaceful and legitimate means' - a
clear echo of the recent past when peaceful expansionism
had been the guiding principle of American foreign
policy. The Democrats were not opposed to expansion.
But they saw the administration's Philippine policy as a
subversion of traditional expansionism and a betrayal
of American values and interests. William Jennings Bryan,
once again the Democratic candidate, reiterated his anti-
imperialist themes throughout the summer and fall of
1900. 'We cannot set a high and honorable example for
the emulation of mankind,' he wrote for the 'North
American Review,' 'while we roam the world like beasts
of prey seeking whom we may devour.' (4) In speech after
speech he castigated the Republicans for their acceptance
of colonialism, no matter what their justification. Such
a policy, Bryan asserted, only profited special interest
groups at home. The country stood to gain nothing by
acquiring territory to govern, nor by achieving the
status of a world power. They only complicated things
for America. By adopting imperialism, the United States
was losing its identity and becoming less and less
American.

Imperialism, however, was only one of the issues that
divided national opinion in 1900. Unfortunately from
the standpoint of the anti-imperialists, Bryan and the
Democratic Party were neither able nor willing to
concentrate on the foreign policy debate. Bryan and his
followers were still far more interested in the silver
question, and their rigid monetary stand drove away
would-be supporters of the Democratic Party. It is to
be noted, for instance, that the leadership in the
nationwide anti-imperialist movement was mostly well
educated, affluent, and conservative, who would be
frightened away by Bryan's advocacy of free silver.
Prominent lawyers, educators and politicians, including a
number of senior Republicans, were members of the Anti-
Imperialist League, which sprang in the Boston area and

whose major strength was in New England. There was an
air of conservatism, respectability and tradition about
the movement. Edward Atkinson, editor of the 'Anti-
Imperialist' magazine, castigated the administration's
policy of committing a 'criminal aggression' on other
peoples as bringing 'dishonor' to America. Such a sense
of outrage persuaded some anti-imperialists to cast
their ballots for Bryan, but most of them could not
conscientiously vote for him. He seemed just as alien
to American tradition as McKinley. (In fact on monetary
matters the latter commanded the support of conservative
businessmen and professional groups.)

Under the circumstances, McKinley's overwhelming
victory over Bryan could not be viewed as a popular
mandate for imperialism. Nevertheless, no presidential
election is fought on a single issue, and McKinley's
success could be said to reflect general acceptance
of his foreign and domestic policies. Most important,
his re-election confirmed the impression abroad that
the United States was now a world colonial power and that
it would not go back to the pre-1898 years of general
passivity in international relations. It remained to be
seen specifically how the country would govern the newly
acquired empire, and how it would conduct its foreign
policy in various parts of the world.

1 GOVERNING AN EMPIRE

The United States had never had a colony before. It had
expanded territorially by annexing lands through war,
purchase, settlement and other means, but the newly
acquired territories had been governed with a view to
their eventual incorporation into the United States.
That had been the pattern in the Old Northwest, the lands
obtained in the Louisiana purchase, those acquired from
Mexico in 1848, or Alaska. American political and
economic institutions were made applicable to them,
although there was usually a period of preparation before
a region gained an autonomous status as a state of the
United States. No such pattern was perceived with
respect to the lands ceded to America by Spain. Hawaii,
before 1898 an independent republic seeking annexation
to the United States and not a colony of another power,
was something of an exception. A formal treaty of
annexation preceded Hawaii's incorporation into the
United States, but at the same time the white minority
on the islands did not want statehood if that implied
the giving of citizenship to other races. Consequently,

a territorial regime was set up to administer the islands under an appointive governor. No statehood was foreseen in the near future. At the same time, however, citizenship was granted all those who had been citizens of the Hawaiian republic as of 12 August 1898, the specific date of the annexation. Moreover, Hawaii was fully integrated into the national economy, and goods passed freely between the islands and the continent without being subject to customs and other charges. Laws of the land were applied to the former as to the latter. Thus in most essential respects Hawaii was now part of the United States. The fact gave the islands a sense of permanence lacking in other parts of the empire.

The situation was very different elsewhere, but there was no uniformity in the governance of the rest of the empire. In Puerto Rico, for instance, the American forces of occupation had established military government in October 1898. It was maintained until the middle of 1900. Since even Bryan accepted the annexation of the island by the United States, its administration was a relatively simple affair, unrelated to the debate on empire. Still, the government in Washington had to devise a method for dealing with Puerto Rico in the absence of any precedent. Quite predictably, those in charge of colonial government turned to Britain for guidance. Elihu Root, a prominent New York attorney who was asked by McKinley to head the War Department with specific responsibilities for administering the recently annexed territories, avidly read books on British colonial systems for precedents that might help the United States in its new task. And there were numerous writings on the British empire in India, Egypt and other areas as well as more general discussions on tropical colonies. During the 1890s, John Foreman, Andrew Clarke, James Bryce and others had published books on these subjects, and they were extremely valuable to such men as Root, John Hay and William Howard Taft as they undertook to work out a strategy for the governing of the American empire as well as a persuasive rhetoric of empire to convince themselves and their countrymen of the justice of the new imperialism.

Root was impressed with the 'crown colony' concept which Britain applied to Hong Kong, and thought the same arrangements could be made for Puerto Rico. In other words, the latter would not be turned into a territory of the United States, which implied an eventual amalgamation with the rest of the country, but be made a colony under American civil administration. Military occupation seemed unnecessary since there was no turbulent

populace unlike Cuba or the Philippines. Thus in 1900
a civil government was inaugurated under a governor
appointed by the President and endowed with veto power.
There was to be a bicameral legislature, with an
elected house of delegates and an appointed upper house.
Those inhabitants of the island who had at least
twenty-five dollars worth of property would be allowed
to vote. All Puerto Ricans would be entitled to
protection of the United States, and one of them would
go to Washington to sit in Congress as a resident
representative without a vote. But Puerto Ricans would
not become American citizens.

By far the most controversial issue at this time was
the status of the economic relationship between Puerto
Rico and the United States. McKinley, Root and others
favored a free trade between them, virtually integrating
the island's economy with that of the mainland. This
seemed desirable as it would enable the free entry of
Puerto Rican coffee, sugar and tobacco, the main staples
of the island, into the United States and assist in the
economic rehabilitation of Puerto Rico. Some ardent
imperialists, including Senator Beveridge, supported
free-trade arrangements as a matter of duty on the part
of the mother country, and some anti-imperialists,
notably Bryan, also argued that all taxes must be
uniform throughout the enlarged American dominion and
that the Puerto Ricans could not be made to pay taxes
(duties on their exports) without their consent. But
protectionists in Congress were opposed to free trade
with the colonies, especially because such a policy
would bring about an influx of cheap Philippine goods
to compete with domestic products. The result was a
compromise, whereby the Puerto Rico tariff bill of
1900 imposed 15 per cent of the Dingley tariff rates
upon all imports from the island. The Dingley tariff
of 1897 had been a Republican measure and scaled the
average rate down to 39.9 per cent. Thus while Puerto
Rican products were definitely favored over foreign
commodities, they were still discriminated against in
comparison with domestic American goods. The question of
economic relationship was to prove one of the most vexing
in the subsequent history of American colonialism.

The governing of the Philippines was an even more
complicated affair not only because of the turmoil caused
in American politics by the annexation, but also because
the archipelago was much farther away, larger, and
socially more complex than Puerto Rico. American
leaders, casting about for the best ways of administering
the Philippines, started out from the shared assumption

that American control over the former Spanish colony was
justified on every conceivable ground. They accepted
the prevailing racial theory which characterized
Filipinos as not fit for self-government. The matter
was of more than academic interest, as bands of
Filipinos began challenging American authority as soon
as Spain was expelled from the archipelago. Under the
leadership of Emilio Aguinaldo, they refused to put
down their arms and co-operate with the American army
of occupation in establishing a new framework of
government for the Philippines. Instead, they set up
their own regime, more a military dictatorship than a
representative form of government, and insisted on the
end to American rule and the grant of independence. The
bulk of the Filipino population was unaffected, and the
majority of the 'ilustrados,' men of education and wealth,
were opposed to Aguinaldo and his followers, considering
them ignorant and incompetent. Fighting was endemic
among these groups as well as between American and
insurgent forces.

The administration in Washington convinced itself that
Aguinaldo's call for independence was mere rhetoric,
little related to the realities of Philippine life and
history, and ill-suited to bring about law, order and
welfare to the inhabitants. As Root declared in a speech
in October 1899,

Are we fighting the Philippine nation? No. There is
none. There are hundreds of islands, inhabited by
more than sixty tribes, speaking more than sixty
different languages, and all but one are ready to
accept American sovereignty ... Are we fighting the
whole of the single tribe [the Tagalos] with which
alone we are engaged? No; for the vast majority of
that tribe want peace, law, order, and are ready and
anxious for the protective government of the United
States. The men who own the property, the men who
do the business, the men of intelligence among
them are anxious that the Government of the United
States shall protect them in their interests and their
industries.

Given the inability of the Filipinos to unite and
establish their own workable government, a strong outside
power had the duty and responsibility to help them
maintain law and order. This was another essential part
of the ideology of colonialism that was accepted in
Washington. In Root's words, 'The immutable laws of
justice and humanity require that people shall have
government, that the weak shall be protected, that
cruelty and lust shall be restrained, whether there be

consent or not.' This last assertion, justifying empire,
seemed to follow logically from the twin premises of
imperialism: racial characteristics of a weaker people,
and the need for law and order in any community. The
doctrine, which Aguinaldo was asserting, that the
Filipinos were entitled to government with their consent
should not be allowed to obscure these two, more
fundamental principles. The Jeffersonian dictum about
government with the consent of the governed did not
apply to the Philippines any more than it had been
applied by Jefferson himself to the territory included
in the Louisiana purchase, or by Lincoln to the South.
The ultimate justification, then, was that the United
States had something to offer to the Filipinos which
the latter were bound to accept because it was in their
own interest to do so. As Root said in a speech
supporting McKinley's re-election in 1900,

> When I consider the myriads of human beings who have
> lived in subjection to the rule of force, ignorant
> of any other lot, knowing life only as the beast of the
> field knows it, without the seeds of progress, without
> initiative or capacity to rise, submissive to
> injustice and cruelty and perpetual ignorance and
> brutishness, I cannot believe that, for the external
> forces of civilization to replace brutal and oppressive
> government, with which such a people in ignorance are
> content, by ordered liberty and individual freedom
> and a rule that shall start and lead them along the
> path of political and social progress, is a violation
> of the principle of Jefferson, or false to the highest
> dictates of liberty and humanity. (5)

Colonialism, of course, was also good for the United
States, in the thinking of men who devised policies for
the Philippines. American power and prestige were bound
up with the retention of the islands. 'What President
McKinley has done,' declared Root, 'has been to defend
and assert the sovereignty of the United States.' Once
American power had been extended to the Philippines, the
nation must maintain and defend its position. The
Secretary of War approvingly cited newspaper editorials
that agreed with such an assertion of American
sovereignty. The 'New Orleans Picayune,' for instance,
said in 1899, 'It will now be necessary to crush the
insurrection and firmly establish the American control
before the future form of government for the islands can
be for a moment considered.' The 'Nashville American'
echoed the same sentiment when it declared, 'We must
make them [the rebels] know that our power is supreme,
otherwise we cannot give to them the blessings freedom

and individual liberty have in store.' (6)   In such
thinking, the Philippine question became a test of
American nationalism.

Others stressed more specific benefits of colonialism.
The colonies, some asserted, were the new frontier.   Just
as the frontier in America had challenged the nation's
imagination and produced certain strains of national
character, the overseas frontiers would provide
opportunities to Americans to create civilization out of
wilderness and to develop organized communities out of
primitive conditions of like.   The experience would be
invaluable in training men in problems of organization,
sanitation, agriculture and other pursuits, just as the
colonial service in Great Britain had been a training
school for generations of statesmen.   'I would rather
take part in organizing our colonial system,' said
Senator Beveridge, 'than to do anything else on this
earth.' (7)   Pro-colonialist spokesmen also emphasized
the economic benefits that would accrue to the United
States as a result of Philippine annexation.   There
was little new in their argument.   According to Senator
Henry Cabot Lodge, the Philippines 'would furnish a
large opportunity for the investment of surplus capital,
and thus reduce the competition of accumulated capital
at home, which is tending to lower very much the rates
of interest and to create, in many places, needless
competition by establishment of plants which cannot hope
to earn any decent return.' (8)   In addition, the value
of the Philippines as a market and as a base for
expanding trade with China was reiterated after 1899,
just as it had been stressed in 1898.   On the whole,
however, comparatively little was made of the economic
argument once the United States acquired the islands.
Because of the urgency of settling the revolt staged by
Aguinaldo, the most immediate need was for a political
framework to cope with the situation, and there was little
time to make good the promises of the Philippine market
for American goods and capital.

Fortified with these ideas, the United States set about
establishing rudiments of government for the colony in
the Southwestern Pacific.   It is of considerable interest
that the administration in Washington solicited, and was
in turn inundated by, advice from academic circles.
There was a great deal of excitement at various
universities about imperialism, colonial administration
and world politics, subjects which had not been
systematically taught except by a handful of specialists.
But they saw an obvious need and a challenge to the
academic profession as a result of the Spanish-American

War, to establish new chairs and create new courses in these subjects so that students as well as faculty members might learn something about them to make a constructive contribution to official policy. It was one such academic leader, Jacob Gould Schurman, president of Cornell University, who was asked by President McKinley to head a commission of inquiry into the Philippine situation.

The Schurman commission, sent to Manila in March 1899, was generally inclined to be conciliatory toward the Filipinos. Interviewing mostly representative 'ilustrados', the commission was naturally influenced by the latter's hostility toward the insurgents and their moderate demands for rights and general peace in the Philippines. Schurman thus was able to see 'a complete harmony between the aspirations and needs of the Filipinos and the desire and capacity of the Americans to satisfy them,' as the report of the commission said. More specifically, Schurman proposed that the United States accommodate the Filipino leaders' wishes for provincial and municipal autonomy. The hope was that by making such gestures of goodwill the United States would be able to put an end to the insurrection.

The basic approach and framework for government which the Schurman commission proposed were similar to those eventually adopted. In 1899, however, the administration was more preoccupied with crushing the rebels and with the forthcoming presidential election. McKinley waited till the middle of 1900 to take definite steps to establish a rubric of American administration in the islands, and he did so by asking William Howard Taft, a prominent judge in Ohio, to go to the Philippines to organize a government. The second Philippine commission under Taft arrived in Manila in June 1900, when some Filipinos had hopes of seeing Bryan become president. Many of them were fearful of co-operating with Taft lest Americans elect the Democratic candidate and withdraw from the Philippines after 1901. Once the election was over, however, both the United States government and the Filipinos had to assume that American power would stay on the islands for the indefinite future. Taft was instrumental in devising a scheme of government for the archipelago, confident that the insurrection would soon be put down and that government through him as governor-general was the best institutional framework in which the islanders could mature politically and economically. Following Schurman's recommendation and in response to the desires of moderate Filipino leaders, Taft permitted a measure of local autonomy at the provincial and municipal

levels. But his stress was on economic improvement and
educational reform. As he wrote in June 1900, 'making
internal improvements and giving a good school system'
were 'the most important agencies in bringing about
contentment, and law, and order throughout the islands.'
(9) As can be seen in such remarks, Taft was hopeful
of governing the new colony by demonstrating to the native
population that the American presence was designed to
help the Filipinos as much as the United States. They
would see how American capital and technology would
transform the islands' economy, creating job opportunities
and removing obstacles in modernization. Educational
reform, in the meantime, would awaken Filipinos from their
bondage to the past and make them appreciate the benefits
of modern civilization. Such measures would tend to
create in Filipino society an increasing number of
educated and affluent people whose outlook and interests
would tie them closely to American government. Since
this was his goal, Taft felt he was justified in
restricting Filipine participation in the central
administration at Manila, and in stationing a large
number of American troops to protect the native
population from disorder.

In this way, Hawaii, Puerto Rico and the Philippines
exhibited different patterns of governing newly acquired
lands. They represented three models of American
overseas management, and it was not clear if a uniform
system of colonial service were ever to be developed. At
this time the United States was merely experimenting with
various alternatives, and the major element which tied
the parts of the empire together was the military. It
was no accident that the War Department's bureau of
insular affairs kept control over colonial affairs,
dealing with and through the governors sent to these
possessions and assuming responsibility for their
security.

Cuba was yet another case. Strictly speaking it was
not turned into an American possession, but the United
States retained a large measure of control even after
its forces were withdrawn. Initially, some argued for
keeping Cuba indefinitely. Leonard Wood, for instance,
who in 1900 was to replace General John R. Brooke as
commander of the American occupation force in Cuba,
believed that the nation should not be bound by the
Congressional pledge before going to war against Spain
that the United States did not seek annexation as a
result of the military conflict. But President McKinley
felt the pledge must be honored. At the same time, he
was as unconvinced of Cuban abilities for self-government

and self-protection as of those of Puerto Ricans or
Filipinos. As he said in the annual message of 1899, 'we
must see to it that free Cuba be a reality, not a name,
a perfect entity, not a hasty experiment bearing within
itself the elements of failure.' (10) He saw no hope of
complete Cuban independence without a period of American
involvement to reform Cuban politics and develop its
economy. Turning once again to Root for advice, McKinley
concluded that the best strategy was for a settlement
somewhere in between independence and colonialism. The
United States would not hold the island as a colony but
would look forward to its ultimate sovereignty. In the
interim, however, America would concern itself with the
welfare and security of Cuba as well as with its own
interests. These ideas were incorporated into the
amendment which Senator Orville Platt attached to the
Cuban appropriation bill in 1901. The Platt amendment
derived its inspiration from Root, Wood and others and
established a framework for the degree of formal American
control over Cuba even while the latter was technically
accorded the status of a sovereign state. According
to the Platt formula, the United States was to relinquish
political control over Cuba and end the military
occupation. But America was to retain the right to
'guarantee' Cuban 'independence.' More specifically,
the United States would have the right to intervene in
Cuba should its independence be threatened by internal
turmoil or foreign invasion. Furthermore, the island
republic would pledge not to cede part of its territory
to a third power, while leasing to the United States some
naval bases in perpetuity. The United States navy was
particularly interested in using Guantanamo bay as a key
naval base for its Caribbean strategy, and its lease to
the United States would be a vital condition for ending
the military occupation. These terms were duly accepted
by the provisional Cuban government, and the brief period
of American suzerainty over Cuba came to an end in 1901.
    The Cuban example came closest to 'informal
imperialism' in so far as it did not involve direct
government by the United States of an alien population.
But American interests and power were fully secured, and
for all practical purposes Cuba entered an American sphere
of influence. It was ironical that the one island which
generations of Americans had eyed as a possible addition
to the United States retained its formal sovereignty,
while colonial government was established in the
Philippines and Puerto Rico, lands virtually ignored by
American expansionists before 1898.

2   THE OPEN DOOR DOCTRINE

Hawaii, Puerto Rico, the Philippines and Cuba constituted
the new American empire born of the war with Spain,
the constituent elements being related to the United
States in varying degrees of intimacy and control.   But
beyond this core of territories now integrated into the
American sphere of power, there lay vast regions of the
world, and it became a major task of the United States
diplomacy to define approaches to them in accordance
with the new status it had gained as a colonial power.

In Asia, the key question after 1899 was whether the
United States should go on extending the limits of formal
empire beyond the Philippines.   This was not merely a
question of strategy or tactics, since many considered
American expansion to be primarily aimed at the direction
of Asia and the Pacific.   Newspaper and magazine
articles, heralding the coming of the new epoch in
American foreign relations, almost invariably referred
to the nation's destiny in Asia and viewed the colonial
empire as part of the West's expansion into the East.
Thus Americans had to decide whether to live up to their
vision of Asian empire, or to consider other ways of
implementing their ideas in that part of the world.

In January 1899 Charles Denby, formerly minister to
China, wrote an essay for 'Munsey's Magazine' and
declared, 'Asia is our Eldorado.   Here are hundreds of
millions of the human race to be civilized, Christianized,
if possible, and clothed and fed.'   By Asia he meant
China, Japan, Korea, and Siam, the major countries that
had escaped Western colonization.   The implication was
that the United States should consider it a particular
task to extend its influence and interests in those
regions.   'The races of the east look up to us ... With
our flag go our literature, our laws, and our religion.'
Denby was not specifically calling for outright
colonization by America in the East, but he would insist
on some positive measures to be taken by Americans to
expand in that direction.   As he said, 'it may well be
that it is the decree of an overruling Providence that
has opened to us, in a grand and astounding way, the
door of the far east, for us to enter therein, as we
would enter into a land prepared for us long ago.' (11)

Andrew Raymond, president of Union College, saw also
larger implications in the destiny for America that was
opened up in the East as a result of the Spanish war.
It was a stage in human history which was essentially
a record of 'the conflict of civilizations ... the
conflict that will not and cannot cease until the

worthiest ideals and noblest purposes and truest
conceptions of life and duty dominate the world.'
Echoing Pearson and Mahan, he characterized the nineteenth
century in terms of the conflict between East and West.
The century, according to Raymond 'by reason of its
discoveries and inventions, multiplying facilities for
intercourse, has brought face to face as never before,
and in mutual antagonism, the two great types of
civilization described in general terms as the Eastern
and Western world.' The English-speaking peoples
represented the best in the latter, in fact 'the highest
civilization in the world today.' Their 'aggressive
energy' was merely a concomitant of their 'superior form
of life,' as was their expansion throughout the world.
He continued,

> [The American flag in the Philippines] represented
> ability to protect and teach and develop, an ability
> that carried with it responsibility ... This pressure
> of obligation is the sign of a higher life than the
> world has ever before known, and it marks the
> beginning of a new era in which might is to make,
> not right, but duty, and the greater blessings of the
> Western world are to be given to the peoples of the
> East ... The inevitable conflict of civilizations in
> the Far East will call for all the intelligence and
> strength and high purposes of the Western world. (12)

These writers were confident that the United States
was amply justified in continuing its energetic expansion
in East Asia. Most observers would have agreed. The
problem was specifically how to do it. Some favored the
extension of formal empire by means of acquiring more
bases, spheres of influence and colonies. The United
States navy, in particular, was interested in going
beyond Manila into Chinese waters to complete a chain of
bases across the Pacific. For several years after 1898
naval strategists in Washington pressed the State
Department to negotiate for a cession or lease of such
Chinese locations as Samsah bay and Chusan island which
might be turned into American bases on the east coast
of China. From Peking Minister Edwin Conger wrote in
support of such a scheme. In 1899 he suggested to the
State Department that the United States might take a
port in Chihli province, which included Peking and
Tientsin, with a view to establishing an American sphere
of influence there.

Conger's superiors in Washington, as well as civilian
officials in general, were not persuaded that it would be
necessary or desirable to take such steps. While agreeing
that American power and influence in East Asia were now

greater than ever before, they did not think the
establishment and extension of formal control in China
was what was called for in the aftermath of the Spanish-
American War. To begin with, most of the Ch'ing empire
had already been carved up into spheres of influence by
other imperialist powers, and for the United States to
establish its own sphere it would be necessary to encroach
upon another power's. The result might be an involvement
in the diplomacy of imperialism to a greater extent than
the American people wanted. Moreover, a naval base or a
sphere of influence in China necessitated a larger
military force than was available to the United States
at the time. The bulk of American troops in the East was
engaged in suppressing the uprising in the Philippines,
calling forth a fierce national debate on the future of
American imperialism. To establish a viable zone of
power in China, the United States would have to develop
a force at least comparable to that of the German navy
which was turning Shantung province into a semi-colony
by a large-scale infusion of manpower and technology.
The forces then available did not warrant such action.
For these reasons, most civilian officials opposed the
acquisition of more bases or colonies in Asia. But this
did not mean that they opposed some positive initiatives
by the United States. They wanted the country to play a
greater role in Asian politics and extend its interests
farther than had been the case before 1898, but they did
not think the establishment of formal territorial control
was necessary to bring about these ends. Merchants
should redouble their efforts to penetrate the Chinese
market, investment opportunities should be explored with
vigor, missionary and educational activities should be
encouraged and protected, and the United States should
make its views heard as an Asian power. But the country
should not overextend itself in territorial terms.

It should also be noted that a third group of men -
perhaps a majority of those who expressed themselves on
Asian questions - preferred the traditional policy of
primarily expanding trade opportunities in China, to
departing from it in an aggressive way. To them Asia,
in particular China, was of great importance in
commercial relations. American exports to China had
begun to show signs of recovery from several decades of
stagnation, and toward the end of the 1890s trade
figures were registering impressive gains - all this
without a base or a sphere of influence. It seemed
perfectly possible, then, to continue the traditional
emphasis on commerce without incurring new risks or
venturing into the unknown territory of imperialistic

diplomacy in East Asia. As Bryan said in 1900, other
nations might try to 'slice the Chinese melon,' but the
United States must not depart from a policy of justice
and fair dealing in protecting its interests in China.
He warned traders and missionaries against acting as
forerunners of an imperialistic policy. (13) From such
a point of view, all that was needed to promote the
national interest in Asia was to maintain the traditional
framework for expansion of commerce and for safeguarding
the security of Americans. The treaty rights must be
upheld, but there was no need to go beyond them, as
other countries were doing.

The McKinley administration at this time did not
single out any one of these various approaches as the
sole guide to policy in Asia. Instead it combined them
as it sought to define America's relations with China,
Japan and other countries on the aftermath of the
Spanish-American War. The traditional principle of
commercial expansion was reaffirmed by the State
Department when Secretary of State John Hay enunciated
his famous 'open door' policy in September 1899. It
took the form of sending an identic note to various
governments inviting them to adhere to the principle of
equal commercial opportunity in China. More specifically,
the note said that while the United States recognized
the existence of spheres of influence in the Ch'ing
empire, it insisted on non-discrimination regarding
railway tariffs, harbor dues and related matters within
each sphere.

The policy was traditionalist, but its enunciation
was a departure from the past in that it clearly
established the United States as a country which wished
to have a say and play a role in Asian politics. Only
a little over a year earlier, just before the outbreak
of the Spanish war, Washington had rejected a British
proposal for a joint declaration of just such a principle.
But now Hay, McKinley, and others judged the time was
opportune for clarifying America's stand as an Asian
power. Secretary Hay was fully aware that the open door
proclamation would serve to impress upon the world the
identity of interests and policies between Britain and
the United States. This was but another instance of
Anglo-American co-operation, and he was happy to use the
opportunity presented by China's crisis to further the
cause.

The open door policy also acquired fresh meaning in
that the United States navy would henceforward have a
fairly well defined policy - at least as it appeared -
to defend in Asia. It was added to the Monroe Doctrine

as one of the basic objectives of the nation, in pursuit
of which the armed forces must develop their strategies.
For the navy, in particular, its 'raison d'être' in
Asian waters and in the Western Pacific would now be
quite clear. In addition to safeguarding American
possessions and protecting American lives in that part
of the world, it would have to be concerned with
upholding the open door. This was a new commitment,
and the navy soon began to foresee a future war as
result of a conflict arising out of a third power's
challenge to the open door. (14) In other words, Hay's
doctrine, itself an old-fashioned idea, was coupled with
the growing power and self-consciousness of the navy
and in time developed into a rationale for the presence
not only of American political influence in China but of
military power in Asia and the Pacific. From the
military's point of view, the acquisition of the
Philippines was admirably fitted into the whole scheme.
American power and control over the archipelago made
its foreign policy more plausible, and the open door
policy seemed to provide a perfect framework in which to
tie together disparate aspects of American dealings
in all parts of the region.

As initially announced in 1899, the Hay notes did
not mention foreign bases and leases in China. The
United States navy certainly saw no contradiction
between the open door policy and its own search for a
base somewhere on the China coast. The Boxer affair of
1899-1900, however, necessitated further clarification
of American policy and strategy in Asia, and the United
States confused its own stand by reacting in two
contradictory ways; it joined the other powers to
suppress the Boxers by force and to occupy parts of
China, while at the same time it issued a second open
door note, explicitly denying an intention to seek
bases or spheres of influence in that country. In the
end, however, the United States emerged as a power
with special ties with China, a country whose influence
there would not primarily be based on military power or
formal territorial control.

When the Boxers - armed bands practicing unique rites
and opposed to foreign presence - spread out of Shantung
province where they had begun by attacking Germans, and
entered Chihli province, with two key centers of foreign
population (Tientsin and Peking), the powers became
alarmed and prepared contingency plans to protect or
evacuate their nationals. There was a fear that the
Boxers might engage in a wholesale attack on all foreign
residents in China, cutting them off from the outside

world. The situation became utterly tense when
communication between Peking and Tientsin was severed,
as the railroad traffic between the two cities was stopped
by the Boxers and the latter marched to the capital.
The legation headquarters of the powers were all under
siege, and the Ch'ing court, under momentary pressures
from anti-foreign groups, added to the crisis by
declaring war upon these powers.

Washington was besieged with frantic calls for help
from its representatives as well as American businessmen
and missionaries throughout China, and as far as the
McKinley administration was concerned, there was little
hesitation to act. The use of force seemed not only
justified but absolutely necessary to rescue Americans
in China. Fortunately, there was a large military
contingent in the Philippines, engaged in fighting
against Aguinaldo's rebels, and it could be diverted
to China, with reinforcements to be shipped from the
United States to fill the gaps in the Philippines.
Altogether 2,500 American troops participated in an
international expedition that was organized hastily in
the summer of 1900 to retake Peking from Boxer control.
American forces engaged themselves in military action
against Chinese, although American commanders on the
spot, as well as their superiors in Washington, did
not want to act in close co-operation with the other
expeditionary powers for fear of diplomatic entanglement.
'Whatever you do,' the Navy Department cautioned
Admiral Louis Kempff, commanding the American naval
task force in China, 'let the Navy Department know plan
of concerting powers in regard to punitive or other
expeditions.' Secretary of War Root likewise ordered
General Adna Chaffee, commanding officer of the American
expeditionary force, to 'avoid entering into any joint
action or undertaking with other powers tending to
commit or limit this Government as to its future course
of conduct.' (15)

The decision to use force in China, combined with a
reluctance to be seen in collusion with the other
imperialist powers, was characteristic of America's
China policy in 1900. There was no question that force
would be employed 'to protect American interests as well
as the interests of individual Americans,' as the Navy
Department's instruction to Kempff said. On the basis
of American participation in the Boxer expedition, the
United States became one of the 'protocol powers,'
negotiating with the Ch'ing court for the settlement of
the affair and signing the Boxer protocol. The presence
of American troops entitled the United States to a voice

in the final arrangement, and the United States sought to moderate harsher demands brought forth by some countries, especially Germany. Among the terms of the settlement was China's agreement to have the powers station troops along the route between Peking and Tientsin, in order to keep open the communication between the capital and the sea. As one of the protocol powers, the United States would now maintain several thousand marines in north China, a symbol of its determination to protect its nationals by force.

At the same time, there was considerable reluctance to identify American policy in China with that of other governments. Even as American forces joined the international expedition, and its diplomats conferred with their colleagues in Peking to settle the Boxer incident jointly, the idea of the United States as somehow different from others became more and more influential. With respect to bases and leaseholds in China, for instance, the State Department under Secretary Hay decided to publish a circular - the 'second Hay note' - in July 1900, expressing the policy of the United States to respect China's 'territorial and administrative entity.' Unlike the open door notes of 1899, the declaration did not invite other powers to act likewise. But it clarified America's official stand as much toward them as toward voices within the country calling for a more ambitious policy in China. The principle of upholding Chinese 'entity' - the word 'integrity' would come to be used more frequently - was rather abstract, in view of the presence of foreign troops and the absence of an effective central government in China, and it was not even clear how the United States proposed to prevent the imperialist countries from further encroaching upon the country. As Hay himself confessed, 'we do not want to rob China ourselves, and our public opinion will not permit us to interfere, with an army, to prevent others from robbing her. Besides, we have no army.' (16) Nevertheless, the second Hay note served to present American policy as somehow distinct from that of others. The United States had a real interest in Chinese affairs and its own rights and prerogatives to protect, but it would act in its own way, not as a member of a group of imperialists.

Although Hay probably never saw all the possible implications of such an approach, and although the first and second Hay notes were not calculated responses to domestic opinion, the policy the administration adopted during 1899-1900 proved to be enormously popular with a public whose interest in Asian matters had been aroused

anew by the Spanish-American War. Advocates of power
politics were pleased that the United States was playing
an active role in Chinese affairs, while champions of
the national interest were able to see that the State
Department as well as the armed forces were doing all
they could to protect American lives and property,
without becoming entangled in international complications
in the process. By far the most interesting development
after 1900, however, was the emergence of the idea of
a special friendship between the United States and China.
Such an idea appealed enormously not only to those who
conceived of American policy and interests in a
geopolitical or a nationalistic framework, but also
to those who imputed something ideological and moralistic
to the bilateral relationship.

   'Our interests in China are identical with the
interests of the Chinese themselves,' declared the
'Memphis Commercial Appeal' in June 1900. (17) 'It
would be in the best interests of both the United States
and China,' said the 'Cleveland Leader,' 'if a united,
progressive, independent, and popular government existed
in China.' (18) John Barrett, former minister to Siam,
wrote in the 'Independent,' 'If China maintains her
independence through our support, the United States in
another decade will have greater material and moral
influence than all other nations combined.' (19) These
words were expressed during the height of the Boxer
crisis, when American forces were being dispatched to
China to lift the siege of the legations. Thus at the
very moment of the heaviest military involvement thus
far by the United States in China, there was emerging a
distinct view of Chinese-American relations which
stressed their positive aspects and sought to transform
the calamities of a Boxer uprising into hopeful
beginnings of a new friendship. The July 1900 circular,
stressing America's commitment to Chinese integrity, was
announced just at such a juncture and seemed to confirm
the new approach to China.

   The idea of special ties between China and the United
States, which was to have an enormous impact on the
subsequent history of American-Asian relations, was an
ingenious one, well calculated to appeal to various
schools of thought concerning United States foreign
policy. First of all, it meant that the United States
was going to remain an Asian power, playing a special
role in the affairs of that region. Second, America
would be different from other countries, and its
influence would be derived from a sense of this
difference. Third, the United States would not demand

territory or use a large force to back up its policy in
China, but it would turn to the feeling of the identity
of Chinese and American interests and policies in order
to promote commercial and other objectives. Fourth, an
independent China would 'ipso facto' mean a China
friendly to the United States since the latter, alone of
all the major powers, stood for Chinese integrity.
Fifth, such being the case, the Chinese would look to
America for advice and support, a development further
designed to cement ties between the two. Lastly, the
United States would be an ideologically oriented power
in China, and use the idea of close ties with China as a
weapon, rather than armed forces, to carry out its
policy. In sum, the idea of the United States as a
power on the continent of Asia virtually necessitated
an image of China that was friendly and closely bound
to America. What the latter lacked in military force,
it would make up through such an ideal. In this way
the Open Door policy became an idealistic symbol of
America's approach to China. Already in 1904,
Elihu Root was referring to the Open Door as a historic
policy:

> Carefully guarded by the wise statesman who had
> secured its acceptance, it brought a moral force of
> recognized value to protect peaceful and helpless
> China from dismemberment and spoilation, and to
> preserve the 'open door' in the Orient for the commerce
> of the world ... None other [than the United States]
> had won confidence in the sincerity of its purpose,
> and none other but America could render the service
> which we have rendered to humanity in China during
> the past four years. (20)

The United States, then, was not going to expand
territorially in Asia beyond the Philippines, nor would
it engage in 'realpolitik,' intent upon enlarging its
exclusive zones of prerogatives in China. But it would
continue to extend its interests and influence all the
same. It would do so within the framework of a new Open
Door diplomacy which had ideological as well as commercial
implications. This was the direction the United States
government decided to take in response to the tumultuous
events of 1899-1900 in Asia.

3   CARIBBEAN INTERVENTIONISM

In the Caribbean region, in contrast to Asia, the United
States was far more willing to entrench its power despite
the decision not to turn Cuba into its colony. The region

had for decades been of immediate strategic and economic concern to the United States, but after 1898 America's Caribbean policy became bound up with its emergence as a colonial power. There was greater psychological readiness to employ force than earlier. The military occupation of Cuba and Puerto Rico set a precedent for such action as well as for testing the feasibility of deploying large numbers of American forces in the area. Moreover, the Platt formula adopted for Cuba revealed that the United States did not have to assume formal control over another country in order to enjoy special rights and prerogatives. For all these reasons, the years immediately after 1898 produced some long-range plans and strategies for protecting and promoting American interests in the Caribbean. There were three basic concerns at this time, at least two of which were implemented soon after the turn of the century. First, the United States considered it more than ever urgent to build an isthmian canal and to control the waterway without obstacles. Second, an expanding role of the navy would require additional bases and coaling stations in the Western Hemisphere. Third, political and economic stability in the Caribbean would be of crucial importance to the United States in order to minimize chances for outside interference in the region.

Of the three objectives, the canal question was of the most immediate relevance, now that the United States was emerging as a colonial and world power whose navy would assume far larger obligations than in the past. The experiences of the war with Spain had demonstrated the utmost necessity to build a canal so as to enable American warships to be shifted from one ocean to another without having to go around Cape Horn. There was virtual consensus both within and outside the American government that an isthmian canal must be built with the greatest possible speed. Financing and technology seemed readily available. The only obstacles were the still unresolved question of location and the existence of the Clayton-Bulwer treaty of 1850 which had specified that neither the United States nor Great Britain should obtain or exercise exclusive control over the isthmian canal, and that they would guarantee its neutrality at all times. These obstacles must first be removed before an American canal could be dug.

Regarding the Clayton-Bulwer treaty, sentiment in the United States for several decades had been overwhelmingly in favor of abrogating it. Its provisions for joint control and neutrality had been considered an infringement on America's freedom of action, and several preceding

administrations had tried, unsuccessfully, to modify
or abrogate the treaty. The situation appeared more
urgent in the aftermath of the Spanish-American War,
and this time the McKinley administration was determined
to wage an all-out campaign to have America's wishes
accepted by Britain. The latter, too, was willing to
oblige, but not to give up a complete free hand to the
United States. Despite the generally pro-American foreign
policy of the British cabinet, it was not ready to
concede total US control in Central America, which
an unconditional abrogation of the treaty would have
entailed. The result was a compromise, known as the
first Hay-Pauncefote treaty, signed in November 1900.
It was negotiated by Secretary Hay and the British
ambassador, Sir Julian Pauncefote. The agreement gave
the United States sole rights to construct, control and
maintain a canal. At the same time, it reaffirmed the
principle of neutrality and non-fortification, and also
invited other countries to adhere to the principle. This
appeared an eminently reasonable compromise, explicitly
assigning to the United States the right to build an
isthmian canal, while at the same time making sure that
the canal would remain an international waterway, open
to peaceful commerce at all times.

Much to the chagrin of Secretary Hay and the British
government, opinion in America was not favorable. Both
in and out of the Senate where the treaty came up for
a debate, there was a very strong sentiment against
any compromise of American sovereignty. Perhaps it
reflected the sense of confidence and nationalism
following the victory over Spain. It also was an
expression of the traditional hostility toward Britain
and misgivings about foreign complications. Thus
William Jennings Bryan attacked the first Hay-Pauncefote
treaty as a submission to British imperialism, and others
argued that its clause about inviting foreign powers to
adhere to the neutrality principle was a violation of the
Monroe Doctrine. Nationalists asserted that under the
non-fortification provision of the treaty the nation
would be prevented even from stopping a potential
enemy fleet from passing through the canal to attack
San Francisco or New Orleans. Imperialistic expansionism
in Central America would be barred, since the treaty
retained the provision in the original Clayton-Bulwer
treaty forbidding the signatories to colonize in the
area.

There might have been an impasse on the matter but for
Britain's difficulties with other European powers,
especially Russia and Germany, which inclined its

officials to accept a virtual surrender to the United
States on the canal question. It was not an easy
decision, for there could be no end to American
intransigence if Britain continued to yield to its
demands. But there was really no choice. Even the
acknowledged friends of Britain such as John Hay and
Henry White admitted that it would be impossible to
change American opinion on the matter and that the only
way to settle the dispute was through Britain's
concession. They urged London to yield for the sake of
removing one of the last major obstacles to Anglo-
American understanding. Finally, toward the end of
1901, the 'second Hay-Pauncefote treaty' was signed,
this time explicitly abrogating the Clayton-Bulwer
treaty. The new accord did not mention fortification
of the canal route, but by a separate note the British
government recognized America's right to fortify the
canal.

As if to demonstrate the new freedom and prestige
the canal agreement gave the United States, a Caribbean
squadron was organized in 1902, with instructions to
ensure law and order in the isthmus. The only thing
now lacking was a canal, but before construction began a
decision had to be made as to its location. The 'battle
of the routes' was waged with increasing heat between
exponents of a Nicaraguan and a Panamanian route.
Traditionally, Americans had looked to the building of
a canal across Nicaragua, in part because a French
concern (the New Panama Canal Company) had held a
concession from Colombia to construct a Panama canal.
A number of American firms had acquired rights to a
Nicaraguan alternative, in part because the Southern
states favored the route which was closer to them than
a Panama canal and could conceivably bring blessings to
their economy. This view was opposed by some Republican
Party leaders, most notably Senators Mark Hanna,
John C. Spooner, and Henry Cabot Lodge, who argued that
the Panamanian route was cheaper and less complicated
to build. The movement to reverse public sentiment
gained momentum as the Colombian government became
interested in giving the canal-constructing concession
to the United States to prevent the latter from building
one through Nicaragua, and as bondholders of the New
Panama Canal Company sought to sell the firm's franchise
and assets to the American government. Now that
America's determination and capability to construct an
isthmian canal were clear, these groups stepped up their
campaign to route it across Panama rather than Nicaragua.
Their lobbying and the concerted efforts by Hanna,

Spooner and others resulted in the passage of a Spooner act in 1902, looking toward negotiations for a Panama canal.   It also stipulated that in the event such negotiations failed the President was to be authorized to go back to the Nicaraguan alternative.

It was a reflection of the imperialistic temper of the times that the debate on the canal routes took little cognizance of the possible political and economic implications of America's canal building for the governments and peoples of Nicaragua and Colombia.   It was assumed that these countries would be so eager to have such a canal that they would accept almost any terms which the United States was prepared to offer. Moreover, now that the Clayton-Bulwer treaty had been abrogated, it was taken for granted that the prospective canal would in fact be an extension of American sovereignty.   The United States navy, for instance, was not interested in the question of routes but insisted that the United States should obtain bases at both ends of the canal.   Since the country would be responsible for the security of the waterway, it seemed obviously necessary to turn the region into part of the American strategic system.   The same considerations induced the State Department, in negotiating with the Colombian government for the sale of the New Panama Canal Company's rights, to seek the establishment of a zone on both sides of the contemplated canal where American forces would be stationed to maintain law and order.   The American-Colombian treaty of January 1903 specified that such a canal zone would be ten kilometers wide on each side of the waterway.   In exchange, the United States would pay Colombia an initial lump sum of ten million dollars and an annual rent of 250,000 dollars thereafter.

Had negotiations been with Nicaragua, the United States would have sought and offered similar terms.   In either case, there was bound to be an extension of American power in Central America.   The basic consideration was the security, interests and prestige of the United States.   Wherever the canal was built, such a policy had overwhelming public support, derived as it was from a tradition of Caribbean regionalism and from the new sense of national power.

Against such a background, the Panamanian episode of 1903 offered a good example of how far the United States was willing to go to implement its strategy.   When the Colombian senate refused to ratify the canal treaty, considering its provisions an infringement on national sovereignty and an inadequate compensation in financial terms, the United States had a choice of either

approaching Nicaragua for similar rights or going ahead
with canal construction regardless of Colombia's
opposition. There was no guarantee that Nicaragua would
accept the conditions which Colombia rejected, and in the
end some sort of overt American action might have been
inevitable. In view of the records of United States
military involvement in Cuba, the Philippines and
elsewhere after 1898, and in view of the readily
available rhetoric of imperialism to justify such acts,
the use of force to carry out what was considered
essential to national security and interests was never
far from the policy makers' sights.

The United States was spared an undue delay in coming
to a decision one way or another when on 3 November an
uprising erupted in the Panamanian province of Colombia,
presumably led by those who sought an American
construction of a canal. Colombian troops that were
sent to put down the rebellion were unable to move
across the isthmus as the Panama Railroad, an American
concern, refused to provide transportation, and the
USS 'Nashville', arriving in the area immediately after
the uprising was reported, forbade the passage of
Colombian forces in either direction between the
Atlantic and the Pacific coasts of the isthmus. The
Republic of Panama was recognized by the United States.
Philippe Bunau-Varilla, an executive of the New Panama
Canal Company, now became Panamanian envoy to the
United States and quickly concluded a new canal treaty
with Secretary Hay. On 18 November the Panamanian
government duly ratified it. The agreement was even more
favorable to the United States than the Colombian treaty;
it gave America virtual sovereignty in the canal zone,
which was now to be ten miles wide, as well as the
right to intervene at the two terminal cities of Panama
and Colon.

The Roosevelt administration's handling of the
Panamanian uprising proved to be an embarrassment to
the United States, which seemed to engage precisely in
the same kinds of gun-boat diplomacy and secret
machinations that were associated with European
imperialism. The frankly high-handed manner in which
the canal treaty was secured gave ammunition to the
Democrats and anti-imperialists in America who accused
Roosevelt of being more imperialistic than Europeans.
Nevertheless, there was no national division comparable
to the great debate of 1898. The Democratic Party might
have made an issue out of it in the presidential election
of 1904, but it did not provide a focus for any sort of
nationwide opposition to Roosevelt's leadership in

American foreign affairs. Bryan, the Democrat most
directly associated with anti-imperialism, did not run
for the White House, and he was out of the country
through much of 1904, meeting Leo Tolstoy to discuss
pacifism and otherwise looking at the American scene
from the outside. Since the Democrats as well as
Republicans had consistently advocated American
construction of, and control over, an isthmian canal,
whatever criticism one had about the means employed had
to be moderated by a sense of gratification that at
last the country had obtained full rights to carry out
the project. Administration spokesmen like Hay and
Root vigorously defended its policy toward the Panamanian
episode, asserting that American intervention had been
necessary to keep open the land communication between
the two oceans in order to provide law and order in the
isthmus, and that 'the general interests of mankind'
(Root's phrase) had had to be considered in responding
to the uprising. In other words, the United States
could not afford to keep its hands off Panama, especially
when intervention could be expected to result in a
successful consummation of the canal-related
negotiations.

A canal, then, was finally going to be built across
Panama. Whether the United States should try further to
extend its power was the inevitable next question that
had to be faced. Both the army and the navy strongly
urged that action be taken to ensure the safety of
Panama against possible attacks by Colombia. Admiral
George Dewey recommended that if the United States became
involved in a war for the defense of Panama, American
forces must occupy not only the entire line of the
railroad but also the 'strategic area' of the Yavisa. (21)
In addition to establishing American control over the
isthmus, the navy was interested in obtaining bases in
the Caribbean, especially in Santo Domingo. In 1903 two
junior naval officers were sent by the Navy general board
on a clandestine mission to that country to survey its
military data and possible uses for the United States.
They recommended the establishment of a coaling station at
Samana bay, the location which the American navy was to
continue to consider the most desirable object for
acquisition. According to a memorandum by the general,
it should be feasible to work things out in such a way
that the Dominican Republic would be induced 'to develop
a request for some sort of occupation by the United
States, and this would virtually secure to us control of
this most important strategic point in the
Caribbean.' (22)

President Roosevelt and the State Department, however, decided against territorial seizure at this time. As Roosevelt said in relation to Dewey's recommendation for taking Yavisa, 'The military reasons for taking possession of Yavisa are strong, yet it seems to me that they may be outbourne by the political reasons, so as to make it inadvisable to take it just now.' (23) By 'political reasons' were meant possible domestic opposition to further acts of imperialistic expansionism as well as the fear of becoming involved in local politics in Caribbean or Central American countries where conditions were very unstable. The United States would act resolutely to protect the canal and to safeguard the lives and activities of its citizens in these areas, but it did not seem desirable to extend the limits of America's territorial domain at this time. The only exception at the turn of the century was the Danish West Indies, lying to the east of Puerto Rico. The State Department under John Hay revived Seward's dream of adding these islands to the United States for strategic and prestige reasons. The islands' economy, primarily sugar production based on indigenous labor, was closely tied to the rest of the Caribbean and to the United States, and Denmark had periodically been interested in selling them. Negotiations, however, were broken off in 1902 as the Danish legislature rejected a treaty of purchase as insufficiently generous in financial terms. But Americans assumed, as Henry White wrote, that the 'islands eventually must come to us, and for less money probably.' (24) For the time being, at any event, there would be no further attempt to add territory to the United States.

Eschewing territorial acquisitions and yet intent upon strengthening American power and control over the Caribbean, the Roosevelt administration devised other means for ensuring the protection of American interests and security in the region. The basic concern was with stability, a traditional theme going back to the Monroe Doctrine and even beyond. To this was added the Social Darwinian assumption that countries at lower stages of development were politically more immature and less economically stable than advanced countries, and that the latter had the responsibility to preserve law and order throughout the world. According to Root, the United States must act to prevent conditions of 'continuous revolution and disorder' in Latin American countries, which must be brought up from the 'stage of militarism into the stage of industrialism.' (25) This was the rationale for empire which the European

imperialists had employed in Asia, Africa or the Middle
East, and it justified America's Caribbean interventionism.

At the beginning of the twentieth century, the United
States was particularly worried about the weak financial
condition of some of the American republics. It could
lead to revolution, disorder or foreign intervention.
Now that the United States was a military power and a
canal was finally going to be built, it was imperative
to do something about the situation lest conditions of
weakness and instability should pose a direct threat to
national security. Roosevelt was particularly impressed
with the importance of this when in 1902 British, German
and Italian ships blockaded the Venezuelan coast to
obtain payment of debts owed the three powers. Conditions
inside the country were chaotic, and damage had been
inflicted upon foreign property. In the process of the
blockade, two Venezuelan ships were sunk, and according
to the commander of an American warship in the area,
stability was restored. (26) There was no visible
damage to American interests in the country, and the
diplomats felt there was no need for the United States
to become alarmed. In Washington, however, Roosevelt
considered the blockade as a forerunner of things to
come unless financial instability and irresponsibility
in the Caribbean were checked. Similar demonstration
of force by European powers could take place, and there
was no guarantee that they would not compromise American
supremacy in the area. Fortunately for the Roosevelt
administration, the blockade was terminated when
Venezuela appealed to the United States for mediation,
and the latter offered its good offices to bring about
an arbitration of the debt dispute. But the incident
seemed to dramatize the need for the United States to
concern itself with the solvency of Central American
countries.

One way of achieving that objective was tried in
Santo Domingo in 1905. It was to establish a customs
receivership. The United States would take over the
collection of customs in the Dominican Republic and
distribute the revenue collected in such a way as to
meet interest payments on outstanding debts. Such
measures would ensure the solvency of the country and
tend to discourage the kind of European involvement that
had occurred in Venezuela. The establishment of the
customs receivership in Santo Domingo was occasioned
by political instability in that country after the
assassination of President Ulises Heureaux. The
government was bankrupt as Heureaux had contracted heavy

loans which remained unpaid. In order to forestall
European intervention, President Roosevelt enunciated the
policy that the United States would henceforth be
responsible for financial stability of the Dominican
Republic. This was the 'Roosevelt corollary' to the
Monroe Doctrine and was intended as a statement of
national policy to use United States power and authority
to ensure debt payments by another government. According
to an American-Dominican agreement of January 1905, the
United States was to appoint a customs receiver for the
Dominican Republic, who was to distribute the customs
receipts in such a way that not more than 55 per cent of
them would be applied to redeem existing debts.

The customs receivership idea, which was to be
extended to other countries in the succeeding years,
was a compromise between non-intervention and
imperialistic control. Roosevelt was weary of involving
the United States in internal Dominican politics, and
the State Department took a negative view of adding
more political obligations and territory to the United
States. The navy, too, was now less eager than earlier
for a vast network of overseas bases; it came to stress
the concentration of available forces rather than
globally scattered bases. And yet non-intervention was
never a practical alternative in view of the building
of the canal and the power of the United States in
the region. Neither did the administration wish to be
a passive observer of American financiers who sought to
expand and protect their enterprises overseas and often
entered into exclusive arrangements with local regimes.
To bring some sort of order to the scene, to prevent
European interference, and to promote stability, all
short of outright colonialism, it seemed best to provide
for some degree of supervision of Caribbean finances
by the United States.

Caribbean interventionism, then, was American's
response to the region in the Age of Imperialism. It
was a particular form of imperialism, without involving
outright colonization or territorial seizure. Instead,
the United States turned the region into its sphere
of influence through its military presence, canal
construction and economic influence. While the use of
force and the establishment of colonies were kept to a
minimum, there was a distinct departure from the
traditional approach which had generally emphasized
informal control in the Caribbean region. The United
States was little different from the other imperialist
powers in thus having various kinds of approach and
maintaining several levels of control over foreign lands.

Just as the European powers and Japan were extending
their power to less developed areas of the world, American
empire was being defined in Asia, the Pacific and the
Western Hemisphere. It did not embrace Africa or the
Middle East, but by almost any definition, the United
States was now a full-fledged member of the community
of imperialists.

4   EUROPEAN POLITICS AND AMERICA

In thus emerging as an imperialist power, the United
States became inevitably drawn into the vortex of
European 'Machtpolitik' (power politics). Hitherto the
European powers had engaged in the 'diplomacy of
imperialism' among themselves, generally irrespective of,
and unconcerned with, trends in American policy and
opinion. One major question after 1898 was the extent
to which this would change, and the degree to which the
United States would be willing to involve itself in
imperialist diplomacy. Through its sheer presence,
American power now appeared to be a factor which other
countries would have to take into consideration as they
evolved their own policies in Europe, Asia and elsewhere.
    It is well to recall that the 'diplomacy of
imperialism' had certain characteristics which produced
both stability and instability in the international
system. Because of their constant struggle for greater
power and their consciousness of relative respective
positions throughout the world, the imperialists engaged
in armament rivalries and colonial competition, factors
which caused friction and instability in international
relations. At the same time, the very multiplicity of
powers produced a degree of stability because any
combination of alliances and ententes was possible.
Until after 1907 or thereabout, there was no rigid
pattern of European alignments, and thus some sort of
equilibrium existed amid flux at any given moment. There
were few, if any, permanent antagonisms or friendships.
Moreover, all parts of the world were becoming
incorporated into the European state system as a result
of their imperialistic rivalries. This, too, could bring
about stability in so far as events outside Europe
would be related to European politics, and too radical
a shift in colonial balances would be resisted by
equilibrium-conscious metropolitan powers.
    Until after the Spanish-American War, such a system of
imperialist diplomacy had tended to operate without
involving the United States. The latter held to its

predominant position in the Caribbean, and this
geopolitical principle was well recognized by the European
powers. But elsewhere on the global scene America's role
had been minimal. Certainly American presence in
European politics had been generally unnoticed. After
1898, however, the functioning of the diplomacy of
imperialism required that the United States be somehow
incorporated into world politics.

Great Britain was the power most solicitous of having
the United States participate more actively in international affairs, but it was by no means the only one.
Britain's interest in American power and influence must be
seen against the background of its evolving world policy.
It had maintained its superior position on the basis
of two principles: 'splendid isolation' or the policy
of forming no alliance, and the two-navy standard,
sustaining a navy larger than the combination of the
navies of any two nations. The latter principle was
coming under strain because of the rapid build-up of
other countries' navies, especially Germany's. As for the
no-alliance policy, it was ideally fitted to keep
European diplomacy in a state of flux, but increasingly
it came to be seen as too rigid a dogma in view of the
growing power of potential rivals such as Russia,
France and Germany. It was imperative to prevent a
hostile combination among two or three of these powers.
Since France and Russia were allies in accordance with the
dual alliance of 1894, the most pressing need was to avoid
the possibility that one of them, or both together, might
befriend Germany. There was no real conflict between
Britain and Germany in colonial areas, whereas British
imperial interests often clashed sharply with those of
Russia in Asia and of France in the Mediterranean and
North Africa. Under the circumstances, Britain might have
sought out an entente with Germany to prevent the latter
from moving closer to France and Russia. At the turn of
the century, however, Britain did not want permanent
antagonisms and friendships which such a move might
imply. Because of the apparent inadequacy of the two-
navy standard, it could not remain aloof from European
alliance systems, but it wanted to retain freedom of
action to maintain its superior position throughout the
world.

It is not surprising, then, that given these
considerations British officials should have adopted
the policy of seeking regional understandings in
different parts of the world. In order to minimize the
danger of colonial clashes and at the same time to retain
flexibility, the best approach was to enter into various

agreements in various regions of the globe. This was
the background of the Anglo-Japanese alliance of 1902
and the Anglo-French entente of 1904. In the end,
however, these agreements tended to introduce an element
of rigidity into international relations, and both had
the effect of defining the way the United States would
respond to developments in world politics.

The Anglo-Japanese alliance was a typical regional
understanding born of a pragmatic search for a partner
in stability in the Far East. Britain might also have
turned to Russia or France for such an understanding, but
Japan showed greater interest at this time because it
was concerned over the growth of Russian power in
Manchuria. Thus a marriage of convenience was consummated
which initially was envisaged as a temporary device by
both sides. The two countries would recognize each
other's sphere of influence in China and Korea, and
agree to maintain their combined naval power superior to
that of others'. Similarly, Britain and France came to
an understanding over Morocco in 1904. France's interest
in such an entente was a good indication that it did not
want to be bound by its Russian alliance everywhere in
the world. In fact, the French government was alarmed
over the implications of the Anglo-Japanese alliance,
since the latter specified that should one of the allies
(most probably Japan) become involved in war with a
power (Russia), and should the latter be supported by
another (France), the other signatory (Britain) would
enter the war to honor the alliance. In order to
minimize the danger of premature hostilities with
Britain, France considered it imperative to reach some
understanding between the two colonial powers. The
resulting entente of 1904 removed one source of friction
by recognizing British predominance in Egypt and French
rights in Morocco.

These same forces that were driving the European
powers and Japan to enter into regional agreements did
not fail to affect the United States, which was emerging
as an Asia-Pacific power while consolidating its leading
position in the Caribbean. Russia wanted the United
States as a check against Japan in Asia, and Germany
sought to restrain Britain in Europe and Latin America
by using the United States as a potential partner. It
was Britain, however, that took specific steps to obtain
American understanding and co-operation in the Western
Hemisphere and Asia. British efforts were successful,
and by the beginning of the twentieth century, the two
countries became associated in various policy questions
to a far greater extent than ever before. British

rapprochement with the United States, it is true, had
started during the 1890s, but it had been largely
confined to recognizing American prerogatives in the
Caribbean. This policy continued, and Britain deferred
to American wishes concerning Panama, Venezuela and
other matters. It was considered necessary, in view of
the fluctuations in European politics, to remove chances
of friction with the United States in the Western
Hemisphere, even to the point of recognizing the region
as an American sphere of influence. Anglo-American
accord would enable Britain to reduce its naval force in
the Caribbean, just as the Japanese alliance meant that
its Asiatic contingents could be moved elsewhere.

Britain, however, was desirous of obtaining American
understanding not only in the Western Hemisphere but
also in Asia. From London's point of view, an Anglo-
American entente in Asia, coupled with the Japanese
alliance, would contribute immensely to preserving the
status quo in China and the rest of the area, thus
enabling Britain to concentrate its diplomatic efforts
and strategic planning on other parts of the world.
Ultimately, moreover, the pattern of Anglo-American
association might be extended even to these regions, and
the United States might develop its world policy in
close co-operation with Great Britain. This was the
hope of some officials in London, although at that time
few visualized active American involvement in Europe,
the Middle East or Africa.

At the turn of the century, then, the United States
found itself washed by various currents of imperialist
politics. Some redefinition of its role in world affairs
was called for, especially in connection with British
overtures for an entente. Its policies in the Caribbean
and Asia were fairly well established by 1904, as we
have seen, but there remained the question of American-
European relations, particularly with regard to the role
of the United States in the diplomacy of imperialism.

American opinion of European politics at that time
was affected by the imperial and colonial experiences
following the Spanish-American War. With a few
exceptions, those who favored the country's overseas
expansion tended to support the idea of a pro-British
foreign policy. There were a number of reasons for this.
Such supporters of imperialism as John Hay and
Alfred Thayer Mahan were persuaded through geopolitical
reasoning that considerations of power politics made it
inevitable for the United States to act closely with
Britain. Otherwise, the long reign of British supremacy
would be challenged, most likely by Germany or Russia,

and the balance of power that had sustained world
politics for decades would fall into disequilibrium.
Mahan, in particular, expressed his convictions in his
'The Problem of Asia' (1900), which summed up
geopolitical thinking on international affairs. The
world, he argued, was an arena of contest between sea
and land powers, the former led by Britain and the
latter by Russia. Continued stability of the international system required that the sea powers remain
preponderant. For this reason, Mahan called upon the
United States to act as one of the sea powers in close
collaboration with Great Britain. He was particularly
concerned over the future of Asia, especially China,
since such a huge land mass under the control of Russia
would definitely bring about a shift in the world balance
of power. The sea powers, then, must co-operate to
prevent China from being absorbed into the Russian
empire. American expansion into the western Pacific
was opportune from such a point of view. The United
States should not hesitate to work together with the
British empire in furthering the two powers' influence
in that part of the world.

Mahan had also an ideological affinity with Britain
which he shared with other proponents of Anglo-American
understanding. In the above book, he discussed the
Asian problem not only in geopolitical terms but also
in the context of the Westernization of Asia, in
particular China. The incorporation of the mass of
Chinese, he wrote, 'into our civilization, to the spirit
of which they have hitherto been utter strangers, is
of the greatest problems that humanity has yet had to
solve.' (27) In Mahan's view, 'our civilization' was
defined essentially as Anglo-Saxon civilization, which
he distinguished from Slavic civilization. He in fact
characterized the latter as Asiatic, so that the
Westernization of China would be a way of preventing
Russian influence from retaining its hold upon the rest
of Asia. England was a foremost representative of
Anglo-Saxon civilization, but the United States should
do its share in the common task.

There were more explicitly imperialist types of
affinity which writers found between Britain and the
United States, providing them with a rationale for
supporting a policy in favor of British imperialism and
world policies. Of all the colonial powers, Britain
appeared to be the one that might serve as a model for
America's own imperial experience. The British empire
impressed observers as an epitome of efficiency and
organizational skill, and its colonial service an

enviable institution for training young Englishmen for
work overseas. Articulate American opinion overwhelmingly
supported British policy during the Boer War, indicating
that because of their own colonial ventures, Americans
were finding it reassuring to have Britain as a point of
reference. As Theodore Roosevelt said, 'I feel it is
to the interest of civilization that the English-speaking
race should be dominant in South Africa, exactly as it is
for the interest of civilization that the United States
themselves, the greatest branch of the English-speaking
race, should be dominant in the Western Hemisphere.' (28)
The idea here was that the two countries, sharing so much
in common, should act together, or support one another,
in the interest of world order and stability. These
were the very concepts which the exponents of expansion in
Britain had developed in the last decades of the nineteenth century. Americans now had little hesitation
in appropriating the vocabulary of British imperialism.
They were coming to accept British perceptions of the
world with greater and greater ease and even eagerness.
One obvious corollary was the readiness with which they
would support an explicitly pro-British foreign policy.

The growing pro-British orientation of American
thinking was abetted by the cooling off of American
relations with Britain's European rivals, in particular
Germany and Russia. While Mahan considered the former
at least potentially a naval power which might join other
sea powers in coalition against Russia, the turn of the
century saw the erosion of a once pro-German sentiment
in the United States. This was due to the conjunction of
events that took place in rapid succession and
simultaneously with America's emergence as a colonial
power. The unusually keen interest shown by the American
press in the Chinese question in the winter of 1897-8,
as noted earlier, had a strongly anti-German component
in so far as the German seizure of Tsingtao and Kiaochow
had triggered the scramble for bases and spheres of
influence in China. Three years later, the Kaiser was
roundly condemned for taking a harsh stand during the
Boxer crisis. These reports, reinforced by the allegedly
unfriendly attitudes of the German naval commander in
Manila harbor during the Spanish war and by the German
participation in the blockade of Venezuela in 1902,
definitely brought about the worsening of American-German
relations. Although these specific instances did not
apply to Russia, the latter, too, was viewed as hostile
toward the United States. Such an image was very often
a product of a view of civilization which assigned a
lower status to Russia. Writers generally shared Mahan's

characterization of that country as Oriental and
therefore backward, a threat to the progress of
civilization. In terms of world politics, the need for
Russian friendship, quite strong during the Civil War,
was disappearing because of the improved relations with
Great Britain. The United States and Britain seemed to
be standing together in Asia against further Russian
encroachment.

The development of pro-British sentiment did not mean,
however, that there was widespread support for a policy of
co-operation with Britain in world affairs. John Hay
wrote in 1900, 'If it were not for our domestic politics,
we should join with England, whose interests are identical
with ours, and make our ideals prevail.' (29) As such
a remark indicates, the government was not persuaded
that an openly pro-British foreign policy was domestically
feasible. In part this was because of the persistence
of the traditionalist and idealistic strains in American
thinking. Former President Cleveland restated traditional
nationalism when he wrote in 1902, 'The popular
apprehension of the evils of aggressive expansion, and
its incompatibility with what has always been regarded as
safe Americanism, is constantly growing and cannot fail to
become, in the near future, a most important factor in the
political thought of our people.' (30) Such an attitude
would shun innovation and adventurism in foreign policy.
So would the type of idealistic nationalism which Bryan
had embodied during the 1890s. While he spoke less and
less on foreign affairs, his basic attitude, when he was
called upon to express it, remained the same. He would
oppose involvement in power politics as not only
unnecessary but evil, an embodiment of Old World vice.
He still felt that the United States stood for different
principles from those that would pursue geopolitical
goals, and that simple virtues of morality and love
should suffice as guides to the country's foreign policy.
When he left for a tour of Europe in 1904, his basic
objective was not to study European politics first hand,
but to meet Leo Tolstoy in order to exchange with him
visions of an ideal world.

Others resisted pro-British foreign policy for special-
interest or for geopolitical reasons. Irish Americans
continued to be sensitive to any appearance of a change
in the policy of non-entanglement overseas, since it could
only imply a rapprochement with Britain. The more some
leaders became self-consciously pro-British, defining
American society as Anglo-Saxon and identifying themselves
with their counterpart in England, the more determined
grew Irish politicians, journalists, and labor union

leaders to try to maintain America's separate existence
and oppose co-operation with Britain in the international
arena.   The extent of their influence cannot be stated
precisely, but at least they were successful in
reinforcing the impression that the American people
would not tolerate any kind of close understanding with
Britain.   In negotiating with Ambassador Pauncefote over
such issues as Canadian fishery rights and the Alaska-
Canadian boundary, Secretary of State Hay was acutely
conscious of the pressure to resist compromise, since
it would only alienate non-English groups in the United
States.

On more geopolitical grounds, a minority disagreed
with the anti-Russian orientation of most writers as
they discussed America's role in international affairs.
Senator Beveridge, for instance, was an outspoken
supporter of an entente with Russia.   In his book,
'The Russian Mastery,' which he published in 1903 after a
world tour, Beveridge found much in common between
Russia and America: their frontier life, openness, and
'democratic' outlook.   Most fundamentally, however, he
was concerned with trends in world power politics.   At
a time when British power was supreme and was seeking
further to extend itself, Beveridge considered it foolish
to try to befriend that country.   Rather, Russia and
America had much to gain by standing together, especially
in Asia where Britain was trying to establish its
hegemony in alliance with Japan.   An Asia under British-
Japanese control would be forever closed to American
goods and influence.   The United States, he said, should
co-operate with Russia to undertake Asian development.
The Russian market for American goods alone, he added,
would be sufficient to justify such a policy.

Actual United States policy was generally more pro-
British than earlier, but it did not involve any
spectacular initiative on its part to develop a world
strategy.   Rather, the Roosevelt administration sought
to protect American interests by taking advantage of the
evolving patterns of international relations, without
defining a bold new role for the United States in world
politics.   The result was that during the years
immediately following the Spanish-American War, the
country still remained an unknown quantity in the drama
of European 'Machtpolitik.'

The international environment was actually quite
favorable to the United States to ensure the protection
and promotion of national interests with a minimum of
effort.   British solicitude for American understanding
was especially valuable in settling some outstanding

disputes between the two countries in America's favor.
The most important among them was the Alaskan-Canadian
boundary question. Although it involved Canada and
therefore made it difficult for the British government
to make concessions to the United States at the expense
of Canadian nationalism, in the end London was forced
to sacrifice the latter's pride in order to ensure the
former's understanding. The Roosevelt administration
was so certain of obtaining British compliance with the
American definition of the boundary - simply put, the
United States insisted on defining the 'Alaskan panhandle'
to include mouths of bays and inlets, whereas Canadians
sought to exclude Americans from such harbors - that it
indulged in some unsubtle tactics. Armed forces were
sent to push the American claim, and when in 1903 the
two countries agreed on arbitration, Roosevelt appointed,
as one of the American representatives, Senator Lodge,
an outspoken exponent of Alaskan expansionism. Even
Secretary Hay was adamant, exclaiming, 'If the Tribunal
should disagree [the President] will feel that he has
done his utmost, and will make no further effort to settle
the controversy. He will hold the territory, as we have
held it since 1867, and will emphasize the assertion of
our sovereignty in a way which cannot but be disagreeable
to the Canadians.' (31) In the event, no such drastic
measure was necessary, as the commission of arbitration,
consisting of three Americans, two Canadians and one
Englishman, voted four to two in favor of the American
contention. The British representative, Lord Alverstone,
sided with the Americans, an indication that Roosevelt,
Lodge and Hay were correct in assuming that Britain was
so desirous of American understanding that it would
yield on the Alaskan question.
    The satisfactory settlement of the boundary dispute,
coupled with the successful negotiations to terminate
the Clayton-Bulwer treaty and to end the European
blockade of Venezuela, demonstrated that the international
environment was favorable to the United States to assert
and expand its interests and influence in the Western
Hemisphere. Likewise, in Asia and the Pacific, British
policy was such as to enable the United States to look
after its interests without the burden of itself
engaging in power politics. American commercial
interests in Manchuria and China appeared threatened
by Russian penetration southward after the Boxer affair,
but the United States had to do very little by itself
besides identifying its policy with that of Britain and
Japan. These countries were entering into a partnership
in order actively to oppose Russian policy, and American

interests could be protected in the process. In naval
strategy, too, some sort of harmony was assumed to exist
among the navies of Britain, Japan and America. In the
Pacific Ocean the potential danger was perceived to lie
in German naval power, and in the Sea of Japan the
Russian navy seemed to be the major obstacle to the
safeguarding of American commerce. Under the
circumstances, developments in world politics all but
ensured an environment in which the United States would
stand together with Britain and, to a lesser extent,
Japan, without ever having to enter into a closer
relationship.

   Roosevelt's strategy, then, was to maintain a foreign-
policy orientation that assumed a basic harmony of
interests with these countries. But he did not want
to go a step further at this time and to impress the
United States more firmly upon international politics.
Rather, he concentrated on building up American naval
power and consolidating the country's hold upon
Central America. Toward European politics he would be
diffident, taking advantage of shifts and turns in the
balance of power to accommodate the national interest,
but he would not directly intervene. As his first
administration came to an end in 1905, then, the
United States was definitely the leading American power,
and it was also defining itself as an Asia-Pacific
power. But it could not be called a European or a
Middle Eastern power. In these regions the basic thrust
of American policy was still economic, concerned with
the promotion of commercial and other activities rather
than with power politics. But already in 1905 there were
indications that the external environment was fast
changing, and that the United States would be forced
sooner or later to clarify its position as a world
power.

Chapter 5

Co-operation and Competition

In a few short months, remarked President McKinley in
1900, 'we have become a world power.' (1) Obviously
impressed with the abrupt transformation of his country
in the world arena, he, like so many of his countrymen,
sought to define what the world-power status entailed.
The idea that America was 'a great power' went back to
Alexander Hamilton, but now the term most often used
was 'world power.' As Archibald Cary Coolidge, professor
of diplomatic history at Harvard University and one of
the most influential writers on international affairs,
wrote in 1909, 'Twenty years ago the expression "world
power" was unknown in most languages; today it is a
political commonplace, bandied about in wide discussion.'
(2) In trying to articulate just what the term implied,
McKinley could only think of added prestige accruing to
the country as a possessor of the new status. If, he
said, the United States had only taken a coaling station
or an island instead of the entire Philippines, thus
presumably stopping short of becoming a world power,
'we would have been the laughing stock of the world ...
I know ... with what added respect the nations of the
world now deal with the United States.' (3) At the
mundane level, this meant that American lives and
interests overseas would be better protected because
they counted for more now that their country was regarded
as a world power. But even the attainment of these
practical benefits implied that such things as national
prestige, respectability and influence went hand in hand
with power, and therefore that world-power status was
a valuable asset to possess.
     A key to the understanding of the ramifications of the
concept of world power is the generally accepted
assumption that only a handful of nations had achieved
that status. These were the powers; according to

Coolidge, the world powers were nations 'which are
directly interested in all parts of the world and whose
voices must be listened to everywhere.' (4) The view
that the United States had attained that status
necessitated, therefore, a conception of international
relations, an image of the world to accommodate that fact.
There were thus two levels of international relations:
intra-power relations and those between a great power and
a lesser country. By emerging as a world power, the
United States had to define its policies and attitudes
toward these two groups of countries. Common to both
types of relationships, however, was the assumption
that the great powers had certain 'responsibilities' to
maintain peace, law and order throughout the world.
World peace and stability seemed to depend both on an
equilibrium among the great powers and on a degree of
control over less civilized peoples. The strong nations
were engaged in a struggle for power among themselves,
but at the same time they had some sort of collective
responsibility; a common burden, to work for the
maintenance of peace, order and stability in all parts
of the globe. In this way, the idea of world power
entailed a concept of international politics in which
the themes of competition and co-operation were subtly
interwoven. The major countries were related to one
another both in terms of military, political and economic
competition, and of collective responsibilities to
preserve the international system as a whole. That
system contained a host of unstable regions and
irresponsible governments, and it was incumbent upon
the stronger powers to try to prevent such de-stabilizing
and de-equilibrating influences from gaining an upper
hand. As a world power, the United States would both
compete and co-operate with other world powers.
    In the years of Roosevelt's second presidency
(1905-9), such a dual characteristic of American foreign
affairs became clearly visible. Having, during his first
administration, ensured the establishment of United
States predominance in the Caribbean region, President
Roosevelt was ready to venture into the realm of world
politics. As a major power, the United States would
inevitably engage in competition with other powers, but
at the same time it would play a role commensurate with
its status, to contribute to world peace and stability.
One may study the evolution of American diplomacy in such
a framework through two notable examples: estrangement
from Japan and friendship with Great Britain. While
these were never simplistic phenomena susceptible of
mono-causal explanations, they illustrate the kinds of

challenges as well as opportunities confronting the
United States in the age of world politics.

1   PACIFIC ESTRANGEMENT

A major challenge to American perceptions and· policies
came from Japan, and various strands of United States
foreign relations became intertwined with the emerging
crisis across the Pacific. It was as if the American
view of world politics had difficulty fitting in Japan.
Somehow in its emphasis on global co-operation, stability
and law and order, the American perception of international affairs failed to make room for the type of
relationship embodied in the growing sense of crisis
and estrangement between the United States and Japan.
Before 1904, the two countries had developed more
or less in a parallel fashion, expanding territorially
and joining the ranks of the imperialist powers in the
last decade of the nineteenth century. The two powers
nearly collided in Hawaii in 1897, but after 1898 Japan
had accepted the fact of America's Pacific empire, while
the United States accommodated Japanese penetration of
Korea and opposition to Russian ambitions into its
scheme of Asian policies. The Open Door policy defined
both America's insistence on equal commercial opportunity
in China and its reluctance to extend its territorial
control over the continent of Asia. These policies
were compatible with Japan's own objectives in the Asia-
Pacific region, and for a while after the Boxer affair,
the two countries pursued similar goals in trying to
resist further Russian expansionism. Virtual, if not
actual, co-operation characterized their mutual relations
in this period.
Throughout these years, contact between the two
countries remained fairly superficial, and Americans were
not particularly disturbed by trends in Japanese policy.
Whatever points of friction there were - such as
commercial rivalry or colonial competition - could be
dealt with within a framework familiar to practicians of
conventional diplomacy and of power politics. There was
little that was not susceptible of solution in ordinary
manners. Moreover, in ideological terms as well, Japan's
growth as an advanced industrial nation was generally
greeted favorably, even enthusiastically, by American
opinion.
The Russo-Japanese War (1904-5) drastically introduced
discordant elements and altered the situation. At the
level of geopolitics, to be sure, the Roosevelt

administration saw no need for a new Asian policy. At its
inception, at any event, the war between Russia and Japan
could be fitted into the existing definition of American
interests on the Asian continent. The war came about
fundamentally as a result of the clash between Russian and
Japanese ambitions, the former intent upon consolidating
its rights and interests in Manchuria, and the latter
trying to entrench its power in Korea. The two objectives
might have been reconciled by a sphere-of-influence
agreement, with Russia confining its ambitions to
Manchuria and recognizing Japanese control over the
Korean peninsula. Such an agreement would have been
similar to the British-French entente of 1904 regarding
Morocco and Egypt. Geography and psychology, however,
ruled out such a compromise in the Far East. The Korean
peninsula protruded from southern Manchuria, separating
the Sea of Japan from the Yellow Sea, and from the
Russian point of view Japan's political and military
control over Korea would pose a serious threat to
Russia's position both in Manchuria and the Maritime
Province. A demilitarized Korea seemed to be an essential
condition for the security of the Russian fleet in Asian
waters and Russian commercial enterprises in southern
Manchuria. From the Japanese point of view, on the other
hand, such a weakened position in Korea would only make
the peninsula vulnerable to Russian penetration.
Throughout 1903 negotiations were carried on between the
two governments to reconcile their differences, but in
the end the psychological factor - mutual mistrust and a
sense of inevitable conflict - proved decisive. In
Tokyo, in particular, the feeling grew that further
delays would make the solution of the Korean problem that
much more difficult. The nation's very survival seemed
to be at stake. War was the only way to prove that the
nation was still a viable entity. The Japanese attack
on Russian ships at Port Arthur on 8 February 1904,
brought the two countries to war.

These developments were neither unexpected nor
unwelcome by the United States. The latter stood to gain
by the weakening of Russian hold upon Manchuria, and it
had no objection to the consolidation of Japanese control
over Korea. As the war continued and Japan gained
victories at sea and on land, the Roosevelt administration
remained calm, generally satisfied with the turn of
events. Japan, as Roosevelt said, was fighting America's
battle in the sense that one ostensible objective of the
war was to put an end to the Russian policy of turning
Manchuria into its exclusive sphere of influence.
Moreover, the continental thrust of Japanese policy would

be perfectly satisfactory from the point of view of
American security and interests, since Japan, in the event
of victory, would be absorbed in entrenching itself in
Korea, Manchuria and China, face to face with other
ambitious powers, and thus have little time or interest
in expanding into the Pacific Ocean. Roosevelt's
conception of Pacific affairs included an image of the
ocean as an arena for assertive American action, in terms
of its territorial possessions and expanding fleet. It
did not mean American hegemony over the Pacific Ocean,
but it assumed an equilibrium among the naval powers. Too
extensive a growth of Japanese naval power would therefore
be a threat to the American position. After the
Japanese combined fleet annihilated the Russian Baltic
fleet in the spring of 1905, it was more than ever urgent
to make sure that Japan would not emerge as the
predominant power in the western Pacific. Such a
development would make American territories vulnerable
to attack.

There was thus a coherence in Roosevelt's image of
Asian-Pacific politics. He would hope to keep Japan in
check in the Pacific, but would encourage the growth of
Japanese power and influence on the Asian continent.
So long as Japan's expansionist energy was turned
westward, the two countries could maintain a relationship
of understanding on the basis of power factors. With
such an aim in view, although it was not always
articulated in this way, President Roosevelt took certain
steps to help define a new stable system of post-war
Asian politics. First, he involved himself actively in
the making of the peace treaty between the combatants. He
fully approved of Japan's terms for peace, calling for the
cession of Russian rights in Manchuria as well as the
recognition of Japanese hegemony in Korea. Neither of
these objectives seemed extravagant or incompatible with
American interests. In demanding the transfer of Russian
railways, bases and other concessions in Manchuria, it is
true, Japan was going much beyond the pre-war insistence
on a free hand in Korea, but such a redrawing of the
political map of Northeast Asia could be viewed as a
redefinition of the status quo within the framework of
imperialistic politics, not a challenge to the system
itself.

Second, President Roosevelt assured the Japanese
that he well recognized their role in that part of the
world and supported a 'Monroe Doctrine for Asia.' Given
his perception of that doctrine as it applied to American
rights and influence in the Caribbean, it is clear that he
was willing to assign to Japan the same kind of position

in East Asia which he visualized for the United States
in the Western Hemisphere. Other nations would continue
to engage in commercial and political activities in
Asia, but Japan would have an added role as the key
stabilizer, and as a power that would help the less
developed countries to transform their political and
economic lives. Third, in order to ensure peaceful
relations between Japan and the United States, Roosevelt
considered it desirable to have some understanding
regarding their respective interests in the Pacific
Ocean. He was particularly concerned with the growing
power of the Japanese navy. The Anglo-Japanese alliance
was renewed in early 1905, thus further consolidating
the two sea powers' ties in the East. Theoretically
at least, the British and Japanese navies could combine
against a third nation. The Philippines were now more
vulnerable than ever, unless Japanese ambitions could
somehow be checked and turned in the direction of the
continent. While such 'Realpolitik' considerations were
not explicitly spelled out, they were undoubtedly the
meaning of the oral understanding which Secretary of War
Taft reached with Prime Minister Katsura Tarō at the end
of July, when Taft was on a mission to Manila. The
Taft-Katsura agreement specified that Japan had no
desire for the Philippines, and that the United States
would not interfere with Japanese plans in Korea. As a
direct outgrowth of this policy, the United States
became the first country to withdraw its legation from
Seoul when, through a Japanese-Korean treaty of November
1905, Japan took over Korea's diplomatic affairs. Foreign
governments were to conduct their relations with Korea
through Japan, and they were therefore to abolish
diplomatic representation in Seoul.

Such a policy on the part of the Roosevelt
administration implied an image of Asian-Pacific affairs
in which solid understanding between Tokyo and Washington
in power terms was of fundamental importance. Such
understanding, coupled with the Anglo-Japanese alliance
and the principle of the Open Door, would, it was thought,
contribute to regional stability and development.
Clearly, China played a minor role in such a scheme of
things. It would be an object of America's and others
countries' commercial expansion, and these powers would
work out some framework for an equilibrium on the Asian
continent. But China would not be one of the responsible
civilized powers on whose co-operation peace and order
depended.

This view of China was seriously challenged by the
anti-American boycott of 1905, but the episode if anything

confirmed Roosevelt's belief in the need to deal firmly
with that country. The boycott was a product of Chinese
resentment with American immigration laws and regulations
that were discriminatory. The Age of Imperialism had,
if anything, made the matter worse for overseas Chinese
as they were considered inferior to advanced peoples
physically, mentally and morally. The racist strain in
American imperialist and anti-imperialist thought, as seen
earlier, confirmed and strengthened anti-Chinese
practices in the United States, where Chinese were often
arbitrarily denied entry, subjected to humiliating
searches and arrests, and castigated by labor unions
and other groups for their way of life. Such practices,
however, now encountered the opposition of nationalistic
Chinese opinion.

The period immediately after the Boxer affair saw the
appearance of what may be termed 'modern' viewpoints in
Chinese policy and opinion, and one of their earliest
targets was the United States. At the policy level,
Ch'ing officials considered it imperative to recover
rights lost to foreigners and to carry on active
diplomacy to take advantage of potential and actual
conflicts among the imperialist powers. Such efforts
were supported by public opinion which emerged in China
at this time. Although not quite the equivalent of
public opinion in a Western democracy, Chinese students,
journalists, merchants, and gentry self-consciously
proclaimed their voice as that of the public and
portrayed themselves as the bridge between state and
society. They published newspapers and periodicals,
organized mass meetings and demonstrations, and
agitated for local assemblies to institutionalize
popular opinion as part of the decision-making process.

Although officials and opinion leaders were not
always in agreement, they both showed remarkable
interest in foreign affairs during the Russo-Japanese
War. After all, a foreign war was being fought on
Chinese soil, and the powers appeared more concerned
with protecting their own rights than with China's
sovereignty. With such aroused sensitivity, it was not
surprising that consideration should have been given to
transforming Chinese relations with the United States.
Some advocated closer ties between the two countries.
Yüan Shih-k'ai, for instance, was coming to the view that
American support was going to be very important if China
were to maintain its sovereign rights, especially in
Manchuria. On the other hand, many officials considered
the United States a suitable object of the 'rights
recovery' policy, which at this time involved efforts to

get back railroad and mining rights that had been granted to foreigners as concessions. Americans had obtained a right to build a railroad between Canton and Hankow, but only a few miles had been built and the concession stood as a symbol of foreign power: concessioneering for its own sake even when there was no intention of making good the rights obtained. As was to be the case in Mexico after 1917, China would insist that Americans give up such concessions unless they were willing to implement their terms.

By far the most spectacular development in 1905, however, was the anti-American boycott, lasting from spring to the end of the year. Carried out in various coastal cities, the movement was an expression of nationalistic opinion as well as a test of whether it could be effectively organized. The boycott had little official support, and some, notably Yüan, suppressed it as it ran counter to his advocacy of American friendship and support against other powers. For that very reason, the movement was significant; it was a manifestation of public sentiment which found some organizational expression as a new force in Chinese politics. Henceforth, no government in China nor foreign power would be able to ignore it.

American policy under Roosevelt was based on the assumption that China was weak and irresponsible, an assumption that was clearly challenged by the boycott movement of 1905. Still, President Roosevelt saw nothing in it that would compel him to alter his image of Asian politics. If anything, the anti-American movement and the apparent unwillingness of the Chinese officials to suppress it, if not their tacit encouragement of the boycott, confirmed his view of China. The only plausible response to such a situation, therefore, was to demonstrate American determination to protect its merchants and their interests. The United States would hold Ch'ing officials accountable for the protection of American rights, and should they fail to do so, warships would be dispatched as a show of will. Likewise, Roosevelt insisted that the American concession to build a Canton-to-Hankow railroad not be given up. Such action would indicate lack of determination on the part of the United States to maintain its rights and interests in China. Finally, to the overtures from some quarters in China to seek an understanding with the United States, the government in Washington turned deaf ears. It was not interested in playing power politics with China at the expense of the overall framework of imperialist diplomacy in the Far East.

At the geopolitical level, then, the United States would conduct its Asian policy in a framework that was comprehensible and acceptable to Japan, rather than trying to find a new basis for a balance of power through some positive action in China. To that extent, neither in the Pacific Ocean nor in the Asian continent was there a serious conflict between Japan and the United States. The two countries seemed headed for a continued period of understanding and harmony.

Such, however, did not prove to be the case. Within less than two years after the conclusion of the Russo-Japanese War, there was growing talk of war between the United States and Japan. The crisis was the first of its kind in the annals of American diplomacy, entailing a serious, seemingly unmanageable problem that could not be easily resolved in a conventional manner. Fundamentally, the crisis involved the confrontation of two major powers across the Pacific, representing different races, cultures and traditions. While this would be true of American relations with Mexico, or Japanese relations with Russia and other Western countries, the sense of tension and conflict was greater between the United States and Japan because of their simultaneous emergence as expansionist world powers, and in particular because of the immigration dispute which touched all aspects of their relations: economic, social, racial, as well as military.

The immigration dispute became a serious issue between the two countries because it was not merely a matter involving the mistreatment of a few thousand Japanese by a handful of American groups. Rather, it came to affect all other aspects of American-Japanese relations and developed as a symbol of the two countries' ability or inability to work out a framework of harmony and understanding as they emerged as the leading Pacific powers.

Numerically, Japanese residents in the United States were not at all conspicuous. Only about 50,000 of them lived in America, mostly on the West Coast, at the time of the Russo-Japanese War. But they were highly visible in various cities, where they worked as merchants, laborers or 'school-boys.' As recent arrivals, they were a tightly knit group, with their own associations, forums and newspapers. Most important, however, was not so much what they themselves said or did, but what other Japanese wrote about them. According to the then prevailing ideology of Japanese expansionism, these immigrants in America were the spearhead of the country's limitless expansionist activity which was to result in

the creation of 'new Japans' everywhere on the globe.
Writers spoke of 'the new Japan in North America,'
envisioning the establishment of a community of
cosmopolitan Japanese who would settle and develop the
Pacific coast economically and culturally, so that the
region would become a bridge between East and West.
The result would be not only to benefit Japan economically
but also the cause of world civilization. Japanese
and Americans, one author noted, 'are the most progressive
peoples in the world today.' Accordingly, the coming
of Japanese to the United States and their association
and co-operation would surely advance peace, prosperity
and harmony, and serve as an example of internationalism
to the rest of the world. (5)

The depth of the feeling of dismay, frustration and
ultimately anger felt by Japanese, not only on the West
Coast but even more strongly in Japan, toward the
mistreatment of their countrymen by some Americans in
California during 1905-6, can be fully understood only
when one takes such background factors into consideration.
Contrary to the romantic image of Americans welcoming
the coming of thousands of Japanese with open arms,
especially now that the Japanese nation was proving
itself superior to Russia, a Western country, the
Russo-Japanese War conincided with the appearance of a
powerful anti-Japanese movement in California. Even
before the end of the war, various groups, such as
labor unions, political parties and ad hoc bodies, began
calling for an end to Japanese immigration. They
considered the Japanese a threat to American standards
of living and ways of life. While this was the argument
that had been used against Chinese workers, there was
now a sense of urgency because of Japanese victories over
Russia. It was feared that after the war the Japanese,
feeling self-confident and arrogant, would emigrate en
masse to the United States. Discharged officers and
soldiers would especially find it attractive to settle
in America instead of going back to the less affluent
homeland. They could never be assimilated into American
life, and would thus remain an alien element, secretly
if not overtly retaining their allegiance to the
Emperor and without any intention of becoming American
citizens. But even if they should seek naturalization,
they should not be permitted to become citizens since
they would come to outnumber white Americans, as had
threatened to happen in Hawaii. The West Coast, and by
implication the rest of the country, could not afford
the luxury of multiracial living. The United States
already had enough racial problems, and it had every

right to insist on retaining a certain racial characteristic.

The enumeration of such types of argument against Japanese immigration makes it clear that the movement had a much wider appeal than just to local groups on the West Coast. If it had been a purely localized issue, it would not have caused much damage to the geopolitically defined relationship between the two countries. But the anti-Japanese campaign gained momentum as it seemed to affect various aspects of United States foreign affairs and thus question the assumption of the Roosevelt administration that stability and harmony could be maintained in American-Japanese relations.

First of all, the traditional concern with national security and commercial interests was involved because of a particular perception of Japanese immigrants. They were viewed by concerned Americans not merely as foreign laborers who came to work for larger pay but rather as agents of a foreign government intent upon establishing positions of influence within the United States. Similar ideas were held regarding Japanese in Hawaii and the Philippines, thus creating an image of the Japanese as loyal subjects of the Emperor who would never shake off their patriotic commitments and continue to work for their country even after they reached American soil. The most extreme of this type of suspicion held that Japanese immigrants were in fact thinly disguised spies, sent by the military to collect intelligence material that would be useful in the event Japan should decide to attack the United States or its territory. The White House, the State Department and the War Department constantly received reports of suspicious-looking Japanese who appeared to be secretly surveying a strategic area or sketching army forts. Japanese who were employed by railroads or in private businesses could not be trusted; some of them might be scheming to take over control of transportation and commercial systems in parts of the country. The fact that Americans conveyed such reports from all over the United States indicates the widespread acceptance of the image of the Japanese immigrant as at worst a spy, and at best a loyal subject of his government doing what he was told to do in preparation for an eventuality. All of a sudden, there was the fear that the country's peace and security were being compromised.

The suspicion seemed justified in view of the growing military power of Japan. Although the Roosevelt administration sought a geopolitical solution, chances of

friction could not be altogether ruled out, any more than
similar chances could be disregarded vis-à-vis other
powers. Even so, there was no idea that Germans or
Italians or Englishmen in the midst of American society
were secret agents of their governments. In order for
Americans to have an exaggerated notion of the threat
posed by Japanese in the United States, another factor
had to play a crucial role. This was the racial,
cultural or psychological factor derived from the fact
of Japan's being an Asian nation. This was the first
time that Americans came face to face with an image of
an impending crisis with Japan, and because Japanese
were Orientals, representing something unfamiliar and
therefore sinister, tension and fear were all the greater.
There was a sense of unpreparedness; the American people
were not ideologically and psychologically prepared to
cope with a potentially hostile alien force which
represented a different culture and tradition. It is
interesting to note that many Americans, from the
highest officials to private citizens, tried to
generalize about Japanese character in order better to
understand the nature of the impending crisis. According
to Secretary of State Root, the Japanese 'are particularly
sensitive about everything which questions [their]
equality; one-tenth of the insults which have been
visited upon Chinese by the people of the United States
would lead to immediate war.' The Japanese government,
he went on, 'always conducts its affairs like a military
commander planning a compaign and it has extraordinary
capacity for prompt and sudden action. If they see that
the tendency of events is going to lead to war, they will
not hesitate an instant to bring it on at the time most
favorable to them.' The picture of Japanese discipline
and cohesiveness was shared by virtually all who
expressed their concern over the deteriorating situation.
A man wrote President Roosevelt from Los Angeles that
Japanese on the West Coast were fast acquiring all
necessary information for making war. 'They are silent,
sly, inquisitive, and toward Americans inclined to be
sullen ... They are observers of "every foot of ground"
so to speak, from Alaska to South Dakota.'
   Couched in such ways, the language of Pacific
estrangement revealed awareness that the United States
was dealing with a different culture, not simply with
another military power. It was not surprising, then,
that many spoke of the American-Japanese tension in
terms of the confrontation of two civilizations, two
races, and two ways of life. As an editorial for the
'San Francisco Call' put it, 'the irreconcilable conflict

between occidental and oriental civilizations' was the root of the California immigration crisis. The two civilizations simply could not mingle, and the purity of Western civilization must be maintained by excluding non-Westerners from coming to America. Archibald Cary Coolidge was more blunt and noted that the basic problem was the question: 'Is the future population of the Pacific coast to be white or is it to be Oriental?' Proceeding from the assumption that 'white men and Mongolians cannot live side by side in the same land,' Coolidge justified the decision by Americans to 'reserve territory for the people of their own blood.'

In this way, the immigration dispute developed into a wholesale debate on the nature of American relations with Japan. From various angles observers noted the incompatibility of the two countries and therefore the impossibility of obtaining a stable relationship along traditional lines. This was, of course, profoundly disturbing from the point of view of Japan, interested as it was in maintaining an understanding with the United States while undertaking expansion in all directions. It was as if the latter were not recognizing Japan as a great power of equal status. If it could not expand in certain directions, if it could not carry on the task of establishing 'new Japans' throughout the world, then it would not be playing the same role as the Western powers. For this reason, Japanese felt humiliated, and some of them talked of revenge.

For the time being, however, both Washington and Tokyo were eager to avoid a calamitous showdown. They could not easily settle the immigration issue; it was insoluble, given two fundamentally opposed views concerning Japanese in the United States. But the two governments decided to 'co-operate' to prevent matters from deterioration; Japan would undertake to restrict emigration of laborers to the United States, while the latter tried to seek better treatment of Japanese already in the country. In addition, the two powers would reconfirm their geopolitical understanding regarding their territorial possessions in the Asia-Pacific region. This was the framework of the modus vivendi that was worked out during 1907-8. The solution was superficial, based on a tacit agreement that the two governments would refrain from fundamental disputes on embarrassing questions of racial and cultural diversity. Crisis was bound to recur from time to time, as foreign policy publics in both countries would never be silenced.

The immigration dispute indicated the difficulty of achieving 'co-operation' with a country that was

culturally significantly alien to America. Hitherto,
the United States had dealt with Japan politically,
economically and ideologically on American terms.   There
had been no major contradiction between these various
aspects of American-Japanese relations since Japan had
fitted into such aspects of United States foreign affairs
as power politics, commerce and missionary activities.
'Co-operation' had tended to be unidirectional.   The
immigration episode revealed that the two countries could
share basic concerns in terms of geopolitical considerations, but that American concepts of economic interdependence by means of the Open Door and commercial
expansion, or American notions about Western civilization
would not necessarily be accepted by a country like Japan.
The latter was articulating its own visions of economic
and cultural interrelationships which took account of
Japan's role to expand, not simply remaining a receptacle
of Western expansion. From the Japanese viewpoint,
economic interdependence included the right of emigration
to all parts of the world, and cosmopolitanism was to be
founded upon the meeting of East and West in actual
physical proximity. Thus the very 'raisons d'être' of
the two countries became involved. It was as much a
question of the compatibility of national cultures as of
formal policies. It is little wonder that both Americans
and Japanese said and wrote a great deal about national
character at this time. The crisis forced self-
consciousness, and the awareness of their different ways
of life and thought gave rise to some serious questioning
about the future of their relations. Obviously, an era
was passing in American diplomacy.

2   ANGLO-AMERICAN SOLIDARITY

The appearance of tension and rift across the Pacific
worried the British government. Having, at the turn of
the century, already taken steps to conciliate and
befriend the United States, officials in London were
hopeful of maintaining a framework of co-operation and
solidarity with America in international affairs. The
need was considered to be all the greater after 1905
because the implications of the Russo-Japanese War for
European politics were all too evident. British
officials were eager to establish a stable framework
of the European and colonial status quo, since Russia's
defeat by Japan could be expected to turn the attention
of the European powers to Europe, Africa, and the Middle
East, areas where Britain and Germany had many overlapping
and conflicting interests.

British officials became convinced anew of the
wisdom of maintaining American goodwill during the
Moroccan crisis of 1905, brought about by Germany's
attempt to test the strength of the entente cordiale in
safeguarding French rights in Morocco. Although the
United States had no substantial stake in that country,
President Roosevelt chose to intervene, just as he had
in the Russo-Japanese War. Basically, he wanted the
United States to demonstrate its status and role as a
world power. The European governments approached him
for support against their potential enemies, and it was
considered prudent to participate in the international
conference at Algeciras, convened by the Sultan of
Morocco, to discuss the crisis. American policy was non-
commital, siding neither with Germany nor with France,
but the very fact that its representatives participated
was an indication that American wishes and interests
could not be disregarded. The Kaiser was particularly
interested in forming a joint front with Roosevelt
against France and Britain, whom he accused of violating
the principle of the Open Door. The Algeciras
conference in fact ended up by endorsing the principle,
although it did not result in a clear-cut German victory.
Still, the episode revealed what the United States could
and might do in the future, and it seemed urgent for
Great Britain to remain on friendly terms with it lest
it should enter into special arrangements with Germany
or Russia.

British friendship simultaneously with France and with
America did not present immediate problems. But the
continuation of the alliance with Japan gave rise to
complications because of the American-Japanese crisis.
Britain still needed Japan in China and elsewhere in
Asia, at least until conditions became stabilized after
the Russo-Japanese War in such a way as to ensure the
security of the Empire. But the Japanese alliance was an
embarrassment vis-à-vis the United States which might
consider it an unfriendly instrument to isolate it.

The British dilemma was serious, but it also served to
cement ties, political and psychological, between the two
English-speaking peoples. For the triangular difficulties
involving Britain, Japan and the United States forced
officials in London and Washington to raise some
fundamental questions about the nature of their respective
foreign policies. The Liberal cabinet in London was less
enthusiastic about the Japanese alliance than the
preceding Conservative government which had negotiated
it, and Foreign Secretary Sir Edward Grey was much more
interested in amicable relations with France and with the

United States. Still, it was not considered wise to give
up the Anglo-Japanese alliance. It could be an essential
instrument for maintaining the status quo in Asia, since
no other power, not even America, was willing to commit
itself to safeguard British Imperial security. Under the
circumstances, Britain had to be on friendly terms
both with Japan and the United States.

There was no question, however, that with regard to the
immigration dispute between these two countries, Britain
would not invoke the alliance with Japan against the
United States. It would accept the Asian status quo on
the basis of the Anglo-Japanese alliance, but concerning
Japanese emigration to the Pacific territories, it would
not support Japan. In fact, it made sense to ensure the
security and racial homogeneity of the Commonwealth
countries. In this respect, British and American
policies were quite close. Just as Roosevelt hoped that
Japan's continentalism and the 'Monroe Doctrine for Asia'
would preoccupy that country's postwar energies, thus
minimizing chances of friction in the Pacific or on the
American continent, Grey was convinced that Japanese,
Americans, Canadians and other members of the British
Empire could maintain cordial relations so long as
Japanese expansion was directed toward the Asian
continent. As Grey wrote in 1908,

> the people on the Pacific side of North America had
> very greatly over-rated the possible danger from
> Japan. They had worked themselves up into a belief
> that the Japanese Government had a deep design for
> the annexation of some part of the Pacific coast,
> and that they were preparing the way for this by
> large settlements of Japanese. I was sure the
> Japanese Government never had any such intention.
> On the contrary, they did not wish their people to
> cross the Pacific at all. They wished very much to
> keep them nearer home, in order to strengthen their
> position in Korea and their trade in Manchuria. (6)

This was a theme the British foreign secretary repeatedly
mentioned to American and Canadian officials in order to
allay their suspicion of Japan and fear of Japanese-
American altercations involving Britain and its empire.
Nevertheless, he was alive to the dangerous implications
of such suspicions. As he wrote to Lord James Bryce,
'the Pacific slope is in a state of high fever, and what
I fear is that suspicion may arise among the people
that, when the pinch comes, we shall not support them in
resisting Japanese immigration. Should such a suspicion
get hold of them, there would be no limit to the untoward
political consequences which might ensue.' Grey had in

mind the possibility that Canada and the United States might join in a common cause and become alienated from Britain.   Should the immigration dispute ever lead to such a critical point, the Foreign Office had no hesitation to affirm Britain's support of the positions taken by these countries. (7)

Shortly after he took over as foreign secretary, Grey wrote to Ambassador Durand in Washington,

I hope that a bond of union between ourselves and the United States will be found ... in our tendency to take the same view of events in the world generally.   If the two countries think alike about public events, they will be found acting together in foreign countries where they have mutual interest; and even where only one of them is interested, its policy and action will be understood by the other. ... What I should like to hear from you ... is, what are the subjects of foreign policy which are interest- ing to the American mind most, and what is their point of view and outlook on things which are taking place in the world?   I am anxious to keep in touch with American feeling and especially with the President. (8)

This was a good example of official British thinking at the time; one of the key principles of the country's foreign policy was to 'take the same view of events in the world' as the United States - a principle which in turn was related to the hopeful assumption that 'the two countries think alike'.   The Japanese-American crisis demonstrated that the assumption was not quite realistic, but certainly the Foreign Office did all it could 'to keep in touch with American feeling' in order to prevent a serious collision in the Pacific.

Although Ambassador Durand did not respond directly to Grey's query - 'what are the subjects of foreign policy which are interesting to the American mind most?' - he noted that Americans 'are curiously ignorant of foreign countries.   Many of them seem to think the world practically began with the Declaration of Independence, and to look upon "the effete monarchies of Europe" much as we look upon Persia'.   Durand was undoubtedly right to point out the general lack of interest in external events on the part of the American public.   The size of the attentive foreign policy public in the United States may have actually shrunk after around 1905, although the Japanese crisis of 1906-7 would soon reawaken and revitalize consciousness of foreign affairs.   To the extent that there were individuals and groups concerned with these matters, Durand was able to report that 'in

general the feeling towards England has become much more
friendly since the Spanish war, and is steadily
improving'. As for President Roosevelt, the ambassador
reported in January 1906 his remark that 'he regarded
England to be the one country with which America ought
to be in terms of close and confidential friendship'. (9)
    Durand's reports and observations accurately reflected
one prominent feature of American thinking at the time.
Britain's interest in acting together with the United
States throughout the world was reciprocated by an
administration in Washington which took 'co-operation'
very seriously, and by a people whose outlook was becoming
self-consciously more Anglo-American than ever before.
Roosevelt, to be sure, couched 'co-operation' primarily
in power terms and visualized global stability and peace
on the basis of great-power co-operation. The Japanese
immigration crisis, however, convinced him that there
were some qualitative differences between America's
relations with Japan and with Britain. Whereas with the
former the United States might maintain a stable relationship on the basis of a regional status quo, with the
latter co-operation entailed similar definitions of
economic interests as well as common cultural outlooks.
Thus both Britain and America would pursue an Open Door
policy without including the principle of open
immigration, and they would develop their respective
societies in terms of the values of Anglo-Saxon
civilization. Japanese policy was obviously at odds with
such dimensions of American and British policies.
Co-operation with Japan, then, would be more limited in
scope than was visualized for the latter two. It was this
awareness which often served to check the pessimistic
forecast that Britain and Japan might join their navies
and attack the United States. It seemed more and more
incredible that British ships would consent to carry
Japanese soldiers to invade America to turn the latter
into a haven of Oriental races. On the contrary,
Roosevelt believed that the unity of race and traditon
would keep Americans and Englishmen together as providers
of world stability and protectors of civilization.
    These ideas found eloquent expression among various
popular writers who published books and essays on the
subject of the United States as a world power.
    One of the clearest discussions of the subject was a
book by John Halladay Latañe, a historian at the
Johns Hopkins University, entitled 'America as a World
Power' (1907). By 'a world power' the author meant
much more than a nation possessed of physical, military
power. The United States, he asserted, 'has always been

a world power in a sense: as the great exponent of civil
liberty its influence has gone out to the remotest bounds
of the earth; in its dealings with other nations it has
always been an upholder of legality and an advocate of
arbitration.' Although of dubious historical accuracy,
such an assertion indicated the possibility of combining
nationalism, internationalism and geopolitical factors
to produce an image of the United States as a world power
in ideological as well as military terms. Latañe was
aware that the Spanish-American War had added weight and
prestige to America which 'has now command not only of its
own fortunes but of the fortunes of others.' In this
situation, its foreign relations had inevitably become
complex and burdensome. 'Strained relations with Japan
have already resulted, and the future doubtless has in
store burdens and responsibilities from which it is not
possible to shrink.' Even so, the author's counsel was
that the nation adhere to the 'ancient ideals of peace ...
traditional frankness and fair dealing' even as it
augmented its armed forces and added colonial possessions.
Given these ideas, Latañe's Anglo-Americanist conclusion
was not surprising:

> the course of world politics is destined to lead to
> the further reknitting together of the two great
> branches of the Anglo-Saxon race in bonds of peace
> and international sympathy, in a union not cemented
> by any formal alliance, but based on community of
> interests and of aims, a union that will constitute
> the highest guarantee of the political stability and
> moral progress of the world. (10)

The United States, in such a view, was to be a world power
that was morally oriented. More specifically, the content
of that moral orientation was defined in terms of the
pursuit of liberty, law and order. These were self-
consciously Anglo-Saxon concepts, aspects of the
combination of power and liberty that went back to the
seventeenth century but which now seemed relevant as
America groped for a role in international affairs.
Co-operation with Britain was a perfect combination of
geopolitical and idealistic considerations and functioned
as a guide to action in the world.

As an example of popular thinking on the matter, one
may consider Ernest Hugh Fitzpatrick's 'The Coming
Conflict of Nations, Or the Japanese-American War,'
published in 1909 in Springfield, Illinois. It was one
of the earliest war novels depicting an imaginary conflict
between Japan and the United States. The war, in this
novel, was couched in racial and cultural terms. 'By
their geographical positions, the United States of America

and Canada stood as a barrier between the western
civilization of Europe and the ancient civilization of
Asia.' The key to the conflict, as might be expected,
was held by Great Britain whose government, Fitzpatrick
wrote, urged the people not to take sides in the war in
view of the obligations under the Anglo-Japanese
alliance. 'The hearts of the British people were
nevertheless with their kinsmen, and they longed for a
just and proper excuse to join hands across the seas
to help to expel the invaders from American soil. Were
not the United States but an expansion of Great Britain?
An expansion of Anglo-Saxon civilization?' In this
account, the Japanese invasion of the Panama canal zone
finally brought about Britain's decision to breach the
Japanese alliance and enter into an American alliance.
This was the decisive turning point, as the British navy
destroyed the Japanese fleet, as other European powers
entered into 'modus vivendi' with Britain and observed
neutrality. 'The news of the great sea fight spread
rapidly over the world ... striking terror and
consternation into the enemies of civilization.'
Throughout England and America 'the people congregated in
churches and halls to return thanks to Providence for
the victory and deliverance from the yoke of an
oriental civilization.' Quite appropriately, the victory
was followed by a postwar system of international
relations which included a new confederation of all
English-speaking peoples. This was the aim of this
imaginary tale; the author sought to induce the readers,
as he said, 'to seriously consider the boundless and
inestimable benefits that would accrue to mankind
through this and succeeding ages by the confederation of
the English-speaking peoples of the world.' (11)

Although few at that time agreed with Fitzpatrick
that such a confederation was feasible or necessary, his
Anglo-Saxonism was considered axiomatic by policy-makers
and publicists alike. Americans and British seemed to
perceive the world similarly if not identically, and it
followed that they should co-operate as best they could in
their common interests. Even where the two countries did
not explicitly act together, it was becoming less and
less likely that their policies and outlooks would be so
divergent as to cause serious trouble. From Europe the
United States stood aloof after the Moroccan crisis, but
the years after 1906 were a period of intensive British
diplomatic initiatives, and America's virtual non-
involvement in European politics had the effect of
supporting the British definition of the status quo.
London's foreign policy was becoming more definitely

antagonistic toward Germany, and the 1907 entente between
Britain and Russia, terminating their long rivalry over
Persia and Afganistan, further served to isolate Germany.
The latter had no potential ally outside Europe, and the
Roosevelt administration did not help Germany prevent
the growing rigidity of European politics.   In Latin
America, moreover, the United States began to fear
Germany more than any other European power, as that
country's economic activities and political influence
were in the ascendant in South America and Mexico.   In
this region Britain fully co-operated with America in
accordance with the spirit of the Hay-Pauncefote
agreements.   In Asia, the two countries were more
equally involved, and there were instances of mutual
suspicion, as Americans disliked Britain's tacit
endorsement of Japan's policy in China, whereas British
officials were often exasperated by what they took to be
the naiveté of Americans in the East.   Even so, as
Henry Hoyt, counsellor for the State Department, wrote
in 1909, 'the natural alliance in the East in many cases
is between America and England.' (12)   Their co-operation
would inevitably weaken the Anglo-Japanese alliance and
benefit China through the implementation of the Open Door.
Activist American officials like Consul General Willard
Straight at Mukden energetically sought to undermine
Japan's hold upon Manchuria through working closely with
their British counterpart in China.   The efforts were not
always fruitful.   Nevertheless, investment bankers and
firms in both countries were interested in exploring
commercial opportunities in China, and the two governments
often stood together as champions of the Open Door against
Japanese policy.

   Summing up Rooseveltian foreign policy, then, it may be
said that it was derived from a view of the world as made
up of great powers which would be perpetual competitors
but which would also co-operate to maintain stability and
equilibrium in various regions of the globe.   In terms
of power, such an approach produced a geopolitical outlook
which defined America's spheres of influence in the
Western Hemisphere and parts of the Pacific Ocean.   The
Japanese crisis revealed that a power-orientated policy
was not sufficiently equipped to deal with newer problems.
By the same token, it tended to bring America and Britain
closer together than ever before.   It was left to
Roosevelt's immediate successors to define a more
comprehensive foreign policy to take account of all these
dimensions and relate the United States in more than one
way to the rest of the world.   The foreign policies of
Presidents William Howard Taft (1909-13) and

Woodrow Wilson (through 1914) may be comprehended in
such a framework.

3   THE DOLLAR DIPLOMACY

Taft was ideally fitted to provide the leadership that
was required of the country as it entered the second
decade of the post-1898 era in its foreign affairs.
Perhaps more than any other public figure in the country,
he had accumulated experience and expertise in international relations. 'I visited Japan four times,' he
remarked just before entering office, 'Siberia and Russia
once, China three times, Rome once, the Isthmus of Panama
seven times, Cuba twice, and Porto Rico once ... Such an
experience has ... given me a less provincial view of
many international questions than one is likely to have
who learns of foreign countries by books.' (13) It was
in part because of this reason that Roosevelt preferred
Taft to other Republicans as his heir apparent. Although
Taft had little experience in American politics, he had
dealt extensively with colonial peoples. It is also to be
noted that his foreign travels and missions had heavily
concentrated on the Caribbean and the Far East, areas
where he was to pursue active policies.
  Administratively, he was a rather strict constitutionalist who liked to maintain a sense of institutional
regularity and integrity, letting various organs of the
Executive branch handle their affairs in an orderly
fashion without interference by the White House. For the
State Department, he selected Philander Knox as its
head, an unfortunate choice since the latter, a
corporation attorney, had little experience in foreign
relations. The result was that much of the day-to-day
functioning of the Department devolved on its first
assistant secretary, Fred M. Huntington Wilson, a
professional diplomat who had served in Japan. He had
strong views not only about bureaucratic organization,
which led him to support and initiate the geographical
compartmentalization of the State Department, but also
about specific instances of decision-making. The
situation was thus in contrast to the Roosevelt years
when the president often took personal charge of American
diplomacy. Despite Taft's keen interest in foreign
affairs, they occupied a comparatively minor part in the
history of his administration in comparison with his
predecessor's. This may have been due to a shrinking of
the foreign policy public; diplomatic disputes were far
less frequently related to domestic politics than earlier,

and few politicians now made a career - unlike a Lodge
or a Beveridge during the 1890s - out of strong views on
external matters. Domestic affairs such as the control
over the trusts, conservation and the Negro question
became more prominent in the Taft years. Even his
speech accepting the presidential nomination in 1908
was overwhelmingly concerned with domestic matters and
only casually touched on diplomatic questions.

Nevertheless, the Taft presidency left a distinct mark
on the annals of American foreign policy, and it is
possible to discuss the period 1909-13 as having a unity
of its own. Fundamentally this was because Taft, Knox,
Wilson and their subordinates, despite their personality
differences and despite Wilson's tendency to dominate
the State Department machinery, shared an outlook on
world affairs which provided a basis for American policy.
That outlook or policy is commonly referred to as 'the
dollar diplomacy'. It is a good designation of the
Taft-Knox-Wilson approach, but it bears close scrutiny
as a definition of that particular stage in the
evolution of American diplomacy.

As the term 'dollar diplomacy' implied, the Taft
administration self-consciously pursued commercial
objectives. The rationale was simple. Espousal of
American economic interests, a nationalistic goal going
back to the eighteenth century, could now be considered
a major contribution to international peace and harmony.
After all, as Taft said, it was far better to use dollars
than bullets as means of achieving national goals.
Moreover, the world was a stage where wars were becoming
obsolete and economic interdependence more and more
apparent. American commercial interests were but aspects
of the globalization of the world economy, a trend which
was conducive to creating an atmosphere of order, harmony,
and goodwill among peoples. 'The development of commerce
and industry,' said Knox, 'and the necessary exchange of
commodities have caused nations to see that their
interests are similar and interdependent, and that a like
policy is often necessary as well for the expansion as
for the protection of their interests.' (14) In an
address delivered at the Third National Peace Conference
held in Baltimore in 1911, Huntington Wilson reiterated
the theme: 'commerce means contact; contact means
understanding; and if one is worthy enough to be
respected and liked, if understood, international
commerce conduces powerfully to international sympathy.'
The dollar diplomacy, he continued, 'means the creation
of a prosperity which will be preferred to predatory
strife ... It recognizes that financial soundness is a

potent factor in political stability; that prosperity
means contentment and content means repose.' (15)
   Such an outlook put less emphasis on geopolitics and
more on universalistic concepts. It upheld an image of
the world that was not divided geopolitically in terms
of power but was integrated through the unifying forces
of economic interests. National interests were linked
more to economic expansion than to power politics.
Peace and stability in the world would depend less on a
temporary balance of power than on the nations' pursuing
economic goals and opening up further opportunities
for expansion. Particularism would give way to
universalism. Thus compared with Roosevelt's world
policy, the Taft administration was far more interested
in universalizing American foreign relations. The
United States would be less a great military power than
a leader in promoting world order and unity through
prosperity and interdependence.
   The new approach, of course, could be just as
interventionist as Roosevelt's geopolitics. As
Huntington Wilson said,
      In these days the interests of one nation are so
      intertwined with those of all others that the
      financial recklessness or heresy of one becomes the
      peril of all. As well leave the slum to manage
      its own sanitation and thus infect the whole city,
      as to allow an unenlightened government, unopposed
      to create or maintain a financial plague spot to the
      injury of the general interest. (16)
Nations that were not reckless or heretical, then, had
the responsibility to help those that were. This was no
'old-fashioned selfish exploitation' according to Wilson,
but 'the new and sincere and practical effort to help.'
The United States would use its diplomacy to bring about
a more interrelated world in which all countries behaved
responsibly and in accordance with certain rules of
economic competition. While Theodore Roosevelt had
anticipated such a doctrine and rationalized his action
in Santo Domingo and elsewhere by using similar language,
the Taft administration went a step farther and developed
a rhetoric of American foreign policy in which national
interests and an economically interdependent world
became virtually synonymous. Special-interest groups
at home were also seen as an instrument of official policy
policy, rather than the other way round. The government
was willing to take the initiative to have these groups
serve the larger purpose of bringing about a more
orderly, stable international community.
   Given such an orientation, it was to be expected that

the United States after 1909 would be much more actively
involved in the Western Hemisphere, the Far East and
other relatively undeveloped regions than in European
politics. American relations with the countries of
Europe had developed along traditional lines, and the
new administration's economic emphasis did not alter the
picture. The United States and Europe were still the
closest economic partners, and commercial relations
among the advanced civilized countries could go on as
they had been in the past. At this time, about 60 per
cent of America's total imports come from Europe.
Compared with the situation at the turn of the century,
the relative importance of Europe as a market for
American goods was slowly but steadily declining; in
1900 the European countries purchased 74.6 per cent of
American exports, whereas the percentage for 1913 was
59.9 per cent. This relative decline was due in part to
the changing content of American export trade. Foodstuffs
which accounted for 40 per cent of the total exports in
1900 declined to only 21 per cent thirteen years later,
whereas the share of manufactured items increased from
35 per cent to 49 per cent. Since the European countries
were able to manufacture most if not all of the finished
products exported by the United States, the importance
of Europe as an American market was bound to diminish.
Even so, the steady growth of America's export trade,
which nearly doubled between 1900 and 1914, was possible
only because Europe continued to purchase commodities
made in the United States. Moreover, American financiers
were beginning to invest in Europe, and some multinational corporations were being established. Although
the United States was still a net importer of capital,
some ambitious firms such as the Standard Oil Company
were eager to set up branches and joint partnerships
in Europe. In 1912 $180,000,000 worth of direct
investments was recorded in that part of the world. This
was considerably smaller than investments in Canada,
Mexico and the rest of the Western Hemisphere. But these
were important beginnings in multinational corporations,
not just investments in raw materials and plantations
as was the case in the Western Hemisphere. All in all,
Europe remained the key to America's economic expansion.
   Because their economic ties were close and there were
few problems of outright discrimination or difficulties
resulting from cultural differences, it was natural that
America and Europe should have shown real interest in
concluding arbitration treaties. The basic idea was that
American-European relations were mostly economic, without
involving serious territorial disputes or imperialistic

rivalries, and therefore that what disputes or quarrels they had should be susceptible of peaceful solution rather than armed conflict. No civilized country should be so selfish and arbitrary that it would refuse to come to terms with another through some compromise. There should be no issue, however important in narrowly nationalistic terms, that a country could not consider for arbitration, so long as the other countries that were party to the arbitration maintained the same standards of international conduct. It was thus tautological to argue that since Britain, France and several others in Europe seemed to be at an advanced stage of development politically as well as economically, the United States could trust them to deal fairly with international disputes. In accordance with such thinking, President Taft urged the Senate ratification of arbitration treaties the United States negotiated with Britain and France in 1911. He was even willing to consider matters of 'national honor' justifiable, for he felt that the civilized countries should take the lead and offer exemplary moral conduct in identifying their respective national interests with the welfare of the whole community of nations and peace and harmony throughout the world.

There was a good deal of receptivity in America to such ideals. It is interesting to note that many of the erstwhile anti-imperialists as well as exponents of empire supported Taft's efforts to negotiate arbitration treaties. By 1909 the distinction between imperialism and anti-imperialism had become blurred, for the status of the country as a world power was a fact. Opinion leaders who had earlier divided so sharply on the Philippine question and debated so fiercely about the future of America were now eager to join forces in various peace movements. Men ranging from the anti-imperialist Andrew Carnegie and William Jennings Byran to the imperialist Nicholas Murray Butler and Elihu Root became central figures in giving moral and intellectual support to the Taft policy. They shared an evolutionist view, looking at world events in terms of the responsibilities of the civilized powers. The United States, as one such power, was considered to have a role to play to maintain peace and order in the world in co-operation with other countries. Among the most important roles was to set an example by agreeing to peaceful settlements of disputes with other civilized countries. One of the best expressions of such a viewpoint was an article in the 3 June 1911 issue of 'Outlook', where the writer made a critical comment on Homer Lea's much talked-about book,

'The Valor of Ignorance'. In that book Lea had tried
to awaken the American people to dangers facing the
nation because of their military unpreparedness. The
reviewer for 'Outlook' took issue with the book's
assumption that the nations of the world were still at a
stage of progress where only force counted and therefore
that military measures were the ultimate solution so long
as human nature remained unchanged. On the contrary,
the writer asserted,

> The world of men is moving forward from an earlier
> and savage state to a future and truly civilized
> state ... Historically, man has ... emerged from a
> lower animal condition, passed through the various
> states of barbarism ... to his present semi-
> Christianized, semi-civilized stage of development ...
> [We] are coming into that stage of society in which
> the nations are increasingly recognizing their
> international relations and looking forward to some
> form of true international unity.

In contrast to Lea's pessimism, the article expressed the
faith of some prominent American writers on international
issues that old rules of diplomacy and warfare were
becoming obsolete in an increasingly peaceful and
interdependent world. From such an idea of history it
was just a step to argue that arbitration rather than
war should be the means of solving disputes at least
among the nations that had reached the higher stages of
development. As the above article concluded, 'International arbitration assumes that certain nations have
reached such a stage of civilization that any questions
which are likely to arise between them may be safely
submitted to the judgment of an independent court in
which other nations of equal degree of civilization are
represented.' The last qualifier is important. It was
not maintained that power was no longer necessary or that
arbitration was possible with countries which a civilized
nation shared no common concepts of vital interests or
principles. Still, the emphasis on peaceful and
economically oriented international relations was a
dominant theme in American thinking at that time. The
generally favorable reviews the American press gave an
English book in the same idealistic vein, Norman Angell's
'The Great Illusion' (1909), indicates sympathy, if not
complete agreement, with such a theme. This book, too,
reiterated the idea that the time was long past when
nations could reap benefits by fighting wars. The only
profitable way of conducting in international affairs was
through peaceful competition, an idea which American
supporters of arbitration found entirely congenial.

Unfortunately for the Taft administration and the
exponents of arbitration, the United States Senate was
not willing to go along. The Senators rejected the
treaties of arbitration with Britain and France for fear
that they might usurp their treaty-making power, and
opposed an agreement that would bind the country to
arbitrate disputes without first deferring to the Senate
as to the issues to be arbitrated. From Taft's point of
view, the Senate acted irresponsibly, in consideration
only of its particularistic rights. He was also unhappy
over the Republican tariff of 1909 which lowered the
import duties to the average of 38 per cent, down
almost 20 per cent from the Dingley tariff of 1987. Even
this concession to economic expansionism was not
sufficient from Taft's point of view, who wanted to
penetrate the world's markets by taking the initiative
to lower America's own customs rates. These instances
annoyed Taft as interferences by special-interest
groups with his grand scheme of the dollar diplomacy.
All the same, they reveal the thrust of his foreign
policy with regard to the European countries. He was
ready to take them into a partnership in which they
would co-operate with the United States in increasing
the levels of international economic relations as well
as political behavior.
   It is also clear, however, that such a stand did not
impel Taft and his advisors to involve the United States
in the intricacies of European diplomacy. Although his
presidency coincided with the Balkan crisis which led
inexorably to the general European conflagration of 1914,
the United States played virtually no role in that
scenario. The story was essentially confined to Britain,
France, Germany, Austria-Hungary, Russia and Turkey, with
an increasingly rigid line of demarcation separating the
entente powers (Britain, France, Russia) from Germany,
Austria and eventually Turkey. Britain and Germany were
the respective leaders on the two sides, and the latter's
fear of encirclement coupled with Britain's determination
to prevent German control over France to break that
sense of encirclement hardened their mutual relations,
creating an atmosphere of fundamental hostility. For
that very reason Germany needed Austria as an ally and
supported the latter's ambitions in the Balkans, thus
drawing in Russia and Turkey into the vortex. Wherever
one turned, there mounted a sense of an impending crisis.
But it is possible to write the history of the coming of
the First World War with little mention of the United
States. It did not become part of a coalition in
European politics. Neither did European powers solicit

active American participation in their affairs. They
all assumed that the United States would remain aloof
from purely European questions. It was only when they
pursued various policies outside Europe that they had to
reckon seriously with American interests and proclivities.
Thus the United States during the Taft years persisted
in a non-political approach to Europe, stressing
economic relations and avoiding power considerations.
It was symbolic of the times that Lewis Einstein, a
professional diplomat, warned of a German-British war in
a book in 1912 and urged American military preparedness
to cope with a possible breakdown in the European balance
of power, but that he was never able to find a publisher
in the United States. The book was published in England,
a lone dissenting voice from America where his countrymen
would not share his concerns with power politics.

It was, then, outside Europe that Taft's dollar
diplomacy resulted in greater American involvement than
hitherto. In the Western Hemisphere, the Far East, and
to an extent in the Middle East, the administration was
anxious to implement the policy of economic expansion
and espouse the principles of orderly conduct and
political responsibility. In the Western Hemisphere, it
is true, President Roosevelt had already applied such a
policy to Panama, Cuba, Santo Domingo and Venezuela. But
he had tended to concentrate on two main objectives in
his Caribbean region: security of the canal area and the
avoidance of European interference. President Taft and
the State Department, in contrast, were eager to go
beyond such specific concerns and promote the principles
of the dollar diplomacy throughout the hemisphere. Thus
they sought the establishment of a customs receivership
in Nicaragua and Honduras, in addition to the Dominican
Republic where the Roosevelt administration had
inaugurated the system in 1905. Moreover, in order to
make such arrangements more durable, Taft was desirous
of negotiating formal treaties and having Congress approve
them, rather than establishing customs receiverships
through executive agreement.

The Nicaraguan case was rather complicated because of
its domestic crisis. The long reign of José Santos
Zelaya, viewed with growing alarm by Washington because
of his tendency to cancel foreign debts arbitrarily, came
to an end in 1910, when a revolt took place against him.
Zelaya resigned and was succeeded by José Madriz, but the
United States refused to recognize him, considering him
as no less irresponsible than Zelaya. Finally, Madriz
was overthrown by Estrada, whom Washington recognized
when he agreed to certain conditions such as the holding

of free elections and the reconstruction of Nicaraguan
finances on the basis of American loans to be secured
on customs revenues. Estrada was soon succeeded by
Adolfo Diaz, once an employee of an American firm doing
business in Nicaragua. An agreement was signed between
the new government and the United States for adjudicating
all existing loan claims held by Americans, and for
establishing a customs receivership. When Diaz's war
minister, Luis Mena, revolted, American troops were
sent to control Nicaraguan railroads, allowing only
Diaz's forces to use them. Seven American soldiers
were killed, but the presence of United States forces
was maintained in order to prevent the downfall of the
Diaz regime.

American military intervention in Nicaragua went a
step beyond Rooseveltian policy in that neither the
security of the canal zone nor alleged intervention by
European powers was involved. Rather, the United States
took action in order to restore political and financial
stability in a country that was apparently falling into
the control of reckless and irresponsible men. Zelaya
and Madriz were termed 'destructive', and Mena
'uncivilized and savage' by Taft and Knox. The United
States had a 'moral mandate,' they declared, 'to Central
America and duty to civilization,' and the country could
best discharge its moral obligations by spreading the
reign of stability and responsibility throughout the
region. (17) American bankers and financiers were an
instrument of governmental policy; they were to be used
to promote these goals through extending loans to the
Nicaraguan government under Diaz. The use of American
troops was, in view of Taft and his officials, of
decidedly minor importance. Both financiers and soldiers
were instruments of the dollar diplomacy, and if the
United States did not have to employ force, so much the
better. The goal was the establishment of workable
arrangements to provide a framework for economic
interdependence and political stability. To do so of
course necessitated dealing with a local regime that was
willing to work with the United States in this manner,
and the Nicaraguan episode demonstrated that overt
interference might become necessary to keep in power a
government that was predisposed to do so.

Elsewhere in the Western Hemisphere, the United States
under Taft tried to apply similar means to bring to
fruition the ideals of the dollar diplomacy. In Costa
Rica the State Department passed favorably on a loan
proposal by an American, Minor Keith, only after it
consulted Charles Conant, a New York financial expert, to

see whether the proposal was 'fair and reasonable as
regards the Government and people of Costa Rica, as well
as in no way detrimental to American interests.' (18)   In
Haiti the State Department objected to an international
loan scheme, in which American bankers would participate,
for reorganization of the country's finances, on the
grounds that it seemed to be unfair to the Haitian
government and people.   In Guatemala the State Department
tried to rehabilitate its finances through methods
similar to those employed in Santo Domingo and
Nicaragua, but for once it met with failure, as the
government of Estrada Cabrera was adamantly opposed to
any plan for fiscal reform.   Little was done to alter
the situation during the Taft administration.   Mexico
was also a problem because of the downfall of Porfirio
Diaz in 1911.   Although the situation inside Mexico was
considered critical, Taft did not authorize outright
military intervention by the United States.   The safety
of 40,000 Americans residing in that country was a matter
of grave concern, but the administration felt it best
to avoid reckless measures which would only exacerbate
the situation.   American forces were mobilized along the
Mexican border, but they were to desist from intervention
unless American lives in Mexico were jeopardized.   In
the meantime, as Diaz was succeeded by Francisco Madero
and the latter by Victoriano Huerta, President Taft
almost decided to recognize him, considering his regime
capable of providing law and order.   Before the final
step was taken, however, Taft was succeeded by Woodrow
Wilson in the White House.   Farther southward, the Taft
administration successfully concluded a sale agreement
with Argentina, resulting in a sale of 23 million
dollars worth of American warships to that country.   This
was but an extreme example of Washington's eagerness to
spread America's economic interests with a view to
entrenching its political influence.

In the Far East, Taft's departure from Rooseveltian
policy was even more remarkable.   The Roosevelt years
had been characterized by power-political arrangements
with Japan, coupled with the immigration crisis with
that country.   The situation was wholly unsatisfactory
from the point of view of the exponents of the dollar
diplomacy.   In Asia as elsewhere they sought to
emphasize economic and ideological aspects of international relations and to create an environment where
countries would relate to one another not in terms of
'realpolitik' experiences but of common interests and
principles.   Such a shift of emphasis meant that the
United States would now be more interested in China and

less preoccupied with problems of Japanese power and
immigration.

The coming of Taft to power coincided with a strong
movement inside and outside government to adopt a more
active policy in Asia to maximize economic opportunities
in China and enhance American influence against the
particularism of Japan and other powers. Taft himself
had been identified by American merchants and officials
in China as the one member of the Roosevelt administration
who did not entirely accept the policy of belittling
Chinese nationalism and stressing understanding with
Japan. When he visited Shanghai in November 1907,
Taft was given a rousing reception by the American
community in that city, and his visit was made an
occasion for an intensive campaigning by the community
to reinvigorate American policy. Taft's speech before
the American Association of China indicates his own
trends of thought:

> The American Chinese trade is sufficiently great to
> require the Government of the United States to take
> every legitimate means to protect it against
> discrimination or injury by the political preference
> of any of its competitors ... I am not one of those
> who view with alarm the effect of the growth of China
> with her teeming millions into a great industrial
> empire. I believe that this, instead of injuring
> trade with China, would greatly increase it ... A
> trade which depends for its profit on the backwardness
> of a people in developing their own resources ... is
> not one which can be counted upon as stable or
> permanent ... [It] is a pleasure to know and to say
> that in every improvement which she aims at, [China]
> has the deep sympathy of America, and that there never
> can be any jealousy or fear on the part of the United
> States due to China's industrial or political
> development, provided always that it is directed along
> the lines of peaceful prosperity and the maintenance
> of law and order and the rights of the individual,
> native or foreign. (19)

This was a fair summation of how Taft would think and act
toward China after 1909. The United States, he believed,
had an obligation to encourage Chinese industrialization
so that China would join the international community not
only in name, but in terms of the principles of peaceful
prosperity, law and order, and individual rights,
principles whose espousal defined the ideological and
idealistic aspect of American policy. Such a development
would tie China and the United States closer together,
create an environment of harmony and the Open Door, and
serve America's own economic interests.

Taft was not alone in thus hoping to alter the
'realpolitik' orientation of Roosevelt's Asian policy.
Young diplomats such as Willard Straight, William
Phillips, E.T. Williams, as well as Fred M. Huntington
Wilson were ardent advocates of a positive approach to
Asia, cultivating economic and political opportunities
to bind China and America together, even if this meant
alienating Japan. In their view, the growth of American
influence in China was a far more exciting prospect and
much more desirable goal to pursue than the maintenance
of a Pacific balance of power vis-à-vis Japan or the
policy of encouraging Japanese continental expansion as
part of the Asian regional scheme. As Phillips wrote in
1908, 'China is looking to us to help her out of her
difficulties ... Shall the United States use its influence
to preserve the integrity of China or shall we let
Manchuria go to Russian and Japanese influences?' (20)
This was the language not so much of power politics as
of economic and political internationalism, which had
strongly ideological and moralistic connotations. With
Phillips and others who shared such views in key
positions of the State Department under Secretary Knox,
Taft's conception of a benevolent and activist policy
toward China was certain of serious attempts at
implementation. Outside the government, one of the
most vocal and persistent spokesmen for special ties
between the United States and China was Thomas F. Millard,
a journalist of long residence in China and a close
friend of Straight's. When Taft gave the above speech
in Shanghai, Millard followed him to the rostrum and
declared,

> [We] have a hopeful interest, through commerce, in
> the enormous, the almost incalculable material
> development which the application of modern western
> influence and methods to the teeming resources of China
> is sure to bring about ... Am I going too far to
> declare that China and America need each other, that
> in some important matters their futures are
> inseparably linked? ... The time has arrived in our
> national history when our statesmanship must climb
> a lofty intellectual mountain, survey the world,
> and plan for the glorious future which the Americans
> believe stretches ahead of our country. It is not
> possible that such a survey can fail to include the
> Orient, where two-thirds of the inhabitants of the
> earth, just waking to new conditions and opportunities,
> are congregated. (21)

Millard was to continue to sound such a theme in his
writings, echoing almost exactly the ideas Taft, Knox and

other officials entertained about the prospects for
Chinese-American co-operation. The two countries seemed
standing at an opportune moment for such co-operation,
and it was America's moral obligation as well as an
economically advantageous enterprise to offer its
assistance for the development of China as a modern
industrial country, away from the domination of the
imperialist powers.

Unfortunately, the 'lofty' vision was never actualized
during the Taft administration. As Williams wrote to
Knox in 1910, 'Our policy in Manchuria has won us the
ill will of Russia, irritated Japan, and failed of support
in France and Great Britain; should we now turn back, we
shall have to count on the enmity of China also, and
reckon with a decided loss of prestige throughout the
Far East.' (22) The dollar diplomacy as applied to the
Far East was to have challenged the spheres of influence
of Japan and Russia in Manchuria, and actively
participated in loan arrangements there and in the rest
of China so as to promote a more orderly process of that
country's transformation. Specifically, the United States
undertook several measures after 1909; it sought
participation in international loans to the Chinese
government for railway construction and currency reform,
and it proposed the building of a trunk-line across
Manchuria running parallel to the South Manchuria
Railway. When that project fell through, the Taft
administration suggested a scheme for 'railway neutralization' in Manchuria, which was to create an international syndicate to enable China to buy back all
railways in the region. Obviously, such projects were
designed to involve American finance and political
influence far more extensively than hitherto in China
proper and Manchuria. They would take the United States
a step beyond John Hay's conception of economic
expansionism and establish unique ties between the two
countries.

It was not surprising that other powers would strongly
object to most of these schemes which were in fact
intended to augment American power and influence in Asia
at their expense. Japan, in particular, was an object
of the China aspect of the dollar diplomacy, Secretary
Knox declaring a desire to 'smoke Japan out from her
dominant position' in China. The projected trunk-line
in Manchuria, running between Chinchow and Aigun, would
take business away from the Japanese-controlled South
Manchuria Railway, while the neutralization scheme would
diminish Japan's special position in Manchuria which would
be opened up to foreign investments as well as to Chinese

efforts at modernization in accordance with the principles
of equal opportunity and Chinese integrity. Japan
adamantly opposed these proposals, as did Russia which
still retained the Chinese Eastern Railway and other
interests in northern Manchuria. These two countries
were so impressed with the American offensive that they
drew together and signed a protocol in 1910, secretly
dividing Manchuria into their respective spheres of
influence. With Japan and Russia thus determined to
squash American proposals, Britain and France were
unwilling to jeopardize their good relations with those
two powers. When, in February 1911, an international
banking consortium was organized by the United States,
Britain, France and Germany - a development conspicuous
by the absence of Japan and Russia from the initial
membership - London and Paris took care to ensure that
it would not impair Japanese and Russian special
interests in Manchuria.

Such opposition from the other imperialist powers
was not unexpected. What was discouraging from the
American point of view, as exemplified by Williams's
remark quoted above, was the rather lukewarm reception
of the various financial schemes by Chinese authorities.
The idea as put forth by Wilson, Straight and others was
to work closely with those Ch'ing officials who were
considered pro-American and enlist their support in
reducing Japan's and other powers' hold upon China, in
particular Manchuria. As Straight wrote to the State
Department as early as 1907, urging American trade and
investment activities in Manchuria in co-operation with
certain Chinese officials, 'by allying ourselves, at
the outset, with the officials who ... represent the most
progressive and, at the present time, most influential
party in China, we would aid them in this trying time,
and later from Manchuria as a starting point ... might
extend our influences and activity to other portions of
the Empire.' (23) And there were some high officials,
most notably Yüan Shih-k'ai, T'ang Shao-yi and Hsi-liang,
who were eager to reciprocate such overtures from the
United States. They perceived the American policy of
the Open Door as an instrument with which to counter the
dangerously expanding influences and power of Japan,
Russia and other countries in Manchuria. Some kind of
alliance between China and the United States to keep the
latter involved in Manchurian affairs seemed a good
solution to the problems besetting the Ch'ing empire.
Nevertheless, in the end little came of such proposals,
and the Chinese were disillusioned with the meager
results of American efforts in Asia.

The fundamental obstacle in the way of Chinese-
American co-operation was the domestic situation in
China. Taft's policy was designed to stabilize financial
conditions in China, promote its economic opportunities
through the Open Door, encourage educational reform and
strengthen political authority. All these had the
implication of augmenting the power of the central
government in Peking and those local officials loyal to
the Ch'ing regime. The timing was most inopportune from
the point of view of Americans who sought close ties with
Chinese, for there were serious moves within China
just at that juncture to question established authority
and resist further tendency toward political and
economic centralization. Groups in the country that
opposed the Ch'ing policy of centralization were
increasing in number and geographical spread: the gentry
alienated from Peking and intent upon railway and mining
development at the local level, provincial leaders who
were more interested in regional than national modernization, students and journalists driven by various
types of radical ideology, army officers and soldiers
coming under the influence of anti-Ch'ing ideas, radicals
and reformers who believed that the alien dynasty of the
Manchus was an obstacle to rights recovery, and many
other groups that combined anti-imperialism with
opposition to Ch'ing power at home.
The drama of Chinese politics intensified just as the
Taft administration was trying to bring about an era of
understanding and co-operation between the two countries.
Although it cannot be argued that the dollar diplomacy
brought about the Republican revolution of 1911-12 which
put an end to the three-hundred year rule of the Manchus,
American policy ran counter to forces within China that
demanded greater provincial autonomy and resisted the
centralizing tendency of the Ch'ing government after the
deaths of the Emperor and the Empress Dowager in 1908.
By proposing plans for financial assistance to Peking
or for railway nationalization, the United States began
to appear as a power behind the throne, intent upon
perpetuating its control against the tides of nationalism,
regionalism and republicanism. The October revolt of
1911 which triggered the revolution was derived from the
provincial gentry's opposition to the four-power loan of
thirty million dollars for railway development under
Peking's supervision and control. By doing so much to
participate in the loan, and by actually providing about
one-fourth of the amount, American officials and bankers
became involved in the last act of the downfall of the
Ch'ing dynasty, much to their surprise and chagrin.

American officials and businessmen were perturbed and
dismayed by the revolt of 1911, for they feared the demise
of a stable government in China which they had sought to
support through its pro-American members. Yet just as
swiftly the Taft administration was able to adjust its
dollar diplomacy to take account of the new development.
Yüan Shih-k'ai provided one key link between the old
regime and the new. He had been a favorite of American
officials because of his receptivity to their overtures.
Although the Manchu dynasty turned to him to suppress the
rebellion, he refused to step in to save a dying regime,
and the last Ch'ing emperor had no alternative but to
resign. Yüan seemed the only strong man capable of
preventing anarchy in China, and all factions courted him.
Neither provincial gentry nor radical factions could
emerge as a victorious revolutionary power with an
ability to restore law and order in the country, and real
power devolved upon local military leaders. Under the
circumstances, Yüan's prestige could be counted upon to
unite factions and organize a provisional government.
This was done in 1912, and the Republic of China was born
with him as provisional president. From the American
point of view, such a situation was not unwelcome, as
the United States had in Yüan a man it had dealt with in
the past and found co-operative with American policy. As
a token of support, the United States joined the other
consortium powers to offer a loan to the new Chinese
government.
More important, the Republican revolution was viewed
in America as a momentous event of historic significance.
For the first time since 1848, there was excitement over
the birth of another 'sister republic,' and it seemed
particularly important that it was an Asian republic, the
first of its kind save for the ill-fated Taiwan republic
of 1895. The 'New York Tribune' echoed the sentiment
of public opinion in the United States when it declared,
'The Chinese are the most democratic people in the world.'
Public and Congressional pressure mounted for recognizing
the new Chinese republic, and the Taft administration
was not averse to the idea. After all, one could readily
read into events in China the assumptions and ideas one
had entertained about the close relationship between the
two countries. The ideal, as Taft, Millard and others
had expressed it, of the United States helping China
modernize itself through close co-operation in policy and
financial matters, could now be applied to the new
republic, the more easily because the latter seemed to
augur a wholesale transformation of the ancient country.
It was much like the story of America's response to the

Meiji Restoration half a century earlier. Today
historians may question whether China after 1912 was
really more modernized or enlightened than it had been
before 1911. 'In fact a good case could be made for
arguing that late Ch'ing China had begun to move toward
reform and transformation, steps that were set back by
the events of the Republican revolution. But to Americans
at that time, the most important thing was the rhetoric
of Chinese revolution as well as the vision of vast
opportunities which it appeared to have opened up to
American enterprise, both commercial and cultural. It
did not take long for the Taft administration, therefore,
to decide to continue to apply the principles of the
dollar diplomacy to the republic as it had to the
Chinese empire. The United States would do all it could
to speed up the recognition of the new government in
Peking, to extend to it the financial assistance it
needed, and otherwise to establish close relations
between the officials of the two countries.
   Most of these projects were to be left to the
succeeding administrations, and Taft and Knox did not
even accomplish the cherished object of recognizing the
new Chinese government as they failed to obtain the
concurrence of other countries. Still, definite
beginnings were made to establish a framework for
Chinese-American understanding at the outset, a legacy
of the dollar diplomacy in the Far East. This was in
marked contrast to Roosevelt's policy of seeking power-
oriented understandings with Japan. American relations
with Japan during the Taft administration were distinctly
of minor importance. There were few serious crises
comparable to the immigration dispute, and the signing of
a Japanese-American treaty of commerce and navigation
in 1911 attested to the generally peaceful and commerce-
oriented relationship between the two countries. The
renewal of the Anglo-Japanese alliance, also in 1911, did
not cause as much alarm in America as earlier as both
London and Tokyo took pains to reassure Washington that
the alliance was not directed against the United States.
Nevertheless, America's deepening involvement in Asian
politics through assertive policies in China implied
that in terms both of 'realpolitik' and ideological
considerations the United States would stand opposed to
Japan. The tension between the two would not be confined
to the immigration problem but would embrace other aspects
of their relations. Competition for influencing the
destiny of China and rivalry in shaping the future course
of Asian politics, rather than big-power collaboration for
regional equilibrium, would characterize American-Japanese

relations. This was the legacy of the Taft
administration's Asian policy.

American diplomacy was much less active in the Middle
East than in the Far East, but even in that region the
Taft administration sought to broaden the base of United
States policy from the traditional one of safeguarding
the national interest narrowly defined in terms of
protecting American merchants and missionaries in the
Ottoman Empire and elsewhere. In accordance with the
principle and spirit of the dollar diplomacy, the State
Department became interested in turning the region into
yet another realm for entrenching American influence so
that it, too, would become more closely integrated into
the world of stability and interdependence which the
United States was to help create. The Middle East,
traditionally an area of European diplomacy and during
the Taft presidency a focus of imperialistic rivalry,
would engage American economic resources to a far
greater extent than earlier so that the United States
would do its share in the region's modern transformation
much as in China. Unfortunately, Middle Eastern
politics was if anything more complex than Chinese
affairs, and some promising American initiatives bore
little fruit at this time.

It is interesting to note that in Persia, an American,
Morgan Shuster, was employed as treasurer-general. He had
served as a financial advisor in the Philippines and Cuba,
and was thus one of the small group of colonial
administrators. Three of his four assistants in Persia
had also worked in America's newly won colonies and
represented the extension of the country's recently
acquired status as an empire. President Taft was
enthusiastic about Shuster's work and considered his job
in Persia a great opportunity to help its government
toward efficiency and fiscal responsibility, as well as
to create a good market for American goods and capital.
(24) Unfortunately, Shuster's energetic activities drew
Russian displeasure. Russia and Britain had divided
Persia into spheres of influence, and neither of them
cherished the idea of growing American influences that
could threaten the status quo. Under their pressure
the Persian government terminated Shuster's services
in 1912, and the State Department decided against
supporting him, not wanting to become more deeply involved
in big-power politics in that part of the world. The
Department, however, was more assertive in Turkey where
Admiral Colby M. Chester organized an Ottoman-American
Development Company in 1909 with a view to building
railways in the empire. Here the major objection came

from Germany which was developing its own system of
railways from Europe to Baghdad through Turkey. The
United States government interceded on Chester's behalf,
and the young Turks, coming to positions of influence
after the revolution of 1908, were interested in using
America as a check on Germany and other European powers.
Although knowledgable American diplomats cautioned
against further involvement in Ottoman politics, the
State Department wanted to see how far the dollar
diplomacy could be pushed. Here again, the realities
of domestic politics in Turkey and European imperialistic
rivalries proved to be too discouraging. The United
States was no match for a Germany determined to assert
its influence through offering inducements to Turkish
leaders, or an Austria-Hungary intent upon strengthening
its hold upon the Balkans through rapprochement with the
Ottoman empire. The Taft administration had no
intention of becoming involved in that region's power
politics. Nevertheless, it is significant that for the
first time the United States was going beyond traditionalism in its approach to the Middle East. Here too, one
sees the global nature of Taft's foreign policy. It
was universalistic in imagination as well as application.
He was paving the way for the coming of Wilsonian
internationalism.

4   THE MEANING OF WILSONIANISM

Because the dollar diplomacy of Taft and Knox embraced
all aspects of America's foreign relations, it was bound
to evoke reaction at home. But the very criticism it
gave rise to tells as much about the accomplishments as
about the problem of that diplomacy. Wilsonian foreign
policy was not so much a rejection of Taft's approach
as an attempt to overcome some of these problems without
throwing away the accomplishments.

   In terms of power politics, the Taft administration
had continued the emphasis on America's special interests
in the Caribbean. But it came under attack from men like
former President Roosevelt who denounced Taft's Asian
policy for undermining the subtle framework of understanding with Japan and other powers. From the point of
view of 'realpolitik' advocates, it did not make much
sense to seek to expand American influence irrespective
of the power realities of specific regions of the globe.
But those opposed to power politics also expressed
unhappiness over the dollar diplomacy, viewing it as
imperialistic. Senator William Jennings Bryan condemned

the dollar diplomacy as serving only a handful of
banking interests. Some Democrats criticized Taft's
acceptance of a Panama canal toll system which exempted
American coastal shipping from paying tolls, and others
attacked the administration's loan arrangements with
Nicaragua's Diaz regime.

On the other hand, those concerned with the protection
of national interests failed to appreciate Taft's
rhetoric of the new age or his stress on arbitration.
Senator Henry Cabot Lodge, for example, represented those
who urged that active steps be taken to protect Americans
in Mexico when the latter was thrown into political
turmoil after the revolution of 1910. Nationalistic
Senators passed the protectionist Payne-Aldrich tariff
over Taft's objection, and they rejected arbitration
treaties with Britain and France as too impinging on
national sovereignty as well as Senatorial prerogatives.
Special-interest groups, too, had their complaints; the
military were unhappy over Taft's non-interventionist
policy in Mexico, and small bankers resented what they too
took to be the administration's preference for large
Wall Street firms in organizing international consortia.

Above all, Taft had to contend with public indifference
to foreign affairs. To be sure there were moments of
excitement such as the Republican revolution in China
which rekindled public interest in Asia. But even that
did not become a political issue at home comparable
to the great debate of 1898-9 or Roosevelt's Caribbean
policy. The electorate during the Taft years was far
more preoccupied with domestic problems, and the 'new
middle class' of professionals and technicians concerned
themselves far more with coping with such issues as
urbanization, industrialization and immigration than with
settling international disputes or extending the limits
of American empire. Walter Lippmann, perhaps the most
articulate commentator on the changing mood of the
nation, spoke of the erosion of tradition and the coming
of the new era, but it was described in a domestic context
in terms of 'the new type of administrator, the
specialist, the professionally trained business man' or
'the larger, collective life upon which the world is
entering.' To adjust themselves to the situation, the
American people, Lippmann wrote, would have to look to
'the infusion of scientific method, the careful
application of administrative technique, the organization
and education of the consumer for control.' (25) Very
little was said about America's external affairs which
seemed all but irrelevant to the key question of the day.
The Presidential election of 1912, pitting Taft against

Theodore Roosevelt and Woodrow Wilson, generated unusual
excitement, but the campaign was not fought on diplomatic
issues.   It was more a matter of three perceptions of the
changing America, and Wilson won a close victory by
appealing to the mass sentiment against big business and
larger organizations. He talked of the 'new freedom,'
but it had at first little implication for foreign
affairs.

Wilson himself was keenly sensitive to the mood of
the country and to its tradition. He was aware of the
different types of criticism heaped upon Taft's foreign
policy. He had no experience in foreign affairs
comparable to his predecessor. He had been generally
guided by traditional nationalism and nineteenth-century
idealism when thinking of America's external affairs.
He was not an anti-imperialist like Bryan, and had
supported the acquisition of the Philippines. In 1902
writing the last volume of his 'History of the American
People,' Wilson justified the acquisition of empire in
1898 in traditional ways, in terms of commercial
opportunity and national interest.

> A quick instinct [he said] apprised American statesmen
> that they had come to a turning point in the progress
> of the nation, which would have disclosed itself in
> some other way if not in this, had the war for Cuba
> not made it plain. It had turned from developing
> its own resources to make conquest of the markets of
> the world. The great East was the market all the world
> coveted now, the market for which statesmen as well as
> merchants must plan and play their game of competition,
> the market to which diplomacy, and if need be power,
> must make an open way.

He concluded the book with a vision of the immediate
future which was equally traditionalist and nationalistic:

> Sections began to draw together with a new understand-
> ing of one another. Parties were turning to the new
> days to come and to the common efforts of peace.
> Statesmen knew that it was to be their task to release
> the energies of the country for the great day of trade
> and of manufacture which was to change the face of
> the world: to ease the processes of labor, govern
> capital in the interest of those who were its
> indispensable servants in pushing the great industries
> of the country to their final value and perfection,
> and make law the instrument, not of justice merely,
> but also of social progress. (26)

Such an idealized image of America was at first little
related to international affairs. The Wilsonian
perception of American virtues was different both from

Roosevelt's geopolitical image and from Taft's vision of
economic interdependence. 'A nation is not made of
anything physical,' Wilson said in 1912, '[but] of its
thoughts and its purposes. Nothing can give it dignity
except its thoughts.' (27) This was an internally
directed view, stressing the purity of American principle
and not really concerned with the rest of the world.

And yet it was Woodrow Wilson more than anyone else
who came to symbolize America's concern with the welfare
of mankind and to embody the idea that the interests of
the country and of the world were identical. As
President he did far more than Roosevelt or Taft to
associate the United States with other countries
militarily, politically and economically, and to
articulate the internationalist vision as a basic
framework of American foreign policy.

Circumstances exterior to the country played a role in
bringing about such a result, but most fundamentally the
emergence of Wilsonian internationalism was a product of
American environment and history, and can best be
comprehended as a fruition of the various strands that had
characterized United States foreign relations since the
eighteenth century. If, before 1913, Wilson's perceptions
were traditionalist, derived from an interest in
commercial expansion and in maintaining the purity of
American institutions, he soon learned to accept the fact
of the country's enormous power when he became its leader.
Whether he liked it or not, the United States ranked
third as a naval power, it had far-flung territorial
possessions, it was involved in the politics of Latin
America, Asia and even the Middle East, and it was
outstripping the European countries in industrial
production. The United States, in short, was a world
power whose moves, policies and attitudes had an impact
on developments in all parts of the globe. Roosevelt
had tried to use power much as the European nations did,
to contribute to a global balance of power. Taft had
sought to promote a stable and interdependent international society through extending American economic
and political influence overseas. It was Wilson's turn
to harness the power of the United States in some new
fashion, and he did so by combining it with his
traditional ideals and aspirations. He would use
American power in the service of certain ideals as well
as for more narrowly nationalistic objectives.

This last goal was never absent from Wilsonian foreign
policy. He was never forgetful of such traditional goals
of diplomacy as the protection of nationals overseas or
the safeguarding of territorial security. But he was also

keenly interested in basing foreign policy on liberty,
justice and other principles which he pictured as having
brought greatness to the country. He would look outward
and see other lands in the same framework as in domestic
history. There seemed to be no reason why one could not
apply identical ideas and assumptions to foreign as well
as to internal matters. In the end national interests
and world interest would become almost synonymous in
Wilson's mind, and he would come to view himself not
simply as president of a country but as a world leader,
concerned as much with the welfare and happiness of the
masses in Europe, Asia and the Middle East as in the
United States.

   That transformation would take time, and the story of
Wilsonian internationalism largely belongs to another
volume, dealing with United States foreign policy after
1914. But even during his first year in office,
President Wilson began to espouse ideas that combined
traditional nationalism and idealism with the consciousness of power and the concern for the application of
America's ideals to other lands as well as to itself.
In the Caribbean, he sought to remove the stigma of
American imperialism by offering Colombia an apology for
the way the Panama canal route had been obtained and by
reversing Taft's policy of exempting American ships
from the canal tolls. In the Pacific, Wilson had
concluded that the Philippines should be granted
independence sooner or later, as continued bondage was
repugnant to his image of America as a liberator. In
Asia, he reprimanded the military for taking the threat
of war with Japan too seriously on the wake of another
immigration dispute following California's enactment of
the alien land act in 1913. Wilson saw little need for
preparedness at this time. In China he acted
independently of other powers and recognized the regime
of Yüan Shih-k'ai, considering it America's duty to
support the fledgling Chinese republic. He was keenly
interested in providing China with America's technical and
educational advisors as well as financial assistance.
But he opposed the international consortium, viewing
it as an imperialistic instrument. He caused the
disbandment of the American group in the consortium and
instead turned to independent bankers and businessmen to
extend loans to China.

   In Mexico, in the meantime, Wilson acted in a way
that was to characterize his diplomacy during much of his
two administrations. The government of Victoriano Huerta,
who became president shortly before Wilson entered the
White House, was recognized by most powers by the summer

of 1913, and President Taft had also favored recognition, considering the regime sufficiently stable and responsible. But Taft left the matter to his successor who, much to his dismay, adopted a different approach. Wilson considered Huerta a dictator who had come to power through illegal means and against the wishes of the Mexican people. The United States was not going to be party to wrongdoing by recognizing a government that denied the rule of law, restraint, constitutionalism, liberty and all those principles to which Wilson attributed the greatness of the United States. The more he thought about the Mexican episode, the more convinced he became that a firm policy there was the only alternative open to him. He was not merely trying to ensure the safety of Americans in Mexico. In fact, purely on grounds of national interest, he might have followed Taft's example and extended recognition to Huerta. But the experience seemed to show that America's dignity and self-respect depended not only on a narrowly defined set of national interests but on acting on behalf of other peoples' interests and wellbeing. 'We will serve the Mexican people without first thinking how we shall save ourselves,' he declared in 1913, 'we must show ourselves friends [of Mexicans] by comprehending their interest whether it squares with our own interest or not.' (28) Substitute Mexico for any other country, and one has the essence of Wilsonian internationalism.

Wilsonian vision thus embraced the whole of mankind through the prism of certain ideas and ideals that went back to the eighteenth century, and it was backed up by the consciousness of power. President Taft, it will be recalled, had been primarily interested in integrating Asia, Latin America and the Middle East into a larger economic system. He had applied internationalism primarily to less advanced parts of the world. Wilson was destined to go a step further and try to apply internationalist concepts and ideals to the advanced countries of Europe and Japan so as to transform them as liberal members of a new co-operative world order. The Wilsonian administration was the first to develop a systematic scheme for the whole world derived from a vision of the relationship between advanced and less developed countries. The former would co-operate peacefully so as to assist the latter's economic and political development, and the two halves of mankind would together contribute to peace, progress and prosperity. The American people would have a role to play in this drama. They would become world citizens

interested in peace, liberty, and orderly change abroad
as at home. Special-interest groups, instead of
competing with one another for a larger share of the
domestic market or for governmental favors, would
co-operate together so as to serve the interests of the
nation which, in turn, would contribute to making the
world more perfect and more open to progressive forces.

Wilsonian policy was thus a culmination of all the
strands that had developed and characterized American
foreign relations since the eighteenth century.
Initially strongly nationalistic and defined in terms of
the national interest, United States diplomacy had also
exhibited concern with the world balance of power and
with certain ideals. Domestically, special-interest
groups as well as mass opinion had been determinants of
policy in so far as they acted as constraints upon policy-
makers. Wilson was a traditionalist in embodying all
these strands, but he went beyond tradition to define
a new approach for United States foreign relations. He
would stress the idealistic strain, but he would integrate
other aspects of the country's external affairs into
one coherent whole, to develop an internationalistic
framework that would appeal both to disparate groups and
individuals at home and to the governments and peoples
overseas. It was a grand vision, rooted in the American
experience and reflecting the newly acquired sense of
power and influence.

In July 1914, as Europe was on the brink of an
unprecedented calamity, Colonel Edward M. House was
visiting the statesmen of the Old World to persuade them
to co-operate together for the economic development of
'undeveloped countries.' It was symbolic that such an
effort, a concrete manifestation of Wilsonian internationalism should go unheeded by the European powers.
In time, however, they would be forced to follow
America's lead to reconstruct world order. In time, too,
they would be faced with the challenge of yet another
internationalist doctrine which assumed a fundamental
conflict, not harmony, between the interests of advanced
and underdeveloped societies. The resulting clashes
between divergent forces of 'internationalism' were to
shape the subsequent course of world history as well as
the evolution of US foreign policy.

Selected Documents

I have selected eighty documents as illustrations of
various stages of American foreign policy and types of
ideas that underlie specific decisions. Rather than
trying to be comprehensive in a textbook fashion, I have
chosen these documents, most of which are not usually
found in similar collections, because they provide
interesting examples of the kinds of observations that
are made in 'From Nationalism to Internationalism'.

1 INTRODUCTION

1 Washington on national defence

(The Napoleonic Wars confronted the American Republic
with its first major crisis in foreign relations. This,
a 1791 report by President Washington to Congress, and
several other documents that follow illustrate the ideas
and assumptions that underlay official policy in
Washington as the leaders grappled with the question of
how to define and protect the interests of the young
nation.)

I cannot recommend to your notice measures for the
fulfilment of *our* duties to the rest of the world, without
again pressing upon you the necessity of placing
ourselves in a condition of complete defence, and of
exacting from *them* the fulfilment of *their* duties towards
us. The United States ought not to indulge a persuasion,
that, contrary to the order of human events, they will,
for ever, keep at a distance those painful appeals to
arms, with which the history of every other nation
abounds. There is a rank due to the United States among
nations, which will be withheld, if not absolutely lost,

by the reputation of weakness. If we desire to secure
peace, one of the most powerful instruments of our rising
prosperity, it must be known that we are at all times
ready for war.
(From 'State Papers and Publick Documents of the United
States', Vol. 1 (Boston, 1817), pp. 40-1.)

2 The policy of commercial internationalism

(Washington's 'farewell address' of 1796 was a
justification for his policy of neutrality during the
European war. But it also offered a formulation for
universalizing the country's economic relations with the
rest of the world while minimizing political links.)

Taking care always to keep ourselves, by suitable
establishments, in a respectable defensive posture, we
may safely trust to temporary alliances for extraordinary emergencies.
    Harmony and a liberal intercourse with all nations,
are recommended by policy, humanity, and interest. But
even our commercial policy should hold an equal and
impartial hand; neither seeking nor granting exclusive
favors or preferences; consulting the natural course of
things; diffusing and diversifying by gentle means the
streams of commerce, but forcing nothing; establishing,
(with powers so disposed, in order to give trade a stable
course, to define the rights of our merchants, and to
enable the government to support them,) conventional
rules of intercourse, the best that present circumstances
and mutual opinion will permit, but temporary, and liable
to be from time to time abandoned or varied, as
experience and circumstances shall dictate; constantly
keeping in view, that it is folly in one nation to look
for disinterested favors from another; that it must pay
with a portion of its independence, for whatever it may
accept under that character; that, by such acceptance,
it may place itself in the condition of having given
equivalents for nominal favors, and yet of being
reproached with ingratitude for not giving more. There
can be no greater error than to expect or calculate
upon real favors from nation to nation. It is an
illusion which experience must cure, which a just pride
ought to discard ...
    The duty of holding a neutral conduct may be inferred,
without any thing more, from the obligation which justice
and humanity impose on every nation, in cases in which it
is free to act, to maintain inviolate the relations of
peace and amity towards other nations.

The inducements of interest for observing that conduct
will best be referred to your own reflections and
experience. With me, a predominant motive has been to
endeavour to gain time to our country to settle and mature
its yet recent institutions, and to progress without
interruption to that degree of strength and consistency,
which is necessary to give it, humanly speaking, the
command of its own fortunes.

3   Hamilton's perception of the United States

(In arguing against involvement in the European war, the
leaders of the country shared certain assumptions about
the position and character of the United States in the
world. The following excerpts from Hamilton's 1794
pamphlet offer a clear vision.)

The United States, rooted as are now the ideas of
independence, are happily too remote from Europe to be
governed by her; dominion over any part of them would
be a real misfortune to any nation of that quarter of the
globe ...
    There are two great errors in our reasoning upon this
subject [i.e. American policy toward the war]: one, that
the combined powers will certainly attribute to us the
same principles which they deem so exceptionable in
France; the other, that our principles are in fact the
same.
    If left to themselves they will all, except one,
naturally see in us a people who originally resorted
to a revolution in government, as a refuge from
encroachments on rights and privileges *antecedently*
enjoyed, not as a people who from choice sought a radical
and entire change in the established government, in
pursuit of new privileges and rights carried to an
extreme, irreconcilable perhaps with any form of
regular government. They will see in us a people who have
a due respect for property and personal security; who,
in the midst of our revolution, abstained with exemplary
moderation from every thing violent or sanguinary,
instituting governments adequate to the protection of
persons and property; who, since the completion of our
revolution, have in a very short period, from mere
reasoning and reflection, without tumult or bloodshed,
adopted a form of general government calculated, as well
as the nature of things would permit, to remedy antecedent
defects, to give strength and security to the nation, to
rest the foundations of liberty on the basis of justice,

order, and law; who have at all times been content to
govern themselves without intermeddling with the affairs
or governments of other nations; in time, they will see
in us sincere republicans, but decided enemies to
licentiousness and anarchy; sincere republicans, but
decided friends to the freedom of opinion, to the order
and tranquility of all mankind. They will not see in us
a people whose best passions have been misled, and whose
best qualities have been perverted from their true
direction by headlong, fanatical, or designing leaders,
to the perpetration of acts from which humanity shrinks,
to the commission of outrages over which the eye of reason
weeps, to the profession and practice of principles which
tend to shake the foundations of morality, to dissolve
the social bonds, to disturb the peace of mankind, to
substitute confusion to order, anarchy to government ...

Let us content ourselves with lamenting the errors
into which a great, a gallant, an amiable, a respectable
nation has been betrayed, with uniting our wishes and our
prayers that the Supreme Ruler of the world will bring
them back from those errors to a more sober and more just
way of thinking and acting, and will overrule the
complicated calamities which surround them, to the
establishment of a government under which they may be
free, secure, and happy. But let us not corrupt ourselves
by false comparisons or glosses, nor shut our eyes to the
true nature of transactions which ought to grieve and warn
us, nor rashly mingle our destiny in the consequences of
the errors and extravagances of another nation.
(From Henry Cabot Lodge, ed., 'The Works of Alexander
Hamilton', vol. V (New York, 1904), pp. 92-6.)

4   John Adams and the crisis with France

(United States relations with France worsened in 1797
when the French authorities interfered with American
shipping and refused to negotiate a new treaty of
commerce. This document, addressed by President
John Adams to various heads of cabinet departments,
referred to the difficulties American commissioners were
encountering in Paris and asked specific questions about
foreign policy options.)

The President of the United States requests the Secretary
of State, the Secretary of the Treasury, the Secretary of
War, and the Attorney-General, to take into their
consideration the state of the nation, and its foreign
relations, especially with France. These, indeed, may be

so connected with those with England, Spain, Holland, and others, that perhaps the former cannot be well weighed without the other. If our envoys extraordinary should be refused an audience, or, after an audience, be ordered to depart without accomplishing the objects of their mission,

1. They may repair to Holland; or, 2. Two of them may return home, leaving one abroad; or, 3. All of them may return to America.

In the first case, will it be prudent to call them all home? And, in the second, to recall the one?

In any of these three cases, what will be necessary or expedient for the executive authority of government to do here?

In what manner should the first intelligence be announced to Congress; by message or speech?

What measures should be recommended to Congress? Shall an immediate declaration of war be recommended or suggested? If not, what other system shall be recommended more than a repetition of the recommendations heretofore repeatedly made to both houses? Will it in any case, and in what cases, be advisable to recommend an embargo?

What measures will be proper to take with Spain? What with Holland? What with Portugal? But, above all, what will policy dictate to be said to England, and how shall it be said? By Mr. King, or to Mr. Liston? And how shall it be conveyed to Mr. King? By packet, or any ordinary conveyance; or by some special, trusty, and confidential messenger? Will it not be the soundest policy, even in case of a declaration of war on both sides, between France and the United States, for us to be totally silent to England, and wait for her overtures? Will it not be imprudent in us to connect ourselves with Britain, in any manner that may impede us in embracing the first favorable moment or opportunity to make a separate peace? What aids or benefits can we expect from England by any stipulations with her, which her interest will not impel her to extend to us without any? On the brink of the dangerous precipice on which she stands, will not shaking hands with her necessitate us to fall with her, if she falls? On the other hand, what aid could we stipulate to afford her, which our own interest would not oblige us to give without any other obligation? In case of a revolution in England, a wild democracy will probably prevail for as long a time as it did in France; in such case, will not the danger of reviving and extending that delirium in America, be increased in proportion to the intimacy of our connection with that nation?
(From Charles Francis Adams, ed., 'The Works of John Adams', vol. VIII (Boston, 1853), pp. 561-2.)

5   Jefferson and France

(One of the first foreign policy crises that confronted
President Jefferson was the Spanish retrocession of
Louisiana to France. In the following famous letter to
Robert R. Livingston, United States minister in Paris,
dated 18 April 1802, Jefferson sought to redefine his
perceptions of American-French relations in light of
these developments.)

The session of Louisiana and the Floridas by Spain to
France works most sorely on the U. S. On this subject
the Secretary of State has written to you fully. Yet I
cannot forbear recurring to it personally, so deep is the
impression it makes in my mind. It compleatly reverses
all the political relations of the U. S. and will form
a new epoch in our political course. Of all nations of
any consideration France is the one which hitherto has
offered the fewest points on which we could have any
conflict of right, and the most points of a communion
of interests. From these causes we have ever looked to
her as our *natural friend,* as one with which we never
could have an occasion of difference. Her growth
therefore we viewed as our own, her misfortunes ours.
There is on the globe one single spot, the possessor of
which is our natural and habitual enemy. It is New
Orleans, through which the produce of three-eighths of
our territory must pass to market, and from its
fertility it will ere long yield more than half of our
whole produce and contain more than half our inhabitants.
France placing herself in that door assumes to us
the attitude of defiance. Spain might have retained
it quietly for years. Her pacific dispositions, her
feeble state, would induce her to increase our facilities
there, so that her possession of the place would be
hardly felt by us, and it would not perhaps be very long
before some circumstance might arise which might make the
cession of it to us the price of something of more worth
to her. Not so can it ever be in the hands of France.
The impetuosity of her temper, the energy and restlessness
of her character, placed in a point of eternal friction
with us, and our character, which though quiet, and
loving peace and the pursuit of wealth, is high-minded,
despising wealth in competition with insult or injury,
enterprising and energetic as any nation on earth, these
circumstances render it impossible that France and the
U. S. can continue long friends when they meet in so
irritable a position. They as well as we must be blind
if they do not see this; and we must be very improvident

if we do not begin to make arrangements on that
hypothesis. The day that France takes possession of
N. Orleans fixes the sentence which is to restrain her
forever within her low water mark. It seals the union
of two nations who in conjunction can maintain exclusive
possession of the ocean. From that moment we must marry
ourselves to the British fleet and nation. We must turn
all our attentions to a maritime force, for which our
resources place us on very high grounds: and having
formed and cemented together a power which may render
reinforcement of her settlements here impossible to
France, make the first cannon, which shall be fired in
Europe the signal for tearing up any settlement she may
have made, and for holding the two continents of America
in sequestration for the common purposes of the united
British and American nations. This is not a state of
things we seek or desire. It is one which this measure,
if adopted by France, forces on us, as necessarily as
any other cause, by the laws of nature, brings on its
necessary effect. It is not from a fear of France
that we deprecate this measure proposed by her. For
however greater her force is than ours compared in the
abstract, it is nothing in comparison of ours when to be
exerted on our soil. But it is from a sincere love of
peace, and a firm persuasion that bound to France by the
interests and the strong sympathies still existing in the
minds of our citizens, and holding relative positions
which ensure their continuance we are secure of a long
course of peace.
(From Paul Leicester Ford, ed., 'The Writings of Thomas
Jefferson', vol. VIII (New York, 1897), pp. 144-5.)

6 Madison and France

(James Madison, Jefferson's secretary of state, instructed
Livingston to initiate negotiations for the purchase of
New Orleans and the Floridas from France. In the
instruction, dated 2 March 1803, Madison developed an
interesting argument for the integrity of the American
union.)

The French Government is ... mistaken if it supposes that
the Western part of the United States can be withdrawn
from their present Union with the Atlantic part, into a
separate Government closely allied with France.
    Our Western fellow citizens are bound to the Union not
only by the ties of kindred and affection which for a
long time will derive strength from the stream of

emigration peopling that region, but by two considerations
which flow from clear and essential interests.

One of these considerations is the passage thro' the
Atlantic ports of the foreign merchandize consumed by the
Western inhabitants, and the payments thence made to a
Treasury in which they would lose their participation
by erecting a separate Government. The bulky productions
of the Western Country may continue to pass down the
Mississippi; but the difficulties of the ascending
navigation of that river, however free it may be made,
will cause the imports for consumption to pass thro' the
Atlantic States. This is the course thro' which they
are now received, nor will the impost to which they will
be subject change the course even if the passage up the
Mississippi should be duty free. It will not equal the
difference in the freight thro' the latter channel. It
is true that mechanical and other improvements in the
navigation of the Mississippi may lessen the labor and
expense of ascending the stream, but it is not the least
probable, that savings of this sort will keep pace with
the improvements in canals and roads, by which the
present course of imports will be favored. Let it be
added that the loss of the contributions thus made to a
foreign Treasury would be accompanied with the necessity
of providing by less convenient revenues for the expense
of a separate Government, and of the defensive
precautions required by the change of situation.

The other of these considerations results from the
insecurity to which the trade from the Mississippi would be
exposed, by such a revolution in the Western part of the
United States. A connection of the Western people as a
separate state with France, implies a connection between
the Atlantic States and Great Britain. It is found from
long experience that France and Great Britain are nearly
half their time at War. The case would be the same with
their allies. During nearly one half the time therefore,
the trade of the Western Country from the Mississippi,
would have no protection but that of France, and would
suffer all the interruptions which nations having the
command of the sea could inflict on it.
(From Gaillard Hunt, ed., 'The Writings of James Madison',
vol. VII (New York, 1908), pp. 12-14.)

7   The War of 1812

(In this message to Congress, dated 1 June 1812, President
Madison enumerated specific grievances against Britain
which, he thought, justified a declaration of war by the
United States.)

It has become ... sufficiently certain that the commerce of the United States is to be sacrificed, not as interfering with the belligerent rights of Great Britain; not as supplying the wants of her enemies, which she herself supplies; but as interfering with the monoply which she covets for her own commerce and navigation. She carries on a war against the lawful commerce of a friend that she may the better carry on a commerce with an enemy - a commerce polluted by the forgeries and perjuries which are for the most part the only passports by which it can succeed ...

In reviewing the conduct of Great Britain toward the United States our attention is necessarily drawn to the warfare just renewed by the savages on one of our extensive frontiers - a warfare which is known to spare neither age nor sex and to be distinguished by features peculiarly shocking to humanity. It is difficult to account for the activity and combinations which have for some time been developing themselves among tribes in constant intercourse with British traders and garrisons without connecting their hostility with that influence and without recollecting the authenticated examples of such interpositions heretofore furnished by the officers and agents of that Government.

Such is the spectacle of injuries and indignities which have been heaped on our country, and such the crisis which its unexampled forbearance and conciliatory efforts have not been able to avert. It might at least have been expected that an enlightened nation, if less urged by moral obligations or invited by friendly dispositions on the part of the United States, would have found its true interest alone a sufficient motive to respect their rights and their tranquility on the high seas; that an enlarged policy would have favored that free and general circulation of commerce in which the British nation is at all times interested, and which in times of war is the best alleviation of its calamities to herself as well as to other belligerents; and more especially that the British cabinet would not, for the sake of a precarious and surreptitious intercourse with hostile markets, have persevered in a course of measures which necessarily put at hazard the invaluable market of a great and growing country, disposed to cultivate the mutual advantages of an active commerce.

Other counsels have prevailed. Our moderation and conciliation have had no other effect than to encourage perseverance and to enlarge pretensions. We behold our seafaring citizens still the daily victims of lawless violence, committed on the great common and highway of nations, even within sight of the country which owes them protection. We behold our vessels, freighted with the products of our soil and industry, or returning with the honest proceeds of them, wrested from their lawful destinations, confiscated by prize courts no longer the organs of public law but the instruments of arbitrary edicts, and their unfortunate crews dispersed and lost, or forced or inveigled in British ports into British fleets, whilst arguments are employed in support of these aggressions which have no foundation but in a principle equally supporting a claim to regulate our external commerce in all cases whatsoever.

We behold, in fine, on the side of Great Britain, a state of war against the United States, and on the side of the United States a state of peace toward Great Britain.

(Ibid., vol. VIII (1908), pp. 196, 198-9.)

8 Clay and the rhetoric of nationalism

(The crisis with Britain coincided with the emergence of younger political leaders, those who had not participated in the events of the 1770s and the 1780s themselves. They avidly engaged in nationalistic oratory. Typical was this speech by Henry Clay in the House of Representatives on 31 December 1811).

For argument's sake, let us concede the fact, that the French Emperor is aiming at universal empire; can Great Britain challenge our sympathies, when, instead of putting forth her arms to protect the world, she has converted the war into a means of self-aggrandizement; when, under pretence of defending them, she has destroyed the commerce and trampled on the rights of every nation; when she has attempted to annihilate every vestige of the public maritime code of which she professes to be the champion? Shall we bear the cuffs and scoffs of British arrogance, because we may entertain chimerical fears of French subjugation? Shall we swallow the potion of British poison, lest we may be presented with the imperial dose? Are we called upon to bow to the mandates of royal insolence, as a preparation to contend against Gallic usurpation? Who ever learned in the school of base submission, the lessons of noble freedom, and courage, and independence? Look at Spain. Did she secure her independence by submitting, in the first instance, to the dictates of imperial usurpations? No, sir. If she had resisted the first intrusion into her councils, her

monarch would not at this time be a miserable victim in
the dungeons of Marseilles. We cannot secure our
independence of one power, by a dastardly submission to
the will of another. But look at our own history. Our
ancestors of the Revolution resisted the first encroachments of British tyranny. They foresaw that by submitting
to pay an illegal tax, contemptible as that was in
itself, their liberties would ultimately be subverted.
Consider the progress of the present disputes with
England. For what were we contending the other day? For
the indirect colonial carrying trade. That has vanished.
For what are we now deliberating? For the direct export
and import trade; the trade in our own cotton, and
tobacco, and fish. Give this up, and to-morrow we must
take up arms for our right to pass from New York to New
Orleans; from the upper country on James River to
Richmond. Sir, when did submission to one wrong induce
an adversary to cease his encroachments on the party
submitting? But we are told that we ought only to go to
war when our territory is invaded. How much better than
invasion is the blocking of our very ports and harbours;
insulting our towns; plundering our merchants, and
scouring our coasts? If our fields are surrounded, are
they in a better condition than if invaded? When the
murderer is at our doors, shall we meanly skulk to our
cells? Or shall we boldly oppose him at his entrance?
(From 'The Life and Speeches of Henry Clay', vol. I (New
York, 1842), pp. 18-19.)

9   John Quincy Adams and Latin America

(Beginning in 1822, the United States proceeded to
recognize Latin American republics that had become
independent of Spain. John Quincy Adams, President
James Monroe's secretary of state, was confident that
European intervention in American affairs could be
prevented so long as the United States did nothing to
provoke them. He thus opposed the efforts by those in the
government who favored taking more definite measures, as
can be seen in these excerpts from his diary.)

[21 November 1823] I mentioned [at a cabinet meeting] my
wish to prepare a paper to be delivered confidentially
to Baron Tuyl [the Russian minister] ... My purpose
would be in a moderate and conciliatory manner, but with a
firm and determined spirit ... to assert those
[principles] upon which our own Government is founded,
and, while disclaiming all intention of attempting to

propogate them by force, and all interference with the
political affairs of Europe, to declare our expectation
and hope that the European powers will equally abstain
from the attempt to spread their principles in the
American hemisphere, or to subjugate by force any part
of these continents to their will.

The President approved of this idea; and then taking up
the sketches that he had prepared for his message, read
them to us. Its introduction was in a tone of deep
solemnity and of high alarm, intimating that this country
is menaced by imminent and formidable dangers, such as
would probably soon call for their most vigorous
energies and the closest union ... Of all this Mr. Calhoun
[secretary of war] declared his approbation. I expressed
as freely my wish that the President would reconsider the
whole subject before he should determine to take that
course. I said the tone of the introduction I apprehended
would take the nation by surprise and greatly alarm them.
It would come upon them like a clap of thunder. There
had never been in the history of this nation a period
of so deep calm and tranquillity as we now enjoyed. We
never were, upon the whole, in a state of peace so
profound and secure with all foreign nations as at this
time ... For more than thirty years Europe had been in
convulsions; every nation almost of which it is composed
alternately invading and invaded. Empires, kingdoms,
principalities, had been overthrown, revolutionized, and
counter-revolutionized, and we had looked on safe in our
distance beyond an intervening ocean, and avowing a total
forbearance to interfere in any of the combinations of
European politics. This message would at once buckle
on the harness and throw down the gauntlet. It would
have the air of open defiance to all Europe, and I should
not be surprised if the first answer to it from Spain and
France, and even Russia, should be to break off their
diplomatic intercourse with us. I did not expect that the
quiet which we had enjoyed for six or seven years would
last much longer. The aspect of things was portentous;
but if we must come to an issue with Europe, let us keep
it off as long as possible. Let us use all possible
means to carry the opinion of the nation with us, and
the opinion of the world.

Calhoun said that he thought there was not the
tranquillity that I spoke of; that there was great
anxiety in the thinking part of the nation; that there
was a general expectation that the Holy Alliance would
employ force against South America, and that it would be
proper that the President should sound the alarm to the
nation. A time was approaching when all its energies

would be needed, and the public mind ought to be
prepared for it ...

[22 November] I spoke to [President Monroe] again
urging him to abstain from everything in his message
which the Holy Allies could make a pretext for
construing into aggression upon them. I said there were
considerations of weight which I could not even easily
mention at a Cabinet meeting. If he had determined to
retire from the public service at the end of his present
term, it was now drawing to a close. It was to be
considered now as a whole, and a system of administration
for a definite term of years. It would hereafter, I
believed, be looked back to as the golden age of this
republic, and I felt an extreme solicitude that its end
might correspond with the character of its progress; that
the Administration might be delivered into the hands
of the successor, whoever he might be, at peace and in
amity with all the world. If this could not be, if the
Holy Alliance were determined to make up an issue with
us, it was our policy to meet, and not to make it. We
should retreat to the wall before taking to arms, and
be sure at every step to put them as much as possible
in the wrong ... [At] the time when Mr. Clay so urgently
pushed for the South American independence, his main
object was popularity for himself and to embarrass the
Administration. It did not appear that this object was
now so important to him, and, as he had some prospect
of coming to the succession himself, I should not suppose
he would wish it encumbered with a quarrel with all
Europe ... The ground that I wish to take is that of
earnest remonstrance against the interference of the
European powers by force with South America, but to
disclaim all interference on our part with Europe; to
make an American cause, and adhere inflexibly to that.
(From Charles Francis Adams, ed., 'Memoirs of John Quincy
Adams', vol. VI (Philadelphia, 1875), pp. 194-7.)

10 Calhoun and the tariff question

(Protectionism became a heated issue in national
politics in the second quarter of the century. As this
speech by John C. Calhoun in the Senate on 5 August 1842
indicates, the tariff debate was related to an image of
American development and its foreign relations.)

Among [the reasons put forward by exponents of the tariff
bill of 1842], one of the most plausible, is that the
competition, which is asked to be excluded, is that of

foreigners. The competition is represented to be between
home and foreign industry; and he who opposes what is
asked, is held up as a friend to foreign, and the enemy
to home industry, and is regarded as very little short
of being a traitor to his country. I take issue on the
fact. I deny that there is, or can be, any competition
between home and foreign industry, but through the latter;
and assert that the real competition, in all cases, is and
must be, between one branch of home industry and another.
To make good the position taken, I rely on a simple fact,
which none will deny - that imports are received in
exchange for exports. From that, it follows, if there be
no export trade, there will be no import trade; and that
to cut the exports, is to cut off the imports. It is,
then, not the imports, but the exports which are
exchanged for them, and without which they would not be
introduced at all, that causes, in reality, the
competition. It matters not how low the wages of other
countries may be, and how cheap their productions, if we
have no exports, they cannot compete with ours.

The real competition, then, is with that industry which
produces the articles for export, and which purchases
them, and carries them abroad, and brings back the
imported articles in exchange for them; and the real
complaint is, that those so empolyed can furnish the
market cheaper than those who manufacture articles similar
to the imported; and what, in truth, is asked, is, - that
this cheaper process of supplying the market should be
taxed, by imposing high duties on the importation of the
articles received in exchange for those exported, in order
to give the dearer a monopoly - so that it may sell its
products for higher prices. It is, in fact, a warfare on
the part of the manufacturing industry, and those
associated with it, against the export industry of the
community, and those associated with it ...

We have, Senators, reached a remarkable point in the
progress of civilization, and the mechanical and chemical
arts - and which will require a great change in the
policy of civilized nations. Within the last three or
four generations, they have received an impulse far beyond
all former example, and have now obtained a perfection
before unknown. The result has been a wonderful
increased facility of producing all articles of supply
depending on those arts; that is, of those very articles
which we call, in our financial language, protected
articles; and against the importation of which, these
high duties are, for the most part, intended. In
consequence of this increased facility, it now requires
but a small part, comparatively, of the labor and capital

of a country, to clothe its people, and supply itself
with most of the products of the useful arts; and hence,
all civilized people, with few exceptions, are producing
their own supply, and even overstocking their own market.
It results, that no people, restricted to the home
market, can, in the present advanced state of the useful
arts, rise to greatness and wealth by manufactures. For
that purpose, they must compete successfully for the
foreign market, in the younger, less advanced, and less
civilized countries. This necessity for more enlarged and
freer intercourse between the older, more advanced, and
more civilized nations, and the younger, less advanced,
and less civilized, at a time when the whole globe is
laid open to our knowledge, and a rapidity and facility
of intercourse established between all its parts
heretofore unknown, is one of the mighty means ordained
by Providence to spread population, light, civilization,
and prosperity, far and wide over its entire surface.

The great problem then is, how is the foreign market
to be commanded? I answer, by the reverse means proposed
in order to command the home market - low, instead of
high duties; and a sound currency, fixed, stable, and as
nearly as possible on the level with the general currency
of the world, instead of an inflated and fluctuating one.
Nothing can be more hostile to the command of foreign
trade, than high prohibitory duties, even as it regards
the exports of manufactures.
(From Richard K. Crallé, ed., 'Speeches of John C.
Calhoun,' vol. IV (New York, 1861), pp. 181-2, 192-4.)

11 War, expansion, and politics: Benton

(Apart from the tariff question, territorial expansion
became bound up with domestic politics and the struggle
for power between Whigs and Democrats, between North
and South, and among various interest groups. The
following several documents, all taken during the crisis
with Mexico, reveal the intricate connections between
considerations of national and particularistic interests.
The first excerpt is taken from a speech by Senator
Thomas Hart Benton of Missouri, objecting to the 1844
treaty annexing Texas to the United States.)

The war with Mexico, and its unconstitutionality, is
fully shown: its injustice remains to be exhibited, and
that is an easy task. What is done in violation of
treaties, in violation of neutrality, in violation of an
armistice, must be unjust. All this occurs in this case,

and a great deal more. Mexico is our neighbor. We are
at peace with her. Social, commercial, and diplomatic
relations subsist between us, and the interest of the two
nations requires these relations to continue. We want a
country which was once ours, but which, by treaty, we
have acknowledged to be hers. That country has revolted.
Thus far it has made good its revolt, and not a doubt
rests upon my mind that she will make it good for ever.
But the contest is not over. An armistice, duly
proclaimed, and not revoked, strictly observed by each
in not firing a gun, though inoperative thus far in the
appointment of commissioners to treat for peace: this
armistice, only determinable upon notice, suspends the
war. Two thousand miles of Texian frontier is held in
the hands of Mexico, and all attempts to conquer that
frontier have signally failed: witness the disastrous
expeditions to Mier and to Santa Fé. We acknowledge
the right - the moral and political right - of Mexico
to resubjugate this province, if she can. We declare
our neutrality: we profess friendship: we proclaim our
respect for Mexico. In the midst of all this, we make a
treaty with Texas for transferring herself to the United
States, and that without saying a word to Mexico, while
receiving notice from her that such a transfer would be
war. Mexico is treated as a nullity; and the province
she is endeavoring to reconquer is suddenly, by the magic
of a treaty signature, changed into United States domain.
We want the country; but instead of applying to Mexico,
and obtaining her consent to the purchase, or waiting a
few months for the events which would supersede the
necessity of Mexican consent - instead of this plain and
direct course, a secret negotiation was entered into with
Texas, in total contempt of the acknowledged rights of
Mexico, and without saying a word to her until all was
over. Then a messenger is despatched in furious haste to
this same Mexico, the bearer of volunteer apologies, of
deprecatory excuses, and of an offer of ten millions of
dollars for Mexican acquiescence in what Texas has done.
Forty days are allowed for the return of the messenger;
and the question is, will he bring back the consent?
That question is answered in the Mexican official notice
of war, if the treaty of annexation was made! and it is
answered in the fact of not applying to her for her
consent before the treaty was made. The wrong to Mexico
is confessed in the fact of sending this messenger, and
in the terms of the letter of which he was the bearer.
That letter of Mr. Secretary Calhoun, of the 19th of
April, to Mr. Benjamin Green, the United States chargé
in Mexico, is the most unfortunate in the annals of human

diplomacy! By the fairest implications, it admits
insult and injury to Mexico, and violation of her
territorial boundaries! It admits that we should have had
her previous consent - should have had her concurrence -
that we have injured her as little as possible - and that
we did all this in full view of all possible consequences!
that is to say, in full view of war! in plain English,
that we have wronged her, and will fight her for it.
(From [Thomas Hart Benton], 'Thirty Years' View', vol. II
(New York, 1856), pp. 603-4.)

12 Tyler and Texas

(President John Tyler sought to counter the argument that
the annexation of Texas and the acquisition of adjoining
lands from Mexico were designed to appeal to the sectional
interest of the South. In his message to Congress in
December 1844, he insisted that his policy deserved the
support of all segments of the population.)

I must express frankly the opinion that had the treaty [of
Texas annexation] been ratified by the Senate [which had
rejected it in June] it would have been followed by a
prompt settlement, to the entire satisfaction of Mexico,
of every matter in difference between the two countries.
Seeing, then, that new preparations for hostile invasion
of Texas were about to be adopted by Mexico and that these
were brought about because Texas had adopted the suggestions of the Executive upon the subject of annexation, it
could not passively have folded its arms and permitted a
war, threatened to be accompanied by every act that could
mark a barbarous age, to be waged against her because she
had done so.
    Other considerations of a controlling character
influenced the course of the Executive. The treaty which
had thus been negotiated had failed to receive the
ratification of the Senate. One of the chief objections
which was urged against it was found to consist in the
fact that the question of annexation had not been
submitted to the ordeal of public opinion in the United
States. However untenable such an objection was esteemed
to be, in view of the unquestionable power of the
Executive to negotiate the treaty and the great and
lasting interests involved in the question, I felt it to
be my duty to submit the whole subject to Congress as the
best expounders of popular sentiment. No definitive
action having been taken on the subject by Congress, the
question referred itself directly to the decision of the
States and people. The great popular election which has

just terminated afforded the best opportunity of ascer-
taining the will of the States and the people upon it ...
A controlling majority of the people and a large majority
of the States have declared in favor of immediate annexation. Instructions have thus come up to both branches
of Congress from their respective constituents in terms
the most emphatic. It is the will of both the people and
the States that Texas shall be annexed to the Union
promptly and immediately ...

The subject of annexation addresses itself, most fortunately, to every portion of the Union. The Executive
would have been unmindful of its highest obligations if it
could have adopted a course of policy dictated by sectional interests and local feelings. On the contrary, it was
because the question was neither local nor sectional, but
made its appeal to the interests of the whole Union, and
of every State in the Union, that the negotiation, and
finally the treaty of annexation, was entered into; and it
has afforded me no ordinary pleasure to perceive that so
far as demonstrations have been made upon it by the people
they have proceeded from all portions of the Union. Mexico
may seek to excite divisions amongst us by uttering unjust
denunciations against particular States, but when she
comes to know that the invitations addressed to our
fellow-citizens by Spain, and afterwards by herself, to
settle Texas were accepted by emigrants from all the
States, and when, in addition to this, she refreshes her
recollection with the fact that the first effort which
was made to acquire Texas was during the Administration of
a distinguished citizen from an Eastern State, which was
afterwards renewed under the auspices of a President from
the Southwest, she will awake to a knowledge of the
futility of her present purpose of sowing dissensions
among us or producing distraction in our councils by
attacks either on particular States or on persons who are
now in the retirement of private life.
(From James D. Richardson, ed., 'A Compilation of the
Messages and Papers of the Presidents,' vol. IV
(Washington, 1897), pp. 343-4, 355.)

13 The Oregon question

(In his annual message to Congress, on 2 December 1845,
President James K. Polk reiterated America's opposition
to European interference with hemispheric affairs. He
also insisted on the settlement of the dispute with
Britain over Oregon in terms favorable to the United
States. His diary recorded Congressional responses to
the message.)

Wednesday, 3rd December, 1845. Many members of Congress
called today; the Democratic members all expressing in
strong terms their approbation of the message ... These
gentlemen and many others who called assured me that there
was a universal approval among all the Democratic
members and that the Whigs generally had but little to say
on the subject, some of them expressing approbation in
relation to Oregon ...

Wednesday, 24th December, 1845 ... Hopkins L. Turney
of the Senate from Tennessee called about 6 o'clock P.M.,
having previously written to me that he desired to see
me on the subject of the Oregon question. He opened the
conversation by saying that he wished to ascertain my
views and intentions on the Oregon question with a view
to regulate his own conduct as a Senator by them, and
expressed his intention to support my administration on
that and all other subjects. I told him the question
stood precisely as it did when I delivered my message
to Congress, the British Minister having taken no steps
since that time. He spoke of the difference of opinion
among the Democratic Senators, and among other things
said that before Mr. Calhoun's arrival in Washington he
had been assured by some of his friends that he would
support the views of the administration on the Oregon
question, but that since his arrival he had had some
conversation with him and was satisfied he would not do
so. He found too that Mr. C.'s friends, who had given
him the assurance above referred to, since his arrival
had changed their opinions, and he mentioned two Southern
Senators who had done so. He said that Mr. Benton would
not support the administration on the question, and that
Mr. Benton and Mr. Calhoun in his opinion would be found
acting together in opposition, whenever they thought it
safe to break ground against the administration. He said
many members of Congress from the South were opposed to
war and would follow Mr. Calhoun, while some members from
the West were almost mad on the subject of Oregon, and
that I was between these two fires and whatever I might
do I must dissatisfy the one or the other of these
sections of the party. He then asked me (if I did not
think it improper to answer the question) if I had made
up my mind what course I would take if Great Britain
should renew the offer of the 49° or something equivalent
to it. To this I answered that my opinions on the whole
subject were candidly set forth in the message, and that
I adhered to the opinions there expressed; but that if
such a proposition as he had supposed was made, the
decision upon it would probably involve the question of
peace or War. I told [him] in event of such propositon

being made I would feel inclined to take the advice of
the Senate confidentially before I acted on it. This
Mr. Turney heartily approved and said he would conform
his action on the subject to this view of the case.
(From Milo Milton Quaife, ed., 'The Diary of James K.
Polk', vol. I (Chicago, 1910), pp. 111-2, 140-1.)

14 Polk and the Mexican War

(These further excerpts from Polk's diary reveal the
American leader's fascination with the connection
between the Oregon and Mexican disputes, and between
foreign policy and domestic politics.)

Saturday, 18th April, 1846 ... Mr. Calhoun ... inquired
about the state of our relations with Mexico. I told
him that Mr. Slidell [special emissary to Mexico] had,
on being rejected as Minister of the U. States, returned,
and that our relations with Mexico had reached a point
where we could not stand still but must assert our rights
firmly; that we must treat all nations whether weak or
strong alike, and that I saw no alternative but strong
measures towards Mexico. Mr. Calhoun deprecated war &
expressed a hope that the Oregon question would be first
settled, and then we would have no difficulty in
adjusting our difficulties with Mexico. He thought the
British Government desired to prevent a war between the
U.S. & Mexico, and would exert its influence to prevent
it. I told him I had reason to believe that the British
Minister in Mexico had exerted his influence to prevent
Mr. Slidell from being received by the Mexican government.
He said the British Government desired to prevent a war,
but did not desire a settlement between the U.S. and
Mexico until the Oregon question was settled. He then
expressed an earnest desire to have the Oregon question
settled ...
  Tuesday, 21st April, 1846 ... Mr. Calhoun intends to
oppose my administration. He has embarrassed the
administration on the Oregon question. He is playing a
game to make himself President and his motives of action
are wholly selfish. I will observe his future course &
treat him accordingly.
  Wednesday, 22nd April, 1846 ... The speech of
Mr. Webster, Mr. Calhoun, and others in the Senate
advocating peace and the British title to a large portion
of the country, have made the British Government & people
more arrogant in their tone and more grasping in their
demands. If war should be the result, these peace

gentlemen & advocates of British pretensions over those
of their own country will have done more to produce it
than any others.

The truth is that in all this Oregon discussion in the
Senate, too many Democratic Senators have been more
concerned about the Presidential election in '48, than
they have been about settling Oregon either at 49° or
54°40'. 'Forty-eight' has been with them the Great
question, and hence the divisions in the Democratic
party. I cannot but observe the fact, and for the sake
of the country I deeply deplore it. I will however do
my duty whatever may happen. I will rise above the
interested factions in Congress, and appeal confidently
to the people for support ...

Monday, 11th May, 1846. [The House declared that a
state of war existed between the United States and
Mexico.]. Col. Benton came in [and] said that the [House]
had passed a Bill to-day declaring war in two hours, and
that one and [a] half hours of that time had been occupied
in reading the documents which accompanied my message,
and that in his opinion in the 19th Century war should
not be declared without full discussion and much more
consideration than had been given to it in the Ho. Repts.
Mr. Buchanan then remarked that War already existed by
the act of Mexico herself & therefore it did not require
much deliberation to satisfy all that we ought promptly
and vigorously to meet [it]. Mr. Marcy and Mr. Buchanan
discussed the subject for some time with Mr. Benton, but
without any change of the opinions which he had expressed
to me in conversation this morning. I saw it was useless
to debate the subject further with him & therefore I
abstained from engaging further in the conversation.
After remaining near an hour Col. Benton left.
Mr. Buchanan, Mr. Marcy, and myself were perfectly
satisfied that he would oppose the Bill which had passed
the House to-day, and that if the Whigs on party grounds
acted with him the Bill might be defeated.

Gov. Yell of Arkansas, Senator Houston, & other
members of Congress called in in the course of the
evening, and were highly gratified at the action of the
House in passing the Bill by so overwhelming a majority.
The part taken by Mr. Calhoun in the Senate to-day
satisfies me that he too will oppose the Bill passed
by the House to-day if he thinks he can do so safely in
reference to public opinion. The Whigs in the Senate will
oppose it on party grounds probably, if they can get
Mr. Calhoun, Mr. Benton, and two or three other Senators
professing to belong to the Democratic party to join them,
so as to make a majority against the Bill. Should the

Bill be defeated by such a combination, the professed
Democratic members who by their votes aid in rejecting
it will owe a heavy responsibility not only to their
party but to the country. I am fully satisfied that
all that can save the Bill in the Senate is the fear
of the people by the few Democratic Senators who wish
it defeated.
(Ibid., pp. 337-8, 344-5, 392-3.)

15   Buchanan and Caribbean regionalism

(James Buchanan, Polk's secretary of state, was a strong
advocate of American expansion into and dominion over the
Caribbean and Central America. The following instruction
to R. M. Saunders, United States minister in Madrid,
dated 17 June 1848, fully spells out his reasoning in
connection with an abortive scheme to purchase Cuba from
Spain.)

Cuba is almost within sight of the coast of Florida.
Situated between that State and the Peninsula of Yucatan
and possessing the deep, capacious, and impregnably
fortified harbor of the Havana, if this Island were
under the dominion of Great Britain, she could command
both the inlets to the Gulf of Mexico. She would thus
be enabled in time of war effectively to blockade the
mouth of the Mississippi and to deprive all the western
States of this Union, as well as those within the Gulf,
teeming as they are with an industrious and enterprising
population, of a foreign market for their immense
productions. But this is not the worst. She could, also,
destroy the commerce by sea between our ports on the
Gulf and our Atlantic ports - a commerce of nearly as
great a value as the whole of our foreign trade.
    Is there any reason to believe that Great Britain
desires to acquire the Island of Cuba?
    We know that it has been her uniform policy throughout
her past history to seize upon every valuable commercial
point throughout the world whenever circumstances have
placed this in her power. And what point so valuable
as the Island of Cuba? The United States are the chief
commercial rival of Great Britain. Our tonnage at the
present moment is nearly equal to hers; and it will be
greater within a brief period, if nothing should occur
to arrest our progress. Of what vast importance would it
then be to her to obtain the possession of an Island
from which she could at any time destroy a very large
proportion both of our foreign and coasting trade.

Besides, she well knows that if Cuba were in our possession, her West India Islands would be rendered comparatively valueless. From the extent and fertility of this Island and from the energy and industry of our people, we should soon be able to supply the markets of the world with tropical productions at a cheaper rate than these could be raised in any of her possessions.

The disposition of Great Britain to extend her dominion over the most important commercial positions of the globe has been clearly manifested on a recent occasion. Tempted by the weakness and disunion of the Central American States, and acting under the mask of a protector to the King and Kingdom of the Mosquitos - a miserable, degraded, and paltry tribe of Indians - she is endeavoring to acquire permanent possession of the entire coast of the Caribbean Sea from Cape Honduras to Escuda de Veragua ...

But let me present another view of the subject. If Cuba were annexed to the United States, we should not only be relieved from the apprehensions which we can never cease to feel for our own safety and the security of our commerce whilst it shall remain in its present condition, but human foresight cannot anticipate the beneficial consequences which would result to every portion of our Union. This can never become a local question.

1. With suitable fortifications at the Tortugas, and in possession of the strongly fortified harbor of Havana as a naval station on the opposite Coast of Cuba, we could command the outlet of the Gulf of Mexico between the Peninsula of Florida and that Island. This would afford ample security both to the foreign and coasting trade of the Western and Southern States which seek a market for their surplus productions through the Ports on the Gulf.

2. Under the Government of the United States, Cuba would become the richest and most fertile Island of the same extent throughout the world ...

Were Cuba a portion of the United States, it could be difficult to estimate the amount of breadstuffs, rice, cotton, and other agricultural, as well as manufacturing and mechanical productions - of lumber, of the products of our fisheries, and of other articles, which would find a market in that Island, in exchange for their coffee, sugar, tobacco, and other productions. This would go on, increasing with the increase of its population and the development of its resources; and all portions of the Union would be benefited by the trade.

Desirable, however, as the possession of this Island

may be to the United States, we would not acquire it
except by the free consent of Spain. Any acquisition
not sanctioned by justice and honor would be too dearly
purchased. Whilst such is the determination of the
President, it is supposed that the present relations
between Cuba and Spain might incline the Spanish
Government to cede the Island to the United States, upon
the payment of a fair and full consideration ...

The apprehensions which existed for many years after
the origin of this Government, that the extension of our
federal system would endanger the Union, seem to have
passed away. Experience has proved that this system of
confederated Republics, under which the Federal
Government has charge of the interests common to the
whole, whilst local Governments watch over the concerns
of the respective States, is capable of almost
indefinite extension, with increasing strength. This,
however, is always subject to the qualification that the
mass of the population must be of our own race, or must
have been educated in the school of civil and religious
liberty. With this qualification, the more we increase
the number of confederated States, the greater will be
the strength and security of the Union; because the more
dependent for their mutual interests will the several
parts be upon the whole and the whole upon the several
parts.

It is true that of the 418,291 white inhabitants
which Cuba contained in 1841, a very large proportion
is of the Spanish race. Still many of our citizens have
settled on the Island, and some of them are large
holders of property. Under our Government it would
speedily be *Americanized* - as Louisiana has been.

Within the boundaries of such a federal system alone
can a trade exempt from duties and absolutely free be
enjoyed. With the possession of Cuba, we should have,
throughout the Union, a free trade on a more extended
scale than any which the world has ever witnessed, -
arousing an energy and activity of competition which
would result in a most rapid improvement in all that
contributes to the welfare and happiness of the human
race. What state would forego the advantages of this
vast free trade with all her sisters, and place herself
in lonely isolation!

But the acquisition of Cuba would greatly strengthen
our bond of Union. Its possession would secure to all the
States within the valley of the Mississippi and Gulf of
Mexico free access to the ocean; but this security could
only be preserved whilst the ship-building and navigating
States of the Atlantic shall furnish a navy sufficient to

keep open the outlets from the Gulf to the Ocean. Cuba,
justly appreciating the advantages of annexation, is now
ready to rush into our arms. Once admitted, she would be
entirely dependent for her prosperity, and even existence,
upon her connexion with the Union; whilst the rapidly
increasing trade between her and the other States would
shed its benefits and its blessings over the whole. Such
a state of mutual dependence, resulting from the very
nature of things, the world has never witnessed. This
is what will insure the perpetuity of our Union.
(From John Bassett Moore, ed., 'The Works of James
Buchanan,' vol. VIII (Philadelphia, 1909), pp. 90-1,
94-5, 99-100.)

16   The Pacific Ocean: Japan

(Next to Latin America, the United States developed a
strong interest in the Pacific Ocean for commercial,
strategic and cultural reasons. Daniel Webster, secretary
of state in the Whig administrations of W. H. Harrison,
John Tyler, and Millard Fillmore, was an articulate
spokesman of this interest. This excerpt is from his
instruction to Commodore John H. Aulick, dated 10 June
1851, as the latter embarked on a mission to Japan
which proved to be abortive.)

The moment is near when the last link in the chain of
oceanic steam navigation is to be formed. From China and
the East Indies to Egypt, thence through the Mediterranean
and Atlantic ocean to England, thence again to our happy
shores, and other parts of this great continent; from our
own ports to the southernmost part of the isthmus that
connects the two western continents; and from its Pacific
coast, north and southwards, as far as civilization has
spread, the steamers of other nations and our own carry
intelligence, the wealth of the world, and thousands of
travellers.
    It is the President's opinion that steps should be
taken at once to enable our enterprising merchants to
supply the last link in that great chain which unites all
nations of the world, by the early establishment of a
line of steamers from California to China. In order to
facilitate this enterprise, it is desirable that we should
obtain, from the Emperor of Japan, permission to purchase
from his subjects the necessary supplies of coal, which
our steamers on their out and inward voyages may require.
The well known jealousy with which the Japanese empire
has, for the last two centuries, rejected all overtures

from other nations to open its ports to their vessels,
embarrasses all new attempts to change the exclusive
policy of that country.

The interests of commerce, and even those of humanity,
demand, however, that we should make another appeal to
the sovereign of that country, in asking him to sell to
our steamers, not the manufactures of his artisans, or
the results of the toil of his husbandmen, but a gift of
Providence, deposited, by the Creator of all things, in
the depths of the Japanese islands for the benefit of
the human family.
(From 'The Writings and Speeches of Daniel Webster',
vol. XIV (Boston, 1903), pp. 427-8.)

17   The Pacific Ocean: Hawaii

(Already by the 1850s the United States government had
come to view the Hawaiian islands as a country of
special concern, applying to it some of the language used
in connection with the Western Hemisphere. A good
example is this instruction by Webster to Luther
Severance, American commissioner in Hawaii, dated
14 July 1851.)

This Government still desires to see the nationality of
the Hawaiian Government maintained, its independent
administration of public affairs respected, and its
prosperity and reputation increased.

But while thus indisposed to exercise any sinister
influence itself over the counsels of Hawaii, or to
overawe the proceedings of its Government by the menace or
the actual application of superior military force, it
expects to see other powerful nations act in the same
spirit ...

The Hawaiian Islands are ten times nearer to the
United States than to any of the powers of Europe. Five-
sixths of all their commercial intercourse is with the
United States, and these considerations, together with
others of a more general character, have fixed the course
which the Government of the United States will pursue in
regard to them. The annunciation of this policy will not
surprise the governments of Europe, nor be thought to be
unreasonable by the nations of the civilized world, and
that policy is that while the Government of the United
States, itself faithful to its original assurance,
scrupulously regards the independence of the Hawaiian
Islands, it can never consent to see those islands taken
possession of by either of the great commercial powers of

Europe, nor can it consent that demands, manifestly
unjust and derogatory and inconsistent with a *bona fide*
independence, shall be enforced against that
Government ...

You inform us that many American citizens have gone to
settle in the islands; if so, they have ceased to be
American citizens. The Government of the United States
must, of course, feel an interest in them not extended
to foreigners, but by the law of nations they have no
right further to demand the protection of this
Government. Whatever aid or protection might under any
circumstances be given them must be given, not as a
matter of right on their part, but in consistency with
the general policy and duty of the Government and its
relations with friendly powers.

You will therefore not encourage in them, nor indeed
in any others, any idea or expectation that the islands
will become annexed to the United States. All this, I
repeat, will be judged of hereafter, as circumstances
and events may require, by the Government at Washington.
(Ibid., pp. 438-41.)

18   The Civil War: the Northern view

(The Civil War put an end to the period of self-confident
assertiveness and expansion in American foreign relations.
Both the Union and the Confederate regimes sought
sympathy and understanding abroad. Lincoln's secretary of
state, William Seward, sent the following instruction to
Minister Cassius Clay in Russia on 6 May 1861.)

Nations, like individuals, have three prominent wants;
firstly, freedom; secondly, prosperity; thirdly, friends.
The United States early secured the first two objects by
the exercise of courage and enterprise. But, although
they have always practised singular moderation, they
nevertheless have been slow in winning friends.

Russia presents an exceptional case. That power was
an early, and it has always been a constant friend. This
relationship between two nations, so remote and so unlike,
has excited much surprise, but the explanation is
obvious. Russia, like the United States, is an improving
and expanding empire. Its track is eastward, while that
of the United States is westward. The two nations,
therefore, never come into rivalry or conflict. Each
carries civilization to the new regions it enters, and
each finds itself occasionally resisted by states jealous
of its prosperity, or alarmed by its aggrandizement.

Russia and the United States may remain good friends
until, each having made a circuit of half the globe in
opposite directions, they shall meet and greet each other
in the region where civilization first began, and where,
after so many ages, it has become now lethargic and
helpless. It will be your pleasing duty to confirm and
strengthen these traditional relations of amity and
friendship ...

If nations were now, as in ancient times, morally
independent and unsocial, the President would not have
occasion to address our representatives in Europe on the
painful events which are subjects of intense solicitude
at home. But the world has, in a measured degree, become
one commonwealth. Nations favor or discourage political
changes in other nations, and exercise influences upon
their success and fortunes, sometimes from interest,
sometimes from sympathy, and sometimes from caprice ...

What would be the consequences of the revolution [i.e.
rebellion by the Southern states] if it could be
successful? The answer is obvious. At first, division
of this great and hitherto peaceful and happy country
into two hostile and belligerent republics. Later, a
resolution of each of those two republics into an
indefinite number of petty, hostile, and belligerent
states. Local jealousies, continually agitated, would,
early or late, be aggravated by the horrors of a servile
war, filling the whole country with desolation. The end
would be military despotism, compelling peace where free
government had proved an absolute and irretrievable
failure.

The equilibrium of the nations, maintained by this
Republic, on the one side, against the European system on
the other continent, would be lost, and the struggles of
nations in that system for dominion in this hemisphere
and on the high seas, which constitutes the chief portion
of the world's history in the eighteenth century, would
be renewed. The progress of freedom and civilization,
now so happily inaugurated, would be arrested, and the
hopes of humanity which this the present century has
brought forth would be disappointed and indefinitely
postponed.

What will be the consequences of the failure of the
revolution? The continuance of the country in the happy
career that it has pursued so auspiciously, to the repose
of nations and to the improvement of the condition of
mankind.

What does the President require or expect from the
Emperor of Russia? That sovereign is expected to do just
what this government does in regard to Russia and all

other nations. It refrains from all intervention whatever
in their political affairs; and it expects the same just
and generous forbearance in return. It has too much
self-respect to ask more, and too high a sense of its
rights to accept anything less.
(From George E. Baker, ed., 'The Works of William H.
Seward', vol. V (Boston, 1890), pp. 246-7, 251.)

19   The Civil War: the Southern view

(President Jefferson Davis of the Confederacy gave this
report on the South's foreign relations to the Confederate
Congress on 7 December 1863.)

For nearly three years this Government has exercised
unquestioned jurisdiction over many millions of willing
and united people. It has met and defeated vast armies
of invaders, who have in vain sought its subversion.
Supported by the confidence and affection of its citizens,
the Confederacy has lacked no element which distinguishes
an independent nation according to the principles of
public law. Its legislative, executive, and judicial
Departments, each in its sphere, have performed their
appropriate functions with a regularity as undisturbed
as in a time of profound peace, and the whole energies
of the people have been developed in the organization of
vast armies, while their rights and liberties have rested
secure under the protection of courts of justice. This
Confederacy is either independent or it is a dependency
of the United States; for no other earthly power claims
the right to govern it. Without one historic fact on
which the pretention can rest, without one line or word
of treaty or covenant which can give color to title, the
United States have asserted, and the British Government
has chosen to concede, that these sovereign States are
dependencies of the Government which is administered at
Washington. Great Britain has accordingly entertained
with that Government the closest and most intimate
relations, while refusing, on its demands, ordinary
amicable intercourse with us, and has, under arrangements
made with the other nations of Europe, not only denied
our just claim of admission into the family of nations,
but interposed a passive though effectual bar to the
knowledge of our rights by other powers ...
    I am well aware that we are unfortunately without
adequate remedy for the injustices under which we have
suffered at the hands of a powerful nation, at a juncture
when our entire resources are absorbed in the defense of

our lives, liberties, and independence, against an enemy
possessed of greatly superior numbers and material
resources. Claiming no favor, desiring no aid, conscious
of our own ability to defend our own rights against the
utmost efforts of an infuriate foe, we had thought it not
extravagant to expect that assistance would be withheld
from our enemies, and that the conduct of foreign nations
would be marked by a genuine impartiality between the
belligerents. It was not supposed that a professed
neutrality would be so conducted as to justify the
Foreign Secretary of the British nation in explaining, in
correspondence with our enemies, how 'the impartial
observance of neutral obligations by Her Majesty's
Government has thus been exceedingly advantageous to the
cause of the more powerful of the two contending parties.'
The British Government may deem this war a favorable
occasion for establishing, by the temporary sacrifice of
their neutral rights, a precedent which will justify the
future exercise of those extreme belligerent pretensions
that their naval power renders so formidable ... But we
cannot permit, without protest, the assertion that
international law or morals regard as 'impartial
neutrality' the conduct avowed to be 'exceedingly
advantageous' to one of the belligerents ...

The events of the last year have produced important
changes in the condition of our Southern neighbor. The
occupation of the capital of Mexico by the French army,
and the establishment of a provisional government,
followed by a radical change in the constitution of the
country, have excited lively interest. Although
preferring our own Government and institutions to those
of other countries, we can have no disposition to contest
the exercise by them of the same right of self-government
which we assert for ourselves. If the Mexican people
prefer a monarchy to a republic, it is our plain duty
cheerfully to acquiesce in their decision and to evince
a sincere and friendly interest in their prosperity. If,
however, the Mexicans prefer maintaining their former
institutions, we have no reason to apprehend any obstacle
to the free exercise of their choice. The Emperor of the
French has solemnly disclaimed any purpose to impose on
Mexico a form of government not acceptable to the nation;
and the eminent personage to whom the throne has been
tendered declines its acceptance unless the offer be
sanctioned by the suffrages of the people. In either
event, therefore, we may confidently expect the
continuance of those peaceful relations which have been
maintained on the frontier, and even a large development
of the commerce already existing to the mutual advantage

of the two countries.
(From Dunbar Rowland, ed., 'Jefferson Davis,
Constitutionalist: His Letters, Papers and Speeches',
vol. VI (Jackson, Miss., 1923), pp. 104-5, 107.)

2 EUROPEAN IMPERIALISM AND US EXPANSIONISM

20 Seward and Alaska

(The Alaskan purchase of 1867 was the only instance of
substantial territorial acquisition by postbellum
America, but Secretary of State Seward had an even
grander vision of expansion, as can be seen in these
excerpts from his speech at Sitka, Alaska, on 12 August
1869.)

You, the citizens of Sitka, are the pioneers, the
advanced guard, of the future population of Alaska; and
you naturally ask when, from whence, and how soon,
reinforcements shall come, and what are the signs and
guarantees of their coming? This question, with all its
minute and searching interrogations, has been asked by
the pioneers of every state and territory of which the
American Union is now composed; and the history of those
and territories furnishes the complete, conclusive, and
satisfactory answer. Emigrants go to every infant state
and territory in obedience to the great natural law that
obliges needy men to seek subsistence, and invites
adventurous men to seek fortune where it is most easily
obtained, and this is always in the new and uncultivated
regions. They go from every state and territory, and
from every foreign nation in America, Europe, and Asia;
because no established and populous state or nation can
guarantee subsistence and fortune to all who demand them
among its inhabitants.
    The guarantees and signs of their coming to Alaska are
found in the resources of the territory, which I have
attempted to describe, and in the condition of society in
other parts of the world. Some men seek other climes
for health and some for pleasure. Alaska invites the
former class by a climate singularly salubrious, and the
latter class by scenery which surpasses in sublimity that
of either the Alps, the Apennines, the Alleghanies, or the
Rocky Mountains. Emigrants from our own states, from
Europe, and from Asia, will not be slow in finding out
that fortunes are to be gained by pursuing here the
occupations which have so successfully sustained races of
untutored men. Civilization and refinement are making

more rapid advances in our day than at any former period.
The rising states and nations on this continent, the
European nations, and even those of Eastern Asia, have
exhausted, or are exhausting, their own forests and mines,
and are soon to become largely dependent upon those of
the Pacific. The entire region of Oregon, Washington
Territory, British Columbia, and Alaska, seem thus
destined to become a ship-yard for the supply of all
nations. I do not forget on this occasion that British
Columbia belongs within a foreign jurisdiction. That
circumstance does not materially affect my calculations.
British Columbia, by whomsoever possessed, must be
governed in conformity with the interests of her people
and of society upon the American continent. If that
territory shall be so governed, there will be no ground
of complaint anywhere. If it shall be governed so as to
conflict with the interests of the inhabitants of that
territory and of the United States, we all can easily
foresee what will happen in that case. You will ask me,
however, for guarantees that the hopes I encourage will
not be postponed. I give them.

Within the period of my own recollection, I have seen
twenty new states added to the eighteen which before that
time constituted the American Union, and I now see,
besides Alaska, ten territories in a forward condition of
preparation for entering into the same great political
family. I have seen in my own time not only the first
electric telegraph, but even the first railroad and the
first steamboat invented by man. And even on this
present voyage of mine, I have fallen in with the first
steamboat, still afloat, that thirty-five years ago
lighted her fires on the Pacific ocean. These, citizens
of Sitka, are the guarantees, not only that Alaska has
a future, but that the future has already begun. I know
that you want two things just now, when European monopoly
is broken down and United States free trade is being
introduced within the territory: These are, military
protection while your number is so inferior to that of the
Indians around you, and you need also a territorial civil
government. Congress has already supplied the first of
these wants adequately and effectually. I doubt not that
it will supply the other want during the coming winter.
(From 'Works of Seward', pp. 567-8.)

21 Grant and Santo Domingo

(President Grant was an advocate of Dominican annexation.
In this document, dated 31 May 1870, he gave reasons why

the Senate should ratify a treaty of annexation which had been signed by the two governments. Grant's efforts bore no fruit, as the majority of Senators did not support territorial expansion in the Caribbean.)

I feel an unusual anxiety for the ratification of this treaty, because I believe it will redound greatly to the glory of the two countries interested, to civilization, and to the extirpation of the institution of slavery.

The doctrine promulgated by President Monroe has been adhered to by all political parties, and I now deem it proper to assert the equally important principle that hereafter no territory on this continent shall be regarded as subject of transfer to a European power.

The Government of San Domingo has voluntarily sought this annexation. It is a weak power, numbering probably less than 120,000 souls, and yet possessing one of the richest territories under the sun, capable of supporting a population of 10,000,000 people in luxury. The people of San Domingo are not capable of maintaining themselves in their present condition, and must look for outside support.

They yearn for the protection of our free institutions and laws, our progress and civilization. Shall we refuse them?

I have information which I believe reliable that a European power stands ready now to offer $2,000,000 for the possession of Samana Bay alone. If refused by us, with what grace can we prevent a foreign power from attempting to secure the prize?

The acquisition of San Domingo is desirable because of its geographical position. It commands the entrance to the Caribbean Sea and the Isthmus transit of commerce. It possesses the richest soil, best and most capacious harbors, most salubrious climate, and the most valuable products of the forests, mine, and soil of any of the West India Islands. Its possession by us will in a few years build up a coastwise commerce of immense magnitude, which will go far toward restoring to us our lost merchant marine. It will give to us those articles which we consume so largely and do not produce, thus equalizing our exports and imports.

In case of foreign war it will give us command of all the islands referred to, and thus prevent an enemy from ever again possessing himself of rendezvous upon our very coast ...

The acquisition of San Domingo is an adherence to the 'Monroe doctrine;' it is a measure of national protection; it is asserting our just claim to a

controlling influence over the great commercial traffic
soon to flow from east to west by the way of the Isthmus
of Darien; it is to build up our merchant marine; it is
to furnish new markets for the products of our farms,
shops, and manufactories; it is to make slavery
insupportable in Cuba and Porto Rico at once and ultimately
so in Brazil; it is to settle the unhappy condition
of Cuba, and end an exterminating conflict; it is to
provide honest means of paying our honest debts, without
overtaxing the people; it is to furnish our citizens with
the necessaries of everyday life at cheaper rates than
ever before; and it is, in fine, a rapid stride toward
that greatness which the intelligence, industry, and
enterprise of the citizens of the United States entitle
this country to assume among nations.
(From 'Messages and Papers of Presidents', vol. VII
(Washington, 1898), pp. 61-3.)

22   Fish and the Cuban uprising

(The Cuban uprising of 1868-78 was a major foreign
policy issue of the Grant administration. Many,
including President Grant, were inclined to support the
rebels by recognizing their belligerency, but Secretary
of State Hamilton Fish succeeded in having the administration maintain a cautious policy of neutrality. The
following document, a report by Grant to Congress, dated
13 June 1870, was drafted by Fish.)

Mr. Monroe concisely expressed the rule which has
controlled the action of this Government with reference
to revolting colonies pending their struggle by saying:
    As soon as the movement assumed such a steady and
    consistent form as to make the success of the Provinces
    probable, the rights to which they were entitled by
    the laws of nations as equal parties to a civil war
    were extended to them.
The strict adherence to this rule of public policy has
been one of the highest honors of American statesmanship,
and has secured to this Government the confidence of the
feeble powers on this continent, which induces them to
rely upon its friendship and absence of designs of
conquest and to look to the United States for example and
moral protection. It has given to this Government a
position of prominence and of influence which it should
not abdicate, but which imposes upon it the most delicate
duties of right and of honor regarding American questions,
whether those questions affect emancipated colonies or
colonies subject to European dominion ...

The insurgents hold no town or city; have no established seat of government; they have no prize courts; no organization for the receiving and collecting of revenue; no seaport to which a prize may be carried or through which access can be had by a foreign power to the limited interior territory and mountain vastnesses which they occupy. The existence of a legislature representing any popular constituency is more than doubtful.

In the uncertainty that hangs around the entire insurrection there is no palpable evidence of an election, of any delegated authority, or of any government outside the limits of the camps occupied from day to day by the roving companies of insurgent troops; there is no commerce, no trade, either internal or foreign, no manufactures ...

There is not a *de facto* government in the island of Cuba sufficient to execute law and maintain just relations with other nations. Spain has not been able to suppress the opposition to Spanish rule on the island, nor to award speedy justice to other nations, or citizens of other nations, when their rights have been invaded.

There are serious complications growing out of the seizure of American vessels upon the high seas, executing American citizens without proper trial, and confiscating or embargoing the property of American citizens. Solemn protests have been made against every infraction of the rights of our flag upon the high seas, and all proper steps have been taken and are being pressed for the proper reparation of every indignity complained of.

The question of belligerency, however, which is to be decided upon definite principles and according to ascertained facts, is entirely different from and unconnected with the other questions of the manner in which the strife is carried on on both sides and the treatment of our citizens entitled to our protection. (Ibid., pp. 66-8.)

23 A Centennial oration

(In 1876 Americans recalled the past century and looked forward to the future in an optimistic frame of mind. Their orations inevitably referred to the place of the United States in the world. A typical example was the following, delivered at Columbus, the capital of Ohio, by George L. Converse.)

Can there be any doubt that the nations are profiting by

our example? If the world's progress during the last
century is any criterion, what will be the condition of
affairs at the end of the next? In another century there
will be from sixty to a hundred sovereign States. Our
Southern border will be the isthmus; our Northern, the
frozen seas; and East and West our flag will float far
enough to cover with its protecting shadow the adjacent
islands.

In other centuries, perhaps, this whole continent will
be locked in the embrace of one common brotherhood of
States. Under the representative principle and home rule,
the Union is capable of great expansion, and could with
time and education be made to embrace the continent.
American citizenship shall everywhere be a panoply and a
shield to its possessor. Our population may become as
countless as the sands on the sea shore, but science shall
unlock to them the secret storehouse of wealth. The earth
under their manipulation shall yield her products more
abundantly and with greater regularity. Science shall
discover to them the door that leads to the rich deposits
of silver, gold and precious stones. By its aid, her
commerce may float in the air above the mountain top and
the cloud, or be guided on glistening rails beneath the
ocean. The arcana of nature will be explored - the air,
the water - the very elements shall give up their secret
treasures of power and of motion, at the command of
science, to the sons of freedom.

In the march of coming generations, the thundering
tread of American freemen, whether in war or in peace,
shall echo from the distant ocean shore on either side,
and be heard and heeded alike by Caucasian and Mongolian.

In the clash of ideas and political principles sure to
come in the distant future, America will represent one
type of civilization, with free and popular government,
while Russia, having swallowed the lesser kingdoms around
or combining with them, shall represent the other, with
centralization and despotism.

When the two systems meet, as meet they will, it will
be in the shock of dreadful war, and like the meeting of
two clouds surcharged with the elements of storm, the
land will be deluged in blood. The sons of freedom shall
prevail, and out of the conflict shall arise the sweet
and lasting peace that shall characterize the millennium.
(From Frederick Saunders, ed., 'Our National Centennial
Jubilee' (New York, 1877), pp. 614-15.)

24   Blaine and pan-Americanism

(James G. Blaine, Secretary of State during the short-
lived presidency of James A. Garfield, made a contribution
to the history of United States foreign relations by
promoting the idea of pan-American congresses and courts
of arbitration. The following instruction of
29 November 1881, was sent to the American minister in
Mexico.)

The attitude of the United States with respect to the
question of general peace on the American continent is
well known through its persistent efforts for years past
to avert the evils of warfare, or, these efforts failing,
to bring positive conflicts to an end through pacific
counsels or the advocacy of impartial arbitration. This
attitude has been consistently maintained, and always
with such fairness as to leave no room for imputing to
our Government any motive except the humane and
disinterested one of saving the kindred States of the
American continent from the burdens of war. The position
of the United States as the leading power of the New
World might well give to its Government a claim to
authoritative utterance for the purpose of quieting
discord among its neighbors, with all of whom the most
friendly relations exist. Nevertheless, the good offices
of this Government are not and have not at any time
been tendered with a show of dictation or compulsion, but
only as exhibiting the solicitous good will of a common
friend.
    For some years past a growing disposition has been
manifested by certain States of Central and South America
to refer disputes affecting grave questions of
international relationship and boundaries to arbitration
rather than to the sword. It has been on several such
occasions a source of profound satisfaction to the
Government of the United States to see that this country
is in a large measure looked to by all the American
powers as their friend and mediator.
    The just and impartial counsel of the President in
such cases has never been withheld, and his efforts have
been rewarded by the prevention of sanguinary strife or
angry contentions between peoples whom we regard as
brethren.
    The existence of this growing tendency convinces the
President that the time is ripe for a proposal that shall
enlist the good will and active co-operation of all the
States of the Western Hemisphere, both north and south,
in the interest of humanity and for the common weal of
nations.

He conceives that none of the Governments of America
can be less alive than our own to the dangers and horrors
of a state of war, and especially of war between kinsmen.
He is sure that none of the chiefs of Governments on the
continent can be less sensitive than he is to the sacred
duty of making every endeavor to do away with the chances
of fratricidal strife. And he looks with hopeful
confidence to such active assistance from them as will
serve to show the broadness of our common humanity and
the strength of the ties which bind us all together as a
great and harmonious system of American Commonwealths.

Impressed by these views, the President extends to all
the Independent countries of North and South America an
earnest invitation to participate in a general congress
to be held in the city of Washington on the 24th day of
November, 1882, for the purpose of considering and
discussing the methods of preventing war between the
nations of America. He desires that the attention of
the congress shall be strictly confined to this one
great object; that its sole aim shall be to seek a way
of permanently averting the horrors of cruel and bloody
combat between countries, oftenest of one blood and
speech, or the even worse calamity of internal commotion
and civil strife; that it shall regard the burdensome
and far-reaching consequences of such struggles, the
legacies of exhausted finances, of oppressive debt, of
onerous taxation, of ruined cities, of paralyzed
industries, of devastated fields, of ruthless
conscription, of the slaughter of men, of the grief of
the widow and the orphan, of embittered resentments that
long survive those who provoked them and heavily afflict
the innocent generations that come after.
(From 'Messages and Papers of Presidents', vol. VIII
(Washington, 1898), pp. 98-9.)

25   Chinese exclusion

(The so-called Burlingame treaty of 1868, giving Chinese
the right to emigrate to the United States, became
increasingly unpopular, and in 1879 Congress passed a
bill restricting the number of Chinese immigrants.
President Rutherford B. Hayes, in this message of
1 March 1879, vetoed it as a violation of the treaty.
But he recognized the need to regulate Chinese
immigration and signed a new treaty in 1880 with China to
supersede the Burlingame provision.)

The lapse of ten years since the negotiation of the

Burlingame treaty has exhibited to the notice of the
Chinese Government, as well as to our own people, the
working of this experiment of immigration in great
numbers of Chinese laborers to this country, and their
maintenance here of all the traits of race, religion,
manners, and customs, habitations, mode of life,
segregation here, and the keeping up of the ties of their
original home, which stamp them as strangers and
sojourners, and not as incorporated elements of our
national life and growth. This experience may naturally
suggest the reconsideration of the subject as dealt
with by the Burlingame treaty, and may properly become
the occasion of more direct and circumspect recognition,
in renewed negotiations, of the difficulties surrounding
this political and social problem. It may well be that,
to the apprehension of the Chinese Government no less
than our own, the simple provisions of the Burlingame
treaty may need to be replaced by more careful methods,
securing the Chinese and ourselves against a larger and
more rapid infusion of this foreign race than our system
of industry and society can take up and assimilate with
ease and safety. This ancient Government, ruling a
polite and sensitive people, distinguished by a high
sense of national pride, may properly desire an
adjustment of their relations with us which would in all
things confirm and in no degree endanger the permanent
peace and amity and the growing commerce and prosperity
which it has been the object and the effect of our
existing treaties to cherish and perpetuate.

I regard the very grave discontents of the people of
the Pacific States with the present working of the
Chinese immigration, and their still graver apprehensions
therefrom in the future, as deserving the most serious
attention of the people of the whole country and a
solicitous interest on the part of Congress and the
Executive. If this were not my own judgment, the passage
of this bill by both Houses of Congress would impress
upon me the seriousness of the situation, when a majority
of the representatives of the people of the whole country
had thought fit to justify so serious a measure of
relief ...

I am convinced that, whatever urgency might in any
quarter or by any interest be supposed to require an
instant suppression of further immigration from China,
no reasons can require the immediate withdrawal of our
treaty protection of the Chinese already in this country,
and no circumstances can tolerate an exposure of our
citizens in China, merchants or missionaries, to the
consequences of so sudden an abrogation of their treaty

protection.   Fortunately, however, the actual recession
in the flow of emigration relieves us from any
apprehension that the treatment of the subject in the
proper course of diplomatic negotiations will introduce
any new features of discontent or disturbance among the
communities directly affected.   Were such delay fraught
with more inconveniences than have ever been suggested
by the interests most earnest in promoting this
legislation, I can not but regard the summary
disturbance of our existing treaties with China as
greatly more inconvenient to much wider and more
permanent interests of the country.
(From 'Messages and Papers of Presidents', VII, 517-18,
519.)

26   The opening of Korea

(The United States signed a treaty of commerce and amity
with the Kingdom of Korea - referred to as Tah-Chosun in
the following document - in 1882.   The following year
the first Korean embassy visited Washington, and President
Chester A. Arthur gave this welcoming address.)

Mr. Minister and Mr. Vice-Minister: It gives me much
pleasure to receive you as the representatives of the
King and Government of Tah-Chosun.   I bid you a cordial
welcome.
      We are not ignorant of your beautiful peninsular
country, with its surrounding islands, or of their
productions, or of the industries of your people, who in
population number more than twice that of the United
States when they became an independent nation.
      The ocean which intervenes between our respective
domains, has, by means of the introduction and perfection
of steam navigation, become a highway of convenient and
safe intercourse.   You are our neighbors.
      The United States from their geographical position,
are, of all others, the nation with which the orientals
should cultivate friendship and a commerce which will
prove to them and to us alike beneficial and profitable,
and which must constantly increase.
      This Republic, while conscious of its power, of its
wealth, and of its resources, seeks, as our history shows,
no dominion or control over other nationalities, and no
acquisition of their territory, but does seek to give
and receive the benefits of friendly relations and of a
reciprocal and honest commerce.
      We know you can be of benefit to us, and we think that

when you become familiar with the improvement we have made
in agricultural implements and processes, and in the
mechanical arts generally, you will be satisfied that we
can give you a fair return for the benefit you may confer
on us; and it may be that in our system of education and
in our laws you will discover some things that you will
be glad to adopt.

It was fit and becoming that you should have made with
us your first treaty of intercourse, amity and commerce.

You will be so good as to present to your King my
respectful regards, and to express to him my gratification
and that of our people that he should have seen proper
to honor us by the visit of this embassy.

Gentlemen, I trust that while you are in our country
you will have health and enjoyment.

It will be the purpose of our Government and people
so to receive you that you shall carry home with you
pleasant recollections of the American Republic.
(From 'Papers Relating to the Foreign Relations of the
United States, 1883' (Washington, 1884), pp. 249-50.)

27   The pork controversy with Germany

(Germany's decision to prohibit the importation of
American pork products was considered discriminatory
against the United States. Special interest groups
affected by the measure wrote urgent memorials to the
State Department, of which an example is the following
letter from Armour & Co. of Chicago, dated 1 March 1883.)

The recent action of the German Government, in prohibiting
the importation of American hog products, it seems to us,
demands some effort towards checking a policy that must
unquestionably result (if persisted in) in disaster to
the farming interests of Illinois and the Northwest. We
know that your familiarity with this subject renders it
unnecessary for us to enlarge upon it for your
information, but recognizing and acknowledging, with
thanks, your former interest in this question, we now
beg to ask your co-operation in the adoption of some
measure calculated to bring about the speedy repeal of
existing prohibitory decrees, or at least to render
their adoption in other quarters less attractive than at
present.

Knowing, as well as ourselves, that the sanitary
pretexts of both the French and German Governments need
no arguments, we feel that you will heartily support any
wise retaliatory measure brought forward to counteract

their disastrous legislation. And while aware that you
are fully informed as to the magnitude of the interests
thus attacked, we may state, from our intimate relations
with this most important Illinois industry, that the time
cannot be far distant when our own and adjoining States
will suffer to the extent of millions of dollars.

We refrain from inflicting upon you at length the
reasons for this conviction, which to us present the
feature of absolute certainty, because we feel that your
own information is ample, and that you must, having
already broadly considered the matter, fully agree with
us.

We therefore confidentially request that you will make
some effort, retaliatory in its character, the details
of which you can much better suggest than ourselves, and
will conclude by saying that while our own interests are
necessarily involved, they are, as you know, secondary
to those enormous interests which involve the welfare
of the State to as great a degree, perhaps, as those of
any other important industry.

The time, we suppose, being short for action during
the present Congress, we, of course, leave the matter
in your hands, hoping you may be able to do something
either before or after the close of the present Congress,
but as promptly as your numerous duties (and the
importance of the subject) will permit.
(Ibid., pp. 355-6.)

28 For an isthmian canal

(The United States-Nicaraguan treaty of 1884 gave the
former a right not only to construct a canal through
Nicaragua, but also to own, operate, and protect it. In
the following to Congress, dated 10 December 1884,
President Arthur urged Senate ratification of the treaty.)

The canal is primarily a domestic means of water
communication between the Atlantic and Pacific shores of
the two countries which unite for its construction, the
one contributing the territory and the other furnishing
the money therefor. Recognizing the advantages which the
world's commerce must derive from the work, appreciating
the benefit of enlarged use to the canal itself by
contributing to its maintenance and by yielding an
interest return on the capital invested therein, and
inspired by the belief that any great enterprise which
inures to the general benefit of the world is in some sort
a trust for the common advancement of mankind, the two

Governments have by this treaty provided for the peaceable use by all nations on equal terms, while reserving to the coasting trade of both countries (in which none but the contracting parties are interested) the privilege of favoring tolls.

The treaty provides for the construction of a railway and telegraph line, if deemed advisable, as accessories to the canal, as both may be necessary for the economical construction of the work and probably in its operation when completed.

The terms of the treaty as to the protection of the canal, while scrupulously confirming the sovereignty of Nicaragua, amply secure that State and the work itself from possible contingencies of the future which it may not be within the sole power of Nicaragua to meet.

From a purely commercial point of view the completion of such a waterway opens a most favorable prospect for the future of our country. The nations of the Pacific coast of South America will by its means be brought into close connection with our Gulf States. The relation of those American countries to the United States is that of a natural market, from which the want of direct communication has hitherto practically excluded us. By piercing the Isthmus the heretofore insuperable obstacles of time and sea distance disappear, and our vessels and productions will enter upon the world's competitive field with a decided advantage, of which they will avail themselves.

When to this is joined the large coasting trade between the Atlantic and Pacific States, which must necessarily spring up, it is evident that this canal affords, even alone, an efficient means of restoring our flag to its former place on the seas.

Such a domestic coasting trade would arise immediately, for even the fishing vessels of both seaboards, which now lie idle in the winter months, could then profitably carry goods between the Eastern and the Western States.

The political effect of the canal will be to knit closer the States now depending upon railway corporations for all commercial and personal intercourse, and it will not only cheapen the cost of transportation, but will free individuals from the possibility of unjust discriminations.

It will bring the European grain markets of demand within easy distance of our Pacific States, and will give to the manufacturers on the Atlantic seaboard economical access to the cities of China, thus breaking down the barrier which separates the principal manufacturing centers of the United States from the markets of the vast

population of Asia, and placing the Eastern States of the
Union for all purposes of trade midway between Europe and
Asia. In point of time the gain for sailing vessels would
be great, amounting from New York to San Francisco to a
saving of seventy-five days; to Hongkong, of twenty-seven
days; to Shanghai, of thirty-four days, and to Callao, of
fifty-two days.
(From 'Messages and Papers of Presidents', VIII, 257-8.)

29 Against an isthmian canal

(President Cleveland opposed the Nicaraguan canal treaty
and withdrew it from the Senate. His reasoning was an
excellent statement of peaceful expansionism, as recorded
in the following message to Congress on 8 December 1885.)

My immediate predecessor [President Arthur] caused to be
negotiated with Nicaragua a treaty for the construction,
by and at the sole cost of the United States, of a canal
through Nicaraguan territory, and laid it before the
Senate. Pending the action of that body thereon, I
withdrew the treaty for reexamination. Attentive
consideration of its provisions leads me to withhold it
from resubmission to the Senate.
    Maintaining, as I do, the tenets of a line of
precedents from Washington's day, which proscribe
entangling alliances with foreign states, I do not favor
a policy of acquisition of new and distant territory or
the incorporation of remote interests with our own.
    The laws of progress are vital and organic, and we
must be conscious of that irresistible tide of commercial
expansion which, as the concomitant of our active
civilization, day by day is being urged onward by those
increasing facilities of production, transportation, and
communication to which steam and electricity have given
birth; but our duty in the present instructs us to
address ourselves mainly to the development of the vast
resources of the great area committed to our charge and to
the cultivation of the arts of peace within our own
borders, though jealously alert in preventing the
American hemisphere from being involved in the political
problems and complications of distant governments.
Therefore I am unable to recommend propositions
involving paramount privileges of ownership or right outside of our own territory, when coupled with absolute and
unlimited engagements to defend the territorial integrity
of the state where such interests lie. While the
general project of connecting the two oceans by means of a

canal is to be encouraged, I am of opinion that any
scheme to that end to be considered with favor should be
free from the features alluded to ...

Whatever highway may be constructed across the
barrier dividing the two greatest maritime areas of the
world must be for the world's benefit - a trust for
mankind, to be removed from the chance of domination by
any single power, nor become a point of invitation for
hostilities or a prize for warlike ambition. An engage-
ment combining the construction, ownership, and operation
of such a work by this Government, with an offensive and
defensive alliance for its protection, with the foreign
state whose responsibilities and rights we would share is,
in my judgment, inconsistent with such dedication to
universal and neutral use, and would, moreover, entail
measures for its realization beyond the scope of our
national polity or present means.

The lapse of years has abundantly confirmed the wisdom
and foresight of those earlier Administrations which, long
before the conditions of maritime intercourse were
changed and enlarged by the progress of the age,
proclaimed the vital need of interoceanic transit across
the American Isthmus and consecrated it in advance to
the common use of mankind by their positive declarations
and through the formal obligation of treaties. Toward
such realization the efforts of my Administration will
be applied, ever bearing in mind the principles on which
it must rest, and which were declared in no uncertain
tones by Mr. Cass, who, while Secretary of State, in 1858,
announced that 'what the United States want in Central
America, next to the happiness of its people, is the
security and neutrality of the interoceanic routes which
lead through it.'
(Ibid., pp. 327-8.)

30   The Congo question

(John A. Kasson, United States minister to Germany in the
mid-1880s, was one of the staunchest advocates of an
aggressive foreign policy that went much beyond
traditional concerns. He attended the Berlin congress
on the Congo, but was disappointed that the government
in Washington decided against submitting the final act
at that conference for ratification by Congress. In an
article for the 'North American Review', Kasson
criticized the administration's timidity.)

... what do we gain by this act of the Conference?

We secure freedom and equality for our vessels and our commerce in all time and through all progressive developments to come, in an area broader than the United States and extending from the Atlantic to the Indian Ocean, together with all its interior waters, and over the canals and railroads connecting them. We secure the abolition of all monopolies, private or corporate. This is to continue, whatever the present sovereign jurisdiction, or the changes of governments to come, and whether they be independent states or colonial dependencies, and in time of war as well as peace. We secure freedom and equal protection for the persons of Americans whether travelling or resident there, for their property, and for the pursuit of their professions and enterprises of every sort. We gain security for the American missionaries, churches, and schools, now or hereafter to be established, and absolute liberty of commerce and freedom of worship. We gain pledges for the extinction of the hateful slave trade. In a word, we gain everything which we could gain by owning the country, except the expense of governing it. What we gain here by adhering to this act is what elsewhere we have been for a hundred years unable to gain by special negotiations with each individual government, from whose colonial possessions we are until this day either excluded or only admitted upon ruinous terms of discrimination.

On the other hand, what do we yield in exchange for this? Neither land, nor soldiers; neither money nor liability to expenditure; neither jurisdiction nor revenue. We simply agreee to recognize in other nations the same rights in Central Africa which are conceded to us; and we agree to use our 'good offices' with the governments on the eastern coast to obtain their consent to apply the liberal provisions of the act to their territories: in other words, to further our own interests. We further agree to lend our 'good offices' - *bons offices*, says the text and only that - to persuade a belligerent having possessions in this free zone, and with the consent of both belligerents, to adopt neutrality for these possessions during any war. These are the engagements, and the only engagements for action, which we assume toward other governments. But this pledge of our 'good offices' is hardly startling enough to shock the timidity of an administration which represents the spirit of the American people.
(From 'The North American Review', 142: 132-3 (February 1886).)

31   Cleveland's concern with national honor

(Grover Cleveland, the first Democratic president after
the Civil War, was a traditonal nationalist, concerned
with the preservation of the country's aggregate welfare
and honor in dealings with foreign countries. The
following is a letter he wrote to an official of the
American Fishery Union, dated 7 April 1887, in connection
with the Canadian fishery dispute.)

A nation seeking by any means to maintain its honor,
dignity, and integrity is engaged in protecting the
rights of its people; and if in such efforts particular
interests are injured and special advantages forfeited,
these things should be patriotically borne for the
public good.

An immense volume of population, manufactures, and
agricultural productions, and the marine tonnage and
railways to which these have given activity, all largely
the result of intercourse between the United States and
British America, and the natural growth of a full half
century of good neighborhood and friendly communication,
form an aggregate of material wealth and incidental
relations of most impressive magnitude. I fully
appreciate these things, and am not unmindful of the great
number of our people who are concerned in such vast and
diversified interests.

In the performance of the serious duty which the
Congress has imposed upon me ... I shall deem myself
bound to inflict no unnecessary damage or injury upon
any portion of our people; but I shall, nevertheless,
be unflinchingly guided by a sense of what the self-
respect and dignity of the nation demand. In the
maintenance of these, and in the support of the honor
of the government, beneath which every citizen may repose
in safety, no sacrifice of personal or private interests
shall be considered as against the general welfare.
(From George F. Parker, ed., 'The Writings and Speeches
of Grover Cleveland' (New York, 1892), pp. 499-500.)

32   Toward tariff reform

(President Cleveland devoted the whole of his annual
message to Congress, delivered on 6 December 1887, to
the question of tariff revision. No lowering of import
duties, however, took place until 1894.)

The difficulty attending a wise and fair revision of our

tariff laws is not underestimated. It will require on
the part of the Congress great labor and care, and
especially a broad and national contemplation of the
subject and a patriotic disregard of such local and
selfish claims as are unreasonable and reckless of the
welfare of the entire country.

Under our present laws more than 4,000 articles are
subject to duty. Many of these do not in any way compete
with our own manufactures, and many are hardly worth
attention as subjects of revenue. A considerable
reduction can be made in the aggregate by adding them
to the free list. The taxation of luxuries presents
no features of hardship; but the necessaries of life
used and consumed by all the people, the duty upon
which adds to the cost of living in every home, should
be greatly cheapened.

The radical reduction of the duties imposed upon raw
material used in manufactures, or its free importation,
is of course an important factor in any effort to reduce
the price of these necessaries. It would not only
relieve them from the increased cost caused by the tariff
on such material, but the manufactured product being thus
cheapened that part of the tariff now laid upon such
product, as a compensation to our manufacturers for the
present price of raw material, could be accordingly
modified. Such reduction or free importation would
serve besides to largely reduce the revenue. It is not
apparent how such a change can have any injurious effect
upon our manufacturers. On the contrary, it would appear
to give them a better chance in foreign markets with the
manufacturers of other countries, who cheapen their wares
by free material. Thus our people might have the
opportunity of extending their sales beyond the limits
of home consumption, saving them from the depression,
interruption in business, and loss caused by a glutted
domestic market and affording their employees more
certain and steady labor, with its resulting quiet and
contentment.

(From 'Messages and Papers of Presidents', VIII, 589.)

33 The new manifest destiny

(Even in the age of Cleveland's traditonalist diplomacy,
some were trying to develop a new outlook to accommodate
the vast changes taking place in the world, both
physically and intellectually. The following excerpt
from an article by John Fiske, entitled 'Manifest
Destiny', is a good example of the way American writers

sought to develop a world view that incorporated recent
history and the sociology of Herbert Spencer as well as
the usual optimism about American experience.)

... The Aryan people, after attaining a high stage of
civilization in Europe, are at least beginning to recover
their ancient homestead. The frontier against barbarism,
which Caesar left at the Rhine, has been carried eastward
to the Volga, and is now advancing even to the Oxus. The
question has sometimes been raised whether it would be
possible for European civilization to be seriously
threatened by any future invasion of barbarism or of
some lower type of civilization. By barbarism certainly
not; all the nomad strength of Mongolian Asia would
throw itself in vain against the insuperable barrier
constituted by Russia. But I have heard it quite
seriously suggested that if some future Attila or Jinghis
were to wield as a unit the entire military strength of
the four hundred millions of Chinese, possessed with
some suddenly conceived idea of conquering the world,
even as Omar and Abderrahman wielded as a unit the newly
welded power of the Saracens in the seventh and eighth
centuries, then perhaps a staggering blow might yet be
dealt against European civilization. I will not waste
precious time in considering this imaginary case further
than to remark that if the Chinese are ever going to try
anything of this sort, they can not afford to wait very
long; for within another century, as we shall presently
see, their very numbers will be surpassed by those of the
English race alone. By that time all the elements of
military predominance on the earth, including that of
simple numerical superiority, will have been gathered
into the hands not merely of Europeans generally, but
more specifically into the hands of the offspring of
the Teutonic tribes who conquered Britain in the fifth
century. So far as the relations of European civilization
with outside barbarism are concerned to-day, the only
serious question is by what process of modification the
barbarous races are to maintain their foot-hold upon the
earth at all. Where once they threatened the very
continuance of civilization, they now exist only on
sufferance ...
    Let us consider now to what conclusions the rapidity
and unabated steadiness of the increase of the English
race in America must lead us as we go on to forecast the
future. Carlyle somewhere speaks slightingly of the fact
that the Americans double their numbers every twenty
years, as if to have forty million dollar-hunters in the
world were any better than to have twenty million

dollar-hunters.   The implication that Americans are
nothing but dollar-hunters, and are thereby distinguish-
able from the rest of mankind, would not perhaps bear too
elaborate scrutiny. But during the present paper we
have been considering the gradual transfer of the
preponderance of physical strength from the hands of the
war-loving portion of the human race into the hands of
the peace-loving portion - into the hands of the dollar-
hunters, if you please, but out of the hands of the
scalp-hunters. Obviously to double the numbers of a
pre-eminently industrious, peaceful, orderly, and free-
thinking community is somewhat to increase the weight in
the world of the tendencies that go toward making
communities free and orderly and peaceful and
industrious ...
[The] work which the English race began when it
colonized North America is destined to go on until every
land on the earth's surface that is not already the seat
of an old civilization shall become English in its
language, in its religion, in its political habits and
traditions, and to a predominant extent in the blood of
its people. The day is at hand when four-fifths of the
human race will trace its pedigree to English
forefathers, as four-fifths of the white people in the
United States trace their pedigree to-day. The race thus
spread over both hemispheres, and from the rising to the
setting sun, will not fail to keep that sovereignty of
the sea and that commercial supremacy which it began to
acquire when England first stretched its arm across the
Atlantic to the shores of Virginia and Massachusetts.
The language spoken by these great communities will not
be sundered into dialects like the language of the
ancient Romans, but perpetual intercommunication and the
universal habit of reading and writing will preserve its
integrity, and the world's business will be transacted
by English-speaking people to so great an extent that
whatever language any man may have learned in his
infancy, he will find it necessary sooner of later to
learn to express his thoughts in English ...
Thus we may foresee in general how, by the gradual
concentration of physical power into the hands of the
most pacific communities, we may finally succeed in
rendering warfare illegal all over the globe. As this
process goes on, it may, after many more ages of
political experience, become apparent that there is
really no reason, in the nature of things, why the whole
of mankind should not constitute politically one huge
federation, each little group managing its local affairs
in entire independence, but relegating all questions of

international interest to the decision of one central
tribunal supported by the public opinion of the entire
human race. I believe that the time will come when such
a state of things will exist upon the earth, when it
will be possible (with our friends of the Paris dinner
party) to speak of the United States as stretching from
pole to pole, or with Tennyson to celebrate the
'parliament of man and the federation of the world.'
Indeed, only when such a state of things has begun to be
realized can civilization, as sharply demarcated from
barbarism, be said to have fairly begun. Only then can
the world be said to have become truly Christian ...
(From 'Harper's Magazine', 70: 580-1, 584-5, 588-90
(March 1885).)

3   THE GROWTH OF NATIONALISTIC EXPANSIONISM

34   Protection and prosperity

('Patriotism, protection, prosperity' was the Republican
Party's cardinal doctrine, according to William McKinley.
In the following annual message, delivered on 6 December
1892, President Benjamin Harrison echoed the same
sentiment - little suspecting that within several months
a major economic disaster would befall the country.)

... A comparison of the existing conditions with those of
the most favored period in the history of the country
will, I believe, show that so high a degree of prosperity
and so general a diffusion of the comforts of life were
never before enjoyed by our people ...
   There never has been a time in our history when work
was so abundant or when wages were as high, whether
measured by the currency in which they are paid or by
their power to supply the necessaries and comforts of
life ...
   If any are discontented with their state here, if any
believe that wages, or prices, the returns for honest
toil, are inadequate, they should not fail to remember
that there is no other country in the world where the
conditions that seem to them hard would not be accepted
as highly prosperous. The English agriculturist would be
glad to exchange the returns of his labor for those of
the American farmer and the Manchester workmen their
wages for those of their fellows at Fall River.
   I believe that the protective system, which has now
for something more than thirty years continuously
prevailed in our legislation, has been a mighty instrument

for the development of our national wealth and a most
powerful agency in protecting the homes of our workingmen
from the invasion of want.   I have felt a most solicitous
interest to preserve to our working people rates of
wages that would not only give daily bread, but supply
a comfortable margin for those home attractions and family
comforts and enjoyments without which life is neither
hopeful nor sweet.   They are American citizens - a part
of the great people for whom our Constitution and
Government were framed and instituted - and it can not be
a perversion of that independence, loyalty, and sense of
interest in the Government which are essential to good
citizenship in peace, and which will bring this stalwart
throng, as in 1861, to the defense of the flag when it is
assailed.
(From 'Messages and Papers of Presidents', vol. IX
(Washington, 1898), pp. 306-9.)

35   The Chilean controversy

(An attack by a Valparaiso mob upon American sailors on
shore leave from the cruiser 'Baltimore', in October
1891, brought United States-Chilean relations to a
crisis.   But the administration's attitude, as revealed
in this special message of 25 January 1891, by President
Harrison, was basically traditionalist.)

... The *Baltimore* was in the harbor of Valparaiso by
virtue of that general invitation which nations are
held to extend to the war vessels of other powers with
which they have friendly relations.   This invitation, I
think, must be held ordinarily to embrace the privilege
of such communication with the shore as is reasonable,
necessary, and proper for the comfort and convenience
of the officers and men of such vessels.   Captain Schley
testifies that when his vessel returned to Valparaiso on
September 14 the city officers, as is customary, extended
the hospitality of the city to his officers and crew.
It is not claimed that every personal collision or injury
in which a sailor or officer of such naval vessel visiting
the shore may be involved raises an international
question, but I am clearly of the opinion that where such
sailors or officers are assaulted by a resident populace,
animated by hostility to the government whose uniform
these sailors and officers wear and in resentment of acts
done by their government, not by them, their nation must
take notice of the event as one involving an infraction
of its rights and dignity, not in a secondary way, as

where a citizen is injured and presents his claim
through his own government, but in a primary way,
precisely as if its minister or consul of the flag
itself had been the object of the same character of
assault.

The officers and sailors of the *Baltimore* were in
the harbor of Valparaiso under the orders of their
Government, not by their own choice. They were upon
the shore by the implied invitation of the Government
of Chile and with the approval of their commanding
officer; and it does not distinguish their case from
that of a consul that his stay is more permanent or that
he holds the express invitation of the local government
to justify his longer residence. Nor does it affect
the question that the injury was the act of a mob. If
there had been no participation by the police or military
in this cruel work and no neglect on their part to extend
protection, the case would still be one, in my opinion,
when its extent and character are considered, involving
international rights ...

If the dignity as well as the prestige and influence
of the United States are not to be wholly sacrificed,
we must protect those who in foreign ports display the
flag or wear the colors of this Government against insult,
brutality, and death inflicted in resentment of the acts
of their Government and not for any fault of their own.
It has been my desire in every way to cultivate friendly
and intimate relations with all the Governments of this
hemisphere. We do not covet their territory. We desire
their peace and prosperity. We look for no advantage in
our relations with them except the increased exchanges
of commerce upon a basis of mutual benefit. We regret
every civil contest that disturbs their peace and
paralyzes their development, and are always ready to
give our good offices for the restoration of peace. It
must, however, be understood that this Government, while
exercising the utmost forbearance toward weaker powers,
will extend its strong and adequate protection to its
citizens, to its officers, and to its humblest sailor
when made the victims of wantonness and cruelty in
resentment not of their personal misconduct, but of the
official acts of their Government.
(Ibid., pp. 217-18, 225.)

36 John Sherman and the conservative tradition

(In 1895 Senator John Sherman of Ohio published a lengthy
memoir, thinking that his public career was coming to an

end. As it turned out, he would serve as President
McKinley's first secretary of state. The last sentences
in the memoir summed up the thinking of those in the
mid-1890s who sought to preserve the tradition of non-
involvement in external affairs.)

'Our country, our whole country, and nothing but our
country' has been the watchword and creed of my public
life. It was the opposite doctrine of 'states' rights,'
allegiance to a state, that led to the Civil War. It
was settled by this war that we have a country limited
in its powers by the constitution of the United States
fairly construed. Since that time our progress and
development have been more rapid than any other country's.

The events of the future are beyond the vision of
mankind, but I hope that our people will be content with
internal growth, and avoid the complications of foreign
acquisitions. Our family of states is already large
enough to create embarrassment in the Senate, and a
republic should not hold dependent provinces or possessions. Every new acquisition will create embarrassments.
Canada and Mexico as independent republics will be more
valuable to the United States than if carved into
additional states. The Union already embraces discordant
elements enough without adding others. If my life is
prolonged I will do all I can to add to the strength and
prosperity of the United States, but nothing to extend
its limits or to add new dangers by acquisition of foreign
territory.
(From John Sherman, 'Recollections of Forty Years in the
House, Senate and Cabinet', vol. II (Chicago, 1895),
p. 1216.)

37 Reaffirmation of the Monroe Doctrine against
European imperialism

(The long-standing boundary dispute between Venezuela
and British Guiana prompted President Cleveland and
Secretary of State Richard Olney to reassert America's
determination to oppose European intervention in
hemispheric affairs. The following long and strongly
worded instruction from Olney to Ambassador Thomas F.
Bayard in London, dated 20 July 1895, can be considered
a traditionalist response in the Age of Imperialism.)

Europe, as Washington observed, has a set of primary
interests which are peculiar to herself. America is not
interested in them and ought not to be vexed or

complicated with them. Each great European power, for
instance, today maintains enormous armies and fleets in
self-defense and for protection against any other
European power or powers. What have the states of America
to do with that condition of things, or why should they be
impoverished by wars or preparations for wars with whose
causes or results they can have no direct concern? If all
Europe were to suddenly fly to arms over the fate of
Turkey, would it not be preposterous that any American
state should find itself inextricably involved in the
miseries and burdens of the contest? If it were, it
would prove to be a partnership in the cost and losses
of the struggle but not in any ensuing benefits ...

Is it true, then, that the safety and welfare of the
United States are so concerned with the maintenance of
the independence of every American state as against any
European power as to justify and require the interposition
of the United States whenever that independence is
endangered? The question can be candidly answered in but
one way. The states of America, South as well as North,
by geographical proximity, by natural sympathy, by
similarity of governmental constitutions, are friends and
allies, commercially and politically, of the United
States. To allow the subjugation of any of them by an
European power is, of course, to completely reverse that
situation and signifies the loss of all the advantages
incident to their natural relations to us ...

The civilized states of Christendom deal with each
other on substantially the same principles that regulate
the conduct of individuals. The greater its enlightenment, the more surely every state perceives that its
permanent interests require it to be governed by the
immutable principles of right and justice. Each,
nevertheless, is only too liable to succumb to the
temptations offered by seeming special opportunities for
its own aggrandizement, and each would rashly imperil
its own safety were it not to remember that for the
regard and respect of other states it must be largely
dependent upon its own strength and power. Today the
United States is practically sovereign on this continent,
and its fiat is law upon the subjects to which it
confines its interposition. Why? It is not because
of the pure friendship or good will felt for it. It is
not simply by reason of its high character as a civilized
state, nor because wisdom and justice and equity are the
invariable characteristics of the dealings of the United
States. It is because, in addition to all other grounds,
its infinite resources combined with its isolated position
render it master of the situation and practically
invulnerable as against any or all other powers.

All the advantages of this superiority are at once
imperiled if the principle be admitted that European
powers may convert American states into colonies or
provinces of their own. The principle would be eagerly
availed of, and every power doing so would immediately
acquire a base of military operations against us. What
one power was permitted to do could not be denied to
another, and it is not inconceivable that the struggle
now going on for the acquisition of Africa might be
transferred to South America. If it were, the weaker
countries would unquestionably be soon absorbed, while
the ultimate result might be the partition of all South
America between the various European powers. The
disastrous consequences to the United States of such a
condition of things are obvious. The loss of prestige,
of authority, and of weight in the councils of the family
of nations, would be among the least of them. Our only
real rivals in peace as well as enemies in war would be
found located at our very doors ... [With] the powers
of Europe permanently encamped on American soil ... [we]
too must be armed to the teeth, we too must convert the
flower of our male population into soldiers and sailors,
and by withdrawing them from the various pursuits of
peaceful industry we too must practically annihilate a
large share of the productive energy of the nation.
How a greater calamity than this could overtake us
it is difficult to see. Nor are our just apprehensions
to be allayed by suggestions of the friendliness of
European powers - of their good will towards us - of
their disposition, should they be our neighbors, to
dwell with us in peace and harmony. The people of the
United States have learned in the school of experience
to what extent the relations of states to each other
depend not upon sentiment nor principle, but upon
selfish interest ... They realize that had France and
Great Britain held important South American possessions
to work from and to benefit, the temptation to destroy
the predominance of the Great Republic in this
hemisphere by furthering its desmemberment might have
been irresistible. From that grave peril they have been
saved in the past and may be saved again in the future
through the operation of the sure but silent force of the
doctrine proclaimed by President Monroe. To abandon it,
on the other hand, disregarding both the logic of the
situation and the facts of our past experience, would be
to renounce a policy which has proved both an easy
defense against foreign aggression and a prolific source
of internal progress and prosperity.
(From 'Foreign Relations of the United States, 1895'
(Washington, 1896), I, 556-9.)

38   Missionaries in China

(The 1890s witnessed a ground swell of interest in mission
work. China attracted particular attention because it was
felt that its defeat by Japan in the war of 1894-5 would
result in reform and modernization of the country. In the
following excerpt from Minister Charles Denby's dispatch,
dated 22 March 1895, one may note a clear connection
between civilization, Christianity, commerce, and
ultimately Western expansionism.)

There are schools and colleges all over China taught by
the missionaries. I have been present often at the
exhibitions given by these schools. They showed progress
in a great degree.

The educated Chinaman, who speaks English, becomes a
new man; he commences to think. A long time before the
present war the Emperor was studying English, and, it is
said, was fast acquiring the language ...

Missionaries are the pioneers of trade and commerce.
Civilization, learning, instruction breed new wants which
commerce supplies. Look at the electric telegraph now in
every province in China but one. Look at the steamships
which ply along the coast from Hongkong to Newchang and on
the Yangtze up to Ichang. Look at the cities which have
sprung up like Shanghai, Tientsin, Hankow - handsome
foreign cities, object lessons to the Chinese ... Will
anyone say that the 1,500 missionaries in China of
Protestants, and perhaps more Catholics, have not contributed to these results?... Someone may say that
commercial agents might have done as much, but they are
not allowed to locate in the interior. The missionary,
inspired by holy zeal, goes everywhere, and by degrees
foreign commerce and trade follow. I suppose that
whenever an uncivilized or semi-civilized country becomes
civilized, its trade and dealings with Western nations
increase. Humanity has not devised any better, or even
any as good, engine or means for civilizing savage people
as proselytism to Christianity. The history of the world
attests this fact ...

It is too early now to consider what effect the
existing war may have on the interests of the missions.
It is quite probable, however, that the spirit of progress
developed by it will make mission work more important
and influential than it has ever been.

(Ibid., pp. 197-8.)

39 The Hawaiian controversy (1)

(The quickening tempo of events in Asia coincided with
the emergence of a serious controversy over the annexation
of Hawaii. President Harrison had favored it and
submitted a treaty of annexation to the Senate. But his
successor, Cleveland, was strongly opposed both to the
policy and the means of annexation, as he explained in
this message to Congress, dated 18 December 1893.)

I suppose that right and justice should determine the
path to be followed in treating this subject. If
national honesty is to be disregarded and a desire for
territorial extension or dissatisfaction with a form of
government not our own ought to regulate our conduct,
I have entirely misapprehended the mission and character
of our Government and the behavior which the conscience
of our people demands of their public servants.
When the present Administration entered upon its
duties, the Senate had under consideration a treaty
providing for the annexation of the Hawaiian Islands to
the territory of the United States. Surely under our
Constitution and laws the enlargement of our limits is a
manifestation of the highest attribute of sovereignty,
and if entered upon as an Executive act all things
relating to the transaction should be clear and free
from suspicion. Additional importance attached to this
particular treaty of annexation because it contemplated
a departure from unbroken American tradition in providing
for the addition to our territory of islands of the sea
more than 2,000 miles removed from our nearest coast ...
I believe that a candid and thorough examination of
the facts will force the conviction that the Provisional
Government owes its existence to an armed invasion by the
United States. Fair-minded people, with the evidence
before them, will hardly claim that the Hawaiian
Government was overthrown by the people of the islands or
that the Provisional Government had ever existed with
their consent. I do not understand that any member of
this Government claims that the people would uphold it by
their suffrages if they were allowed to vote on the
question ...
Believing, therefore, that the United States could not,
under the circumstances disclosed, annex the islands without justly incurring the imputation of acquiring them by
unjustifiable methods, I shall not again submit the
treaty of annexation to the Senate for its consideration
... I mistake the American people if they favor the
odious doctrine that there is no such thing as

international morality; that there is one law for a
strong nation and another for a weak one, and that even
by indirection a strong power may with impunity despoil a
weak one of its territory ...
(From 'Messages and Papers of Presidents', IX, 461, 469,
470.)

40   The Hawaiian controversy (2)

(Senator Henry Cabot Lodge was one of the supporters of
Hawaiian annexation. The following is excerpted from a
speech he gave in the Senate on 22 January 1895.)

It is perfectly obvious, Mr. President, that England, in
pursuance of a well-settled policy, which I think is
perfectly correct, for I have no sympathy with either
the 'Little England' party or its wretched equivalent
in our politics, is taking possession of every island
upon which she can conveniently lay her hands. It is
a part of the conquering and aggressive policy of
England. I am the last to find fault with her. I believe
she is wise in doing so. My criticism is that we do not
exhibit the same spirit, the true spirit of our race, in
protecting American interests and advancing them everywhere and at all times. I do not mean that we should
enter on a widely extended system of colonization. That
is not our line. But I do mean that we should take all
outlying territory necessary to our own defense, to the
protection of the Isthmian Canal, to the upbuilding of our
trade and commerce, and to the maintenance of our
military safety everywhere. I would take and hold the
outworks, as we now hold the citadel, of American
power ...
   [Any] one who is familiar with the condition of
affairs in Hawaii knows that there are over twenty
thousand Japanese in those islands, that they are an
element in the population disposed to be turbulent and to
make trouble, and that they are regarded as very dangerous
by all the people of the white race, English and
Americans alike ...
   Our relations with those islands are totally
different from our relations with any other country
outside of the United States. When we have warned off
other nations in that way, we assume great responsibility;
we say to the people in those islands that nobody else
shall go there, that we shall regard it as an act of
hostility if they do, and I think we owe it to them to
assist them in the maintenance of peace and order. I

believe that the only way now to deal with this question
is to annex those islands. We have got to the point where
we must settle this matter conclusively. I have no
question in my own mind but that to-day there is a
majority for annexation in both Houses of Congress; that
it will be still larger in the next Congress; and that
there is an overwhelming majority of the American people
who believe that we should control those islands, and
put an end to the disorders which exist there. If this
Hawaiian Republic which now maintains order there is
unjust in some of the provisions of law, we can remedy
it if we take the islands; but to stand as we do in the
attitude of a dog in the manger, allowing nobody to go
there, taking our ships away at crucial moments, leaving
the islands open to disorder, a breeder of trouble with
Japan, a breeder of trouble with Great Britain possibly,
is a policy utterly mistaken. It may, perhaps, seem
unintelligible to some Senators, but the only motive I
have in the matter is because I dislike to see American
interests sacrificed. It may be merely a sentimental
feeling, although it is one which I cherish very strongly;
but I cannot bear to see the American flag pulled down
where it has once been run up, and I dislike to see the
American foot go back where it has once been advanced.
(From Henry Cabot Lodge, 'Speeches and Addresses'
(Boston, 1909), pp. 167, 170, 176-7.)

41 The Hawaiian controversy (3)

(A basic annexationist argument, one that proved to be
decisive, was to present the picture of Japanese
invasion, as did Lorrin A. Thurston, Hawaii's representative in Washington, in a pamphlet published in 1897.)

The awakening of Japan has introduced a new element into
the politics of the world, and more especially of the
Pacific. Until within a few years, emigration from Japan
was prohibited. Japan has now reversed this policy, and
emigration, particularly to Hawaii, is encouraged. So
rapidly have the Japanese come to Hawaii that in 1896
they numbered twenty-five thousand; the adult Japanese
males outnumbering those of any other nationality.
    During the latter part of 1896 and the early part of
1897 they came in at the rate of 2000 a month. If this
rate of immigration had continued for a year, they would
have numbered one-half of the population of the entire
country, and before the end of five years would have
outnumbered all of the other inhabitants put together, two

to one. The rate at which they were entering Hawaii, is, as compared with the population of the United States, as though a million Japanese a month were entering San Francisco. It has been well said that 'this was not immigration but invasion.' ...

Under the existing constitution of Hawaii, the Japanese are not citizens and are ineligible to citizenship; but it goes without saying, that an energetic, ambitious, warlike, and progressive people like the Japanese can not indefinitely be prevented from participating in the government of a country in which they become dominant in numbers, and the ownership of property ...

It may be claimed that Europeans and Americans can hold their own in competition with the Japanese. The reply to this is, that experience has demonstrated that there can be no competition between Europeans and Americans on the one side and Japanese or Chinese on the other. The only possible result is the absolute substitution of the Asiatic in the place of the white man, by reason of the fact that the Eastern standard of civilization and living is so much lower than the Western, that the Asiatic can exist and prosper on a margin of profit which means starvation and destitution to a man who attempts to feed, clothe and educate a family in accordance with the American standard.

The issue in Hawaii is not between monarchy and the Republic. That issue has been settled. There are some persons who do not recognize this fact. There are never lacking those who set their faces backward; who mourn every lost cause and vainly hope for the restoration of abused and forfeited power.

The issue in Hawaii today, is the preliminary skirmish in the great coming struggle between the civilization and the awakening forces of the East and the civilization of the West. The issue is whether, in that inevitable struggle, Asia or America shall have the vantage ground of the control of the naval 'Key of the Pacific,' the commercial 'Cross-roads of the Pacific.'
(From Lorrin A. Thurston, 'A Hand-Book on the Annexation of Hawaii' (St Joseph, Michigan, 1897), pp. 6–8.)

42 The Cuban question (1)

(Coinciding with the debate over Hawaiian annexation, the Cuban question forced Americans to pay much greater attention to foreign affairs than earlier. Both interventionists and anti-interventionists had to clarify

national objectives, priorities and interests. In the
following note of 4 April 1896 addressed to the Spanish
minister, Secretary of State Olney offered United States
mediation to Spain.)

What can a prudent man foresee as the outcome of existing
conditions except the complete devastation of the island,
the entire annihilation of its industries, and the
absolute impoverishment of such of its inhabitants as are
unwise or unfortunate enough not to seasonably escape
from it? ...

There are only too strong reasons to fear that, once
Spain was withdrawn from the island, the sole bond of
union between the different factions of the insurgents
would disappear; that a war of races would be
precipitated, all the more sanguinary for the discipline
and experience acquired during the insurrection, and
that, even if there were to be temporary peace, it could
only be through the establishment of a white and a black
republic, which, even if agreeing at the outset upon a
division of the island between them, would be enemies
from the start, and would never rest until the one had
been completely vanquished and subdued by the other.

The situation thus described is of great interest to
the people of the United States. They are interested in
any struggle anywhere for freer political institutions,
but necessarily and in special measure in a struggle
that is raging almost in sight of our shores. They are
interested, as a civilized and Christian nation, in the
speedy termination of a civil strife characterized by
exceptional bitterness and exceptional excesses on the
part of both combatants. They are interested in the
noninterruption of extensive trade relations which have
been and should continue to be of great advantage to
both countries. They are interested in the prevention of
that wholesale destruction of property on the island
which, making no discrimination between enemies and
neutrals, is utterly destroying American investments that
should be of immense value, and is utterly impoverishing
great numbers of American citizens.

On all these grounds and in all these ways the
interest of the United States in the existing situation
in Cuba yields in extent only to that of Spain herself,
and has led many good and honest persons to insist that
intervention to terminate the conflict is the immediate
and imperative duty of the United States. It is not
proposed now to consider whether existing conditions
would justify such intervention at the present time, or
how much longer those conditions should be endured before

such intervention would be justified. That the United
States can not contemplate with complacency another ten
years of Cuban insurrection, with all its injurious and
distressing incidents, may certainly be taken for granted.
The object of the present communication, however, is
not to discuss intervention, nor to propose intervention,
nor to pave the way for intervention. The purpose is
exactly the reverse - to suggest whether a solution of
present troubles can not be found which will prevent all
thought of intervention by rendering it unnecessary.
What the United States desires to do, if the way can be
pointed out, is to cooperate with Spain in the immediate
pacification of the island on such a plan as, leaving
Spain her rights of sovereignty, shall yet secure to the
people of the island all such rights and powers of local
self-government as they can reasonably ask. To that end
the United States offers and will use her good offices
at such time and in such manner as may be deemed most
advisable. Its mediation, it is believed, should not
be rejected in any quarter, since none could misconceive
or mistrust its purpose ...
To attribute to the United States any hostile or
hidden purposes would be a grave and most lamentable
error. The United States has no designs upon Cuba and
no designs against the sovereignty of Spain. Neither
is it actuated by any spirit of meddlesomeness nor by any
desire to force its will upon another nation. Its
geographical proximity and all the considerations above
detailed compel it to be interested in the solution of
the Cuban problem whether it will or no. Its only
anxiety is that that solution should be speedy, and,
by being founded on truth and justice, should also be
permanent.
(From 'Foreign Relations of the United States' 1897
(Washington, 1898), pp. 542-4.)

43   The Cuban question (2)

(President McKinley, who inherited the Cuban question
from Cleveland, at first followed his predecessor's
cautious policy. In this message to Congress of
6 December 1897, he explained why he wanted to let the
new Sagasta cabinet in Madrid try to solve the matter
before the United States decided on intervention.)

The story of Cuba for many years has been one of unrest;
growing discontent; an effort toward a larger enjoyment
of liberty and self-control; of organized resistance to

the mother country; of depression after distress and
warfare and of ineffectual settlement to be followed
by renewed revolt ...

Throughout all these horrors and dangers to our own
peace this Government has never in any way abrogated its
sovereign prerogative of reserving to itself the
determination of its policy and course according to its
own high sense of right and in consonance with the
dearest interests and convictions of our own people
should the prolongation of the strife so demand.

Of the untried measures there remain only: Recognition
of the insurgents as belligerents; recognition of the
independence of Cuba; neutral intervention to end the
war by imposing a rational compromise between the
contestants, and intervention in favor of one or the
other party. I speak not of forcible annexation, for
that can not be thought of. That by our code of
morality would be criminal aggression ...

That the Government of Sagasta has entered upon a
course from which recession with honor is impossible can
hardly be questioned; that in the few weeks it has
existed it has made earnest of the sincerity of its
professions is undeniable. I shall not impugn its
sincerity, nor should impatience be suffered to embarrass
it in the task it has undertaken. It is honestly due
to Spain and to our friendly relations with Spain that she
should be given a reasonable chance to realize her
expectations and to prove the asserted efficacy of the
new order of things to which she stands irrevocably
committed. She has recalled the Commander whose brutal
orders inflamed the American mind and shocked the
civilized world. She has modified the horrible order of
concentration and has undertaken to care for the helpless
and permit those who desire to resume the cultivation of
their fields to do so and assures them of the protection
of the Spanish Government in their lawful occupations.
She has just released the 'Competitor' prisoners
heretofore sentenced to death and who have been the
subject of repeated diplomatic correspondence during both
this and the preceding Administration.

Not a single American citizen is now in arrest or
confinement in Cuba of whom this Government has any
knowledge. The near future will demonstrate whether the
indispensable condition of a righteous peace, just alike
to the Cubans and to Spain as well as equitable to all
our interests so intimately involved in the welfare of
Cuba, is likely to be attained. If not, the exigency of
further and other action by the United States will remain
to be taken. When that time comes that action will be

determined in the line of indisputable right and duty.
It will be faced, without misgiving or hesitancy in the
light of the obligation this Government owes to itself,
to the people who have confided to it the protection of
their interests and honor, and to humanity.

Sure of the right, keeping free from all offense
ourselves, actuated only by upright and patriotic
considerations, moved neither by passion nor selfishness,
the Government will continue its watchful care over the
rights and property of American citizens and will abate
none of its efforts to bring about by peaceful agencies
a peace which shall be honorable and enduring. If it
shall hereafter appear to be a duty imposed by our
obligations to ourselves, to civilization and humanity
to intervene with force, it shall be without fault on our
part and only because the necessity for such action will
be so clear as to command the support and approval of
the civilized world.

(Ibid., pp. xi, xiv-xv, xx-xxi.)

44   The Cuban question (3)

(Consul General Fitzhugh Lee, stationed at Havana, daily
reported on deteriorating conditions in Cuba, and was a
strong advocate of United States intervention. Here are
excerpts from some of the telegraph messages he sent to
the State Department.)

January 12, 1898. Mobs, led by Spanish officers, attacked
today the offices of the four newspapers here advocating
autonomy ... Palace heavily guarded. Consulate also
protected by armed men.

January 13, 1898. After a day and night of excitement,
all business suspended, and rioting, everything quiet at
this hour ... Uncertainty exists whether [Governor General
Ramon Blanco y Arenas, recently appointed] can control the
situation. If [it is] demonstrated he can not maintain
order, preserve life, and keep the peace, or if Americans
and their interests are in danger, ships must be sent,
and to that end should be prepared to move promptly.
Excitement and uncertainty predominates everywhere.

January 24, 1898. Advise visit [by the Maine,
scheduled to call at Havana port in a day or two] be
postponed six or seven days, to give last excitement more
time to disappear ...

January 25, 1898. At an interview authorities
profess to think United States has ulterior purpose in
sending ship. Say it will obstruct autonomy, produce
excitement, and most probably a demonstration ...

Ship quietly arrived 11 a.m. today.   No demonstration so far.

January 26, 1898.   Have just had pleasant visit on *Maine*.

February 4, 1898.   Do not think slightest sanitary danger to officers or crew until April or even May. Ship or ships should be kept here all the time now.   We should not relinquish position of peaceful control of situation, or conditions would be worse than if vessel had never been sent.   Americans would depart with their families in haste if no vessel in harbor, on account of distrust of preservation of order by authorities.   If another riot occurs, will be against Governor-General and autonomy, but might include anti-American demonstration also.   First-class battle ship should replace present one if relieved, as object lesson and to counteract Spanish opinion of our Navy, and should have torpedo boat with it to preserve communication with admiral.

February 16, 1898.   *Maine* blown up and destroyed tonight at 9:40 p.m.   Explosion occurred well forward under quarters of crew; consequence many were lost ... Cause of explosion yet to be investigated.   Captain-General and Spanish army and navy officers have rendered every assistance.

(From 'Foreign Relations of the United States 1898' (Washington, 1901), pp. 1024-9.)

45   Concessioneering in China (1)

(After the Sino-Japanese War, foreign individuals and governments actively began to seek concessions in China, which was soon turned into their spheres of influence. Belatedly, American officials began to stir themselves to go beyond the traditional policy of 'protecting the nationals.'   Minister Denby's efforts on behalf of the American China Development Company, as reported in the following dispatch of 10 January 1897, gives one example.)

I had, day before yesterday, an important interview with the Tsung-li Yamen [the Chinese foreign office] ...

I stated that I came to see the Yamen to discuss with them certain questions in which my countrymen were interested; that while I was not authorized by my Government to demand of the Chinese Government contracts to build railroads or to do any other work, yet it was, as I conceived, my duty to see that the rights of my compatriots should be protected as well in the matter of

contracts as in other matters ... that to one power a
large strip of territory on the Mekong was ceded; that to
another the right to build railroads in Manchuria was
granted; that with another a contract was made to buy
ships; that with all three powers advantageous loans
were made; that it was conceded by all the officials who
had been consulted on railroad questions that Americans
could better than any other people build great railroads;
that the Government had been distinctly advised on all
sides to treat with Americans for building its great
lines of railroads; that it had gone out all over the
world that contracts would be made with Americans; that
from a political point of view it was conceded on all
hands that the work of developing China should be conceded
to Americans, because the United States had and could
have no ulterior designs on Asiatic territory; that to
refuse now to grant contracts to Americans might develop
a bad feeling among our people at home and make them less
friendly than they always had been to China; that a few
weeks ago it was understood that the contract for building
the Hankow-Pekin line was actually let to Americans - a
preliminary contract had been made with the American China
Development Company; that this company was composed of
men who were worth several hundred millions of taels;
that it was beyond all peradventure able to execute any
contract it might make; that at the instance of Sheng
Taotai and other distinguished persons (meaning Li Hung
Chang) well-known experts and financiers had come to
Shanghai; that they were there in consultation with Sheng,
and they had represented to me that Sheng was not
disposed to treat them fairly; that it would be a breach
of good faith to fail to make a contract with these
representatives of American interests, and I had to
demand that they wire to Sheng to contract with the
American company for the building of the Hankow-Pekin
line; that I did not desire to go into details of the
contracts to be made, but would leave them to the parties
concerned.
(From 'Foreign Relations 1897', pp. 56-7.)

46   Concessioneering in China (2)

(The State Department under Secretary of State John
Sherman felt that Denby had gone too far in exerting
himself on behalf of a private firm, as he told the
American official in this instruction of 8 March 1897.)

The Department commends the interest you take in the

advancement of American enterprises in China and the
efforts made by you in their behalf with the Chinese
foreign office, but you should be cautious in giving
what might be understood as this Government's indorsement
of the financial standing of the persons seeking contracts
with that of China. In the present case it appears from
your despatch that you told the Tsung-li Yamen that
the American China Development Company 'was composed of
men who were worth several hundred millions of taels.'
The Department understands that the said company is a
limited liability company, with a very small capital.
The individual financial standing of the various persons
composing the company has, consequently, little to do
with the matter.
(Ibid., pp. 59-60.)

47 The Philippine debate (1)

(All of a sudden, in the spring of 1898, the Philippine
islands became a major issue in United States foreign
policy. America's growing involvement may be traced in
these excerpts from the dispatches by Consul Oscar F.
Williams at Manila.)

March 19, 1898. Matters are in a serious state here. I
have daily communication by cable and letter with
Commodore [George] Dewey [in Hong Kong], but we pass
letters by British and other ship-masters and by private
parties, because cables and letters are tampered with ...
   Rebellion never more threatening to Spain. Rebels
getting arms, money, and friends, and they outnumber the
Spaniards, resident and soldiery, probably a hundred to
one.
   Report says that Holy Week the insurgents plan to burn
and capture Manila. But, if so, you will learn it by
wire before you receive this dispatch ...
   All news comes direct from Washington. I hear nothing
as to relations between United States and Spain, and,
depending upon unofficial reports, I must act as if peace
reigned ...
   March 27, 1898. On Friday morning, March 25, a church
holiday, a meeting of natives was being held near my
consulate in Manila, the natives being unarmed. The
building was surrounded by police and military, the
meeting broken up, twelve natives wantonly shot to death,
several wounded, and sixty-two taken prisoners. Saturday
morning, March 26, the sixty-two prisoners were marched
in a body to the cemetery and shot to death, although it

was shown that several were chance passers-by or
employees in ships adjoining, not being in attendance
at the meeting.

It was cold comfort to the widows and orphans of
innocent men to have Spanish officers present them the
mangled corpses of husbands and fathers.

Such horrors, but usually on a smaller scale, but
at times attended by greater disregard for modern rules
of war, occur almost daily, and the piteous cry goes up,
'Will it ever stop?' ...

Cruelties too horrid for an official report are
detailed to me every day, and it seems that the cry of
outraged humanity would soon compel Spain to abolish
Middle Age methods of warfare.

Christian nations are such only in name when such
atrocities as daily blacken the calendar are known to be
perpetrated here and no effort made to protect the weak.

There is to-day no Christian nation - policy and mock
diplomacy govern all; the vilest cruelties of war are
added to the mangling of old men, women, and children to
make full the measure of iniquity.

The American Indians would not permit one of their
tribes to practice such barbarities. Why should so-
called Christian nations decline to call a halt upon
Spanish outrages? ...

March 31, 1898. During the period when war between
the United States and Spain was expected, which seems
happily now to be disappearing, I daily heard the
assurance that the natives, half-breeds, Chinese
merchants, and such Spaniards as were in business were
all ready to welcome our fleet, fight with it to hoist
over these islands the United States flag, and swear
allegiance to it; and once done, all interests here would
thrive, be settled and happy.

May 4, 1898. At about 5:30 a.m. Sunday, May 1, the
Spanish guns opened fire at both the Manila breakwater
battery and at Cavite from fleet and forts.

With magnificent coolness and order, but with greatest
promptness, our fleet, in battle array, headed by the
flagship, answered the Spanish attack, and for about two
and a half hours a most terrific fire ensued.

The method of our operations could not have shown
greater system, our guns greater effectiveness, or our
officers and crews greater bravery. And while Spanish
resistance was stubborn and the bravery of Spanish forces
such as to challenge admiration, yet they were outclassed,
weighed in the balance of war against the methods,
training, aim, and bravery shown on our decks, and after
less than three hours' perilous and intense combat one of

Spain's war ships was sinking, two others burning, and all
others with land defenses had severely suffered when our
squadron, with no harm done its ships, retired for
breakfast. At about 10 o'clock a.m. Commodore Dewey
renewed the battle and with effects most fatal with each
evolution ...

History has only contrasts. There is no couplet to
form a comparison. The only finish fight between the
modern war ships of civilized nations has proven the
prowess of American naval men and methods, and the glory
is a legacy for the whole people. Our crews were all
hoarse from cheering, and while we suffer for cough drops
and throat doctors we have no use for liniment or
surgeons.

To every ship, officer, and crew all praise be given.
As Victoria was answered years ago, 'Your Majesty, there
is no second,' so may I report to your Department as to
our war ships conquering the Spanish fleet in the battle
of Manila Bay: There is no first; there is no second.
The cool bravery and efficiency of the commodore was
echoed by every captain and commander and down through
the lines by every officer and man, and naval history
of the dawning century will be rich if it furnishes to
the world so glorious a display of intelligent command
and successful service as must be placed to the credit
of the United States Asiatic Squadron under date of
May 1, 1898.

May 12, 1898. An insurgent leader, Major Gonzales,
reported to me last week on the Olympia, that they had
37,000 troops under arms, good and bad, surrounding
Manila, endeavoring to cooperate with us. In the main
they are very poorly armed, but have about 6,600 rifles
taken from the Spaniards. They have captured the entire
railroad line and the River Pasig, thus cutting off
supply lines, while we by cutting off supply by bay and
sea can soon starve Manila into surrender.

These natives are eager to be organized and led by
United States officers, and the members of their cabinet
visited me and gave assurance that all would swear
allegiance to and cheerfully follow our flag. They are
brave, submissive, and cheaply provided for.

To show their friendliness for me as our nation's
only representative in this part of the world, I last
week went on shore at Cavite with British consul, in his
launch, to show the destruction wrought by our fleet. As
soon as natives found me out, they crowded around me,
hats off, shouting 'Viva los Americanos,' thronged about
me by hundreds striving to get even a finger to shake.
So I moved half a mile, shaking continuously with both

hands. The British consul, a smiling spectator, said he
never before saw such an evidence of friendship ...

June 16, 1898. While the Spaniards cruelly and
barbarously slaughter Filipinos taken in arms, and often
noncombatants, women, and children, the insurgent victors,
following American example, spare life, protect the
helpless, and nurse, feed, and care for Spaniards taken
prisoners and for Spanish wounded as kindly as they care
for the wounded fallen from their own ranks.

For future advantage I am maintaining cordial relations
with General Aguinaldo, having stipulated submissiveness
to our forces when treating for their return here. Last
Sunday, 12th, they held a council to form provisional
government. I was urged to attend, but thought best to
decline. A form of government was adopted, but General
Aguinaldo told me to-day that his friends all hoped that
the Philippines would be held as a colony of United
States of America.

It has been my effort to maintain harmony with
insurgents in order to exercise greater influence hereafter when we reorganize government ...

Manila is at the mercy of our fleet, and I believe its
capture may be effected, so far as the fleet's part is
concerned, without the loss of a man or the disabling
of a vessel. Rear-Admiral Dewey only awaits troops to
insure order and good government once we are in possession. We fear the city may fall too soon. For this
reason Admiral Dewey asked me to remain here, where he
could command such service as I may be able to render in
event of his taking the city.

I expect that on July 4 we will celebrate in Manila
under the folds of 'Old Glory,' and write in living
letters a page of history that this magnificent insular
empire has become a part and parcel of the United States
of America.

(From 'A Treaty of Peace Between the United States and
Spain', 55th Congress, 3rd Session, Doc. 62, Part 1,
pp. 320-30.)

48 The Philippine debate (2)

(The following is an excerpt from President McKinley's
instruction to the American commissioners who attended
the peace conference in Paris in October 1898. The
commissioners were: William R. Day [chairman], Cushman
K. Davis, William P. Frye, Whitelaw Reid, and George Gray.
The instruction was dated 16 September.)

[Without] any original thought of complete or even partial acquisition, the presence and success of our arms at Manila imposes upon us obligations which we can not disregard. The march of events rules and overrules human action. Avowing unreservedly the purpose which has animated all our effort, and still solicitous to adhere to it, we can not be unmindful that, without any desire or design on our part, the war has brought us new duties and responsibilities which we must meet and discharge as becomes a great nation on whose growth and career from the beginning the Ruler of Nations has plainly written the high command and pledge of civilization.

Incidental to our tenure in the Philippines is the commercial opportunity to which American statesmanship can not be indifferent. It is just to use every legitimate means for the enlargement of American trade; but we seek no advantages in the Orient which are not common to all. Asking only the open door for ourselves, we are ready to accord the open door to others. The commercial opportunity which is naturally and inevitably associated with this new opening depends less on large territorial possession than upon an adequate commercial basis and upon broad and equal privileges.

It is believed that in the practical application of these guiding principles the present interests of our country and the proper measure of its duty, its welfare in the future, and the consideration of its exemption from unknown perils will be found in full accord with the just, moral, and humane purpose which was invoked as our justification in accepting the war.

In view of what has been stated, the United States can not accept less than the cession in full right and sovereignty of the island of Luzon. It is desirable, however, that the United States shall acquire the right of entry for vessels and merchandise belonging to citizens of the United States into such ports of the Philippines as are not ceded to the United States upon terms of equal favor with Spanish ships and merchandise, both in relation to port and customs charges and rates of trade and commerce, together with other rights of protection and trade accorded to citizens of one country within the territory of another. You are therefore instructed to demand such concession, agreeing on your part that Spain shall have similar rights as to her subjects and vessels in the ports of any territory in the Philippines ceded to the United States.

(From 'Foreign Relations, 1898', pp. 907-8.)

49 The Philippine debate (3)

(At Paris, the commissioners interrogated various
experts on the Philippines. One witness was John Foreman,
an Englishman who had written the widely read book, 'The
Philippine Islands'. Foreman gave one reason why the
whole of the archipelago, not just the island of Luzon,
should be taken by the United States.)

The Chairman [Day]:
Q. Suppose that the island of Luzon were taken, and we
should have a stipulation for free trade, for free intercourse between the islands, and that Spain shall never
alienate any of the islands to any other power, what have
you left of Spanish sovereignty in any of the other
islands, what is left to Spain, practically, in the
islands not taken?
A. Their honor.
Q. Then, you have, practically, the islands deserted
and no right to change the ownership?
A. Yes, sir.
Q. In a case of that kind, would it not be as well to
take the entire property and be done with it?
A. By taking the whole of the islands, it would be a
favor to Europe by setting aside all chance of rivalry.
Q. You do not seem to think it would be much of a
burden?
A. No, sir; only a little more expense of
administration, which I think would be covered by the
islands themselves.
Mr. Reid:
Q. Do you have any doubt that, with a judicious
administration of the revenues of the islands, those
revenues would be sufficient to cover the expenses of
the islands?
A. Yes, sir.
Q. Do you think they would be sufficient?
A. Yes, sir.
Q. Do you think we would be able to recruit a
sufficient number of native soldiers to form a garrison
of sufficient defense?
A. I am in doubt about the island of Mindanao. It is
a large island, and you could not think of recruiting any
Musselmans.
Q. Do you think we could recruit, exclusive of
Mindanao, enough native soldiers to maintain and defend
our sovereignty over the whole group?
A. Yes, sir.

The Chairman:

Q. What would be the effect - suppose we keep Luzon - if Spain should find it too expensive to undertake to maintain her sway and sovereignty over the rest of the islands, of the establishment of some other power there?

A. I should make strenuous efforts to keep out the Germans.

Q. Why?

A. Because Germany is just now Great Britain's very strong competitor in trade, and I think in the next generation will be the same with America. Perhaps it would be all right with this generation, or for twenty-five years, but I think Germany is, with the next generation, destined to be the great competitor.

Q. Your idea, in short, is this: You would prevent the alienation of the rest of the group because, peradventure, Spain might alienate to Germany?

A. Yes, sir. As to France, I always regard France as like taking a map, and it is practically blotted out commercially. It prevents others coming in, but there is nothing to be got out of it. Metaphorically speaking, it is simply blotting out that portion of the map. France does not develop anything; there is no development of any kind, and there is nothing to fear from France in competition of any kind, now or in the future, that I can see. May I make an observation? The name of Japan has been brought up. It is, of course, quite out of the question, because it is a pagan nation. The natives have been brought up as Christians, and I am sure it would be opposed to the popular opinion in Europe, and in America, I should think. That excludes Japan, in my opinion.

Mr. Frye:

Q. Do you not think Japan will improve in that direction as she has in others?

A. I do not think so.

(From 'Treaty of Peace', pp. 470-1.)

50 The Philippine debate (4)

(While the peace commissioners were still undecided on the question, by mid-October President McKinley had decided to demand the Spanish cession of the entire archipelago. The result was the peace treaty of 10 December. McKinley sought to justify his decision in numerous speeches across the United States. These excerpts are taken from a speech he gave in Atlanta, Georgia, on 15 December 1898.)

The peace we have won is not a selfish truce of arms, but one whose conditions presage good to humanity. The domains secured under the treaty yet to be acted upon by the Senate came to us not as the result of a crusade or conquest, but as the reward of temperate, faithful, and fearless response to the call of conscience, which could not be disregarded by a liberty-loving and Christian people ...

We could have avoided all the difficulties that lie across the pathway of the nation if a few months ago we had coldly ignored the piteous appeals of the starving and oppressed inhabitants of Cuba. If we had blinded ourselves to the conditions so near our shores, and turned a deaf ear to our suffering neighbors, the issue of territorial expansion in the Antilles and the East Indies would not have been raised.

But could we have justified such a course? [General cry of 'No!'] Is there any one who would now declare another to have been the better course? [Cries of 'No!'] With less humanity and less courage on our part, the Spanish flag, instead of the Stars and Stripes, would still be floating at Cavite, at Ponce, and at Santiago, and a 'chance in the race of life' would be wanting to millions of human beings who to-day call this nation noble, and who, I trust, will live to call it blessed.

Thus far we have done our supreme duty. Shall we now, when the victory won in war is written in the treaty of peace, and the civilized world applauds and waits in expectation, turn timidly away from the duties imposed upon the country by its own great deeds? And when the mists fade away and we see with clear vision, may we not go forth rejoicing in a strength which has been employed solely for humanity and always tempered with justice and mercy, confident of our ability to meet the exigencies which await us, because confident that our course is one of duty and our cause that of right? [Prolonged applause.]

(From 'Speeches and Addresses of William McKinley' (New York, 1900), pp. 161, 163-4.)

51 The acquisition of Puerto Rico

(There was little public debate on the decision to acquire Puerto Rico from Spain. Most Americans would have agreed with this analysis by Alfred Thayer Mahan.)

[The] estimate of the military importance of Puerto Rico should never be lost sight of by us as long as we have any

responsibility, direct or indirect, for the safety or
independence of Cuba. Puerto Rico, considered militarily,
is to Cuba, to the future Isthmian canal, and to our
Pacific coast, what Malta is, or may be, to Egypt and
the beyond; and there is for us the like necessity to
hold and strengthen the one, in its entirety and in its
immediate surroundings, that there is for Great Britain
to hold the other for the security of her position in
Egypt, for her use of the Suez Canal, and for the control
of the route to India. It would be extremely difficult
for a European state to sustain operations in the eastern
Mediterranean with a British fleet at Malta. Similarly,
it would be very difficult for a transatlantic state to
maintain operations in the western Caribbean with a
United States fleet based upon Puerto Rico and the
adjacent islands. The same reasons prompted Bonaparte
to seize Malta in his expedition against Egypt and India
in 1798. In his masterly eyes, as in those of Nelson, it
was essential to the communications between France, Egypt,
and India. His scheme failed, not because Malta was less
than invaluable, but for want of adequate naval strength,
without which no maritime position possesses value.
(From Alfred T. Mahan, 'Lessons of the War with Spain'
(Boston, 1899), pp. 28-30.)

52 Pacific empire

(The annexation of Hawaii and the cession of the
Philippines raised questions about other Spanish
possessions in the Pacific. Should the United States
complete an island chain of bases and coaling stations
in the ocean? Commander R. B. Bradford, chief of the
bureau of equipment of the navy, strongly answered in
the affirmative when interrogated by the peace
commissioners in Paris.)

The Chairman:
    Q. Then, if we understand you, you do not think the
island in the Ladrones, assuming it to be Guam, the
southern island, is sufficient for a coaling station
between Hawaii and the Philippines?
    A. I do not. Guam has the advantage of being
farther north, and therefore more on the direct route
from Hawaii to the Philippines than the Carolines, but
it has not a very good harbor.
    Q. It is more in the direct line from the Hawaiian
group to the Philippines than any one of the Carolines?
    A. Yes; it has that advantage.

Q. You would not expect to go from the Ladrones to
the Carolines, on the way to the Philippines, would you?

A. No; I should not.

Q. Then what is the disadvantage in not having one
or more of the Carolines, from our point of view?

A. The Carolines possess better harbors; they are on
several highways of commerce; they are uncomfortably near
the Ladrones, and they extend east and west along the
route between the Pacific coast and the China Sea nearly
2,000 miles, affording numerous coaling stations and
harbors of refuge.

Mr. Reid:

Q. That is, in the hands of another nation they would
be troublesome or disagreeable?

A. They might be. Here are the Pelews [indicating on
a chart] about 600 miles from the Philippines. I am
firmly convinced that the Pelews, Carolines, and Ladrones
should all be acquired if we are to possess any territory
near the China Sea.

The Chairman:

Q. If the United States could have one of the
Carolines, which one would you designate as the one best
suited for our purposes?

A. Ponapi

Q. Where is that?

A. It is about 300 miles west of Ualan, in latitude
7° north and longitude 158°20' east.

Mr. Reid:

Q. It is the largest, is it not?

A. No; not the largest, but it has some very good
harbors, is high and well watered and well wooded. Ualan,
or Kusaie, the headquarters of the American missions, has
also good harbors, and is similar in its characteristics
to Ponapi. Yap, the extreme western island, excepting
the Pelews, has good harbors, and is valuable. It is the
seat of government for the western Carolines. Ponapi
is the seat of government for the eastern Carolines.
Truk Islands are the largest group of the Carolines and
the most densely populated. This small group has about
10,000 inhabitants.

The Chairman:

Q. Yap is more in the line of travel to the
Philippines than any of the others of these islands?

A. No; I do not think it is. It is only on the
route between the Fiji Islands and the North China Sea.
Here is a chart showing the usual routes of full-powered
steamers. Upon examination it appears that Ponapi is
more directly on the commercial routes traversed by
steamers than any island of the Caroline group. Guam and

Ponapi are both on the route from the Samoan Islands to the north end of Luzon.

Q. We have a place in Samoa?

A. We hope to have a coaling station there soon. In conjunction with Great Britain and Germany we exercise a protectorate over the Samoan Islands. This is the only claim we have to the vast territory known as the Polynesian Islands.

Mr. Gray:

Q. Is not the great-circle route the shortest from the Pacific coast to the Philippines?

A. Yes. It is 6,300 miles from San Francisco to the Philippines by the great-circle route, and 7,000 miles via Hawaii and Guam.

The Chairman:

Q. We hold the Aleutian Islands?

A. Yes. Unalaska is the best coaling station there.

Mr. Frye:

Q. Any harbor there?

A. Yes; Dutch Harbor, a fairly good one. The great-circle route from San Francisco to the China Sea and its neighboring islands is not often used, because of fogs near the Aleutian Islands in summer and heavy gales during the winter. The regular trans-Pacific steamers avoid the Aleutian Islands for these reasons. The presence of fog also makes it diffiuclt to enter the harbors of the Aleutian Islands ...

Mr. Frye:

Q. Have you stated what, in your opinion, ought to be done relative to these positions in the East and in the Pacific from investigations which you have made?

A. I think that the entire Philippine group of islands, the Carolines, including the Pelews, and the Ladrones should be annexed to the United States.

The Chairman:

Q. Annexed by what means; taken forcibly?

A. Yes, primarily; and if they can not be fairly taken, then purchased. I would like to say that the Carolines and Ladrones are mere dependencies of the Philippines, and it is so stated in the Blue Book of the Captain-General of the latter ...

Mr. Frye:

Q. If we should adopt your line of demarcation, what do you think Spain would do with the balance of those islands?

A. Sell them to Germany.

Q. Is not Germany about as troublesome a neighbor as we could get?

A. The most so, in my opinion. I think it probable

that the balance of the Spanish possessions in the
Pacific not acquired by us will go to Germany. Germany
has long desired to possess the Carolines, and she
hoisted her flag at Yap in 1886. Our missionaries have
been in the Caroline Islands for fifty years, and all
that has been done to educate and civilize the natives
there has been done by American missionaries.
(From 'Treaty of Peace', pp. 475-6, 482, 484.)

4   THE UNITED STATES IN WORLD POLITICS

53   The aftermath of war (1)

(Politicians and officials continued to discuss the
momentous decisions that had been made in 1898. Magazines
and journals that had rarely published articles dealing
with foreign affairs before the 1890s now became
crowded with such articles. The 'North American Review',
one of the most respected journals, provides a good
example. Virtually all the articles on its pages
published during the first half of 1900 dealt with
international events and foreign policy. Four examples
are given below. The first is an army officer's
criticism of the way the occupation of Cuba was being
conducted.)

The history of the American occupation since the day
when the entire island passed into American hands is
simply the story of what has been done at Havana. It is
a record of error and neglect, of folly, ending
necessarily in failure, and, possibly, in shame and
disgrace ...
   It may be stated, in brief, that wherever Cubans, under
nominal American control, have been trusted to exercise
the functions of government, the result has been worse
than failure. The courts are corrupt and incompetent;
the police forces are hopelessly inefficient; the public
schools are unorganized; the municipalities are all
bankrupt dependents on a political machine; the offices
of government, high and low, are filled, very largely,
with unworthy and incompetent officials; the laws, the
courts and the methods of procedure are unreformed; and,
finally, almost every abuse against which Cubans rebelled
and to remedy which the United States intervened is in
operation to-day under American authority. There exists
throughout the island a condition of tame anarchy, which
awaits only the withdrawal of the American forces to burst
out into anarchy of another type.

In two branches only of the public service has there
been great and highly satisfactory advance from the
previously existing conditions. The receipts from the
custom houses have greatly increased, in spite of the
reduction in trade due to the exhausted condition of the
island, and the reductions made in the tariff rates.
This will be understood when it is remembered that an
American, an officer of the regular army, collects and
accounts for the receipts in every custom house in Cuba,
and that a regular officer is treasurer and another is
auditor for the whole island. In the department of
sanitation and public health, also, the American control
has been absolute, and no Cuban has been permitted to
interfere with the operations of that important branch.
The result is seen in the lowest death-rate ever known in
the island. In other words, where Americans have been
allowed to work, with American methods, the result has
been distinguished success. On the other hand, wherever
Cubans have been allowed to proceed, by any methods of
their own choice, they have invariably clung to the
methods of Spain, which they have employed for their own
ends, nor for the public good; and the result is
disastrous failure, for which Americans are responsible.
Not one step has been taken toward a realization of the
purposes of the intervention. The problem has become,
by reason of neglect and incompetency, more difficult
to-day than it was a year ago. The house was swept and
garnished, but the door was left open and the seven other
devils seem to have taken advantage of the opportunity.
If no change occurs soon the last state of Cuba bids
fair to be far worse than the first.
(From Major J.E. Runcie, American Misgovernment of Cuba,
'North American Review', 170: 286, 293 (February 1900).

54 The aftermath of war (2)

(In the following essay, a noted anti-imperialist
ridicules the imperialist argument that commercial
expansion in Asia necessitated colonial possessions.)

We are now seeking to increase our exports and to develop
our commerce with the East. To that end we are
conducting a war in the Philippine Islands at a cost of
at least three dollars per head of our population. That
is to say, the normal cost of this Government for all
purposes, for twenty years prior to the Spanish war, was
five dollars per head, tending to diminish with the
falling in of pensions and the increase of population.

It is now nearly eight dollars per head, and may be more.
The difference of three dollars per head comes to over
two hundred million dollars a year, all of which must
be distributed in the taxes, increasing the cost of
production and diminishing our power to compete with
other countries.   In fact, it would very seriously impair
our power of competition with England, France and
Germany, were they not committing greater folly than
ourselves by increasing their destructive military
expenditures even in greater measure than we are.

Is there not something grotesquely absurd in the
commercial support which is given to this Philippine
war?   It will not in any measure help to increase our
commerce with Japan, with British India, with Borneo or
Sumatra.   The only argument in its favor consist in its
advocates holding up a brilliant expectation of the
development of commerce with the Philippine Islands,
where white men cannot live and work, and as a stepping-
stone to getting larger share of the commerce with China.
Our commerce with the Province of Manchuria has already
increased very greatly since Russia obtained a sphere of
influence.   Our commerce with every part of China that
comes under British influence must greatly increase,
so far as her supervision gives stability and maintains
order.   Any expenditure of our own for warlike purposes
only diminishes our power to sell more goods and to buy
more in return from the Philippine Islands and from
China.   Our exports for the last fiscal year to both
amounted to fifteen million dollars' worth outside the
British possessions, on which it may be assumed that there
was a profit of ten per cent – call it twenty.   Admit
that some merchants in this country made a profit of a
million and a half to three million dollars in the export
of fifteen million dollars' worth of goods in this branch
of Eastern trade, China outside British possessions and
the Philippines, which the advocates of military expansion
and control hold up as a magnificent example of the
possibility of expansion.   It cost the taxpayers two
hundred million dollars to get whatever increase of
traffic has been or may be secured by this method.   Could
anything be more foolish? ...

Another almost ludicrous block to the Administration
policy has appeared in this matter.   The Chinaman is
representative of the only race which maintains habits
of industry, economy and honesty in the tropics.   Skilful
according to their methods, and earnest in their efforts,
they are doing a vital and essential part of the work
of preparing crops for export from the Philippine
Islands.   They number there about one hundred thousand;

yet, under the existing prejudice against Chinese labor
in this country, the Administration has been obliged to
prohibit the further entry of the Chinese into the
Philippine Islands. Thus, while excluding the Chinese
from one of the few places open to them for relief from
their excess of population, the advocates of expansion
are at the same time pretending that the Philippine
Islands will be a great stepping-stone toward our traffic
with China. Could the force of folly go any further?

I would by no means undervalue the development of
Eastern commerce. It is of importance even at its present
measure. We are but witnessing the beginning of the
process of development of Asia, Africa and South America
by the railway and steamship. With that development,
commerce will increase by leaps and bounds, provided
it is not interrupted by war and by criminal aggression.
If we only stand and wait, that commerce is at our feet.
It must come to us in very large measure, because we
hold the paramount control of the iron and steel products
and manufactures of the world, and these give us the
control of shipping and commerce whenever we choose to
free the natural course of trade from obstructive taxes
and repeal our obsolete navigation laws, which only keep
our flag from the sea. Every step that we take in
criminal aggression, or in warfare of any kind, for the
control of commerce only adds to our burden, destroys
the power of those with whom we would trade to buy our
goods, while working a possible profit to the few
promoters and contractors who desire to get the first
plunder out of ignorant people in the construction of
their railways, but at the cost of the mass of the
taxpayers of this country.
(From Edward Atkinson, Eastern Commerce: What Is It
Worth?, ibid., 170: 301-4 (February 1900).)

55   The aftermath of war (3)

(Here a former secretary of war equates the then-raging
Boer War with the Spanish-American War and criticizes
those, such as William Jennings Bryan, who condemned
British imperialism in South Africa.)

It is greatly to be regretted that a man of Mr. Bryan's
position, hoping as he does (I trust and believe in vain)
that he will some day be President of the United States,
should go about the country trying to create a difference
between America and Great Britain. He is the spokesman
of a great American party, and it would not be surprising

if, speaking in that capacity, he placed the country in
a false position before the world in its relations to the
South African situation by passing from place to place,
attempting to further his political ambitions by fanning
into flame whatever anti-British sentiment he may find
among our heterogeneous population. Here, where he is
known, the object of his endeavor to incite the American
people against the British will be understood, and his
statements will be valued at their true worth. So far
as I am aware, he has never contributed anything that has
added to the substantial growth of this country, either
by employing men or doing anything to develop our
industries. To use a little slang, he seems to produce
'nothing but wind and noise.' The course he advocates
with regard to the financial policy of his country
would disgrace us in the eyes of the world, ruin our
credit and place us at the rear, instead of the van,
where we now are, among the great commercial nations of
the world. But abroad, where he is regarded only as a
political leader with a large following, his words as to
the policy of a friendly nation may have greater weight
and effect than they ought to have.

   If, during our war with Spain, the leader of one of
the great political parties in Great Britain had indulged
in frequent denunciation of the United States and of the
motives which animated the United States in their
determination to free Cuba from Spanish control, his
conduct would have aroused the most bitter resentment in
the minds of our people from Maine to California and from
the Canadian frontier to the Gulf. If in the House of
Commons and in the House of Lords prominent British
statesmen had introduced resolutions condemning our
Government and expressing sympathy with the weaker power
against which, under a sense of duty, we had turned the
vast resources of our country, the act would have
excited just indignation in the breast of every American
patriot. But we had no such experience. And I hold that
we should treat Great Britain in 1900 as squarely as she
treated us in 1898.
(From R. A. Alger, America's Attitude toward England,
ibid., 170: 333-4 (March 1900).)

56 The aftermath of war (4)

(Imperialism was an issue in the presidential election of
1900. In the following excerpts the Democratic
candidate, Bryan, outlines his position.)

If the Filipino is to be under our domination, he must be either citizen or subject. If he is to be a citizen, it must be with a view to participating ultimately in our government and in the making of our laws ... If the Filipino is to be a subject, our form of government must be entirely changed. A republic can have no subjects. The doctrine that a people can be kept in a state of perpetual vassalage, owing allegiance to the flag, but having no voice in the government, is entirely at variance with the principles upon which this government has been founded. An imperial policy nullifies every principle set forth in the Declaration of Independence.

The Porto Rican tariff law illustrates this new doctrine. The flag is separated from the Constitution, and the Porto Ricans are notified that they must obey the laws made for them and pay the taxes levied upon them, and yet have no share in our Bill of Rights or in the guarantees of our Constitution. No monarch or tyrant in all history exercised more despotic power than the Republicans now claim for the President and Congress.

The theory that our race is divinely appointed to seize by force or purchase at auction groups of 'inferior people,' and govern them with benevolent purposes avowed and with trade advantages on the side, carries us back to the creed of kings and to the gospel of force ...

There is no doubt that an imperial policy will be advantageous to army contractors, and to owners of ships who rent their vessels to the United States to carry live soldiers to the Philippine Islands and to bring dead soldiers back; and it may be advantageous to carpet-bag governors and to those who can secure good paying positions in the army, but it will be a constant drain upon the wealth producers. The amount already spent upon a war of conquest in a single year would almost construct the Nicaragua Canal; or, if used for the reclamation of arid lands in the West, it would furnish homes for more American citizens than would go to the Philippine Islands in a thousand years.

If an imperial policy is indorsed by the people, a large standing army will always be necessary. The same influences which lead to a war of conquest in the Philippines will lead to wars of conquest elsewhere, and an immense military establishment will not only become a permanent burden upon the people, but will prove a menace to the Republic.

One of the great objections to imperialism is that it destroys our proud pre-eminence among the nations. When the doctrine of self-government is abandoned, the United States will cease to be a moral factor in the world's

progress. We cannot preach the doctrine that governments
come up from the people, and. at the same time, practice
the doctrine that governments rest upon brute force. We
cannot set a high and honorable example for the
emulation of mankind while we roam the world like beasts
of prey seeking whom we may devour.
(From W. J. Bryan, The Issue in the Presidential
Campaign, ibid., 170: 766-9 (June 1900).)

57 McKinley defends the new course

(In a speech delivered at the Ohio Society of New York
on 3 March 1900, President McKinley extolled the virtues
of the imperial republic.)

Within two years there has been a reunion of the people
around the holy altar consecrated to country and newly
sanctified by common sacrifices. [Great applause.]
The followers of Grant and Lee have fought under the same
flag and fallen for the same faith. [Continued great
applause.] Party lines have loosened and the ties of
union have been strengthened. [Applause.] Sectionalism
has disappeared and fraternity and union have been rooted
in the hearts of the American people. Political passion
has altogether subsided, and patriotism glows with
inextinguishable fervor in every home of the land.
[Applause.] The flag - our flag - has been sustained
on distant seas and islands by the men of all parties
and sections and creeds and races and nationalities, and
its stars are only those radiant hope to the remote
peoples over whom it floats. [Great applause.]
    There can be no imperialism. Those who fear it are
against it. Those who have faith in the republic are
against it. [Applause.] So that there is universal
abhorrence for it and unanimous opposition to it.
[Enthusiastic applause.] Our only difference is that
those who do not agree with us have no confidence in
the virtue or capacity or high purpose or good faith of
this free people as a civilizing agency, while we believe
that the century of free government which the American
people have enjoyed has not rendered them irresolute and
faithless, but has fitted them for the great task of
lifting up and assisting to better conditions and larger
liberty those distant peoples who, through the issue of
battle, have become our wards. [Great applause.] Let us
fear not! There is no occasion for faint hearts, no
excuse for regrets. Nations do not grow in strength, and
the cause of liberty and law is not advanced, by the

doing of easy things. [Applause.] The harder the task
the greater will be the result, the benefit, and the
honor. To doubt our power to accomplish it is to lose
faith in the soundness and strength of our popular
institutions. [Applause.]

The liberators will never become the oppressors. A
self-governed people will never permit despotism in any
government which they foster and defend. [Great
applause.]

Gentlemen, we have the new care and cannot shift it.
And, breaking up the camp of ease and isolation, let us
bravely and hopefully and soberly continue the march
of faithful service, and falter not until the work is
done. [Great applause.] It is not possible that
seventy-five millions of American freemen are unable to
establish liberty and justice and good government in our
new possessions. [Continued applause.] The burden is
our opportunity. The opportunity is greater than the
burden. [Applause.] May God give us strength to bear
the one, and wisdom so to embrace the other that we may
carry to our new acquisitions the guaranties of 'Life,
liberty, and the pursuit of happiness'! [Enthusiastic
and long-continued applause.]
(From 'Speeches and Addresses of McKinley', pp. 364-6.)

58 Equal opportunity in China

(China became an important area of America's concern
after the Spanish-American War. In the next document a
noted economist discusses the question.)

For the means of finding new productive employments for
capital ... it is necessary that the great industrial
countries should turn to countries which have not felt
the pulse of modern progress ...

The United States cannot afford to adhere to a policy
of isolation while other nations are reaching out for the
command of these new markets. The United States are
still large users of foreign capital, but American
investors are not willing to see the return upon their
investments reduced to the European level. Interest
rates have greatly declined here within the last five
years. New markets and new opportunities for investment
must, therefore, be found, if surplus capital is to be
profitably employed.

In pointing out the necessity that the United States
shall enter upon a broad national policy, it need not
be determined in just what manner that policy shall be

worked out. Whether the United States shall actually
acquire territorial possessions, shall set up captain-
generalships and garrisons, whether they shall adopt the
middle ground of protecting sovereignties nominally
independent, or whether they shall content themselves
with naval stations and diplomatic representatives as
the basis for asserting their rights to the free commerce
of the East, is a matter of detail. The discussion of
the details may be of high importance to our political
morality and our historical traditions, but it bears
upon the economic side of the question only so far as a
given political policy is necessary to safeguard and
extend commercial interests. The writer is not an
advocate of 'imperialism' from sentiment, but does not
fear the name if it means only that the United States
shall assert their right to free markets in all the old
countries which are being opened to the surplus
resources of the capitalistic countries and thereby
given the benefits of modern civilization. Whether
this policy carries with it the direct government of
groups of half-savage islands may be a subject for
argument, but upon the economic side of the question
there is but one choice - either to enter by some means
upon the competition for the employment of American
capital and enterprise in these countries, or to continue
the needless duplication of existing means of production
and communication, with the glut of unconsumed products,
the convulsions followed by trade stagnation, and the
steadily declining return upon investments which a
negative policy will invoke ...

The present situation in China is such as to call for
energetic political action on the part of all powers
which desire to obtain new openings for their commerce.
Russia, Germany, and France have seized stations and
large tracts of territory in China, with a view to
enforcing there their restrictive policy of shutting up
the market to their own people. It is necessary, if the
United States are to have an unimpaired share in the new
trade of Asia, that they should protest against this
policy of exclusion and seek to limit the area over which
it is applied. Great Britain stands before the world,
as she has done since the days of Huskisson and Peel, as
the champion of free markets. The United States, if they
are not to be excluded from Asia, must either sustain the
policy of Great Britain, or they must follow the narrower
policy of the continental countries in carving out a
market of their own. Silent indifference to what is
going on in Asia is not merely a question of political
and naval prestige, or of territorial extension. It is

a question whether the new markets which are being created there shall be opened to our commerce in any form under any conditions, and nothing but vigorous assertion of American interest in the subject will prevent the obstructions to the natural course of trade which will follow the division of Asia among the exclusionist powers of the European continent.
(From Charles A. Conant, 'The United States in the Orient' (Boston, 1901), pp. 27, 29-30, 32-3.)

59 The Boxer uprising

(The landing of American forces in China in 1900 to protect foreign lives against attacks by the Boxers brought United States-Chinese relations to a crisis. Yet, as these telegraphic exchanges between Secretary of State John Hay and Minister Edwin Conger indicate, the State Department was desirous of acting independently of other powers as much as possible.)

Hay to Conger, June 6, 1900. In concert with naval authorities you are authorized to take all measures which may be practicable and discreet for protection of legation and American interests generally.

Conger to Hay, June 7, 1900. Situation nowhere improved. Tientsin seriously threatened, and railway again cut. Chinese Government still temporizing. If diplomatic corps decides it is necessary to demand special audience with Emperor, shall I join?

Conger to Hay, June 8, 1900. Paotingfu missionaries safe up to the present. Chinese Government has sent troops and promises ample protection, but this does not insure permanent safety. Impossible to send foreign relief from forces now here.

Hay to Conger, June 8, 1900. Act independently in protection of American interests where practicable, and concurrently with representatives of other powers if necessity arise.

Conger to Hay, June 8, 1900. More railway destroyed. Protecting troops withdrawn. Chinese Government becoming more helpless every day. Foreign troops will have to protect railways. Russian, English, and Japanese are ready to do so. Twenty-four foreign war vessels are at Taku. The United States has only one.

Conger to Hay, June 8, 1900. Most of my colleagues propose demanding an audience with Emperor, the demand to be insisted upon, and to state to the Throne that unless Boxer war is immediately suppressed and order

restored foreign powers will be compelled themselves to
take measures to that end. Shall I join? Answer quick.
    Hay to Conger, June 9, 1900. Yes.
    Hay to Conger, June 10, 1900. We have no policy in
China except to protect with energy American interests,
and especially American citizens and the legation. There
must be nothing done which would commit us to future
action inconsistent with your standing instructions.
There must be no alliances.
(From 'Foreign Relations of the United States, 1900'
(Washington, 1902), pp. 142-3.)

60   The partitioning of Samoa

(American involvement in Samoan affairs, dating back
to the 1880s, came to a conclusion in 1899, when the
islands were divided between the United States and
Germany. President McKinley explained the situation
in his annual message of 5 December 1899.)

Important events have occurred in the Samoan Islands.
The election, according to the laws and customs of
Samoa, of a successor to the late King, Malietoa Laupepa,
developed a contest as to the validity of the result,
which issue, by the terms of the General Act, was to be
decided by the Chief Justice. Upon his rendering a
judgment in favor of Malietoa Tanu, the rival chief,
Mataafa, took up arms. The active intervention of
American and British war ships became imperative to
restore order, at the cost of sanguinary encounters. In
this emergency a joint commission of representatives of
the United States, Germany, and Great Britain was sent
to Samoa to investigate the situation and provide a
temporary remedy. By its active efforts a peaceful
solution was reached for the time being, the kingship
being abolished and a provisional government established.
Recommendations unanimously made by the commission for
a permanent adjustment of the Samoan question were taken
under consideration by the three powers parties to the
General Act. But the more they were examined the more
evident it became that a radical change was necessary
in the relations of the powers to Samoa ...
    The arrangement under which Samoa was administered
had proved impracticable and unacceptable to all the
powers concerned. To withdraw from the agreement and
abandon the islands to Germany and Great Britain would
not be compatible with our interests in the archipelago.
To relinquish our rights in the harbor of Pago Pago, the

best anchorage in the Pacific, the occupancy of which
had been leased to the United States in 1878 by the first
foreign treaty ever concluded by Samoa, was not to be
thought of either as regards the needs of our Navy or
the interests of our growing commerce with the East.   We
could not have considered any proposition for the
abrogation of the tripartite control which did not
confirm us in all our rights and safeguard all our
national interests in the islands.

Our views commended themselves to the other powers.
A satisfactory arrangement was concluded between the
Governments of Germany and of England, by virtue of
which England retired from Samoa in view of compensations
in other directions, and both powers renounced in favor
of the United States all their rights and claims over
and in respect to that portion of the group lying to
the east of the one hundred and seventy-first degree of
west longitude, embracing the islands of Tutuila, Ofoo,
Olosenga, and Manua.
(From 'Foreign Relations of the United States, 1899'
(Washington, 1901), pp. xxvi-xviii.)

61   The Hague Conference

(The United States participated in the first Hague
Conference, held in 1899 to discuss disarmament,
prohibition of certain instruments of war, and the
establishment of an international court of arbitration.
These excerpts from Secretary Hay's instructions to
the United States delegates, dated 18 April 1899,
indicate where American policy stood with respect to
these proposals.)

The [question of disarmament] is, at present, so
inapplicable to the United States that it is deemed
advisable for the delegates to leave the initiative
upon this subject to the representatives of those
Powers to which it may properly belong.   In comparison
with the effective forces, both military and naval, of
other nations, those of the United States are at present
so far below the normal quota that the question of
limitation could not be profitably discussed.

The [proposal] relating to the non-employment of
firearms, explosives, and other destructive agents, the
restricted use of existing instruments of destruction,
and the prohibition of certain contrivances employed in
naval warfare, seem lacking in practicability, and the
discussion of these propositions would probably prove

provocative of divergence rather than unanimity of views.
It is doubtful if wars are to be diminished by rendering
them less destructive, for it is the plain lesson of
history that the periods of peace have been longer
protracted as the cost and destructiveness of war have
increased. The expediency of restraining the inventive
genius of our people in the direction of devising means
of defense is by no means clear, and, considering the
temptations to which men and nations may be exposed in
a time of conflict, it is doubtful if an international
agreement to this end would prove effective. The dissent
of a single powerful nation might render it altogether
nugatory. The delegates are, therefore, enjoined not to
give the weight of their influence to the promotion of
projects the realization of which is so uncertain ...

The [suggestion by Russian Foreign Minister Muraviev
for a] wider extension of good offices, mediation and
arbitration, seems likely to open the most fruitful field
for discussion and future action. 'The prevention of
armed conflicts by pacific means,' to use the words of
Count Muraviev's circular of December 30, is a purpose
well worthy of a great international convention, and its
realization in an age of general enlightenment should not
be impossible. The duty of sovereign States to promote
international justice by all wise and effective means
is only secondary to the fundamental necessity of
preserving their own existence. Next in importance to
their independence is the great fact of their interdependence. Nothing can secure for human government
and for the authority of law which it represents so deep
a respect and so firm a loyalty as the spectacle of
sovereign and independent States, whose duty it is to
prescribe the rules of justice and impose penalties upon
the lawless, bowing with reverence before the august
supremacy of those principles of right which give to
law its eternal foundation.
(From 'World Peace Foundation Pamphlet Series', vol. III,
no. 4 (Boston, 1913), pp. 4-5.)

62   Roosevelt on expansion

(Theodore Roosevelt, becoming president after McKinley's
assassination in September 1901, was in tune with the
assertive mood of the time, and he completely accepted
the framework of United States foreign policy that his
predecessor had established after the war. The following
several documents record Roosevelt's ideas on various
aspects of foreign policy. The first is taken from his
speech in San Francisco on 13 May 1903.)

Before I came to the Pacific Slope I was an expansionist,
and after having been here I fail to understand how any
man, convinced of his country's greatness and glad that
his country should challenge with proud confidence in
its mighty future, can be anything but an expansionist.
In the century that is opening the commerce and the
command of the Pacific will be factors of incalculable
moment in the world's history ...

[Our] own mighty Republic has stretched from the
Atlantic to the Pacific, and now in California, Oregon,
and Washington, in Alaska, Hawaii and the Philippines,
holds an extent of coast line which makes it of necessity
a power of the first class in the Pacific. The extension
in the area of our domain has been immense, the extension
in the area of our influence even greater. America's
geographical position on the Pacific is such as to
ensure our peaceful domination of its waters in the
future if only we grasp with sufficient resolution the
advantages of that position. We are taking long strides
in that direction; witness the cables we are laying down,
the steamship lines we are starting - some of them already
containing steamships larger than any freight carriers
that have previously existed. We have taken the first
steps toward digging an Isthmian canal, to be under our
own control, a canal which will make our Atlantic and
Pacific coast lines in effect continuous, which will be
of incalculable benefit to our mercantile navy, and
above all to our military navy in the event of war.

The inevitable march of events gave us the control
of the Philippine Islands at a time so opportune that it
may without irreverence be called Providential. Unless
we show ourselves weak, unless we show ourselves
degenerate sons of the sires from whose loins we sprang,
we must go on with the work we have undertaken ...
(From Theodore Roosevelt, 'Presidential Addresses and
State Papers', vol. I (New York, 1910), pp. 390-4.)

63   Roosevelt on peace and war

(This is taken from a speech by Roosevelt in New York,
delivered on 11 November 1902.)

We have passed that stage of national development when
depreciation of other peoples is felt as a tribute to
our own. We watch the growth and prosperity of other
nations, not with hatred or jealousy, but with sincere
and friendly good-will. I think I can say safely that
we have shown by our attitude toward Cuba, by our attitude

toward China, that as regards weaker powers our desire is that they may be able to stand alone, and that if they will only show themselves willing to deal honestly and fairly with the rest of mankind we on our side will do all we can to help, not to hinder, them. With the great powers of the world we desire no rivalry that is not honorable to both parties. We wish them well. We believe that the trend of the modern spirit is ever stronger toward peace, not war; toward friendship, not hostility, as the normal international attitude. We are glad indeed that we are on good terms with all the other peoples of mankind, and no effort on our part shall be spared to secure a continuance of these relations. And remember, gentlemen, that we shall be a potent factor for peace largely in proportion to the way in which we make it evident that our attitude is due, not to weakness, not to inability to defend ourselves, but to a genuine repugnance to wrongdoing, a genuine desire for self-respecting friendship with our neighbors. The voice of the weakling or the craven counts for nothing when he clamors for peace; but the voice of the just man armed is potent. We need to keep in a condition of preparedness, especially as regards our navy, not because we want war, but because we desire to stand with those whose plea for peace is listened to with respectful attention. (Ibid., I, 197-8.)

64 Roosevelt and the Monroe Doctrine

(This is part of Roosevelt's speech at Chicago on 2 April 1903.)

Ever since the time when we definitely extended our boundaries westward to the Pacific and southward to the Gulf, since the time when the old Spanish and Portuguese colonies to the south of us asserted their independence, our Nation has insisted that because of its primacy in strength among the nations of the Western Hemisphere it has certain duties and responsibilities which oblige it to take a leading part thereon. We hold that our interests in this hemisphere are greater than those of any European power possibly can be, and that our duty to ourselves and to the weaker republics who are our neighbors requires us to see that none of the great military powers from across the seas shall encroach upon the territory of the American republics or acquire control thereover.

   This policy, therefore, not only forbids us to

acquiesce in such territorial acquisition, but also causes
us to object to the acquirement of a control which would
in its effect be equal to territorial aggrandizement.
This is why the United States has steadily believed that
the construction of the great Isthmian Canal, the building
of which is to stand as the greatest material feat of
the twentieth century - greater than any similar feat in
any preceding century - should be done by no foreign
nation but by ourselves. The canal must of necessity
go through the territory of one of our smaller sister
republics. We have been scrupulously careful to abstain
from perpetrating any wrong upon any of these republics
in this matter. We do not wish to interfere with their
rights in the least, but, while carefully safeguarding
them, to build the canal ourselves under provisions which
will enable us, if necessary, to police and protect it,
and to guarantee its neutrality, we being the sole
guarantor. Our intention was steadfast; we desired action
taken so that the canal could always be used by us in
time of peace and war alike, and in time of war could
never be used to our detriment by any nation which was
hostile to us. Such action, by the circumstances
surrounding it, was necessarily for the benefit and not
the detriment of the adjacent American republics ...
The Monroe Doctrine is not international law, and
though I think one day it may become such, this is not
necessary as long as we possess both the will and the
strength to make it effective. This last point, my
fellow-citizens, is all important, and is one which as a
people we can never afford to forget. I believe in the
Monroe Doctrine with all my heart and soul; I am convinced
that the immense majority of our fellow-countrymen so
believe in it; but I would infinitely prefer to see us
abandon it than to see us put it forward and bluster
about it, and yet fail to build up the efficient fighting
strength which in the last resort can alone make it
respected by any strong foreign power whose interest it
may ever happen to be to violate it.
Boasting and blustering are as objectionable among
nations as among individuals, and the public men of a
great nation owe it to their sense of national self-
respect to speak courteously of foreign powers, just as
a brave and self-respecting man treats all around him
courteously. But though to boast is bad, and causelessly
to insult another, worse, yet worse than all is it to
be guilty of boasting, even without insult, and when
called to the proof to be unable to make such boasting
good. There is a homely old adage which runs: 'Speak
softly and carry a big stick; you will go far.' If the

American Nation will speak softly, and yet build, and
keep at a pitch of the highest training, a thoroughly
efficient navy, the Monroe Doctrine will go far. I ask
you to think over this. If you do so, you will come to
the conclusion that it is mere plain common-sense, so
obviously sound that only the blind can fail to see its
truth and only the weakest and most irresolute can fail
to desire to put it into force.
(Ibid., I, 257-9, 265-6.)

65   Roosevelt and the Philippines

(This was a speech Roosevelt delivered in Memphis on
19 November 1902, at a banquet in honor of General Luke E.
Wright, acting governor of the Philippines.)

The events of the last four years have definitely decided
that whether we wish to or not we must hereafter play a
great part in the world. We can not escape facing
the duties. We may shirk them if we are built of poor
stuff, or we may take hold and do them if we are fit sons
of our sires - but face them we must, whether we will or
not. Our duty in the Philippine Islands has simply been
one of the duties that thus have come upon us. We are
there, and we can no more haul down our flag and abandon
the islands than we could now abandon Alaska. Whether
we are glad or sorry that events forced us to go there
is aside from the question; the point is that, as the
inevitable result of the war with Spain, we found
ourselves in the Philippines and that we could not leave
the islands without discredit. The islanders were wholly
unfit to govern themselves, and if we had left there would
have been a brief period of bloody chaos, and then some
other nation would have stepped in to do the work which
we had shirked. It can not be too often repeated that
there was no question that the work had to be done. All
the question was, whether we would do it well or ill;
and, thanks to the choice of men like Governor Wright, it
has been done well. The first and absolutely
indispensable requisite was order - peace. The reign of
lawless violence, of resistance to legitimate authority,
the reign of anarchy, could no more be tolerated abroad
than it could be tolerated here in our own land.
    The American flag stands for orderly liberty, and it
stands for it abroad as it stands for it at home. The
task of our soldiers was to restore and maintain order
in the islands. The army had the task to do, and it did
well and thoroughly. The fullest and heartiest praise

belongs to our soldiers who in the Philippines brought
to a triumphant conclusion a war, small indeed compared
to the gigantic struggle in which the older men whom I
am addressing took part in the early sixties, but
inconceivably harassing and difficult, because it was
waged amid the pathless jungles of great tropic islands
and against a foe very elusive, very treacherous, and
often inconceivably cruel both toward our men and toward
the great numbers of peace-loving Filipinos who gladly
welcomed our advent ...

There is no question as to our not having gone far
enough and fast enough in granting self-government to
the Filipinos; the only possible danger has been lest we
should go faster and further than was in the interest
of the Filipinos themselves. Each Filipino at the present
day is guaranteed his life, his liberty, and the chance
to pursue happiness as he wishes, so long as he does not
harm his fellows, in a way which the islands have never
known before during all their recorded history. There
are bands of ladrones, of brigands, still in existence.
Now and then they may show sporadic increase. This will
be due occasionally to disaffection with some of the
things that our government does which are best - for
example, the effort to quarantine against the plague and
to enforce necessary sanitary precautions, gently and
tactfully though it was made, produced violent hostility
among some of the more ignorant natives. Again, a
disease like the cattle plague may cause in some given
province such want that a part of the inhabitants revert
to their ancient habit of brigandage. But the islands
have never been as orderly, as peaceful, or as prosperous
as now; and in no other Oriental country, whether ruled
by Asiatics or Europeans, is there anything approaching
to the amount of individual liberty and of self-
government which our rule has brought to the Filipinos.
(Ibid., I, 204-8.)

66 Roosevelt and the navy

(In his first annual message to Congress, given on
3 December 1901, more space was devoted to the discussion
of naval matters than to any other subject.)

The work of upbuilding the navy must be steadily
continued. No one point of our policy, foreign or
domestic, is more important than this to the honor and
material welfare, and above all to the peace, of our
Nation in the future. Whether we desire it or not, we

must henceforth recognize that we have international
duties no less than international rights. Even if our
flag were hauled down in the Philippines and Porto Rico,
even if we decided not to build the Isthmian Canal, we
should need a thoroughly trained navy of adequate size,
or else be prepared definitely and for all time to
abandon the idea that our Nation is among those whose
sons go down to the sea in ships. Unless our commerce
is always to be carried in foreign bottoms, we must have
war craft to protect it.

Inasmuch, however, as the American people have no
thought of abandoning the path upon which they have
entered, and especially in view of the fact that the
building of the Isthmian Canal is fast becoming one of
the matters which the whole people are united in
demanding, it is imperative that our navy should be put
and kept in the highest state of efficiency, and should
be made to answer to our growing needs. So far from
being in any way a provocation to war, an adequate and
highly trained navy is the best guaranty against war, the
cheapest and most effective peace insurance. The cost
of building and maintaining such a navy represents the
very lightest premium for insuring peace which this
nation can possibly pay ...

It is not possible to improvise a navy after war
breaks out. The ships must be built and the men trained
long in advance. Some auxiliary vessels can be turned
into makeshifts which will do in default of any better
for the minor work, and a proportion of raw men can be
mixed with the highly trained, their shortcomings being
made good by the skill of their fellows; but the
efficient fighting force of the navy when pitted against
an equal opponent will be found almost exclusively in the
warships that have been regularly built and in the
officers and men who through years of faithful performance of sea duty have been trained to handle their
formidable but complex and delicate weapons with the
highest efficiency. In the late war with Spain the
ships that dealt the decisive blows at Manila and
Santiago had been launched from two to fourteen years,
and they were able to do as they did because the men
in the conning towers, the gun-turrets, and the engine-
rooms had through long years of practice at sea learned
how to do their duty ...

There should be no cessation in the work of
completing our navy. So far ingenuity has been wholly
unable to devise a substitute for the great war craft
whose hammering guns beat out the mastery of the high
seas. It is unsafe and unwise not to provide this year

for several additional battleships and heavy armored
cruisers, with auxiliary and lighter craft in
proportion ...

To send any warship against a competent enemy unless
those aboard it have been trained by years of actual
sea service, including incessant gunnery practice, would
be to invite not merely disaster, but the bitterest
shame and humiliation. Four thousand additional seamen
and one thousand additional marines should be provided;
and an increase in the officers should be provided by
making a large addition to the classes at Annapolis ...

The American people must either build and maintain an
adequate navy or else make up their minds definitely
to accept a secondary position in international affairs,
not merely in political, but in commercial, matters. It
has been well said that there is no surer way of
courting national disaster than to be 'opulent,
aggressive, and unarmed.'
(Ibid., vol. II (New York, 1910), pp. 577-84.)

5   CO-OPERATION AND COMPETITION

67   A new world-view

(Although for a decade after 1904, the United States
was not involved in external adventures comparable to
those in the preceding decade, there were intensive
attempts to develop a stable structure of peace on the
basis of America's recent achievements. Elihu Root,
secretary of state during 1905-9, was typical of the
age in that he perceived, and tried to articulate, what
he considered to be aspirations of the world for
stability, peace, and progress. These passages are taken
from his speeches in Rio de Janeiro and Montevideo on
31 July and 12 August 1906.)

[No] student of our times can fail to see that not
America alone but the whole civilized world is swinging
away from its old governmental moorings and intrusting
the fate of its civilization to the capacity of the
popular mass to govern. By this pathway mankind is to
travel, withersoever it leads. Upon the success of this
our great undertaking the hope of humanity depends ...

[No] nation can live unto itself alone and continue
to live. Each nation's growth is a part of the development of the race. There may be leaders and there may be
laggards, but no nation can long continue very far in
advance of the general progress of mankind, and no nation

that is not doomed to extinction can remain very far behind. It is with nations as it is with individual men; intercourse, association, correction of egotism by the influence of other's judgment, broadening of views by the experience and thought of equals, acceptance of the moral standards of a community the desire for whose good opinion lends a sanction to the rules of right conduct - these are the conditions of growth in civilization. A people whose minds are not open to the lessons of the world's progress, whose spirits are not stirred by the aspirations and the achievements of humanity struggling the world over for liberty and justice, must be left behind by civilization in its steady and beneficent advance ...

I have been preaching for the past few weeks in many places and before many audiences the gospel of international fraternization. I know there are many incredulous; there are many who think practical considerations alone rule the efforts of men - profit in trade, the almighty dollar, the balance of bookkeeping, or the checks in the countinghouse. There are many who think that this is all there is to life and that he is an idle dreamer and insincere orator who talks of the constancy of international friendship, who talks of love of country rising above the love of material things, who talks of sentiment as controlling the affairs of men. That may be true so far as their own short and narrow lives are concerned, but it is not an idle dream that the world through the course of ages is growing up from material to spiritual, to moral, and to intellectual life. It is not an idle dream that moral influences are gradually, steadily in the course of centuries taking the place of brute force in the control of affairs of men. Sentiment rules the world to-day - the feelings of the great masses of mankind; the attractions and repulsions that move the millions rule the world to-day, and as generation succeeds generation progress is ever from the material to the moral. We can not see it in a day; we can not see it in a single lifetime, as we can not see the movement of the tide. We see the waves, but the tide moves on imperceptibly. The progress, the steady and irresistible progress, of civilization is ever on.

(From 'Speeches Incident to the Visit of Secretary Root to South America' (Washington, 1906), pp. 8-9, 116-17.)

68 Colonial administration

(William Howard Taft, secretary of war in the Roosevelt
administration, applied his experiences as governor of
the Philippines to an understanding of international
affairs. His ideas, here excerpted from a lecture at
Yale University, complement those of Root as an integral
part of the same world view.)

The parts of the earth which have been retarded, the
places where there is the greatest field for progressive
work, both material, intellectual, and moral, are in the
tropical countries. The discoveries of medical science,
the knowledge of conditions that promote health, have
improved to such a point that it is much more practicable
now for people of the temperate zone to live an extended
period in the tropics without injury to health than it
was a decade or two decades ago. The land of the
temperate zones is rapidly being absorbed. Profit lies
in the improvement of the tropical countries; agriculture,
mines, and other sources of revenue are there; and it
is inevitable that in the next century the great progress
of the world is to be made among tropical peoples and in
tropical countries. Therefore what we are doing in the
Philippines ·is merely a precursor of what will be done in
other lands near the equator; and if we demonstrate that
it is possible for people purely tropical to be educated
and lifted above the temptations to idleness and savagery
and cruelty and torpor that have thus far retarded the
races born under the equatorial sun, we shall be pointing
another important way to improve the civilization of the
world.
   Hence it is that the value of the work we are doing in
the Philippines rises far above the mere question of
what the total of our exports and imports may be for this
year or for next year or hereafter, or whether they are
at present a burden. The Philippine question is, Can the
dominion of a great and prosperous civilized nation in the
temperate zone exercise a healthful and positively
beneficial influence upon the growth and development of a
tropical people? What we have to do is in a sense to
change their nature; it is to furnish, by developing their
physical and intellectual wants, a motive for doing work
which does not exist under their present conditions. That
this can be done I have no doubt, from what has already
been done in the islands. But it is a question of time
and patience. The tropical peoples cannot lift themselves
as the Anglo-Saxons and other peoples of the cold and
temperate zones, where the inclemency and rigors of the

climate demand effort and require labor, have lifted
themselves. The struggle that these tropical peoples
must go through in reaching better things is far more
difficult; and its outcome must depend, in my judgment,
on the outside aid of friendly and guiding nations. The
principle which our anti-imperialists seek to apply, that
people must acquire knowledge of self-government by
independence, is not applicable to a tropical people. We
cannot set them going in a decade and look to their
future progress as certain. We must have them for a
generation or two generations, or perhaps even three,
in order that our experiment with reference to education,
primary and industrial, shall have its effect, and that
our guiding hand, in teaching them commonsense views of
government, shall give them the needed direction.
(From William Howard Taft, 'Four Aspects of Civic Duty',
(New York, 1906), pp. 86-8.)

69 Economic interdependence (1)

(The economic realities underlying the search for a
stable world order were well described by this speech
by Secretary Root in Kansas City on 20 November 1906.)

Since the first election of President McKinley the
people of the United States have for the first time
accumulated a surplus of capital beyond the requirements
of internal development. That surplus is increasing
with extraordinary rapidity. We have paid our debts
to Europe and have become a creditor instead of a
debtor nation; we have faced about; we have left the
ranks of the borrowing nations and have entered the
ranks of the investing nations. Our surplus energy is
beginning to look beyond our own borders, throughout
the world, to find opportunity for the profitable use
of our surplus capital, foreign markets for our
manufactures, foreign mines to be developed, foreign
bridges and railroads and public works to be built,
foreign rivers to be turned into electric power and
light. As in their several ways England and France and
Germany have stood, so we in our own way are beginning
to stand and must continue to stand towards the
industrial enterprise of the world.
   That we are not beginning our new role feebly is
indicated by the $1,518,561,666 of exports in the year
1905 as against $1,117,513,071 of imports, and by
$1,743,864,500 exports in the year 1906 as against
$1,226,563,843 of imports. Our first steps in the new

field indeed are somewhat clumsy and unskilled. In
our own vast country, with oceans on either side, we
have had too little contact with foreign peoples readily
to understand their customs or learn their languages;
yet no one can doubt that we shall learn and shall
understand and shall do our business abroad, as we have
done it at home, with force and efficiency.

Coincident with this change in the United States the
progress of political development has been carrying the
neighboring continent of South American out of the stage
of militarism into the stage of industrialism. Throughout the greater part of that vast continent revolutions
have ceased to be looked upon with favor or submitted
to with indifference; the revolutionary general and the
dictator are no longer the objects of admiration and
imitation; civic virtues command the highest respect;
the people point with satisfaction and pride to the
stability of their Governments, to the safety of property
and the certainty of justice; nearly everywhere the
people are eager for foreign immigration to occupy their
vacant land. Immediately before us, at exactly the
right time, just as we are ready for it, great
opportunities for peaceful commercial and industrial
expansion to the south are presented. Other investing
nations are already in the field - England, France,
Germany, Italy, Spain; but the field is so vast, the new
demands are so great, the progress so rapid, that what
other nations have done up to this time is but a slight
advance in the race for the grand total. The
opportunities are so large that figures fail to convey
them. The area of this newly awakened continent is
7,502,848 square miles - more than two and one-half
times as large as the United States without Alaska, and
more than double the United States including Alaska. A
large part of this area lies within the Temperate Zone,
with an equable and invigorating climate, free from
extremes of either heat or cold. Farther north in the
Tropics are enormous expanses of high table-lands,
stretching from the Atlantic to the foothills of the
Andes, and lifted far above the tropical heats; the
fertile valleys of the western cordilleras are cooled by
perpetual snows even under the Equator; vast forests
grow untouched from a soil of incredible richness. The
plains of Argentina, the great uplands of Brazil, the
mountain valleys of Chile, Peru, Ecuador, Bolivia, and
Columbia are suited to the habitation of any race,
however far to the north its origin may have been;
hundreds of millions of men can find healthful homes and
abundant sustenance in this great territory.
(From 'Speeches of Root', pp. 272-5.)

70   Economic interdependence (2)

(Taft, becoming president in 1909, agreed with Root's
conception of economic interdependence, especially
between North and South America. His first annual
message to Congress, dated 7 December 1909, is a good
example.)

To-day, more than ever before, American capital is
seeking investment in foreign countries, and American
products are more and more generally seeking foreign
markets. As a consequence, in all countries there are
American citizens and American interests to be
protected, on occasion, by their Government. These
movements of men, of capital, and of commodities bring
peoples and governments closer together and so form
bonds of peace and mutual dependency, as they must also
naturally sometimes make passing points of friction.
The resultant situation inevitably imposes upon this
Government vastly increased responsibilities. This
Administration, through the Department of State and the
foreign service is lending all proper support to
legitimate and beneficial American enterprises in foreign
countries, the degree of such support being measured by
the national advantages to be expected. A citizen
himself can not be contract or otherwise divest himself
of the right, nor can this Government escape the
obligation, of his protection in his personal and
property rights when these are unjustly infringed in a
foreign country. To avoid ceaseless vexations it is
proper that in considering whether American enterprise
should be encouraged or supported in a particular
country, the Government should give full weight not only
to the national as opposed to the individual benefits
to accrue, but also to the fact whether or not the
Government of the country in question in its administration and in its diplomacy [is] faithful to the
principles of moderation, equity, and justice upon which
alone depend international credit, in diplomacy as well
as in finance.
    The Pan-American policy of this Government has long
been fixed in its principles and remains unchanged. With
the changed circumstances of the United States and of the
republics to the south of us, most of which have great
natural resources, stable government, and progressive
ideals, the apprehension which gave rise to the Monroe
Doctrine may be said to have nearly disappeared, and
neither the doctrine as it exists nor any other doctrine
of American policy should be permitted to operate for the

perpetuation of irresponsible government, the escape of
just obligations, or the insidious allegation of
dominating ambitions on the part of the United States.

Beside the fundamental doctrines of our Pan-American
policy there have grown up a realization of political
interests, community of institutions and ideals, and a
flourishing commerce. All these bonds will be greatly
strengthened as time goes on and increased facilities,
such as the great bank soon to be established in Latin
America, supply the means for building up the colossal
intercontinental commerce of the future.
(From William Howard Taft, 'Presidential Addresses and
State Papers' (New York, 1910), pp. 455-6.)

71 International arbitration (1)

(One marked sign of the times was the movement for
international arbitration. One strong exponent was
William Jennings Bryan who attended a conference of the
Interparliamentary Union at London in July 1906. His
speech, supporting a resolution for instituting a
cooling-off period before two countries went to war to
resolve their differences, foreshadowed his own proposal
as secretary of state in the Wilson administration.)

The first advantage ... of [the proposed] resolution is
that it secures an investigation of the facts; and if you
can but separate the facts from the question of honor,
the chances are a hundred to one that you can settle both
the fact and question of honor without war. There is,
therefore, a great advantage in an investigation that
brings out the facts, for disputed facts between nations,
as between friends, are the cause of most disagreements.

The second advantage of this investigation is that it
gives time for calm consideration ... I need not say to
you that a man excited is a very different animal from
a man calm, and that questions ought to be settled, not
by passion, but by deliberation. If this resolution
would do nothing else but give time for reflection and
deliberation, there would be sufficient reason for its
adoption. If we can but stay the hand of war until
conscience can assert itself, war will be made more
remote. When men are mad, they swagger around and tell
what they can do; when they are calm, they consider what
they ought to do.

The third advantage of this investigation is that it
gives opportunity to mobilize public opinion for the
compelling of a peaceful settlement, and that is an

advantage not to be overlooked. Public opinion is coming
to be more and more a power in the world. One of the
greatest statesmen my country has produced, Thomas
Jefferson - and, if it would not offend, I would say I
believe him to be the greatest statesman the world has
produced - said that if he had to choose between a
government without newspapers and newspapers without a
government, he would rather risk the newspapers without
a government. You may call it an extravagant statement,
and yet it presents an idea, and that idea is that
public opinion is to be more and more powerful; glad
that the time is coming when the moral sentiment of one
nation will influence the action of other nations; glad
that the time is coming when the world will realize
that a war between two nations affects others than the
two nations involved; glad that the time is coming when
the world will insist that nations settle their differences by some peaceful means. If time is given for
marshaling the force of public opinion, peace will be
promoted. This resolution is presented, therefore, for
the reasons that it gives an opportunity to investigate
the facts and to separate them from the question of
honor; that it gives time for the calming of passion;
and that it gives a time for the formation of a
controlling public sentiment.
(From 'World Peace Foundation Pamphlet Series', vol. III,
no. 11, part I, Appendix.)

72 International arbitration (2)

(In the following speech at the University of San Marcos,
Lima, given on 14 September 1906, Secretary of State Root
linked arbitration to education.)

We are too apt, both those who are despondent about the
progress of civilization and those who are cynical about
the unselfishness of mankind, to be impatient in our
judgment and to forget how long the life of a nation is,
and how slow the processes of civilization are; how long
it takes to change character and to educate whole peoples
up to different standards of moral law. The principle
of arbitration requires not merely declarations by
governments, by congresses, but it requires that
education of the people of all civilized countries up to
the same standard which exists now regarding the
sacredness of judicial function exercised in our courts.
It does not follow from this that the declaration of the
principle of arbitration is not of value; it does not

follow that governments and congresses are not
advancing the cause of international justice: a principle
recognized and declared always gains fresh strength and
force; but for the accomplishment of the results which
all of us desire in the substitution of arbitration for
war, we must not be content with the declaration of
principles; we must carry on an active campaign of
universal national and international education, elevating
the idea of the sacredness of the exercise of the
judicial function in arbitration as well as in litigation
between individuals. Still deeper than that goes the
duty that rests upon us. Arbitration is but the method
of preventing war after nations have drawn up in
opposition to each other with serious differences and
excited feelings. The true, the permanent, and the
final method of preventing war is to educate the people
who make war or peace, the people who control parliaments
and congresses to a love for justice and regard for the
rights of others. So we come to the duty that rests
here - not in the whims or the preference or the policy
of a monarch, but here, in this university, in every
institution of learning throughout the civilized world,
with every teacher - the responsibility of determining
the great issues of peace and war through the
responsibility of teaching the people of our countries
the love of justice, teaching them to seek the victories
of peace rather than the glories of war, to regard
more highly an act of justice and of generosity than
even an act of courage or an act of heroism.
(From 'Speeches of Root', pp. 246-7.)

73   International arbitration (3)

(President Taft was also a firm believer in arbitration,
even when it concerned matters of national honor. His
ideas are clearly reflected in this speech at Marion,
Indiana, on 3 July 1911.)

The awful consequences to two heavily-armed countries
under modern conditions of war have been a great
deterrent of war; but the irresponsibility of men claiming
to be patriots and desiring to overturn existing
governments where law and order are not well established
has led to a great deal of guerilla warfare and to the
suffering of innocent people who find no real principle
involved in the two contending parties except that of
ambition for power.

Much of this kind of work has occurred in South
America and in Central America, and in that degree of
guardianship which the United States must feel over the
republics of this hemisphere, in maintaining their
integrity against European invasion, we ought to
welcome every opportunity which gives us a legitimate
instrument by which we can make less probable such
internecine strife.   In the assertion of that sort of
guardianship we have to be very careful to avoid the
charge, which is always made by the suspicious, that
we are seeking our own aggrandizement in our interference
with the affairs of other countries of this hemisphere.
It is an unfounded charge, for we envy no power its
territory.   We have enough.   But we have been able to
fend off war in five or more instances of recent date
because of our attitude as an elder brother of these
smaller governments ...

For the further securing of peace, and as an example
to all the world of the possibilities of the use of
arbitration, we have invited England and France and
Germany to make a treaty for the arbitration of all
differences of an international character that in their
nature can be adjudicated, and we have left out in this
treaty those exceptions which have heretofore always
been excluded from arbitrable controversies, to wit,
questions of a nation's honor, and of its vital
interest ...

Objection has been made that an agreement to arbitrate
a question of national honor ought not to be entered
into, for the reason that when one's honor is affected,
one will never consent to have the question arbitrated,
and, therefore, that to agree to do so in advance is to
agree to do something that one will not be willing to
do, and that one does not intend to do, and, therefore,
it savors of hypocrisy and ought not to be adopted as a
national policy.   I can not concede the premises of this
argument.   I look upon a treaty of this sort as a
self-denying ordinance, as a self-restricting obligation
... And so in agreeing to arbitrate questions of national
honor, I see no reason why we may not agree to do so, and
that we may not have moral courage enough, in spite of our
impulse to the contrary, to submit such questions to an
impartial tribunal and await its judgment ...

There is very little probability, as between Great
Britain and the United States, that any occasion will
ever arise in which war would be possible.   The same
thing is true of France and of Germany.   Why, therefore,
it is asked, is it necessary to make a treaty of
arbitration to avoid wars that are only remotely possible?

International law is made up of international customs, traditions, and the formulation of international standards of ethics in treaties between civilized governments. A willingness of great countries like those of England, France, Germany, and the United States to submit their differences, even of honor, to an impartial tribunal will be a step forward in the cause of peace for the world that can hardly be overestimated. (From Address of President Taft at Marion, Ind. , 'Senate Executive Documents', 62nd Congress, 1st Session, Doc. 79 (1911).

74 World power

(In a widely read book, a noted historian, Archibald Cary Coolidge of Harvard University, discussed the emergence of world powers in a short period of time.)

Twenty years ago the expression 'world power' was unknown in most languages; to-day it is a political commonplace, bandied about in wide discussion. But the term is lacking in exactness. Men differ as to its meaning, as to the countries to which it can properly be applied, and as to the moment when it first becomes applicable to them. Sometimes it seems to be appropriately used of a country in one connection, but not in another; and in a certain sense it may be applied to nearly all independent states, for all may be called upon to maintain their particular rights and interests in any quarter of the globe, and all may take part in framing regulations for the general welfare of mankind. And yet, uncertain as the limits of the phrase may be, it conveys a pretty definite conception - a conception that is of recent origin, although there is nothing new in the political sentiments to which it owes its birth.

The idea that one people should control the known world is ancient enough, its most salient expression being found in imperial Rome and equally imperial China; and it is not extinct even now. We may to-day condemn all mere lust of domination, and hope that, as civilization progresses, the stronger peoples will more and more regard the weaker ones as having rights as sacred as their own; but complete equality has never existed, and can never exist, between states of greatly unequal strength. In practice the larger must tend to arrange many matters without consulting every wish of their numerous smaller brethren. The community of nations cannot content itself with anarchy like that of the

Polish republic, and submit to the *liberum veto* of its
most insignificant member. As there have been in the
past, so there will always be, certain leading states
which, when they are agreed, will find some way of
imposing their decisions upon the rest, and by their
mutual jealousies will tend to establish a balance of
power among themselves ...

One effect of the present international evolution
has been to modify certain long-accepted formulas. Among
these is the idea of a continent as a group of states,
each of which has, besides historical traditions of its
own, particular ties and interests common to them all,
but not shared by the rest of mankind. This has in the
past been more or less true of Europe, and as a
sentimental bond it deserves respect. In actual
politics, however, it is becoming a mere figure of speech.
Are we to regard Imperial Britain as a European power,
when the greater part of her external interests and
difficulties are connected with her situation on other
continents? Are not the vast majority of Englishmen
more in touch in every way with Australians, Canadians,
Americans, than they are with Portuguese, Italians, or
Austrians of one sort or another? What strictly
European interests does England represent, she who is
now joined in close alliance with the Asiatic empire of
Japan? Or is Russia European? Although the majority
of her inhabitants live on the western side of the open
range of hills we call the Urals, much the larger portion
of her territory is on the other, and in Europe itself
she has many Asiatic elements. In character and
population, there is indeed hardly more real separation
between European Russia and Siberia than there is between
the eastern and western parts of the United States. Of
late Russia's foreign policy has been chiefly concerned
with Asiatic questions, and it is likely so to continue.
As for France, although her national life is, and will
remain, centered in the European continent, her many
colonies are scattered over the globe. Already some of
them are represented in her chambers, and as time goes
on they will become, more and more, parts of one organic
dominion. A Frenchman born in Algeria regards himself
as a European, and with good right; but he is no more so
than is the white Australian or the Canadian, or, except
in the matter of allegiance, than the American. Under
these circumstances, when people abroad talk about a union
of the European powers against 'the Asiatic peril' or
'the American commercial invasion,' they are appealing to
a community of interests which does not exist ...

If, then, the political destinies of the globe are to

be determined more and more by a few great nations, it is
desirable that we should know as much as possible about
them, and should try to understand the circumstances which
determine their relations with one another. The United
States may be a world in itself, but it is also a part
of a larger world. There is no doubt that its power for
good and for evil is very great. How that power is to
be used is of consequence to all humanity.
(From Archibald Cary Coolidge, 'The United States as a
World Power' (New York, 1908), pp. 1-2, 13-14.)

75 Competition in Asia (1)

(A major crisis of the Taft administration was the
failure of the Open Door policy in China which conflicted
with the interests and ambitions of several powers, in
particular Japan. In his inaugural address, delivered
on 4 March 1909, he indicated a determination to protect
American interests in Asia.)

In the international controversies that are likely to
arise in the Orient growing out of the question of the
open door and other issues the United States can maintain
her interests intact, and can secure respect for her
just demands. She will not be able to do so, however,
if it is understood that she never intends to back up her
assertion of right and her defense of her interest by
anything but mere verbal protest and diplomatic note.
For these reasons the expenses of the army and navy and
of coast defenses should always be considered as
something which the Government must pay for, and they
should not be cut off through mere consideration of
economy. Our Government is able to afford a suitable
army and a suitable navy. It may maintain them without
the slightest danger to the Republic or the cause of
free institutions, and fear of additional taxation ought
not to change a proper policy in this regard.
The policy of the United States in the Spanish war
and since has given it a position of influence among the
nations that it never had before, and should be constantly
exerted to securing to its bona fide citizens, whether
native or naturalized, respect for them as such in foreign
countries. We should make every effort to prevent
humiliating and degrading prohibition against any of our
citizens wishing temporarily to sojourn in foreign
countries because of race or religion.
(From Taft, 'Presidential Addresses', p. 59.)

76   Competition in Asia (2)

(Ambassador Thomas J. O'Brien in Tokyo was a critic of
the administration's Asian policy which, he believed,
tended to antagonize Japan while bringing no particular
advantage to American interests in China.   This
document is excerpted from O'Brien's dispatch to
Secretary of State Philander C. Knox, dated 5 February
1910.)

[However] much well meaning and patriotic Americans and
Japanese may say in public speech that we are to the last
degree friendly, and that nothing can ever occur to
create enmity, I am compelled to believe that enmity
could be created and that the cause need not be great.   It
seems unfortunately to be true that there is a considerable percentage of people in both countries who are not
quite satisfied as to the sincerity and honesty of the
purpose of the other.   It is to be regretted that this
sentiment prevails to a greater extent in the United
States than here [Japan] ...

The symptoms and danger to which I have alluded find
support in the opinion expressed without hesitation in
high places at home that war with Japan is inevitable
and that the plain duty of the United States is to
augment her navy in the Pacific to a point not dreamed
of even five years ago ...

It would not be for the interest of either the United
States or Japan to engage in war.   It will be wise,
therefore, so to manage our relations as to avoid it -
indeed both sides can afford to sacrifice much to this
end ...

The late proposal made by you concerning the railways
in Manchuria - a business proposition pure and simple -
was not welcomed by Japan, and we had no such well
established position of confidence as to protect us from
doubt in many quarters as to the integrity of our
purpose ...

If this enormous population [of China] has a
Government of quality and strength of that of Japan, we
might safely depend upon a compensating support in case
of difficulty here.   We may, in the interest of humanity
and in aid of the proper development of the Chinese
Empire, assist her and interpose ... to protect her from
the aggressions of others ... China furnishes a splendid
opportunity for those who actively help her, to involve
themselves in trouble.   [But] she is not able to meet
her simplest obligations.   She cannot or will not observe
the terms of her solemn treaties, and the Government seems
impotent to enforce its will even in her own provinces ...

[My] purpose is to suggest that a plan to intervene in ordinary matters or to attempt a restraint upon Japan's activities to the extent of alienating the latter, is fraught with dangerous possibilities.
(From 'State Department Archives', 711.94/1910.)

77   Hypothetical war

(In the years preceding World War I, Japan was the one country with which the United States could conceivably be drawn into war because of the immigration dispute and the competition in China. War plans for such an eventuality were drawn up and periodically brought up to date. The following is part of the War Plan Orange - 'Orange' was the code name for Japan - as approved by the War Department.)

Subject: Plan in case of war in the Pacific before the Panama Canal is completed.
    1. The character of such a war will at first be defensive on the part of the United States in the Philippines, Oahu, Panama, Alaska and on the Pacific coast of the United States. On the part of Orange the war will be offensive during the first period and quick, energetic action may be expected against the following points:
    1st. An attack upon Oahu, to deprive the United States of the naval base there, and to establish one for her own use.
    2nd. A naval raid against the Pacific end of the Panama Canal, to cause damage and delay the completion of the work on the canal as much as possible.
    3rd. Seizure of that part of Alaska which would enable Orange to secure the large coal fields near Controller Bay; and for other purposes.
    4th. Seizure and fortification, if possible, of Guam by Orange.
    5th. More or less complete seizure and occupation of the Philippine Islands.
    6th. A descent upon some portion of the Pacific coast of the United States; most probably in the Puget Sound district.
    2. As Orange will soon have practically undisputed control of the Pacific for about three months it is believed that any, or even all, of the above offensive operations are practicable, and must be provided against, as far as possible, by the United States.
    3. The fate of the Philippine Islands must rest with

the present garrison; and the same may be said of
Alaska, if war should come suddenly. The strongest
effort possible should be made to reinforce Oahu,
including increase of the garrison to 6 regiments of
infantry, at war strength, 1 field hospital and 1
ambulance company. Plans for the defense of the
Philippines and Oahu are in the hands of commanders
there.

4. The plan for the defense of Alaska includes 1
regular infantry regiment, and 2 volunteer infantry
regiments to be raised in the vicinity. Arms, ammunition
and equipment for the volunteer regiments should be
shipped to Alaska and a good supply of rations for the
entire force.

5. Guam cannot be defended at all, by the army, as
conditions now are.

6. A naval raid against the Panama Canal should be
provided against at once by the dispatch of 3 regiments
of infantry, 1 battalion of field artillery, 1 squadron
of cavalry, 1 company of engineers and 1 company of
signal troops, to be taken from the most conveniently
situated troops, and form, together with the troops now
at Panama, a reinforced brigade. The garrison heretofore
contemplated is thus increased by one regiment, to
provide for the shortage consequent on the regiments
being below war strength.

7. The provisions for the defense of the Pacific
coast of the United States will include:

(a) The defense of the Puget Sound region
(b) The defense of the San Francisco region
(c) The defense of the Los Angeles region.

(From War Department Archives, Record Group 165.)

78 Wilsonian diplomacy (1)

(Before World War I, President Woodrow Wilson was far more
preoccupied with domestic than with foreign affairs. Yet
some of his speeches were already indicative of the ideas
that he would further develop into a grand vision during
the war. This passage is taken from an address he gave
in Washington on 16 May 1914.)

You do not have to stir your thoughts again with the
issues of the Revolution. Some of the issues of the
Revolution were not the cause of it, but merely the
occasion for it. There are just as vital things stirring
now that concern the existence of the Nation as were
stirring then, and every man who worthily stands in this

presence should examine himself and see whether he has
the full conception of what it means that America should
live her own life. Washington saw it when he wrote his
farewell address. It was not merely because of passing
and transient circumstances that Washington said that
we must keep free from entangling alliances. It was
because he saw that no country had yet set its face in
the same direction in which America had set her face. We
can not form alliances with those who are not going our
way; and in our might and majesty and in the confidence
and definiteness of our own purpose we need not and we
should not form alliances with any nation in the world.
Those who are right, those who study their consciences
in determining their policies, those who hold their
honor higher than their advantage, do not need alliances.
You need alliances when you are not strong, and you are
weak only when you are not true to yourself. You are
weak only when you are in the wrong; you are weak only
when you are afraid to do the right; you are weak only
when you doubt your cause and the majesty of a nation's
might asserted.
(From Woodrow Wilson, 'The New Democracy', vol. I (New
York, 1926), pp. 108-9.)

79 Wilsonian diplomacy (2)

(The following document, excerpted from Wilson's address
in Mobile, Alabama, on 27 October 1913, concerned United
States relations with Latin America, but had implications
for the country's foreign affairs as a whole.)

The future ... is going to be very different for this
hemisphere from the past. These States lying to the south
of us, which have always been our neighbors, will now
be drawn closer to us by innumerable ties, and, I hope,
chief of all, by the tie of a common understanding of
each other. Interest does not tie nations together; it
sometimes separates them. But sympathy and understanding
does unite them, and I believe that by the new route that
is just about to be opened, while we physically cut two
continents asunder, we spiritually unite them. It is a
spiritual union which we seek ...
    There is one peculiarity about the history of the
Latin American States which I am sure they are keenly
aware of. You hear of 'concessions' to foreign
capitalists in Latin America. You do not hear of
concessions to foreign capitalists in the United States.
They are not granted concessions. They are invited to

make investments. The work is ours, though they are
welcome to invest in it. We do not ask them to supply
the capital and do the work. It is an invitation, not a
privilege; and States that are obliged, because their
territory does not lie within the main field of modern
enterprise and action, to grant concessions are in this
condition, that foreign interests are apt to dominate
their domestic affairs, a condition of affairs always
dangerous and apt to become intolerable. What these
States are going to see, therefore, is an emancipation
from the subordination, which has been inevitable, to
foreign enterprise and an assertion of the splendid
character which, in spite of these difficulties, they
have again and again been able to demonstrate. The
dignity, the courage, the self-possession, the self-
respect of the Latin American States, their achievements
in the face of all these adverse circumstances, deserve
nothing but the admiration and applause of the world.
They have had harder bargains driven with them in the
matter of loans than any other peoples in the world.
Interest has been exacted of them that was not exacted
of anybody else, because the risk was said to be greater;
and then securities were taken that destroyed the risk -
an admirable arrangement for those who were forcing the
terms! I rejoice in nothing so much as in the prospect
that they will now be emancipated from these conditions,
and we ought to be the first to take part in assisting
in that emanicpation. I think some of these gentlemen
have already had occasion to bear witness that the
Department of State in recent months has tried to serve
them in that wise. In the future they will draw closer
and closer to us because of circumstances of which I
wish to speak with moderation and, I hope, without
indiscretion.

We must prove ourselves their friends, and champions
upon the terms of equality and honor. You cannot be
friends upon any other terms than upon the terms of
equality. You cannot be friends at all except upon the
terms of honor. We must show ourselves friends by
comprehending their interest whether it squares with our
own interest or not. It is a very perilous thing to
determine the foreign policy of a nation in the terms of
material interest. It not only is unfair to those with
whom you are dealing, but it is degrading as regards your
own actions.

Comprehension must be the soil in which shall grow all
the fruits of friendship, and there is a reason and a
compulsion lying behind all this which is dearer than
anything else to the thoughtful men of America. I mean

the development of constitutional liberty in the world.
Human rights, national integrity, and opportunity as
against material interests - that, ladies and gentlemen,
is the issue which we now have to face. I want to take
this occasion to say that the United States will never
again seek one additional foot of territory by conquest.
She will devote herself to showing that she knows how
to make honorable and fruitful use of the territory she
has, and she must regard it as one of the duties of
friendship to see that from no quarter are material
interests made superior to human liberty and national
opportunity. I say this, not with a single thought that
anyone will gainsay it, but merely to fix in our
consciousness what our real relationship with the rest
of America is. It is the relationship of a family of
mankind devoted to the development of true constitutional
liberty. We know that that is the soil out of which the
best enterprise springs. We know that this is a cause
which we are making in common with our neighbors, because
we have had to make it for ourselves.
(Ibid., pp. 66-8.)

Notes

CHAPTER 1: INTRODUCTION

1 George F. Kennan, 'Memoirs 1950-1963' (Boston, 1972), p. 71.
2 Bruce Kuklick, 'American Policy and Division of Germany' (Ithaca, 1972), p. 238.
3 Walter LaFeber, 'America, Russia, and the Cold War', rev. ed. (New York, 1972), p. 155.
4 'Federalist', no. 11.
5 See Klaus E. Knorr, 'British Colonial Theories' (Toronto, 1944) for an excellent discussion of British colonial theory.
6 Albert K. Weinberg, 'Manifest Destiny' (Baltimore, 1935), p. 31.
7 Ibid., pp. 60-1.
8 Bradford Perkins, 'Castlereagh and Adams', (Berkeley, 1964), p. 201.
9 Among the best studies of the 1840s are Norman A. Graebner, 'Empire on the Pacific' (New York, 1955); Frederick Merk, 'The Monroe Doctrine and American Expansion' (New York, 1966); and Merk, 'Slavery and the Annexation of Texas' (New York, 1972).
10 Henry Blumenthal, 'Reappraisal of Franco-American Relations' (Chapel Hill, 1959), p. 70.
11 Durand Echeverria, 'Mirage in the West' (Princeton, 1967), pp. 167, 169.
12 Ibid., p. 109.
13 A. P. Whitaker, 'The United States and the Independence of Latin America' (Baltimore, 1941), pp. 82, 190.
14 'The Works of William H. Seward', ed. George E. Baker, vol. 4 (Boston, 1889), pp. 165-9.
15 'Democratic Review', 6: 208-9 (September 1839).
16 'American Whig Review', 3: 615-16 (June 1846).

17 'North American Review', 36: 418-48 (April 1833).
18 P. S. Klein, 'President James Buchanan' (University Park, Pa., 1962), p. 235. See also Arthur J. May, 'Contemporary American Opinion of the Mid-Century Revolution in Central Europe' (Philadelphia, 1927).
19 'Southern Literary Messenger', 20: 108 (April 1854).
20 Bayard Taylor, 'The Lands of the Saracen' (New York, 1855), p. 353.
21 Francis Warrier, 'The Cruise of the United States Frigate Potomac Round the World' (New York, 1835), p. 104.
22 'Democratic Review', 15: 65 (July 1844).
23 S. Augustus Mitchell, 'An Accompaniment to Mitchell's Map of the World' (Philadelphia, 1843), p. 466.
24 'Democaratic Review', 6: 216 (September 1839).
25 'DeBow's Monthly', 27: 372 (October 1859).
26 'Knickerbocker', 16: 3 (July 1840).
27 'Christian Examiner', 67: 28 (July 1859).
28 'Harper's Monthly', 21: 342 (August 1860); 'Atlantic Monthly', 5: 722 (June 1860).
29 'New York Times', 21 April 1860.
30 Ibid., 11 June 1860.
31 'New York Journal of Commerce', 14 July 1860.
32 Knorr, 'British Colonial Theories', p. 23.
33 'The Cambridge History of the British Empire' 1: 306-11 (Cambridge, 1929).
34 Alice Tyler, 'Freedom's Ferment' (Minneapolis, 1944), p. 21.
35 See Goetzmann, 'Exploration and Empire' (New York, 1966).
36 Bradford Perkins, 'Prologue to War' (Berkeley, 1961), p. 150.
37 Tyler, 'Freedom', pp. 19-20.
38 Eric Foner, 'Free Soil, Free Labor, Free Men' (New York, 1970), pp. 180-1, 316.
39 'Works of Seward', IV, 603-4.
40 Foner, 'Free Soil', p. 72.
41 Ibid., p. 176.
42 'Works of Seward', IV, 603.
43 Foner, 'Free Soil', p. 267.
44 See William Stanton, 'The Leopard's Spots' (Chicago, 1960) for an excellent discussion of antebellum racial theories.
45 'Encyclopedia Americana' (Philadelphia, 1838), p. 414.
46 Samuel Goodrich, 'The Tales of Peter Parley About Asia' (Philadelphia, 1845), pp. 28, 72-3.
47 Samuel Goodrich, 'A History of All Nations' (Boston, 1851), I, 61-3.
48 'New York Times', 23 April 1860.

49   'New York Times', 28 April 1860.
50   'New York Times', 15 May 1860.
51   'New York Times', 16 May 1860.
52   'Boston Daily Advertiser', 30 May 1860.
53   'Boston Daily Advertiser', 30 June 1860.
54   'New York Times', 15 May 1860.
55   'The First Japanese Mission to America: Diary of
     Yanagawa Masakiyo', trans. by Junichi Fukuzawa and
     Roderick H. Jackson (New York, 1938), pp. 42, 58.
56   'The Works of William H. Seward', ed. George E. Baker,
     vol. 4 (Boston, 1889), p. 122.
57   Eric Foner, 'Free Soil, Free Labor, Free Men', (New
     York, 1970), p. 72.
58   Seward to Pruyn, 15 November 1861, 'Foreign Relations
     of the United States 1861' (Washington, 1862),
     pp. 817.
59   See Mary Ellison, 'Support for Secession' (Chicago,
     1973) for a discussion of British labor's attitudes
     toward the Civil War.

CHAPTER 2: EUROPEAN IMPERIALISM AND US EXPANSIONISM

 1   'Nation', no. 395, p. 52 (23 January 1873).
 2   'Nation', no. 440, pp. 364-5 (4 December 1873), and
     no. 438, p.329 (20 November 1873).
 3   J. A. Logan, 'No Transfer' (New Haven, 1961), p. 251.
 4   Ralph H. Gabriel, 'The Courage of American Democratic
     Thought' (New York, 1940), p. 251.
 5   John L. Motley, 'Historical Process and American
     Democracy' (New York, 1869), pp. 6, 31.
 6   'Nation', no. 549, pp. 4-5 (6 January 1876).
 7   'Nation', no. 392, p. 3 (2 January 1873).
 8   John S. Hittell, 'A Brief History of Culture' (New
     York, 1875), p. 82.
 9   Henry M. Field, 'From Egypt to Japan' (New York,
     1886), pp. 60, 246-8.
10   'Nation', no. 428, p. 17 (11 September 1873).
11   'Galaxy', 8: 194 (August 1869).
12   'Overland Monthly', 14: 254 (March 1875), and 14: 425
     (May 1875).
13   Field, 'From Egypt', pp. 416-17.
14   'San Francisco Daily Evening Bulletin' as quoted in
     Charles Lanman, ed., 'The Japanese in America' (New
     York, 1872), p. 17.
15   'Harper's Monthly', 46: 859 (April 1873).
16   'Overland Monthly', 9: 114 (August 1872).
17   'Nation', no. 563, pp. 41-2 (13 April 1876).
18   'Nation', no. 568, p. 321 (18 May 1876).

19   'American Quarterly Church Review', 1: 274-92 (July 1865).
20   'Nation', no. 438, p. 334 (20 November 1873).
21   Quoted in 'Nation', no. 568, p. 321 (18 May 1876).
22   'North American Review', 125: 37 (July 1877).
23   Eugene Schuyler, 'American Diplomacy and the Furtherance of Commerce' (New York, 1886), passim.
24   Otto zu Stolberg-Wernigerode, 'Germany and the United States in the Period of World Politics' (Philadelphia, 1937), pp. 146-60.
25   'Letters of Grover Cleveland', ed. Allan Nevins (Boston, 1933), pp. 134-5.
26   David M. Pletcher, 'The Awkward Years' (Columbia, Mo., 1962), p. 70.
27   Schuyler, 'American Diplomacy', p. 444.
28   'Letters of Cleveland', p. 197.
29   Edward L. Younger, 'John A. Kasson' (Iowa City, 1955), p. 340.
30   Pletcher, 'Awkward Years', p. 317.
31   Ibid., p. 225.
32   'Harper's Monthly', 70: 581-4 (March 1885).
33   Josiah Strong, 'Our Country' (New York, 1891), rev. ed., p. 225.
34   'Andover Review', 4: 327-29 (October 1885).
35   John Russell Young, 'Around the World with General Grant' (New York, 1879), II, 543-4.
36   E. A. Allen, 'History of Civilization' (Cincinnati, 1888), IV, 5, 726, 733, 750, 752.
37   'American Catholic Quarterly Review' (Philadelphia), 10: 139-40 (January 1885).
38   'North American Review', 138: 214 (March 1884), and 138: 348 (April 1884).
39   'North American Review', 138: 177 (March 1884).
40   Younger, 'Kasson', p. 333.
41   Field, 'From Egypt', p. 427.
42   'Letters of Cleveland', pp. 134-5.
43   Margaret Leech, 'In the Days of McKinley' (New York, 1959), p. 40.
44   Rudyard Kipling, 'American Notes' (New York [1889]), pp. 47, 61, 131, 133-5.

CHAPTER 3: THE GROWTH OF NATIONALISTIC EXPANSIONISM

1   'Letters of Cleveland', p. 221.
2   Leech, 'Days of McKinley', p. 62.
3   'Letters of Cleveland', pp. 365-6.
4   Ibid., pp. 418-19.
5   Paolo E. Coletta, 'William Jennings Bryan', vol. I (Lincoln, Neb., 1964), pp. 84-6.

6   'Letters of Cleveland', pp. 426-8.
7   Allan Nevins, 'Henry White' (New York, 1930),
    pp. 110-11.
8   Ibid., p. 119.
9   See Peter Karsten, 'The Naval Aristocracy' (New York,
    1972) for a good discussion of naval attitudes
    during the 1890s.
10   Akira Iriye, 'Pacific Estrangement' (Cambridge, Mass.,
    1972), pp. 17-25.
11   William A. Russ, 'The Hawaiian Revolution'
    (Selinsgrove, Pa., 1959), p. 135.
12   Ibid., p. 180.
13   Ibid., p. 147.
14   Leech, 'Days of McKinley', p. 150.
15   Ibid., p. 147; Iriye, 'Pacific Estrangement', p. 51.
16   'American Review of Reviews', 17: 146 (February 1898).
17   'Atlanta Constitution', 2 January 1898.
18   'North American Review', 166: 32-3 (January 1898).
19   'New York Times', 7 February 1898.
20   'Atlantic Monthly', 79: 722-32 (June 1897).
21   'Harper's Monthly', 95: 523-33 (September 1897).
22   Leech, 'Days of McKinley', p. 168.
23   'Atlanta Constitution', 2 January 1898.
24   Coletta, 'Bryan', p. 221.
25   John Braeman, 'Albert Beveridge' (Chicago, 1971),
    p. 23.
26   Iriye, 'Pacific Estrangement', p. 55.
27   David Healy, 'U.S. Expansionism' (Madison, Wis.,
    1970), pp. 108-09.
28   Braeman, 'Beveridge', p. 24.
29   Iriye, 'Pacific Estrangement', p. 56.
30   'Outlook', 60: 761 (26 November 1898).
31   'Outlook', 60: 162-3 (19 September 1898).
32   E. Berkeley Tompkins, 'Anti-Imperialism in the
    United States' (Philadelphia, 1970), p. 159.
33   Coletta, 'Bryan', p. 233.
34   Healy, 'U.S. Expansionism', p. 192.
35   H. W. Morgan, 'William McKinley and His America'
    (Syracuse, 1963), p. 403.
36   John Foreman, 'The Philippine Islands' (London, 1892),
    pp. 185-7, 487.

CHAPTER 4: THE UNITED STATES IN WORLD POLITICS

1   Leech, 'Days of McKinley', pp. 356-60. I am
    indebted to David A. Rosenberg's unpublished study for
    data on the Senate ratification of the peace treaty.
2   Braeman, 'Beveridge', p. 44.

3   Coletta, 'Bryan', p. 252.
4   Ibid., p. 254.
5   Elihu Root, 'The Military and Colonial Policy of
     the United States' (Cambridge, Mass., 1916), pp. 9-10,
     42-3.
6   Ibid., pp. 73-4.
7   Braeman, 'Beveridge', p. 26.
8   Peter W. Stanley, 'A Nation in the Making' (Cambridge,
     Mass., 1974), p. 106.
9   Ibid., p. 87.
10 Leech, 'Days of McKinley', p. 394.
11 'Munsey's Magazine', 20: 516-20 (January 1899).
12 'Outlook', 62: 425-32 (24 June 1899).
13 Coletta, 'Bryan', p. 266.
14 Richard D. Challener, 'Admirals, Generals, and
     American Foreign Policy' (Princeton, 1973), p. 18.
15 Ibid., p. 201.
16 Kenton J. Clymer, The Gentleman as Diplomat
     (unpublished manuscript, 1973), pp. 297-8.
17 'Public Opinion', 28: 773 (21 June 1900).
18 'Literary Digest', 21: 74 28 July 1900).
19 'Independent', 52: 1655 (12 July 1900).
20 Root, 'Military and Colonial Policy', p. 105.
21 Challener, 'Admirals', pp. 157-8.
22 Ibid., pp. 120-1.
23 Ibid., p. 158.
24 Nevins, 'Henry White', p. 206.
25 Sondra R. Herman, 'Eleven against War' (Stanford,
     1969), p. 35.
26 Challener, 'Admirals', pp. 115-16.
27 Iriye, 'Pacific Estrangement', p. 71.
28 Ibid., p. 27.
29 Clymer, The Gentleman as Diplomat, p. 293.
30 'Letters of Cleveland', p. 563.
31 Nevins, 'Henry White', p. 198.

CHAPTER 5: CO-OPERATION AND COMPETITION

1   Leech, 'Days of McKinley', p. 464.
2   Archibald Cary Coolidge, 'The United States as a
     World Power' (New York, 1909), p. 1.
3   Leech, 'Days of McKinley', p. 464.
4   Coolidge, 'United States', p. 7.
5   See Iriye, 'Pacific Estrangement', passim.
6   Grey to MacDonald, 14 November 1908, FO 800-68,
     Public Record Office (London).
7   Grey to Bryce, 30 March 1908, FO 800-81, Public
     Record Office.

8   Grey to Durand, 2 January 1906, FO 800-81, Public
    Record Office.
9   Durand to Grey, 15 December 1905, 3 and 26 January
    1906, FO 800-81, Public Record Office.
10 John H. Latane, 'America as a World Power' (New York,
    1907), pp. 261-2, 318-20.
11 Ernest H. Fitzpatrick, 'The Coming Conflict of
    Nations' (Springfield, Ill., 1909), pp. 9, 116, 164,
    197.
12 Michael Hunt, 'Frontier Defence and the Open Door'
    (New Haven, 1973), p. 204.
13 Donald F. Anderson, 'William Howard Taft' (Ithaca,
    1973), pp. 24-5.
14 Iriye, 'Pacific Estrangement', p. 207.
15 Hunting Wilson's address of 4 May 1911, in Fred M.
    Huntington Wilson Papers (Ursinus College).
16 Wilson to Baldwin, 19 January 1910, Wilson Papers.
17 Dana Munro, 'Intervention and Dollar Diplomacy in
    the Caribbean' (Princeton, 1964), pp. 177, 207-08.
18 Ibid., p. 237.
19 'Journal of the American Association of China',
    vol. 2, no. 5, pp. 20-6 (November 1907).
20 Hunt, 'Frontier Defence', pp. 148-9.
21 'Journal of American Association of China', vol. 2,
    no. 5, pp. 27-31.
22 Hunt, 'Frontier Defence', p. 218.
23 Ibid., p. 155.
24 John A. DeNovo, 'American Interests and Politics in
    the Middle East' (Minneapolis, 1963), p. 54.
25 Walter Lippmann, 'Drift and Mastery' (New York, 1914),
    pp. 136, 145.
26 Woodrow Wilson, 'A History of the American People',
    vol. 5, pp. 296, 300 (New York, 1902).
27 Harley Notter, 'The Origins of the Foreign Policy of
    Woodrow Wilson' (Baltimore, 1937), p. 75.
28. Ibid., pp. 257, 269.

Index

For Product Safety Concerns and Information please contact our EU
representative GPSR@taylorandfrancis.com
Taylor & Francis Verlag GmbH, Kaufingerstraße 24, 80331 München, Germany